The Something Delusion

Why is there something rather than nothing?

A surgeon's journey to a Christian worldview

Nigel Jones

DayOne

© Day One Publications 2023

ISBN 978-1-84625-754-4

British Library Cataloguing in Publication Data available

Published by Day One Publications
Ryelands Road, Leominster, HR6 8NZ
Telephone 01568 613 740 FAX 01568 611 473
email—sales@dayone.co.uk
web site—www.dayone.co.uk

Cover design by Kathryn Chedgzoy
Printed by 4edge

To my wife, daughters, sons-in-law
and grandchildren, with love

Endorsements

In a series of well-thought-through short chapters, Nigel Jones has produced a very clear set of essays on why Creation, rather than evolution, is the only way to make sense of the scientific facts in a range of subjects. Writing powerfully from his own experience concerning his journey through his long and successful medical career as a surgeon in the UK, he weaves his own story in a most accessible and delightful manner into his assessment of all the scientific disciplines. He concludes that the theistic evolution position is untenable; that irreducible complexity is real and an impossibility for evolution to explain; and that consciousness is a real witness to the truth of humans being made in the image of the Creator. Nigel speaks eloquently with great authority and his writing is full of carefully weighed factual evidence, brilliantly declaring the truth and majesty of Creation.

Professor Andy McIntosh, DSc, FIMA, C.Math, FEI, C.Eng, FInstP, MIGEM, FRAeS, Emeritus Professor of Thermodynamics, University of Leeds

Aptly subtitled *A Surgeon's Journey*, to travel with the author of *The Something Delusion* is to pass through and contemplate a wide variety of fascinating terrain: the complexities of anatomy and physiology, different views of origins, geological time, miracles, philosophy, chemistry, consciousness, and much more. Along the way, personal anecdotes enliven the discourse. It is difficult to highlight noteworthy 'sites of interest' on such an expansive excursion, but I especially appreciated the chapters on medical ethics. The author taught university students for many years after retiring from his clinical practice, and, as he aptly puts it, 'respect is not enough'. At various stages on the journey, Nigel shows serious shortcomings of the evolutionary worldview, including theistic versions of it. The creation-based worldview is no delusion, rather it is both biblically faithful and intellectually coherent.

Philip Bell, Chief Executive Officer,
Creation Ministries International (UK/Europe).

Acknowledgements

I am very grateful to friends and family who have encouraged me in the writing of this book. Some have very kindly read chapters and made suggestions that have helped in my search for accuracy and truth. I particularly thank Stephen Wright for writing the foreword and I am very grateful to Andy McIntosh and Philip Bell for their kind endorsements. Helen Clark has been an enormous help in editing the book and in her encouragement. My wife Liz has been a constant help. I thank her for her love.

Contents

Contents

'The universe was made out of nearly nothing.'
Professor Richard Dawkins, 2006

'For every house is built by someone, but God is the builder of
everything.'
Hebrews 3:4, NIV

'A super-intellect has monkeyed with physics.'
Professor Fred Hoyle, 1982

Life a 'pilgrimage from nothing to nowhere.'
Robert Louis Stevenson, 1886

'You turn things upside down, as if the potter were thought to be
like the clay! Shall what is formed say to the one who formed it,
"You did not make me"? Can the pot say to the potter, "You know
nothing"?'
Isaiah 29:16, NIV

'With such signs of forethought in the design of living creatures,
can you doubt they are the work of choice or design?'
Socrates, 470—399 BC

'From one man he made all the nations, that they should inhabit
the whole earth; and he marked out their appointed times in
history and the boundaries of their lands. God did this so that they
would seek him and perhaps reach out for him and find him, though
he is not far from any one of us.'
Acts 17:26–27 NIV

10 The Something Delusion

Foreword

What you believe about origins affects your worldview and how you think and live. There is a clash of two worldviews between Secular Humanism—one that says matter came into being without an intelligent cause (more recently popularized by Richard Dawkins' book, *The God Delusion*)—and the claim of the Bible that behind a design there must be a designer, as set out in *Genesis 1:1*: 'In the beginning God created the heavens and the earth.'

As a practicing lawyer for over thirty years, and as a Senior Public Prosecutor, it was my duty to examine the evidence whether to prosecute. One of those tests is the Evidential test; is there sufficient evidence to provide a reasonable / realistic prospect of a conviction. That involves impartially examining the evidence in detail and making a decision.

To many, the claims of secular humanism and atheism is a closed and shut case, but is it? There is a growing body of scholarly work across a broad range of academia that demonstrates evolution is far from being proved beyond all reasonable doubt. In fact, recently it has been described, *A Theory in Crisis*.[1]

I first became fascinated with this subject when I assisted my father, the late Professor Verna Wright MD FRCP, when he researched the evidence on origins as to which of the alternative views the scientific evidence supported. I observed he went on a similar journey to the author of this excellent book.

Nigel Jones is an experienced general surgeon who brilliantly examines the evidence and the underlying assumptions that underpin the atheist worldview and finds them wanting. He rigorously examines the evidence; he looks down the microscope at the biochemical challenges that evolution faces and looks up through the telescope at the fine tuning of the universe. He concurs with Professor Hoyle, when he said, 'A common-sense interpretation of the facts suggests that a super-intellect has monkeyed with physics, as well as with chemistry and biology, and that there are no blind forces worth speaking about in nature. The numbers one calculates from the facts seem to me so overwhelming as to put this conclusion almost beyond question.'[2]

As the Psalmist exclaimed, 'The heavens declare the glory of God; the skies proclaim the work of his hands' (Psalm 19:1).

Nigel Jones helpfully widens his work to consider the evidence of human physiology, anatomy, geology, the fossil record and irreducible complexity, the age of the earth, and discusses the different theological interpretations of the book of Genesis.

This is no dry academic work. Layered between these erudite chapters on different scientific subjects is the personal journey of a surgeon and a Christian, sharing his unique personal insights into his professional life, family life, and spiritual Life. He also shares some interesting stories of the academics he has dialogued with. This is a book forged on the anvil of his medical discipline and personal experience, as he grapples with the ethical and moral dilemmas that confront humanity in the 21st century. As a lecturer in medical ethics and as a former surgeon, he is well qualified to speak into such issues as the sanctity of human life, euthanasia and other profound issues, that are affected by the worldview one holds.

This work is invaluable for those seeking to understand a Christian worldview informed by the Bible and science. It is a resource of succinct scientific, moral, and theological arguments about origins, intertwined with great personal anecdotes.

I know that, on his journey, the author found God's words in Jeremiah 29:13 to be so true: '*You will seek me and find me when you seek me with all your heart.*' Nigel invites us to remember this promise and the Lord Jesus Christ as we continue the journey to find our own worldview. This is an invitation well worth accepting.

Stephen Wright

LL. B Barrister-at-Law

NOTES

1 Denton, Michael, *Evolution: A Theory In Crisis*, (Bethesda, MD: Adler & Adler Publishers Inc., 1986).

2 Fred Hoyle, 'The Universe: Past and Present Reflections', *Annual Review of Astronomy and Astrophysics*, Vol 20, 1982, p. 16.

Introduction

Including the word, 'delusion', in the title of my book may cause any who read it to think of Richard Dawkins' book, *The God Delusion*[1], published in 2006. As I will explain in chapter 19, the seeds of my book were planted by Richard Dawkins himself as I listened to him give a public lecture in the International Centre for Life, Newcastle upon Tyne, in April 2006. When he told the audience that the universe was made from 'nearly nothing' it struck me as a very imprecise remark for a scientist, particularly for one who held the chair of Charles Simonyi Professor of the Public Understanding of Science at the University of Oxford.

Why did I attend his lecture in 2006? Well—as I hope to show in the pages of this book—from my teenage years, I had been keen to understand the purpose of life, the origins of the universe and mankind and whether man has an eternal soul which lives on after his death. I would describe this search for understanding as my being on a journey to find the answers to these questions.

C.S. Lewis said:

> Supposing there was no intelligence behind the universe, no creative mind. In that case, nobody designed my brain for the purpose of thinking. It is merely that when the atoms inside my skull happen, for physical or chemical reasons, to arrange themselves in a certain way, this gives me, as a by-product, the sensation I call thought. But, if so, how can I trust my own thinking to be true? It is like upsetting a milk jug and hoping that the way it splashes itself will give you a map of London.

But if I can't trust my own thinking, of course I can't trust the arguments leading to Atheism, and therefore have no reason to be an Atheist or anything else. Unless I believe in God, I cannot believe in thought: so, I can never use thought to disbelieve in God.[2]

From my teenage years to the present time, at the age of 74, like many of us I have been on a journey of increasing understanding about humanity, myself and our origins. I hope to show the influences upon my developing worldview and how this came to be a settled position. I have been trained in the scientific discipline of Medicine and spent two and a half years in basic research in the Thrombosis Research Unit at King's College Hospital, leading to a higher degree from London University in 1980. I describe my worldview as settled; but that is not the same as saying, 'I have a closed mind,' nor do I claim to have 'all the answers'.

It is well-known that Richard Dawkins is a strong advocate of atheism. I was interested to hear his case for atheism and for the origin of the universe and of man. At the International Centre for Life, I seemed to be listening to a fiction writer, not a scientist. As his wife read extracts from the book he co-authored with Yan Wong, 'The Ancestor's Tale: A Pilgrimage to the Dawn of Life,'[3] I remembered Chaucer's Canterbury Tales, which I had studied for O-level English, on which his book is modelled. His book takes a path backwards through evolution, claiming, as it goes, to celebrate the unity of life. Different groups of organisms are met until the last common ancestor from which all species, including man, are said to have originated. The claimed evidence for this is that organisms share the same genetic code.

How did Richard Dawkins get to his worldview or his system of belief? I would describe his worldview as embracing the ideology of 'Scientism' which claims that science is the only source of knowledge and is the key to understanding the human condition. But how did he get from childhood to his present beliefs as he passed the age of 80 in March 2021?

He learned from his mother, at the age of 9, 'that Christianity was one of many religions and they contradicted each other. They couldn't all be right, so why believe the one in which, by sheer accident of birth, I happened to be brought up?' He explained that his journey to atheism was held up by his hero worship of Elvis Presley and particularly through listening to his recording of, 'I Believe'. Dawkins describes being a strong believer in a creator God at that time. He later dismissed Presley's belief by recognizing that Presley came from a working-class and uneducated family. Because of this, Presley could not avoid being religious, Dawkins stated! By the age of 16, Dawkins tells us that he had thrown off belief in a god. He had personally discovered that Darwinian evolution was a powerful explanation for the beauty and apparent design of life. In his own words: 'It wasn't long then before I became strongly and militantly atheistic.'[4]

While his personal professorial chair is given to help the general public to understand the 'workings' of science, his life's work seems to be more about the public destruction of religion. Many of his pronouncements seem to be about religion, an area in which he holds no academic qualifications. His written and spoken statements about philosophical or theological matters often irritate those better qualified to talk on such matters, who share his atheistic position.

I have given a short account of Dawkins' journey to his settled worldview of atheism. I would like to illustrate to you how all of us, from birth to grave, are on a journey, usually, of increasing understanding and often coming to a settled worldview. My illustration will focus on the author Robert Louis Stevenson, whose adventure books were a source of great pleasure to my brother and I as we grew up in the 1950s. We really enjoyed watching the BBC's dramatizations of Robert Louis Stevenson's books, such as, *Treasure Island*, *Kidnapped* and *The Black Arrow*. Our favourite actor, Patrick Troughton, often featured. The gift which Stevenson had for writing such adventures was clear. We imagined that he had been not only successful as an author, but must have been wise and interesting, like his books.

Born in 1850, Stevenson's father, Thomas, was a famous civil engineer who designed over thirty lighthouses around Scotland; his mother was called Maggie. Robert was their only child. He was brought up in a Christian home and the first book he wrote had a Christian theme. Written when he was sixteen and published in 1866, *The Pentland Rising, a page of history, 1666*[5] remembered the Christian Covenanters being defeated by the forces of Charles II in 1666.

The following year, Stevenson entered Edinburgh University, where he soon turned away from his upbringing. He frequented public houses and read books which 'would have corrupted St Paul'. He formed a frivolous club that believed they should 'ignore everything our parents taught us'.[6] His father, finding a piece of paper recording these words, learnt from his son that he now no longer believed in the Christian religion. Robert's alcohol intake soon had an adverse impact on his health and he suffered from depression.

Stevenson completed a law degree in Edinburgh in 1874 but continued in his ambition to be an author and was soon renowned for many great adventure stories. His father continued to support him financially for many years. Stevenson was introduced to W. E. Henley in 1875 and frequently quoted his famous poem, *Invictus*[7], with the closing words, 'I am the master of my fate: I am the captain of my soul.' Henley was Stevenson's literary agent and friend. As we all know, our friends can influence our choices and decisions in life.

When my wife, Liz, and I were on holiday in Central France, in July 2019, we visited a restaurant in *Le Monastier-sur-Gazeille* for our evening meal. A plaque in the village commemorated the beginning of a twelve-day, 200-mile journey, which Robert Louis Stevenson began on 22nd September 1878 from this village to *Saint-Jean-du-Gard* further south. Stevenson was in his late twenties and still unmarried. The purpose of his journey was to collect material for publication and indeed the resulting book, *Travels with a Donkey in the Cévennes*[8], has been praised as an early travel guide. In preparation for the journey, he had a large sleeping bag made and bought the stubborn donkey, *Modestine*, to carry it for him. The barren and rocky countryside, covered with heather, reminded Stevenson of Scotland and his struggles with *Modestine* added humour to his account. Many have followed the 'Stevenson GR 70 footpath' since that day and still do.

Stevenson wrote, 'For my part, I travel not to go anywhere, but to go. I travel for travel's sake. The great affair is to move; to feel the needs and hitches of our life more clearly; to come down off this feather-bed of civilization, and find the globe granite underfoot and strewn with cutting flints. Alas, as we get up in life, and are more preoccupied with our affairs, even a holiday is a thing that must be worked for. To hold a pack upon a pack-saddle against a gale out of the freezing north is no high industry, but it is one that serves to occupy and compose the mind. And when the present is so exacting who can annoy himself about the future?'[9]

Stevenson, in coming to the guiding principles for his own life, had stubbornly chosen a lifestyle which rejected his parents' worldview and would not reconsider the choice that he had made even when he found 'the globe granite underfoot and strewn with cutting flints'. He described himself as preoccupied with the present and too busy to consider the future. Would you agree that is a dangerous way to live with possible bad consequences? In his words he 'travelled not to go anywhere, but to go'. When he later wrote, in 1886, 'If I could believe in the immortality business, the world would indeed be too good to be true; but … the sods cover us, and the worm that never dies, the conscience sleeps well at last.' He wrote that life was only a 'pilgrimage from nothing to nowhere'.[10]

In 1888, Stevenson and his wife, Fanny, and her son, travelled to make a new home in *Vailima* in the Samoan Islands. There he died at the age of 44 of a cerebral haemorrhage in 1894. Approximately ten years after his death, his wife published a small volume of prayers that he had written. She wrote an introduction in which she explained how Stevenson and his family, living in Samoa at the time, closed each day by gathering for prayer and worship. A photograph of the family, living in Samoa, can be seen on the Internet.

One of Stevenson's prayers in this book begins with the words, 'Lord, behold our family here assembled', and beautifully closes with, 'As the clay to the potter, as the windmill to the wind, as children of their sire, we beseech of Thee this help and mercy for Christ's sake. Amen.'[11] Perhaps at the end he did come to 'believe in the immortality business'. I hope so.

My book title suggests life is a journey. I hope that you do not share Stevenson's view that life is a 'pilgrimage from nothing to nowhere'. I wonder what you think of the metaphor, 'life is a journey'. If one accepts that life is a journey, one presumes that there is also a destination.

My purpose in writing *The Something Delusion* is to describe my own journey to a settled worldview. I will explain the influences that moulded me and the external principles which led me to my own worldview. The book describes my personal journey, so the chapters reflect events, people and influences which I have encountered along the way in chronological order. Hopefully, the Contents page will list the 'stop-off points' on my journey. In early life, the main influences were my parents, schoolteachers and the representatives of the law of our land. In moving to the sixth form in a boarding school, and then on to university, other influences were encountered. I will also examine the journeys and worldviews of others throughout the book. Some of these people have influenced me as my own worldview developed. I recognize and respect that your journey so far may have been very different.

A Christian writer, Paul Tripp, in his Daily Advent Devotional book strikingly states for December 25th,

> All human beings are on a lifelong journey to find wisdom, and all human beings want to think that they are wise. That 3-year-old who endlessly asks, 'Why?' is in the process of putting pieces of a worldview together that will be the means by which she interprets and makes sense out of everything in her life. She's forming some kind of wisdom system that includes ways of thinking about her identity, the meaning and purpose of life, what relationships are about, where happiness is to be found, who God is, what's right and wrong, and a host of perspectives on other things. You see, from birth we are all philosophers, we are all theologians, and we all function like archaeologists, digging through the mound of our existence to make sense of it all.[12]

Paul Tripp justifies these remarks for Christmas Day by saying that the Christmas story is a wisdom story—the best wisdom story ever told. But now I am running ahead of myself! I need to describe in chronological order my own 'surgeon's journey' and how I came to agree with what Paul Tripp has written.

I have been influenced in the style of this book by two excellent books. Firstly, *The Churchill Factor*[13], written by Boris Johnson, and the other, *Seeking Allah, Finding Jesus*[14], by the late Nabeel Qureshi. These are very different books, but both have a similar style of moving from subject to subject in a way that held my attention and interest. It is my hope that this book, written in a similar style, may hold your attention.

Incidentally, when I first wrote this introduction, Boris Johnson, Prime Minister of Great Britain and Northern Ireland was battling for his life in St Thomas' Hospital, where I worked as a Surgical Registrar in 1978. His life's journey so far has been dramatic. His ambition fulfilled, as Prime Minister, but, in Coronavirus, an unseen enemy, completely unexpected, crossed his path.

Journalists aware of Johnson's love of Churchill write to tell him that he is not Churchill! I would guess that he knows that and the reality is that Boris Johnson is on his own journey. His life has certainly been full as a father, journalist and politician. He has been Mayor of London and Prime Minister. He is on his own 'journey of life'—there is a past, there is a present and hopefully for him there is a good future.

Nabeel Qureshi was born in San Diego, USA, to Pakistani Muslim parents and died of stomach cancer, at the age of 34, in September 2017. At university, he studied medicine and Islamic apologetics and engaged Christians in religious discussions. He became a close friend of a Christian called David Wood. Qureshi's subsequent conversion to Christianity was described in his book, *Seeking Allah, Finding Jesus*. This was a New York Times bestseller in 2014.

After completing his medical degree, Qureshi decided to spend his life studying and preaching the Christian gospel and became an international public speaker. He was married with one daughter. He was writing a PhD at the University of Oxford at the time of his death.

G. K. Chesterton, a Christian author, wrote in *The Defendant*[15], in 1901, 'The Iliad is only great because all life is a battle, The Odyssey because all life is a journey, The Book of Job because all life is a riddle.' Chesterton was highlighting that our lives are made up of many different experiences, some are of personal struggle, some are perplexing, but all are part of our journey of life, from birth to grave.

Life has been a battle for Johnson, personally against coronavirus, and as Prime Minister trying to lead a nation out of lockdown. For Qureshi, who loved his parents dearly, he struggled with his search for the truth and the pain it caused them. Finally, he faced a diagnosis of advanced stomach cancer; a riddle, similar to that which Job faced. Johnson's book is a biography of someone else's leadership qualities; Qureshi's book is an autobiography giving insight into his own weaknesses and the strength he found outside himself. For Robert Louis Stevenson, much of life was a battle with parents who he felt were misguided and repressive. His life was moulded by the views he held, the company he chose and the habits he adopted. Whether Stevenson's journey 'from nothing to nowhere' actually ended at a different destination, we cannot say at this time.

I asked the question, 'Does our journey continue after death?' I will address that question in a later chapter. For now, I suggest the following conversation between William Gladstone, when he was Prime Minister of the United Kingdom, and a young man, asking for advice about the future, is challenging:

'Mr. Gladstone, I would appreciate your giving me a few minutes in which I might lay before you my plans for the future. I would like to study law.'

'Yes,' said the great statesman, 'and what then?'

'Then, Sir, I would like to gain entrance to the Bar of England.'

'Yes, young man, and what then?'

'Then, Sir, I hope to have a place in Parliament, in the House of Lords.'

'Yes, young man, what then?' pressed Gladstone.

'Then I hope to do great things for Britain.'

'Yes, young man, and what then?'

'Then, Sir, I hope to retire and take life easy.'

'Yes, young man, and what then?' he tenaciously asked.

'Well, then, Mr. Gladstone, I suppose I will die.'

'Yes, young man, and what then?'

The young man hesitated and then said, 'I never thought any further than that, Sir.'

Looking at the young man sternly and steadily, Gladstone said, 'Young man, you are a fool. Go home and think life through!'[16]

As you read this book and 'think life through,' you may like to look at the contents page and see if some of the questions you wish to ask about life are dealt with in later chapters. The chapters can be read as separate items, if you see a topic you want to consider earlier. My personal journey is woven through the book like a skeleton on which the body of my worldview has grown and developed. Some of the questions I address may, at first sight, seem impossible to answer, for example, 'Where did my mind come from?' or 'Do miracles happen?', but I trust that you will find some answers here.

Thinking of G. K. Chesterton's quote, p. 22, we might ask:

- Life—do you agree that it is a battle or struggle?
- Life—do you personally believe that it is a journey with a destination?
- Life—do you still find that it remains for you a riddle?

How do we make sense of life? Is the answer to be found in something or in Someone?

NOTES

1 Richard Dawkins, *The God Delusion*, (New York: Bantam Books, October 2006).

2 C. S. Lewis, *The Case for Christianity*, (Nashville, Tennessee: B&H Publishing Group, March 1999), p. 32.

3 Richard Dawkins and Yan Wong, *The Ancestor's Tale: A Pilgrimage to the Dawn of Life*, (London: Weidenfeld & Nicolson, April 2016).

4 John Gray, 'The Closed Mind of Richard Dawkins', *The New Republic*, October 3, 2014. https://newrepublic.com/article/119596/appetite-wonder-review-closed-mind-richard-dawkins

5 Robert Louis Stevenson, *The Pentland Rising: a page of history, 1666*, (London/Delhi: Pranava Books, 2020).

6 Iain H. Murray, The Undercover Revolution—How Fiction Changed Britain, (Edinburgh: The Banner of Truth Trust, 2009), p. 12.

7 William Ernest Henley, *Invictus*, 1875. https://www.scottishpoetrylibrary.org.uk/poem/invictus/

8 Robert Louis Stevenson, *Travels with a Donkey in the Cevennes*, (Imprint Illyria Books, February 2009).

9 https://www.goodreads.com/quotes/943857-for-my-part-i-travel-not-to-go-anywhere-but

10 Iain H. Murray, The Undercover Revolution—How Fiction Changed Britain, p. 20.

11 Robert Louis Stevenson, *Prayers Written at Vailima and a Lowden Sabbath Morn*, (London: Chatto & Windus, 1916), p. 1.

12 Paul David Tripp, *Come Let Us Adore Him*, (Wheaton, Illinois: Crossway, 2017), p. 120.

13 Boris Johnson, *The Churchill Factor: How One Man Made History*, (London: Hodder & Stoughton, October 2014).

14 Nabeel Qureshi, *Seeking Allah, Finding Jesus: A Devout Muslim Encounters Christianity*, (Grand Rapids, Michigan: Zondervan, February 2014).

15 G. K. Chesterton, *The Defendant*, (London: J.M. Dent & Sons, 1901). https://www.azquotes.com/quote/458510

16 Leonard Griffith, *This is Living*, (Nashville, Tennessee: Abingdon Press, 1966), pp. 48, 49.

1 Pivotal moments

I am choosing to highlight the summer of 1964 in this opening chapter. For me, as a pupil at Epsom College in Surrey, moving from the fifth form with its O-levels to study Biology, Chemistry and Physics at A-level, in the sixth form, was a pivotal moment. The word, *pivotal*, means of crucial importance in relation to the development or success of something else. I want to explore the idea of *pivotal* moments in my own journey of life. We will see in later chapters that, for all of us, these are of enormous importance.

There are pivotal moments in every human life and these are crucially important. Birth is clearly a pivotal moment: injuries sustained during childbirth, for example causing cerebral palsy, may dictate a person's future experience; inherited genetic diseases, such as cystic fibrosis, may lead to a difficult and shortened life. For some even the opportunity to be born is extinguished because of the choice of others.

Death, at the other end of life, is also clearly a pivotal moment. Many questions are asked during life about what follows death. Some people are confident they have the answers to such questions; others are weighed down with fear. In between birth and death, we will experience many life changing events, some may even be of historic consequence.

On the world stage, in that summer of 1964, such a pivotal moment happened in the lives of two great men: Nelson Mandela and Sir Winston Churchill.

In Nelson Mandela's autobiography, *Long Walk to Freedom*, he describes a pivotal day, during the summer of 1964. On Friday 12 June, he and his six defendant colleagues entered the court in Pretoria, South Africa for the last time. It is no exaggeration to say that the entire world was waiting with bated breath to learn of Judge de Wet's verdicts.

Leonid Brezhnev, President of Russia, had asked for leniency; members of the U.S. Congress protested; fifty members of the British Parliament marched in London; Adlai Stevenson, US representative at the UN, wrote a letter saying that his government would do everything it could to prevent a death sentence.[1]

When the judge indicated that the defendants should stand, his face was pale and he would not look at them—he was breathing heavily. Mandela records, 'We looked at each other and seemed to know: *it would be death,* otherwise why was a normally calm man so nervous?' When he began to speak, the most significant words Mandela and the others heard were: 'I have decided not to impose the supreme penalty ... The sentence in the case of all the accused will be one of life imprisonment.'[2]

Mandela's long walk to freedom—his journey of life—was to continue. He was taken to Robben Island on 13 June 1964 and would remain there until 31 March 1982. He was then moved to a prison on the mainland, near Cape Town. Finally, on 11 February 1990, Nelson Mandela was released from prison. His 10,000 days of imprisonment were at last over. When he later addressed the crowds from the balcony of the old City Hall in Cape Town, he told them 'I place the remaining years of my life in your hands.'[3] In April 1994, Nelson

Mandela became South Africa's first ever black president; his journey of life was continuing, full of purpose.

Winston Churchill had first entered Parliament in February 1901 as a Conservative MP for Oldham. That summer of 1964 witnessed another historic moment when, on 27 July, Sir Winston Churchill, Member of Parliament for Woodford, attended the House of Commons for *the last time*. He spent fifty minutes in the chamber before being assisted to his feet, stopping to bow to the Speaker, and leaving for the last time.

Perhaps the greatest pivotal moment of his life came on 28 May 1940. Churchill was struggling to convince the War Cabinet that Adolf Hitler should be resisted. This pivotal moment was, I believe, the biggest of his life and its outcome, maybe, the most important moment in the history of Great Britain. The Foreign Secretary, Lord Halifax, particularly wanted Churchill to make peace with Hitler. When the meeting adjourned, Winston went to speak to the twenty-five Cabinet ministers outside the War Cabinet to brief them in detail on the current situation faced by Britain. Churchill's speech to them, full of powerful rhetoric, concluded with the sentence:

> We shall go on and we shall fight it out, here or elsewhere, and if this long island story of ours is to end at last, let it end only when each one of us lies choking in his own blood upon the ground.[4]

In the second volume of his memoirs of *The Second World War, Their Finest Hour*, Churchill recalled the Cabinet's response:

> There occurred a demonstration which, considering the character of the gathering—twenty-five experienced

politicians and Parliament men, who represented all the different points of view, whether right or wrong, before the war—surprised me. Quite a number seemed to jump up from the table and come running to my chair, shouting and patting me on the back.

There is no doubt that had I at this juncture faltered at all in the leading of the nation, I should have been hurled out of office. I was sure that every Minister was ready to be killed quite soon, and have all his family and possessions destroyed, rather than give in. In this they represented the House of Commons and almost all the people.[5]

Hitler was resisted and many countries have remained free to this day.

Churchill died at home at the age of 90, on 24 January 1965. The state funeral lasted for four days. The funeral took place at St Paul's Cathedral with Her Majesty the Queen attending. After this, his body was transported along the River Thames to Waterloo station and then, by train, to the burial place in St Martin's churchyard at Bladon.

Three hundred and fifty million people witnessed Churchill's last journey.

My parent's choice to send me to boarding school, in 1961, was a pivotal moment in my life. During my first three years at Epsom College, I decided that I wanted to become a doctor; another pivotal decision. Aiming to become a doctor had many uncertainties along the way, so a second choice was required: mine was to join the Royal Navy, hopefully, as an officer!

NOTES

1 Nelson Mandela, *Long Walk to Freedom*, (Abacus, Little, Brown Book Group, 2007), p. 449.

2 Nelson Mandela, *Long Walk to Freedom*, p. 447–448.

3 Ibid., p. 676

4 The May 1940 War Cabinet Crisis: Churchill's darkest hour? 28th May 1940, https://www.historyextra.com/period/second-world-war/the-may-1940-war-cabinet-crisis-churchills-darkest-hour/

5 Winston S. Churchill, *Second World War Volume II, Their Finest Hour,* (London: Cassell & Co Ltd, 1949), p. 88.

2 A-level choices and the origin of life

I had no idea what life in the Royal Navy would have been like. However, choosing medicine was a clearer path. My mother, Jill, trained as a nurse at Hertford Hospital and later became a theatre sister at Salford Royal Hospital. There was always real order and discipline in the operating theatre. A black-and-white photo in our family album shows her with a dark belt to indicate her seniority and a team of six nurses, masks hiding their identity.

My father, Raymond, was a consultant anaesthetist at Withington Hospital in Manchester. Anaesthetists put people to sleep for operations and care for them, ensuring pain relief and muscle relaxation. My father studied medicine at Guy's Hospital during the Second World War. He was evacuated to Farnborough and Tunbridge Wells, though they went up to Guy's to take their turn at fire watching during German incendiary bombing. He qualified in 1945.

Father did his 'house jobs' (six months Medicine and six months Surgery) at Hertford Hospital where he met Staff Nurse Barnes—my mother; they were married in November 1945. With both my parents working in the operating theatre, my becoming a surgeon was perhaps not a surprising outcome.

Waste anaesthetic gases in the operating theatre have always been a source of concern with suggestions of difficulties in conception, of miscarriages and developmental harm to the offspring of theatre staff. After reading one such report, suggesting that the children of theatre staff were not as clever as they might have been, I understood why I needed extra tuition in Physics and Chemistry. I had been conceived despite a double dose of gas!

Another light-hearted thought about choosing a career in medicine was that it was said that you needed to study Latin. How else would you know that the *flexor pollicis longus* is a long muscle which flexes your pollex (your thumb)? That was a requirement fulfilled because I did study Latin for nine years—though I failed the O-level twice!

Epsom College is a public school in Surrey founded through one man's ambition to improve the lives of those who had fallen on hard times. Dr John Propert provided for elderly doctors, their widows and the orphans of medical families with free housing, clothing and schooling. The school was originally called the Royal Medical Benevolent College. Prince Albert opened the college on the 25th of June 1855. John Propert's desire to care for medical teachers and their offspring, echoed part of the vows of the Hippocratic Oath. Within a few years, the numbers of pupils increased, including those paying fees, and by 1865 there were 300 boys. When I attended, between 1961 and 1966, there were 550 boys.

To prepare for medical school, passes at A-level in Biology, Physics and Chemistry were required. London University granted a so-called 'Certificate of Eligibility' on passing these subjects. So, the choice of these three A-Level subjects was straightforward for me. Many of those at Epsom were the sons of doctors or dentists and each year about 55 boys chose these A-level subjects with a view to studying medicine or dentistry. The father of one boy in my class had been taught by the same Botany teacher who taught us. This boy had his Dad's botany notes, which saved him taking his own! Because I had chosen to study O-level History rather than Biology, my first exposure to Biology was in the A-level course.

As I passed my 16th birthday, I experienced an increasing desire to explore what the world was all about and particularly how it started? If we knew how it started, then we could ask the question, why did it start? Why is the universe as it is and not something else? Why is the universe here at all and does it have a purpose? I think I modelled myself on my own father's pursuit of knowledge and meaning as a young man. He had a lot of blue Pelican books and I would soon have my own collection.

Pelican books, founded in 1937, were low-cost intellectual paperbacks. More than 250 million copies sold worldwide. The founder, Allen Lane, said that there was 'a vast reading public for intelligent books' in this country.[1] There was said to be a thirst for knowledge in the self-educating, post-war generation and Pelican was 'an informal university for "50s Britons".' Subjects such as Music, Literature, History, Physics, Biology, Architecture and many more were covered.

Next to the tuckshop at Epsom College was a shop selling clothing, books and other items. In January 1965, I purchased my first Pelican book from the school shop. This was entitled *The Nature of the Universe* by astronomer, Professor Fred Hoyle and was first published in 1950 by Blackwell. There was a revised edition, published in 1960, and Pelican first published the book in 1963. I thought that this eminent astronomer might be helpful in explaining how and why the universe began.

The preface to the 1960 edition comprises of only three sentences. The middle sentence reads, 'One chapter, that dealing with the origin of the planets, has been entirely rewritten.' I underlined this in blue Biro and wrote, 'Rather significant!'

In his chapter on the origin of the stars, Hoyle wrote, 'Astronomers are generally agreed that the galaxy started its life as a rotating flat disc of gas with no stars in it.'[2] I have always remembered this as saying, 'and there was a cloud of gas'. That is not quite what Hoyle wrote but the reader may decide that this is a fair précis. Hoyle was saying that, at the beginning of the universe, there was something. That something was moving—rotating he said—so this matter was associated with motion and energy.

His book's last chapter is entitled 'A Personal View.'[3] He considered the opinion of the 'out-and-out materialists'[4] whose view he suggests has the appeal of simplicity: the universe is here so let us take it for granted. But Hoyle says, 'there is a great deal more about the universe that I should like to know. Why is the universe as it is and not something else? Why is the universe here at all?'[5] He stated his personal view that, at that time, mankind had no answers to such questions.

Hoyle continued by considering 'contemporary religious beliefs'[6] and noted that there is a good deal of cosmology in the Bible. Hoyle may have been aware of Job 9:9: 'He is the maker of the Bear and Orion, the Pleiades and the constellations of the south,' or of Job 38:4: 'Where were you when I laid the earth's foundation?'

He commented that this understanding, at the time when the book of Job was written, was remarkable. However, he declared this ancient Hebrew cosmology to be the 'merest daub' compared to what modern science reveals. Hoyle asked the following intriguing question: 'Is it in anyway reasonable to suppose that it was given to the Hebrews to understand mysteries far deeper than anything we can comprehend?'[6] In other words, were the Hebrew Scriptures inspired by God?

I wonder whether he had some insight into the Biblical account that the Jews did indeed claim a special relationship with the God of the Bible. When Hoyle stated that mankind does not have answers to the difficult questions about the origin of the universe, 'the Hebrews' may have disagreed and suggested to Hoyle that an eyewitness account of the origin of the universe has been provided in Genesis.

My journey to a more mature worldview and the meaning of the universe and of life had begun. For now, Fred Hoyle, Professor of Astronomy at Cambridge, later Knight and Astronomer Royal, was my guide. Astronomy or Cosmology seemed to be a good place to start. If I understood what the origin of the universe was, I might get an understanding of how I should live for my remaining 52.6 years on planet Earth—in 1965 the life expectancy for men in the UK was 68.6 years!

So, in the next chapter, I will consider the early influences that helped me develop my worldview.

NOTES

1 Sir Allen Lane, *The Literary Shed*, (2013). https://www.theliteraryshed.co.uk/read/the-literary-lounge/penguin-original-ten-the-first-titles-published-by-allen-lane
2 Fred Hoyle, *The Nature of the Universe*, (London: Pelican Books,1963), p. 60
3 Ibid., p. 120.

4 Ibid., p. 118.

5 Ibid., p. 121.

6 Ibid., p. 122.

3 Worldview—unfinished business

worldview is the framework by which we view reality and make sense of life and the world. A personal worldview combines all we personally believe to be true. It has consequences in every area of life: how we think about philosophy, science, medicine, anthropology, theology, law, politics, economics, social order and art for example. Principles may be sincerely held but prejudices may also have been imbibed during our developing years. A framework of values and principles may have been taught to us by those we respect and trust.

Marcus Honeysett, in his book, *Meltdown: Making Sense of a Culture in Crisis*, states, 'Any understanding of the world, or worldview, aspires to correspond to reality (i.e., to describe the world as it really is), to be coherent within itself (i.e., to be consistent), and to have transforming power (i.e., to actually work when we put it into practice). Anything claiming to be a true worldview must satisfy not one, but all three of these criteria.'[1] I found this definition helpful.

Along life's journey, many will have absorbed the prevailing cultural norms of the day, from literature, from the media, from fellow pupils or work colleagues. Some beliefs and practices can contain contradictions and inconsistencies. There may be demands for respect and equality for a number of lifestyles and views, but those making such demands may be intolerant of the lifestyles and views of others.

There is also the problem of fear of isolation and persecution for holding views which go against the majority. Men and women working in academia have been silenced, unfunded and had their appointments terminated. A DVD documentary,[2] hosted by the actor Ben Stein, examines the plight of educators and scientists, silenced for their belief in 'Intelligent Design'. Chesterton's comment that 'life is a battle' is astute. The phraseology in modern conversation of, 'the way all rational people think', or 'what everybody knows', or 'the way we think today', can be very intimidating.

Conduct, that not very long ago might have been thought of as wrong, may now be considered to be right and normal. People holding conservative views may be labelled as bigots for not celebrating the liberal views of a vocal minority. Such tensions exist because of a clash in worldviews.

When I went to school for the first time on Tuesday, 1st September 1953, I was not thinking about developing my own worldview. It was, however, an important day in my life. While I can remember the date because it was my 5th birthday, I cannot truthfully remember my feelings about that day. I think there was certainly an element of pride as I walked to school in my new uniform.

Flixton Infant School was half a mile away and it took ten minutes to walk. On the first day, my mother took me and Mr Platten, the nice policeman who lived in our road, saw us across the main road to the avenue which led to my school. I attended this school for two years. We went home for lunch and returned for the afternoon, before walking home at the end of the school day. Flixton is a suburb of Manchester where, in 1948, I had been born at St Marys Hospital.

Walking home at lunchtime with my friend, we would pass an interesting, old, dilapidated house. Nobody lived there and a rather intriguing notice was displayed saying, 'Wilful damage—trespassers will be prosecuted'. In the summer, there were a lot of windfalls under the apple trees in this property and we would dare each other to take these. There was another sign commenting on the fate likely to be suffered by trespassers. When my parents learned about the apples, I was forbidden from any further stealing! I learned that the 'Wilful damage' sign was a warning and the 'Trespassers will be prosecuted' sign declared the penalty for wrongdoing.

At the age of 5 and earlier, I had learned and understood there were rules in life. I could see these were for my good and for the good of others. Everyone driving on the lefthand side of the road was safer than people just choosing right or left. Similarly, playing football or board games were fun if we all obeyed the rules. I think as a child I realized that an intelligent person had made these rules. If we kept the rules, the world would be a better place.

Looking back, I can see three influences or authorities in my life at that stage. My parents and schoolteachers wanted to help me grow up to be honest, decent, disciplined and educated. Mr Platten, the policeman, who represented the law of our land, was friendly but we were taught not to be cheeky to him, and we learned to respect him and the law which he represented.

I enjoyed infant school, remembering assembly each morning when we loudly greeted the headmistress with, 'Good morning, Miss Mann. Good morning, everybody.' The Christian faith was affirmed in prayers and in hymns such as, *All things bright and beautiful.* I was very pleased to take part in one Christmas Nativity play as the first king, carrying gold! I had a talking part: 'Behold the star'.' The headgear, made from a pudding basin, milk bottle tops and wooden tapers, did not detract from my enthusiasm as I pointed out the star.

As I grew up, my parents were not churchgoers and there was never any suggestion of my brother or me being sent to a Sunday school. Bible stories were learned at school and divinity was treated as any other academic subject. My mother had attended Sunday school at a Baptist Church near her home as a child. Later in life, when I was a medical student, I did have a serious discussion with her about 'religion'. She explained her belief that mankind was evolving and talked a lot about *eugenics*.[3]

My father had been educated as a day boy at Eltham College. This school was founded for the sons of missionaries (incidentally his father was not a missionary). The houses at Eltham were named after famous missionaries: Livingstone, Moffat, Carey and Chalmers. My father had attended a Crusader class (Christian youth group) as a teenager. When I commented earlier that my father collected a lot of Pelican books, this reflected his serious interest in many subjects. One book which seemed to influence him a lot was, *Honest to God* by the Anglican Bishop of Woolwich, John A.T. Robinson, published in 1963 by SCM Press[4]. This criticized traditional Christian theology and seemed to reinforce my father's indifference to Christianity.

In the early 1950s, when I went to infant school, Christianity was accepted and a morning assembly with a hymn and prayers was usual. The school was happy and disciplined. We learned to read and write, and boys and girls mixed happily and safely in the playground. Our favourite game, 'Ticky chain', generated much excitement. Friends were particularly important to my brother and me, and we had several in our road. We went for bike rides, played football and cricket, went fishing, made dens in the 'big field' and watched our local football team, Old Flixtonians, playing in the Lancashire and Cheshire Amateur League.

In primary education, I was learning what was right and wrong; to obey parents, teachers and the law of the land; to play in school games according to the rules; and to take some early responsibility in school and family life. These were all necessary foundations for developing a mature rational worldview. But I had not faced some of the big questions yet. The transition to boarding school and A-levels seemed to open up new issues. Adolescence and puberty also raised the issue of manhood!

I mentioned earlier that, at Epsom College, my first Pelican book purchase introduced me to Fred Hoyle's 'rotating cloud of gas', as I tried to build my own worldview. The same month, I bought my second Pelican book, *Space in the Sixties*,[5] published in 1963 by Patrick Moore. Patrick Moore was a regular TV broadcaster of the monthly programme, *The Sky at Night*. A boy in my house at school was friendly with Patrick Moore and so I gave him my new book in the hope that Patrick Moore would autograph it. This he did: he wrote, 'Nigel Gordon-Jones all best wishes. The Errata slip is the best part! I wonder how right my forecasts are. Regards Patrick Moore 1965 January 26th.'

This entry needs a little explanation. I had written my name as N

A Gordon Jones in the front of the book. Patrick Moore inserted a hyphen between the Gordon and the Jones. When I left home for boarding school in 1961, my mother had carefully sewed multiple *N A Gordon Jones* nametapes into all my clothing. Because of the many Joneses working in the health service, my father had started using his third name, Gordon, in combination with Jones as his surname. My brother and I were both named Gordon Jones at birth but without a hyphen. Gordon was chosen, as my grandfather had served in the 6th Gordon Highlanders from November 1914 to the end of the war.

On my first morning in a classroom at Epsom College, the form master, who taught us French, asked the sixteen boys in the room for their forenames and surnames so that he could compile a list for the school printer. When he came to me, I said, 'Nigel Gordon Jones'. He replied rather abruptly, 'HYPHEN?' I replied, 'No Sir,' to which he said, 'Your name is Jones.' You did not argue in those days and, apart from inscriptions in my own books, my surname has been Jones ever since.

Patrick Moore's book explored the potential for future space travel and exploration of the universe. His opening observations showed the progress that had already been made in travel. For example, Dr D Lardner[6] had said in 1838, 'Men might as well project a voyage to the moon as attempt to employ steam navigation across the stormy North Atlantic Ocean.' Another example was a letter written to P.E. Cleator[7], founder of the British Interplanetary Society, by the Under Secretary of State in 1934, saying, 'We follow with interest any work that is being done in other countries on jet propulsion, but scientific investigation into the possibilities has given no indication that this method can be a serious competitor to the airscrew-engine combination. We do not consider that we should be justified in spending any time or money on it ourselves.' When, ten years later, German V2 rockets began falling on southern England, this comment must have seemed rather foolish.

The first lunar rockets were sent to and around the moon in 1959.[8] On the last page of his book, Moore suggested that, before the end of the 1960s, a manned trip around the moon might take place, though he was dubious if that would happen.[9]

In the event, things moved more rapidly and on 20th of July 1969, the Apollo lunar module, Eagle, touched down on the surface of the moon and Neil Armstrong became the first person to step onto the lunar surface. I remember sitting up most of the night watching it in black and white, listening as President Nixon spoke to the astronauts from the Oval Office.

Patrick Moore's book suggested much about the future but, apart from telling me that the earth was 4,500 million years old, I had not learned anything more about the origin of the earth or of human life. In 1964, as I studied for my Biology A-level, new horizons of knowledge would be opened up for me.

NOTES

1 Marcus Honeysett, *Meltdown: Making Sense of a Culture in Crisis*, (Leicester: Inter-Varsity Press, 2006), p. 31.

2 Ben Stein and Nathan Frankowski, *Expelled: No Intelligence Allowed, (DVD)*, (Timeless International Christi, January 2010).

3 Eugenics is a discredited and immoral idea that one can selectively breed humans to eradicate undesirable traits. While this might be inherited diseases,

eugenics was widely committed to racial discrimination. The Nazis in the Second World War practised eradication of undesirable and unhealthy people.

4 John A.T. Robinson, *Honest to God*, (London: SCM Press, 1963).

5 Patrick Moore, *Space in the Sixties*, (London: Pelican books, 1963).

6 Ibid., p. 7.

7 Ibid. p. 8.

8 Ibid., p. 172.

9 Ibid., p. 218.

4 School biology – introduction to evolution

Although Epsom College had a strong bias toward boys training as doctors, as part of a balanced education we also did one lesson a week of History, one of Music appreciation and one of Art appreciation. The art master had been a Spitfire pilot in Malta in the Second World War and wrote a book about his experiences.[1] He taught us about the history of art and architecture as well as encouraging us to draw.

In the first lesson on a Monday morning, we studied the history of modern China. The history teacher had been a chaplain in the Parachute Regiment and was captured at Arnhem, followed by being a POW for seven months.

The college had a beautiful chapel named after St Luke. In my first year at Epsom, I had been a treble in the choir until my voice broke. We attended chapel every morning, except Wednesdays, and twice on Sundays. One Sunday evening, late in 1964, in a conversation with other boys waiting to go into the evening service, I learned that some of the boys did not believe in Adam and Eve. I can remember one of the boys siding with me, but all the others told us that we had evolved from monkeys. This, at the age of 16, was the first time in my life that I consciously heard the word *evolution*. I did not share the confidence of my peers that we were descended from monkeys; the idea did not appeal to me!

One of my experiences of later life, in moving from house to house, is that old boxes of possessions are re-examined. Thus, the day came for my A-level notes to be tipped in the dustbin. I did however keep my A-level notes on genetics and evolution. As I write this chapter, I have them open in front of me. The handwriting is that of a 16-year-old; the text is full of certainty and, of course, a number of mechanisms by which the evolution of man is said to have taken place.

My notes on genetics begin with a heading: 'The continuity of life'. They read:

> Life is always produced from other life. Louis Pasteur disproved the theory of spontaneous generation. Pasteur showed conclusively that no organism arises except as offspring of pre-existing organisms. But this is negative inductive evidence, and some simple forms of life *certainly must have* arisen spontaneously, although perhaps under very different conditions, early in the Palaeozoic. Modern biochemistry does throw some light upon the possibilities of living organic material being derived from inorganic and the existence of crystalline forms of viruses affords a possible link.

I find that these notes are verbatim from my personal copy of our textbook, *Animal Biology* by Grove & Newell.[2]

The phrase '*certainly must have*', in the light of Pasteur's conclusive proof that life certainly must NOT have arisen from non-life, seemed baffling and suggested a faith in naturalistic processes having miraculous power! I will return to the question as to whether living organisms could arise by 'chemical evolution' from a primordial soup and what part viruses might play, later in this book.

My notes on evolution begin with an incorrect definition of

creation as being, 'All animals and plants were produced as they are now and they have not changed.' Creation was declared untenable because of the existence of fossils and other evidence of change.

Grove & Newell describe *creation*, the alternative view to *organic evolution*, as follows: 'There also exists an equally ancient opposing view for it is found in many mythologies, namely, Special Creation, which postulates that present-day forms were created by some outside influence when life came into existence on this planet and have continued with little alteration ever since.'[3]

However, Grove & Newell's definition of *special creation*, given to us as 16-year-olds, does not do justice to the Bible's account of creation and may be described as a 'straw-man'. The straw-man fallacy is when a person misrepresents his opponent's position and then proceeds to refute that misrepresentation rather than what his opponent actually claims. *Special creation* does *not* say that little alteration has occurred. *Special creation* describes creatures being made according to their kinds or *baramins* but does not claim these have remained unchanged. (*Baramin* is derived from two Hebrew words and means, 'created kind'.)

Grove & Newell were right to say that evolution and special creation are opposing views, but it is important to represent each view fairly and honestly. Evolution embraces three concepts: (1) change over time; (2) universal common ancestry of all living things; and (3) natural selection, which is the process in nature by which organisms better adapted to their environment tend to survive and reproduce more than those less adapted to their environment. Natural selection acts on random variations or genetic mutations. Despite this, we should be clear that Darwinian evolution is an unguided process.

On the other hand, special creation claims that plants, birds, cats, fish or humans did not come from a common ancestor but are all separate created kinds of a Creator. Natural selection or adaptation does operate within creation and leads to changes in the characteristics of animals and plants, whether over time or by breeding, but within the boundaries of each kind.

Much confusion is caused by the use of the term, *micro-evolution*. This is used as another way of describing natural selection. For example, Charles Darwin bred pigeons in his garden and produced many different appearances. Some of his pigeons are displayed in a case in the Natural History Museum in London and are labelled as, 'fancy breeds of pigeons owned by Charles Darwin and which provided evidence for his theory of evolution by natural selection.'

Darwin, using his human intelligence was able to breed pigeons with different characteristics. But these always remained within the boundary of being *pigeons*. His claim, upheld by others today, that this demonstrates evolution (one *kind* of creature changing into another *kind*) cannot be correct. The changes in appearance by breeding pigeons or even by natural selection in the wild, as seen in Darwin's finches on the Galapagos Islands, do not produce new *kinds* of creatures. Pigeons are pigeons and finches are finches. *Macro-evolution* has not been demonstrated in Darwin's pigeons or finches.

In spite of these comments, it is claimed that there is evidence in the fossil record that evolution did produce a developing continuum of animals and plants from *kind* to *kind* and that fossils demonstrate that such changes have taken place.

My A-level notes have several headings for evolutionary evidence: the fossil record; vestigial organs; embryology; physiological evidence; geographical evidence; and morphology. The vestigial organs, listed, were the human appendix; points on our ears known as Darwinian points or tubercles; and the pelvic bones of the whale or dolphin. I will return to several of these headings in a later chapter.

During my two years of A-level Biology study, I did not have any reason to question the reigning paradigm that all life on Earth had come from a common ancestor through the process of evolution. Indeed, there was a possibility that in the A-level examination, I would have had to write an essay based on this evolutionary teaching, so I needed to know the evidence and arguments.

My belief in a literal Adam and Eve as a 16-year-old had been based on Religious Education in school, which raised no doubts about their being the ancestors of all mankind. My parents had not raised any such issues and it was my exposure to A-level Biology that introduced this new tension into my journey of understanding.

NOTES

1 Denis Barnham, *Malta Spitfire Pilot: A Personal Account of Ten Weeks of War, April–June 1942*, (S. Yorkshire: Frontline Books, 2011).

2 Grove & Newell, *Animal Biology*, (London: University Tutorial Press Ltd, 1964, 6th edition reprint), pp. 724–726.

3 Ibid., p. 724.

5 Guy's Hospital – the medical course

During my first year in the sixth form at Epsom College, I applied to study medicine at several London teaching hospitals. I remember catching the train from Epsom Downs to London Bridge to attend an interview at Guy's Hospital. My father had trained there during the Second-World-War years and so I was thrilled to be later offered a place at Guy's Hospital Medical School, part of London University, commencing in October 1966.

When I received my A-level results, I notified Guy's Hospital and they confirmed my place. It was suggested that reading two books in preparation would help. One was called, *Synopsis of Regional Anatomy* by T. B. Johnston[1], formerly Professor of Anatomy at Guy's Hospital. The second book was entitled, *Living Control Systems* by Dr L. E. Bayliss[2] of the Physiology Department of University College Hospital, London. The anatomy book was straightforward, though rather daunting in view of the extent of human anatomy. Anatomy had to be visualized and memorized, and there was a lot of it. For example, each bone of the human body has muscles attached. The point of attachment of these muscles can be recognized on the bare bone and we would soon be embarking on learning these. Later, in the primary examination for my surgical qualification, I was handed a first rib (the top one), asked to name which bone it was, tell the examiner which side the rib came from and name the muscles which had been attached to it.

The physiology book by Dr Bayliss introduced me to the world of homeostasis and biological feedback mechanisms. This is the way that an organism or cell regulates its internal environment and maintains a healthy equilibrium, usually by a system of feedback controls. The feedback mechanisms keep the organism, or cell, functioning within healthy boundaries. All the organs in the human body contribute to homeostasis. Messengers of chemical, thermal, and neural nature interact to help and control the body while it maintains homeostasis.

As I read Dr Bayliss's book today, it refers me back to the great French physiologist, Claude Bernard (1813–1878), who talked in his lectures of 'free and independent life'[3], best seen in the most highly developed animals which are little affected by changes in the physical and chemical properties of their surroundings. Bernard introduced the idea that the living cells of an animal (or plant) were less influenced by the 'external environment' such as the air, sea or lake in which it lives but, more importantly, by an 'internal environment' consisting of a watery solution, often quite different in composition from that of the outside solution or environment. The constancy of the internal environment (homeostasis) is maintained despite interaction with the external environment.

Anatomy needed to be memorized. Physiology to me was more daunting than anatomy and much of Dr Bayliss's book was difficult to understand in 1966 and still is! I draw attention to the complexity of physiology to emphasize the difficulty that I grappled with as my worldview developed. 'How did these complex feedback mechanisms arise?' I had learned that evolution is a non-directed process. How did chance processes, which I had learned about in sixth form biology, turn lifeless chemicals into living creatures with highly complex control systems? Charles Darwin himself was particularly challenged by the complexity of the human eye and expressed serious misgivings about its evolution.

In *The Origin of Species,* he wrote: 'To suppose that the eye with all its inimitable contrivances for adjusting the focus to different distances, for admitting different amounts of light, and for the correction of spherical and chromatic aberration, could have been formed by natural selection seems, I freely confess, absurd in the highest possible degree.'[4]

One may be tempted to think that Darwin was doubtful about the truth of evolution when he made this remark. However, Darwin went on to write: 'Reason tells me, that if numerous gradations from a simple and imperfect eye to one complex and perfect can be shown to exist, each grade being useful to its possessor, as is certainly the case; if further, the eye ever varies and the variations be inherited, as is likewise certainly the case; and if such variations should be useful to any animal under changing conditions of life, then the difficulty of believing that a perfect and complex eye could be formed by natural selection, though insuperable by our imagination, can hardly be considered real.'[4]

The necessity of affirming evolution as the mechanism explaining the origin of life caused Charles Darwin to accept the evolution of the human eye, even when, in his own words, that was clearly absurd. My biology textbook, Grove and Newell, argued for the spontaneous generation of life, even when Louis Pasteur had shown that no organism arises, except as offspring of pre-existing organisms. Grove & Newell stated authoritatively that some simple forms of life *certainly must have* arisen spontaneously![5] What Charles Darwin called absurd, was swept away by the necessity of believing that natural selection has the power to create and modify.

Darwin wrote, in a letter in 1860, to the Harvard Professor of Natural History, Asa Gray: 'The eye to this day gives me a cold shudder, when I think of the fine known gradations, my reason tells me I ought to conquer the cold shudder.'[6] While Darwin had not shown that such gradations[7] exist and did not explain how this supposed progression took place, his worldview caused him to believe something he did not have evidence for and to accept natural selection as an adequate explanation of the human eye.

Darwin's *Zoological Notebook* indicates that, during the voyage of the *Beagle* between 1831–36, he first encountered mantis shrimps.[8] There are 451 species of the mantis shrimp. He might well have commented that the evolution of their eyes was even more absurd! Their vision is enhanced by an amazing control system which endows them with vision that in some respects is superior to human vision. They have the most complex eyes in the animal kingdom. Their eyes are mounted on mobile stalks, which can move independently of each other. Human eyes possess three types of photoreceptor cells but, among the species of Mantis shrimps, we learn that they have between 12 and 16 types of photoreceptor cells in their eyes.

A research team from Bristol University and the University of Western Australia published a paper on the mantis shrimp's eyes, in the Journal of Comparative Physiology A in 2019., partly funded by the Air Force Office of Scientific Research. They concluded that the 'stomatopod (*mantis shrimps are stomatopods*) visual system is unaffected by any potentially image degrading effects due to torsional self-motion and appears robust to ambiguous "apparent motion" cues that are a feature of vision in other animals, including humans. Understanding how stomatopods do this could be valuable for any robotic vision system that needs to maintain visual stability, or track objects, whilst moving with complex or unpredictable trajectories.'[9]

The paper presents foundational research, perhaps, leading to the development of advanced robotic eyes or cameras. Such research is known as *biomimicry*, a practice that learns from and mimics the strategies found in nature to solve human design challenges. The researchers, of course, use human intelligence in their work. However, the design of the mantis shrimp is attributed to naturalistic processes of chance and chaos acting on some matter over a long period of time. It is thought-provoking that these very bright scientists will probably produce a less sophisticated robotic vision system than that of the mantis shrimp, which has been attributed to the undirected process of evolution.

Darwin was challenged by the origin of the complexity of living systems, but I think that my fellow medical students in 1966 were more taken up with the wonder of the structure and working of the human body, which we were learning to understand. Let me quote Bayliss writing in chapter 7 of *Living Control Systems* to show how awesome the human body is.

> In discussing the evidence for the constancy of the internal environment, Claude Bernard (and Barcroft and Cannon after

him) considered its content of water, oxygen, carbon dioxide and other substances used or produced by the living chemical factories; its content of mineral salts; and its temperature. A homeostatic control system is responsible for regulating the exchange of each of these substances, and of heat, with the external world. Each has its receptors and its effectors, hidden for the most part within the animal (or plant): and only rarely are their activities apparent to an external observer (or, by analogy with ourselves, to the animal itself) unless looked for specially. In addition, there are many other control systems, less obviously concerned in homeostasis, but just as important. [10]

The human body has five main senses: vision, hearing, touch, smell and taste. Special sensors are located in the eyes, ears, skin, nose and tongue. We also have sensors which register temperature, body position, balance and blood pH. These sensors send neural messages to areas of our brain which can then initiate regulatory action to protect and maintain homeostasis. Learning about all these was 'mind blowing', particularly if I was to stick with the worldview that they all developed by, what Darwin called, 'fine known gradations', for which there seemed to be little evidence.

I began studying medicine at Guy's Hospital in October 1966. There were 108 students in our year, 25 of whom were girls. For the first year I lived in 'digs' on Crystal Palace Park Road, catching the train from Penge West Station to Guy's Hospital each day. My landlord and landlady, Jim and Rita, were 'Geordies'. I lived on half-board in the week with three meals per day at weekends for £5 a week. Rita did my washing and ironing for two shillings and sixpence! The three-monthly season ticket for the train cost £13.

During the first 18 months at medical school, we studied basic medical sciences. This meant physiology, anatomy and biochemistry. These were studied for five terms and for the last two terms we studied Pharmacology as well. At the end of this time, we took exams in each of the four subjects; the exam was known as 2nd MB.

I really enjoyed the 2nd MB course, which was taught in the Medical School building. Our teachers inspired us, as our understanding of the normal healthy working of the human body grew. The three main professors, Prof. Hunt, Prof. Warwick and Prof. Haslewood ran excellent departments with many good teachers.

There were large lecture theatres for the three main subjects and laboratories for physiology and biochemistry. There was a large anatomy dissecting room where human bodies, donated for dissection, were on tables and covered in sheets to preserve dignity. Six students dissected each body: three to each side of the body. Tutorials in these subjects were held in smaller rooms. Histology (microscopic anatomy) was studied in a laboratory with many microscopes, to look at slides of human organs. Pharmacology was also taught in laboratories as well as in a lecture theatre.

After successfully passing 2nd MB, we embarked on three years of clinical studies. We sometimes called this 'being on the wards'. During the fifth year of study, in 1971, we took the Final MB, BS examination, of London University, in Medicine and Therapeutics, Surgery, Pathology, Obstetrics and Gynaecology.

The three clinical years were divided into three-month blocks when single specialities or combinations of clinical specialities were studied to allow weeks full of teaching and training. For example: General Medicine and General Surgery were studied for three months each in the first year on the wards and again for three months each in the final year. Dermatology, Ophthalmology and Anaesthetics were studied together. Ear, Nose & Throat and Psychiatry were another pairing. Orthopaedics and Urology were paired. Paediatrics stood alone as did Obstetrics and Gynaecology. We each had to deliver twenty babies and we spent one month in a peripheral hospital to allow this target to be met.

We had an elective period for nine weeks, which could be in the UK or overseas. I was fortunate to visit Mulago Hospital in Kampala, Uganda. There, I studied Medicine and Paediatrics and saw many new medical conditions. I travelled and visited three mission hospitals during this time and spent a week at the end of my elective climbing Mount Kilimanjaro in Tanzania and visiting friends who were teaching in a secondary school, north of Nairobi in Kenya.

The clinical years suited my way of learning. Much of our teaching was at the bedside or in a room close to the patients who we had just seen and examined. We were responsible for our own patients, taking their blood for testing and quite often carrying out some of those tests ourselves. I have strong memories of particular patients who we learned about and of the way that we were taught by physicians and surgeons on the 'firms' to which we were attached. (A firm usually consisted of two consultants, a senior registrar, a junior registrar and two house officers.) During these years, I became keen on a career in General Surgery. I had enjoyed anatomy dissection, watching or assisting at operations and seemed to have the manual skills necessary to become a surgeon. I appreciated the challenge of dealing with diagnostic problems such as abdominal emergencies.

In the next three chapters, I will describe some matters of interest encountered during our learning about human physiology, anatomy and biochemistry. These would have a bearing on my developing worldview. I had just turned 18 years old when I began at Guy's Hospital.

NOTES

1   T. B. Johnston, *Synopsis of Regional Anatomy*, (London: Churchill Publishing House, 1968).

2   Dr L. E. Bayliss, *Living Control Systems*, (London: The English Universities Press Ltd, 1968).

3   Dr L. E. Bayliss, *Living Control Systems*, p. 4.

4   Charles Darwin, *The Origin of Species, First Edition*, (Albemarle Street, London: John Murray Publishing House, 1859), p. 217.

5   Grove & Newell, *Animal Biology*, pp. 724–726.

6   Francis Darwin (ed.), *The life and letters of Charles Darwin, including an autobiographical chapter. vol. 2.* (New York: D. Appleton and Co., 1899), p. 67.

7   *Gradations* means a series of successive changes, stages or degrees.

8   https://beagleproject.wordpress.com/2012/09/04/darwins-shrimp/

9   Ilse M Daly et al., 'Gaze stabilization in mantis shrimp in response to angled stimuli', *Journal of Comparative Physiology, A*, volume 205(4), May 16th, 2019, pp. 515–527.

10 Dr L. E. Bayliss, *Living Control Systems*, p. 115.

6 Human physiology

Before we continue, we need to define what *human physiology* is. In simple terms I would say, 'it is how the human body works'. A fuller definition from the internet states, 'Human physiology is the science of the mechanical, physical, and biochemical functions of normal humans or human tissues or organs.' The word, 'normal', is used to imply healthy. The study of humans and their tissues or organs when they are suffering from disease is known as *pathology*.

The Professor in charge of the Department of Physiology at Guy's Hospital, in 1966, was Jack Naylor Hunt MD, PhD, DSc, FRCP. He made valuable contributions to our understanding of the control mechanisms governing the emptying of the stomach and of gastric acid production. In his first lecture to us, he explained what *physiology* is and the various systems that we would study: for example, the respiratory system or the cardiovascular system. I believe he also commented that medical school would double our vocabulary. Some estimates suggest that a medical student learns an extra 15,000 words[1] during his/her training. Prof. Hunt then spent rather a long time discussing one of these new words: *teleology*.

Teleology is the study of the purpose or design of natural occurrences. As an example of this we might ask, 'What is a chair for?' Our response would be, 'for sitting on'. This is a teleological explanation. Prof. Hunt said that we should never use teleology when describing or explaining a physiological process. This would be to imply that there was a designer of the process. He was a precise man and believed that it was unscientific to speak or write in such a way. This meant that one should not ask, 'What is gastric acid for?' but should describe what gastric acid does.

At the time, I accepted this new information, among my many new experiences and knowledge, but I did not realize the significance of his viewpoint. I did, however, get my knuckles metaphorically wrapped, eight months later, when one of the physiology teachers marked an essay of mine entitled, 'Smooth Muscle—with special reference to the Alimentary Tract.' The essay was written on 8 May 1967; I have it in front of me as I write.

I was in trouble with my very first sentence: 'Muscle is specialized for the performance of a definite function.' The word, *for*, was circled in red pen with the comment, 'implies design or purpose'.' In the margin was written again in red pen, 'We can say what something does but not what it is for.' Three more times in the essay the red pen circled the words or phrases, '*purpose*', '*to control*' and '*to have to*'. The final comment on the essay, apart from 'Beta+ fair', was, 'Avoid implying purpose everywhere. We are what we are as a result of evolutionary processes. We can say what a given region does but not what it is for.' This particular teacher certainly agreed with Prof. Hunt!

When I wrote this essay, I had no agenda to challenge Prof. Hunt's teaching. I think you would agree that it is reasonable to ask my earlier question, 'What is a chair for?' The whole of the learning process during childhood is spent asking Mum or Dad, 'What's that for?' The essay title linked the specialization of a particular sort of muscle with a particular definite function. So, it seemed reasonable to me to ask, 'What is smooth muscle for?'

There are three types of muscle: skeletal, smooth and cardiac. They each have a different structure and have a particular role.

Skeletal muscle moves our limbs, our neck and other structures. It is under the voluntary control of our brain and nervous system.

Smooth muscle is found in the walls of hollow organs like the stomach and bladder, allowing a change in size but also propelling contents through or out of the body. This facilitates a bodily function such as digestion. Smooth muscle is involuntary muscle— it is not controlled in the same way as skeletal muscle but works automatically under the control of the autonomic nervous system. In the eye, smooth muscle alters the shape of the lens to bring objects into focus.

Cardiac muscle makes the heart contract to pump blood around the body. Cardiac muscle cells are branched, which allows electrical impulses passing down the cardiac conduction system to also pass around the muscle mass of the heart. Cardiac muscle exhibits rhythmical contractions (even when a portion is removed experimentally from the heart for a period of time in mice) and is controlled by the autonomic nervous system. You do not have to think to make your heart beat—fortunately! The sympathetic nervous system speeds it up and the parasympathetic nervous system slows it down.

In retrospect, I understand Prof. Hunt did not accept that an intelligent *first cause* had designed man and his physiology with a purpose. Clearly his teaching was in line with the prevailing idea of evolution. His view was that teleology must not be allowed in scientific literature. His understanding was that physiology described a chain of causes and effects with no goals or purpose and we should not fall into the trap of making teleological statements. I think that Prof. Hunt must be respected for the consistency of his views, while some modern physiologists could be accused of cheating by speaking in a teleological way when they do not believe in a designer!

There are many current physiology textbooks with teleological explanations in their pages. I have recently spent time in my local medical school library looking in the index of physiology textbooks for the word, *teleology*, and then looking at the relevant passages. The writers of the textbooks accept a teleological explanation for certain physiological properties and rather coyly imply that 'Nature' has inevitably led to these properties.

Bertrand Russell was a 20th century philosopher and atheist. He wrote in his book, *A History of Western Philosophy*:

> When we ask 'why?' concerning an event, we may mean either of two things. We may mean, 'What purpose did this event serve?' or we may mean, 'What earlier circumstances caused this event?' The answer to the former question is a teleological explanation, or an explanation by final causes; the answer to the latter question is a mechanistic explanation. I do not see how it could have been known in advance which of these two questions science ought to ask, or whether it ought to ask both. But experience has shown that the mechanistic question leads to scientific knowledge, while the teleological question does not.[2]

Russell dismissed teleological questions as being unproductive, which of course they will be, if a purposeful designer is totally excluded as an explanation for the origin of all things. His view is a subtle putdown of the search for the first cause of any phenomenon which we observe in the natural world. He implied that looking for a *designer of things* which appear designed will lead to a dead end and certainly not to scientific knowledge. His phrase, 'mechanistic explanation', is synonymous with material causes or naturalistic causes, which are other phrases used to describe this scientific point of view.

Professor Richard Lewontin, an atheist American evolutionary biologist, who died in July 2021, was a researcher at Harvard University. He ruffled many feathers among the scientific fraternity with frank remarks such as, 'We are forced, by our *a priori* adherence to material causes, to create an apparatus of investigation and a set of concepts that produce material explanations, no matter how counter-intuitive, no matter how mystifying to the uninitiated. Moreover, that materialism is absolute, for we cannot allow a Divine Foot in the door.'[3]

Teleology seems to be acceptable today. An interesting comment in Wikipedia's account of *teleology* states: '... some minimal level of teleology might be recognized as useful or at least tolerable for practical purposes even by people who reject its cosmologic accuracy.'[4]

Mark Perlman wrote, in a paper in 2004, 'Teleology has certainly made a comeback in philosophical circles in the last thirty years. It went from a suspect or disreputable notion, ready for elimination, to the hottest topic in philosophy of biology, psychology and mind.'[5]

However, there is clearly some embarrassment among scientists who use teleological explanations in their writing. An outstanding

20th century physiologist, J.B.S. Haldane FRS (1892—1964), was a British-Indian scientist who received many accolades as the most brilliant biologist of his age. Haldane was an atheist and professed Marxist. He was known for his work in the study of physiology, genetics, evolutionary biology, and mathematics. He stated that, 'Teleology is like a mistress to a biologist: he cannot live without her but he's unwilling to be seen with her in public.'[6] Haldane is also reputed to have said, 'If one could conclude as to the nature of the Creator from a study of his creation it would appear that God has a special fondness for stars and beetles.'[7]

This mocking remark fails to appreciate that to create stars and beetles from nothing is an extraordinary achievement which is not belittled by a bright man's sarcasm.

Prof. Hunt introduced new methods in teaching: multiple choice questions, which we did regularly; interpretive questions based on clinical papers; and practical classes where students ran a research project for a full term in conjunction with a member of the staff. As an embryonic surgeon, I wanted to understand physiology—fluid balance, signs of shock or reasons for pain would all become part of my daily work.

I did not need to agree with his view of what is allowed in explaining physiology, but I was beginning to understand the philosophical implications of his teaching. If we take Prof. Hunt's teaching to its logical conclusion, then we should say that there is no purpose in life. This was a tough idea for an 18-year-old medical student who was beginning to look at the human body with wonder. For example, consider the electrical conducting system of the heart which not only has nerves like electrical wires running into and through it, but then has individual muscle cells capable of transferring the electrical impulse to its neighbour, and the whole organ automatically (without conscious decision) filling with blood and emptying regularly to supply far off areas of our bodies.

Prof. Hunt seemed to agree with the message of Bertrand Russell who said, 'Man is the product of causes which had no prevision of the end they were achieving.'[8] The idea that man was not designed was shared by George Gaylord Simpson, a famous US palaeontologist, who was brought up as a Christian but later became an agnostic. Simpson said, 'Man is the result of a purposeless and materialistic process that did not have him in mind. He was not planned.'[9] One could continue with more recent quotes from Richard Dawkins: 'The universe … no design, no purpose,'[10] or Jerry Coyne: 'There is no special purpose for your life.'[11]

But such pessimistic conclusions were the exact opposite of the integrated complexity of the human body that I was seeing through my studies. These 'authorities' seemed to be in denial of the evidence. To claim that something lacking intelligence or even nothing, had made the human body seemed beyond belief. In my next chapter, I will look at the teaching of anatomy at Guy's Hospital.

NOTES

1 How many new words do medical students learn? www.quora.com

2 Bertrand Russell, *A History of Western Philosophy*, (London: Allen & Unwin, 1946), pp. 86–87.

3 Richard Lewontin, *Billions and Billions of Demons*, www.nybooks.com, January 9, 1997. https://www.nybooks.com/articles/1997/01/09/billions-and-billions-of-demons/

4 Teleology, Wikipedia the free encyclopaedia. https://en.wikipedia.org/wiki/Teleology

5 Mark Perlman, 'The modern philosophical resurrection of teleology', *The Monist*, vol. 87, no. 1, 2004, pp. 46.

6 Ernst Mayr, *Toward A New Philosophy Of Biology—Observations of an Evolutionist*, (Cambridge, Massachusetts and London: Harvard University Press, 1988), p. 63.

7 Stephen Jay Gould, 'A Special Fondness for Beetles; Haldane's speech to the British Interplanetary Society 1951', *Natural History* (1) Vol 102, 1993, p. 4.

8 Bertrand Russell, 'The Free Man's Worship', *The Independent Review*, 1 December 1903 pp. 415–24.

9 George Gaylord Simpson, *The Meaning of Evolution. A study of the history of life and of its significance for man*, (Yale University Press, 1950), p. 344.

10 Richard Dawkins, *River Out of Eden*, (New York: Basic Books, 1995), p. 133.

11 Richard Weikart, 'Darwinism, the Meaninglessness of Life, and of Death', *Evolution News*, April 8, 2016. https://evolutionnews.org/2016/04/darwinism_the_m/

7 Anatomy

What is *anatomy*? It is the science of the bodily structure of humans, animals, and other living organisms. Dissection and the separation of parts of the body, are particularly important to its correct understanding. The structural organisation of living things is studied. The word, *anatomy*, is derived from the Greek words, *ana*, meaning 'up' and, *tomia*, meaning 'cutting': hence, 'cutting up'.

The importance of dissection is illustrated by the fact that Galen (AD 129–200) was the most famous physician of antiquity, writing extensively on anatomy and human physiology, though he almost certainly never dissected a human body. His descriptions of human anatomy were often inaccurate, being based on the dissection of pigs and Barbary apes. He did work at a school for gladiators and learned from dealing with their wounds. The Romans had decreed that human dissection was unlawful in approximately 150 BC. Prior to that, human dissection took place in Alexandria from about 300 BC. That all changed with the Roman ban and, for more than a thousand years, Galen's teaching was believed.

In the late 13th century, human dissection began again at Bologna University, though Galen's views still continued to dominate the teaching of anatomy. This all changed when Andreas Vesalius (1514–1564) published his beautiful anatomy book, *De humani corporis fabrica Libri Septem*, in 1543.[1] The book was filled with amazing drawings showing every layer and detail of the human body. I have seen an original copy of this book in the Hagströmer Library of the Karolinska Institutet in Stockholm and it is spectacular. Vesalius produced large anatomical books with several flaps hinged and lying on top of each other to reveal successive layers of dissection. The face of the dissected subject was often his own! Vesalius was a genius with a prodigious knowledge of medicine and very gifted at dissection. He, apparently, made friends with the local judge in Padua, where he worked at the university, to ensure he had a ready supply of bodies from executed criminals.

If we use a microscope to look at the detail of particular tissues in the human body, for example a salivary gland or the spleen, this is known as *histology*. In the preclinical course, we would learn to identify most of the tissues of the human body microscopically. My textbook of histology had 492 pages in it!

The Professor of Anatomy at Guy's Hospital, in 1966, was Roger Warwick BSc, MD, PhD. He had trained in Medicine at Manchester University and served for six years in the Royal Navy during the Second World War, reaching the rank of Surgeon Commander. He was appointed to the chair of Anatomy at Guy's in 1955. He co-edited three editions of Gray's Anatomy.

As students, we were divided, in our preclinical studies, into tutorial groups. There were thirteen in our group and our anatomy tutor was Dr Peter Williams MA, MB, BChir, DSc, FRCS, who was Reader in Anatomy at the time. He was co-editor with Prof. Warwick of Gray's Anatomy. He was an excellent teacher, setting a high standard, and I remember one of our early tutorials, when he was teaching us the anatomy of the groin. The muscles there lie in three layers. He took three sheets of paper, cut them to the shape of the muscles with necessary openings for the passage of the spermatic cord—which was represented by a pencil. Perhaps he got the idea from Vesalius, who used a similar teaching method four hundred years previously. Dr William's obituary, in *The Independent* newspaper dated 10th October 1994, commented that, 'he was one of the first to use overhead transparencies in teaching, in the late 1950s, with multiple overlays to build up complicated diagrams.'[2] If it was good enough for Vesalius, it was good enough for Dr Williams who later became a professor.

Other teaching aids, which we used regularly, were our dissection guides, to help us methodically learn human anatomy in the dissecting room. We dissected the whole body over five terms. These five books were called, *A Manual of Human Anatomy*[3], written by one Professor of Anatomy at the Royal College of Surgeons of England and three Professors of Anatomy at London University: J. T. Aitken, J. Joseph, G. Causey and J. Z. Young.

Dr Jack Joseph MD, DSc, FRCOG was a Reader at Guy's when I was a student and also later became a professor. He was very interested in locomotion—the ability to move from one place to another. He contributed to a *Textbook of Human Anatomy*[4] edited by W J Hamilton, reprinted in 1982. He wrote about the Locomotor System from pages 19 to 200.

Prof. Joseph wrote about the evolution of the locomotor system of Man. What follows is a sample of his writing with much reproduced *verbatim in italics*. He indicated that land-living vertebrates are sometimes known as, Tetrapods. That means creatures with four limbs. *Tetrapods are believed to have been derived from an extinct group of bony fish.* The early tetrapods are known as

Amphibians. *Reptiles are also descended from these early Tetrapods and two specialised offshoots from the earlier reptiles are distinguished as birds and mammals.* He commented that *human evolution seems to have passed through a phase not exactly represented in any living mammal, but possibly most nearly illustrated by a small tree-living animal known as Tupaia,* the common tree shrew about 6 to 8 inches long, found in Thailand, Malaysia and Indonesia.

In the process of evolution, the paired fins of fish were modified into limbs. At an early stage in the course of vertebrate evolution some of the head muscle segments of fish acquired new functions such as the extra-ocular muscles which move the eyeball and the muscles in the floor of the mouth.[5]

The adoption of a relatively upright position of the trunk occurred at an early stage in primate evolution.[6] This "straightening" of the body as a whole…was an evolutionary milestone in the development of Man and resulted in the availability of the hands for the performance of new and more skilled tasks and the consequent development of the forebrain.[7]

On page 196, there is a diagram of the posture of Man and ape. The text confirms *the erect or upright posture of Man is unique. Among the primates Man is the only truly bipedal animal except for the occasional upright posture adopted by the orang-utan … for a few steps.* The text describes the 'centre of gravity of the body' and states *this line invariably passes in front of the transverse axes of the knee joints and slightly behind the transverse axes of the hip joints.*[7] On the next page, '*The vertical line through the centre of gravity of the trunk above the hip joints passes just behind the transverse axes of these joints.*'[8] The text emphasizes that the centre of gravity of the human body lies *slightly* or *just behind* the hip joints. This is of great significance, as the centre of gravity of the apes, claimed to be our nearest relatives, passes in front of the hip joint. According to evolution, humans have gradually evolved an upright stature over millions of years. There are no in-between tetrapods or bipeds either living or extinct. This is not surprising given that, to move the centre of gravity of the body from in front of the hip joint to behind the hip joint would lead to instability at the mid-point.

Professor Verna Wright MD, FRCP, who was the Professor of Rheumatology at the University of Leeds, frequently drew attention to this impossibility in his lectures.[9] Verna Wright was both a clinician and a researcher dealing with diseases which affect our joints and locomotion. Verna Wright was co-director of the Bioengineering Group for the study of Human Joints and collaborated closely with Professor Duncan Dowson CBE, FRS, FREng. Verna was a reliable expert in his field.

The 'in between creature' would be unstable, literally falling over many times in frustration at its poor functional 'design'. I can imagine Verna Wright chuckling as he described a young in-between creature saying to its parent, 'Let's abandon this project, we were better off on four limbs!' When you look at the various pictorial representations of man's evolution from ape to modern man, look closely at the posture of the ape. Usually, the centre of gravity of the ape's body is, correctly, in front of the hip joint but, quite often, there is artistic licence with the ape looking unnaturally upright. The artist is giving the ape a helping hand.

Prof. Joseph, whom I have quoted extensively, wrote a number of other statements which I draw attention to:

> In Man the number of vertebrae has been reduced in the thoracic region to twelve and in the lumbar region to five (thirteen thoracic and seven lumbar our usual in primitive and cursorial mammals). Cursorial mammals are those like deer which are involved in active running. Monkeys retain seven lumbar vertebrae but in the great apes there has also been a reduction in the number. Most large apes have four lumbar vertebrae; the gorilla has thirteen thoracic vertebra and ribs with four lumbar vertebrae.[10]

This of course begs the question of how Man lost a thoracic vertebra and a pair of thirteenth ribs. Prof. Joseph also claimed that some of Man's muscles were vestigial, even when they have a known function. He wrote that 'the plantaris muscle, which acts on the toes as well as the ankle in most animals, is a vestigial muscle in Man with no action on the toes.'[11] This muscle does plantar flex the ankle joint and also flexes the knee joint; Prof. Joseph was wrong to say that it has become functionless (vestigial) in the course of evolution.

'The extensor digitorum longus muscle which in most mammals is attached to the femur has lost this attachment in Man and thus has no action on the femur.'[11] But this muscle does have a perfectly reasonable function to dorsiflex the toes, foot and ankle. This means it pulls the toes and forefoot up off the ground. Just because we have chosen to give the same Latin name to a muscle in Man and other mammals, does not prove that this muscle has 'lost its attachment to the femur' in Man!

As we entered the Anatomy Dissection Room, there was a large, coloured picture of the evolution of man from a crouching ape, in tetrapod style, leading to the upright posture of a man, as alluded to above. When the time came for us to sit the 2nd MB exam, it was rumoured that one of the essays was going to be, 'How did Man achieve his upright posture?' Fortunately, there was a choice of questions in the exam!

When we read of paired fins being modified into limbs by evolution, I am reminded of the *Just So Story* of 'The Elephant's Child' by Rudyard Kipling,[12] who won the Nobel Prize for Literature in 1907. He wrote: 'In the High and Far-Off Times the Elephant, O Best Beloved, had no trunk. He had only a blackish, bulgy nose, as big as a boot, that he could wriggle about from side to side; but he could not pick up things with it. But there was one Elephant—a new Elephant— an Elephant's Child—who was full of "'satiable curtiosity, and that means he asked ever so many questions".' (*curtiosity* is not a misprint!)

The story progresses until one day, 'He asked, "What does the Crocodile have for dinner?" He later, on the bank of the Limpopo River, met the crocodile. He asked the crocodile what he had for dinner and the crocodile caught him by his little nose. A great struggle ensued in which a Bi-Coloured-Python-Rock-Snake helped the Elephant Child pull and eventually the crocodile let go. The Elephant Child waited three days for his nose to shrink but it would not. Soon, however, he was swatting an annoying fly dead, putting lovely cool mud on his hot head and had plucked a large bundle of grass and, after dusting it clean on his knees, put it in his mouth.'

Soon all his family, one by one, went off to the Limpopo River to get new noses from the crocodile. Kipling ends his story by assuring the reader that this is how every elephant that you see and, indeed, those that you do not see got their trunks. Clearly no anatomist would today suggest that this is how the elephant got its trunk. However, Professor Joseph's worldview dictated how he interpreted human anatomy, as he described our Locomotor System rather like a *Just So Story*.

It has been suggested that anatomical vocabulary became cumbersome to include some 50,000 words. Terminological reform brought this down to a modern number of 7,500 anatomical terms.[13] In her foreword to *The Secret Language of Anatomy*, Professor Alice Roberts, anatomist, author and broadcaster, wrote,

> The human body is like a wonderful, mythical landscape. Understanding how all these parts fit together and work together fills you with a sense of profound awe and wonder, and it's not surprising that some people, over the centuries, have ended up believing that someone must have designed all this complexity. And yet it's just evolved to be that way. Evolutionary biology shows how, over eons, the pattern of your body has emerged from the simplest, single-celled beginnings. If you were able to trace your family tree back far enough, you'd find a unicellular organism that was the ancestor of all life on earth—LUCA, the Last Universal Common Ancestor.[14]

As the Professor of Public Engagement in Science at the University of Birmingham, she was affirming the prevailing worldview of evolutionary biology.

As a 19-year-old medical student, I needed to make sense of these 'facts'.

NOTES

1 Andreas Vesalius, *De Humani Corporis Fabrica Libri Septem*, (Padua: School of Medicine, 1543).

2   David Riches, 'Obituary: Professor Peter Williams', *The Independent*, 9th October 1994.

3   J. T. Aitken, J. Joseph, G. Causey and J. Z. Young, *A Manual of Human Anatomy*, Vols 1–5, Second edition, (Edinburgh: E. & S. Livingstone Ltd, 1964).

4   W J Hamilton (ed.), *Textbook of Human Anatomy 2nd edition*, (London: The Macmillan Press Ltd, reprinted in 1982), pp. 19–200.

5   Ibid. p. 20.

6   Ibid. p. 19.

7   Ibid. p. 196.

8   Ibid. p. 197.

9   Verna Wright, *Monkey to Man?* DVD, (Chesterfield: Two by Two Worship Ltd, 1980).

10   W J Hamilton (ed.), *Textbook of Human Anatomy*, 2nd edition, p. 22.

11   Ibid. p. 23

12   Rudyard Kipling, 'Chapter 5, The Elephant's Child', *Just So Stories for Little Children*, (London: Macmillan, 1952 reprint), pp. 59–77.

13   Cecilia Brassett, Emily Evans & Isla Fay, *The Secret Language of Anatomy*, (Chichester: Anatomy Boutique Books, 2017) p. 11.

14   Ibid. p. 7

8 Biochemistry

Biochemistry is the study of the chemical substances and processes that occur within living organisms such as plants, animals and microorganisms. There are four classes of biochemical compounds: carbohydrates, proteins, lipids (fats), and nucleic acids.

Examples of carbohydrates include sugars, starches and cellulose. Proteins are molecules made up of long chains of amino acids including, for example, hormones and enzymes. Lipids are small, hydrophobic (meaning tending to repel or failing to mix with water) molecules built from fatty acids. Nucleic acids are biological polymers made from nucleotides and include DNA (deoxyribonucleic acid) and RNA (ribonucleic acid).

Chemical changes within an organism either degrade substances—usually to gain energy – or build up complex molecules, which are needed for various life processes; these changes are together known as metabolism. Many of these changes require chemicals known as enzymes, which are generated by genetic mechanisms within the cell. Chemical changes seen in disease or due to the action of drugs are part of biochemistry.

Nutrition is understood to be a significant part of biochemistry; many of the things which we buy to eat are labelled with their carbohydrate, fat, protein, vitamin and salt content. Balanced nutrition contributes to a healthy lifestyle in humans. Blood has been investigated from the early days of biochemistry and the normal ranges of the blood's constituents—for example, sodium, potassium, urea or cholesterol—are well known. Variation from normal levels can be detected by blood tests and, therefore, conditions such as diabetes mellitus and kidney failure can be managed effectively.

The biochemistry of plant life is important for man. One early German biochemist, Justus von Liebig, showed, in the 1840s, that animals may disappear from the earth if there were no photosynthesizing plants. Animals need some organic compounds which can only be synthesised by plants.

In this chapter, I will discuss the teachers of Biochemistry at Guy's Hospital, and their views.

The professor who led our biochemistry teaching in the preclinical years was Professor Geoffrey A. D. Haslewood MSc, PhD, AIC. He had a particular interest in bile and bile salts. He authored a significant scientific paper, sixteen pages long, entitled, 'Bile salt evolution', published in the Journal of Lipid Research in 1967.

Bile acids and bile salts are vital in the digestion and absorption of fats. Cholic acid, along with chenodeoxycholic acid, is one of the two major bile acids produced by the liver, where it is synthesized from cholesterol. These two major bile acids are roughly equal in concentration in humans. The different names of the bile acids need not concern the reader but a progression in complexity was described from 'lower animals' to 'higher animals' by Prof Haslewood. The importance of understanding Prof. Haslewood's assumptions will be discussed.

The Abstract of his paper reads as follows:

Viewed against the background of known or supposed

biosynthetic pathways for cholic and chenodeoxycholic acids in man and laboratory animals, the chemical nature of bile salts in more primitive animals clearly *indicates that evolution from C27, 5α-alcohol sulphates to C24, 5β-acids has taken place* ... A closer study of the biochemical mechanisms underlying bile salt differences may be expected to throw *new light on the nature of the evolutionary process itself* (my italics).[1]

In the closing section of the paper entitled, 'General Considerations', he wrote: '*There can be little doubt that bile salts have evolved* and it seems reasonable to suppose that the progression has been from those alcohols nearest cholesterol to cholic, chenodeoxycholic, and related C24 cholanoic acids' (my italics).[2]

'*A curious feature* about bile salt distribution is the occurrence in some animal forms of *small amounts of more advanced bile salts,* although the principal substances are primitive' (my italics).[3]

'It is hard to escape the conclusion that *cholic acid itself has been produced by evolution at least twice,* once in teleosts (any member of a large and extremely diverse group of ray-finned fishes) and once in tetrapods' (my italics).[3]

Before discussing his assumptions, I wish to draw your attention to a paper published in 2010, in *BMC Evolutionary Biology*, with the title, 'Evolutionary diversity of bile salts in reptiles and mammals, including analysis of ancient human and extinct giant ground sloth coprolites', by LR Hagey et al. This long and detailed paper acknowledges using stored samples from the late Prof. Haslewood. In the results section, the following detail about the study of coprolites (fossilized faeces) is included:

Analyses of the approximately 8000-year-old human coprolites yielded a bile salt profile very similar to that found in modern human faeces. Analysis of the Shasta ground sloth coprolites (approximately 12000 years old) showed the predominant presence of glycine-conjugated bile acids, similar to analyses of bile and faeces of living sloths, in addition to a complex mixture of plant sterols and stanols expected from a herbivorous diet.[4]

A sceptic might suggest it is interesting that there was no evolutionary change in human bile over '8,000 years' or in sloth bile over '12,000 years'.

In discussing these two papers, it is helpful to know what bile does, while remembering that Professor Hunt would not allow you to say what it is for. Bile is produced in the liver and stored in the gallbladder; it is then released into the small intestine to help with the digestion and absorption of lipids (fats). In addition, bile is necessary for the absorption of fat-soluble vitamins. Besides its digestive function, bile also serves as a route of excretion of cholesterol and of bilirubin—a pigment produced during the normal breakdown of red blood cells.

The fact that bile acids and salts show an increasing complexity from 'primitive' animals to man was taken by Prof. Haslewood and LR Hagey and his colleagues as proof of evolution. Their pre-existing belief that the only explanation for this progressive complexity is evolution, causes them to say, 'clearly indicates', 'little doubt', and 'hard to escape the conclusion'.

I suggest that such a conclusion might be made, but it is not the only conclusion. Let me explain with an example. When we put our clothes in a washing machine and add soap powder, our intention is that grime, including fat, on our shirt collars will be removed. The emulsifying action of soap allows oil or fat (which attracts dirt and does not normally mix with water) to not only mix with water but to be removed. We often use hot water, which speeds up the process of emulsification of fat.

Where did the soap powder come from? I do not believe any biochemist has ever suggested that Omo evolved into Daz, then to Surf or Tide, later into Persil and finally into Radiant or Bold. No: these washing powders were all intelligently designed to meet a particular need– washing our clothes. Prof. Haslewood and Hagey et al. could not exclude the possibility that an intelligent designer made bile acids and salts using a chemical template with just the right properties of a detergent.

All classes of vertebrate animals need a 'detergent' to emulsify fat in the intestine and to help fat absorption. The basic chemical structure, consistent with the properties of a detergent, is likely to be similar in all these animals. That bile acids and salts are similar can speak of a basic design linked to function. To imply that similarity proves evolution is not proof—the similarities can suggest an intelligent designer with an exceptional knowledge of biochemistry!

You may be interested to learn that horses and some other creatures do not have gallbladders. However, they do produce bile, which is conveyed to the small intestine to aid digestion. There is not a lot of fat in grass but there is some and the horse digests it with the aid of bile. Juliet M. Getty, Ph.D., an internationally respected equine nutritionist, commented in *Horse Illustrated*, 2012, 'Horses don't have a gallbladder because horses are *designed* to eat constantly.' Note the interesting teleological remark![5]

Clearly our worldview influences our conclusions from examining scientific evidence. When we were preclinical students, Dr David Gower BSc, PhD, DSc was *Reader in Biochemistry* in Prof. Haslewood's department. He lectured to us and took many of our practical classes. Dr Gower was a Christian and had a different worldview from Prof. Haslewood. Dr Gower became head of department, later retiring as emeritus professor of steroid biochemistry at the University of London.

Prof. Gower's testimony can be found in a book edited by Dr John Ashton with the title, *In Six Days—Why 50 Scientists Choose to Believe in Creation*. He wrote:

> I am stimulated to criticize evolutionary theory in three areas which are of particular interest to me:
>
> 1. My chemical knowledge has allowed me to understand the criticisms of isotopic dating methods for rock samples and to realize that there are enormous problems with the interpretation of the data. Consequently, my own view is that rocks are nowhere near as old as they are alleged to be.
> 2. From the biochemical point of view, the idea that amino acids, sugars, etc., some of the vital "building blocks" for proteins and deoxyribonucleic acid (DNA), could be formed simply by interaction of electrical discharges with a primitive reducing-type atmosphere, can be criticized in so many ways and at so many levels.
> 3. My own studies in numerous biochemical control mechanisms, especially in the control of steroid hormone formation (for which I was awarded the higher doctorate, D.Sc.) convince me that all these processes are ordered precisely. This order and the extraordinary complexity are entirely consistent, in my own opinion, with the existence of a Creator, who himself must be capable of creating with such design.

Such complexity is also being found in virtually every other branch of science in general and is especially evident in the field of nature. Far from pointing towards formation by the chance processes of evolution, this clearly speaks to me of an Almighty Creator.[6]

As I learned about human physiology, anatomy and biochemistry, Professors Hunt, Joseph and Haslewood were assuming that man had evolved and that I needed to understand this as part of my preparation to become a doctor.

In developing my own worldview, I was not sure that they were right.

NOTES

1 Geoffrey A. D. Haslewood, 'Bile salt evolution', *The Journal of Lipid Research*, 1967, 8: pp. 535–550.

2 Ibid., p. 547.

3 Ibid., p. 548.

4 LR Hagey et al, 'Evolutionary diversity of bile salts in reptiles and mammals, including analysis of ancient human and extinct giant ground sloth coprolites', *BMC Evolutionary Biology* May 2010, 10(1):133.

5 Juliet M. Getty, 'Why don't horses have a gallbladder?' *Horse Illustrated*, 27 December 2012.

6 D.B. Gower, *In Six Days—Why 50 Scientists Choose to Believe in Creation*, Dr John Ashton (Ed.) (Green Forest, Arkansas: Master Books, 2007), pp. 265–267.

9 Becoming a Christian

I started at Epsom College in the autumn of 1961. During my first year, I was a member of the school chapel choir. We rehearsed twice a week and I enjoyed singing, though wearing a cassock, surplice and ruff twice on a Sunday was a little tiresome. Quite a lot of what we sang has remained in my memory. The words of the Magnificat (Luke 1:46–55), Nunc Dimittis (Luke 2:29) and the Jubilate Deo (Psalm 100) were easily memorized. We attended chapel each morning of the week, apart from Wednesday when the whole college attended an assembly which was led by the headmaster. As a result, I was exposed to a significant amount of Christian worship.

I have commented on how, in early life, my parents, my schoolteachers and the local policeman were authorities who directed my understanding of what was right and what was wrong. During primary education, we learned a lot from the Old and New Testaments. We memorized Exodus 20:1–17, Psalm 23, 1 Corinthians 13 and Philippians 2:5–11.

During my primary school years and in the early years at Epsom, I had no reason to doubt that Jesus Christ was both God and man. In the first year of the sixth form, we were offered the opportunity to be confirmed in the Church of England, into which I had been christened as a baby. After conferring with my parents, I took this up. A group of us would walk one evening each week down College

Road to the home of the Rev. Moody, who was one of the college masters.

I remember him being very pleasant and preparing us for the service, which would be conducted by the Bishop of Guildford. We had to learn and recite the Apostles Creed, the Ten Commandments and other sections of the catechism.[1] It was a thorough preparation with opportunity for questions and for discussion. The summary in the catechism of the meaning of the Commandments as, 'my duty towards God and my duty towards my neighbour',[2] made good sense.

In due course, I was confirmed by the Bishop of Guildford, with my parents present, and soon attended my first Holy Communion service. To go to communion, one had to get up early, leave the dormitory, and head for the chapel before breakfast. I was impressed by the seriousness of the service administered by Rev. Menzies. I remember the warning, which asks us to examine ourselves to make sure that we are in a good relationship with God and our neighbour.

Being confirmed and attending communion were important to me, though I was not aware of having a personal relationship with God through Jesus Christ. Indeed, while I was aware of God as my Creator and that his Son, Jesus Christ, had come into the world, this knowledge had minimal daily impact on my life.

At the beginning of my time at Guy's Hospital there was a fresher's event when various student societies came to recruit new members. I had played rugby union at Epsom, usually at fly half. However, I often seemed to end up with my nose bleeding after receiving direct blows and spent a lot of time having my nose cauterised in the sanatorium. So, I joined the soccer club and was soon playing for

Guy's 2nd XI as goalkeeper. After the first year, I became a full-back with rare appearances for the 1stXI as a left-wing! It never crossed my mind to join the Christian Union, who also made their presentation during that fresher's event. I made some good friends in the soccer team and later shared a flat for some years with John, who was the best man at my wedding.

The activities of various student societies were advertised in the Medical School or in the Colonnade. Towards the end of my first term, I noticed a poster advertising a Christian Union meeting entitled, 'Becoming a Christian', with a visiting speaker. This seemed an intriguing title for someone who had been christened and confirmed. I decided to go to the meeting on the following Monday evening, not being sure who I would meet there.

The meeting was upstairs in the facilities provided for the students. Incidentally, there were dental students, trainee physiotherapists and trainee nurses all attending this meeting. The speaker was one of the Inter-Varsity Fellowship Travelling Secretaries. I do not remember the details of his talk but I do remember his two main conclusions: repent and believe. For some reason, which I can only describe as personal deafness or blindness, I had never received these two words into my thought processes when considering Christianity. The warning in the communion service had caused me to fear God's justice, whereas 'repent and believe' seemed to be an invitation to come into a relationship with God.

There was an opportunity for questions at the end of his talk and so I asked, 'What about Adam and Eve and the Genesis account, if evolution is true?' This question reflected my ongoing quest to develop a worldview which explained the world as it is. The speaker replied, 'Oh don't worry about the story of Creation, found in Genesis. That is a poetic description by which God wants to teach us many things.' For the moment, my new interest in Christianity had been kindled and his reply had suggested that the evolutionary viewpoint, supported in the departments of Physiology, Anatomy and Biochemistry, was not in conflict with the Bible. Perhaps Professor Fred Hoyle and the teachers at Guy's were going to help me to arrive at a sensible conclusion. In the light of the message to repent and believe, I could see that I needed to pay greater attention to Christianity and the Bible.

I continued to attend midweek communion in the chapel at Guy's Hospital but also became regular at the Christian Union's meetings. Other students were keen to introduce a newcomer such as myself to churches in London. At that time, there were three special churches attended by students. All Souls, Langham Place, where Rev John Stott was the Minister; St Helen's, Bishopsgate where Rev Dick Lucas was the Minister and Westminster Chapel where Dr Martyn Lloyd-Jones was the Minister.

Two of the girls in my tutorial group, Liz and Alison, shared a bedsit in Pimlico and both attended the Christian Union. Liz and her parents attended a church in Cuckfield, Sussex. Liz's grandfather had been a Baptist minister in Brighton. Liz and Alison would round up other students on a Sunday morning, often including myself, and drive down the A23 in Liz's Mini to the morning service at Cuckfield Baptist Chapel. We would all be invited to lunch at Liz's parents and then drive back up to attend Westminster Chapel in the evening and listen to Dr Martyn Lloyd-Jones.

ML-J or 'The Doctor', as he was often called, studied medicine at St Bartholomew's Hospital. In 1921, he started work as assistant to the Royal Physician, Lord Horder. Sir James Paterson Ross, who was Professor of Surgery at St Bartholomew's, and President of the Royal College of Surgeons of England, said of ML-J, 'One of the finest clinicians I ever encountered.'[3] Despite his abilities as a physician, ML-J felt the call to full-time Christian ministry and so, in 1927, he returned to South Wales, where he had been born, and became a full-time Christian minister at a church in Aberavon.

The minister at Cuckfield Baptist Chapel, was Erroll Hulse, a South African trained architect who, as a young man, had become a Christian with his wife Lynn and moved to London for training at London Bible College. He was very helpful in answering many of my questions. On a Sunday afternoon at Cuckfield, I often went with Liz's father, Stanley, to observe him teaching a large Sunday school. This supplemented my patchy Bible knowledge and taught me a lot of children's choruses, which have stood me in good stead in later life.

I was convinced of the uniqueness of Jesus Christ and did not doubt the historical truth of his death, burial and resurrection or his ability to perform miracles. I was, however, anxious that if I became a Christian, I would let Christ down and bring shame on his people, the Church. I simply did not feel that I could keep it up. I was able to express this to Erroll Hulse who I remember explaining that, when somebody becomes a Christian, the Holy Spirit of God comes to live in them and gives them the power to walk the Christian life in obedience to God's commandments. In John chapter 3, Jesus is recorded as having a conversation at night with Nicodemus, a senior

Jewish religious leader, who also seemed unable to understand how to become a Christian.

Jesus explained to Nicodemus that we must be born again by the Holy Spirit and, as 2 Corinthians 5:17 says, then we will be a new creation. Erroll encouraged me to consider the verse, Philippians 1:6, which says: 'Being confident of this, that he who began a good work in you will carry it on to completion until the day of Christ Jesus.' I was beginning to understand that Christian faith is a gift from God, who equips the Christian to put off old, bad habits and literally, *put on Christ*, with a desire to live according to God's commandments. The perfect righteousness of Christ is reckoned to the Christian's account and all his sins are washed away by the precious blood, which Jesus shed at Calvary.

The Old Testament prophet, Jeremiah, wrote these words long ago: 'You will seek me and find me when you seek me with all your heart' (Jeremiah 29:13). I would go to church each Sunday morning and evening and listen to very helpful preaching. Erroll Hulse was preaching through Exodus and Numbers, telling of the journey of the children of Israel from slavery to freedom with all the emotional ups and downs of human behaviour detailed, as Moses led 600,000 men with their women and children towards the Promised Land of Canaan. I was being taught through expository preaching—which means the minister going logically through a book of the Bible, explaining it within its context.

On Sunday evenings Dr Lloyd-Jones was preaching from Acts chapter 7, where Stephen, the first Christian martyr, was defending himself in front of the Jewish religious leaders of the Sanhedrin. Stephen related the history of the children of Israel up to the building by Solomon of the first Temple. Stephen's crime in the eyes of the Sanhedrin was that he was preaching the gospel of Jesus Christ, who they reckoned was a blasphemer and they thought was dead and buried. Stephen told them that God would no longer be worshipped in the Temple and bluntly described their track record of persecuting all God's prophets. Stephen said that this finally culminated in the coming of 'the Righteous One', who they had recently betrayed and murdered (7:52). The Sanhedrin were furious at Stephen's words, but he 'looked up to heaven and saw the glory of God, and Jesus standing at the right hand of God' (7:55). They dragged him out of the city and stoned him to death.

After these evening services, several medical students from Guy's, and other London medical schools, returned to Liz and Alison's bedsit, in Pimlico and later St George's Square, to discuss the sermon and to get our questions answered. I began attending Dr Lloyd-Jones's Friday night Bible study at Westminster Chapel when he was teaching from Romans chapter 14. I used to go to a café across the road from the Chapel and eat cheese omelette and chips before the Bible study.

I was still collecting Pelican books and was reading one of these—*Freud and Christianity*[4], written by R.S. Lee, Chaplain of St. Catherine's College, Oxford—one evening as I ate my meal. A voice I recognized asked, 'What are you reading Nigel?' I held the book up to Erroll Hulse, who must have come up from Sussex to attend the Bible study that evening. He did not seem very impressed and, two days later, I received in the post an A5 envelope containing a letter from Erroll and, on several A4 sheets of paper, a typed, detailed outline of the whole book of Romans, with the suggestion that it may be more help to me than Freud! I was finding the book fairly difficult to understand anyway and abandoned it immediately. I do remember being grateful that Pastor Hulse was acting pastorally to a young man who was searching for the truth and for a relationship with Jesus Christ.

One Friday evening, in October 1967, I attended the Bible study on Romans 14 but, that evening, my mind was focused on Philippians 1:6. I had come to realize that God could be trusted to help me live the Christian life, forgive me when I faltered and confessed my sins to him, and that God had purposes for my life. I needed to make a commitment to him through repenting and believing. I took that mental step of faith that evening. God, for his part, gave me an assurance that Christ's death on the cross had paid the penalty for my sin and, by his resurrection, assurance of eternal life. This was not self-confidence or arrogance but confidence in the object of my faith, Jesus Christ. The invitation of Christ, recorded in Matthew 11:28–29, 'Come to me, all you who are weary and burdened, and I will give you rest. Take my yoke upon you and learn from me, for I am gentle and humble in heart, and you will find rest for your souls,' confirms his commitment to whoever will repent and believe in him. I had been born again, as John chapter 3 explains. This was the most significant, pivotal moment of my life.

Some may think that my taking a mental step of faith, which changed the whole direction and allegiance of my life, was strange. But this transformation was caused by the work of the Holy Spirit of God in my heart and mind, leading to my repentance and belief in the Christian gospel. It was a supernatural event.

What I am writing about is not a new thing. I would like to quote from Bishop J. C. Ryle's book, *Christian Leaders of the 18th Century*: 'Furthermore, the reformers of the eighteenth century taught constantly the great doctrine of justification by faith. They told men that faith was the one thing needful in order to obtain an interest in Christ's work for their souls; that before we believe, we are dead, and have no interest in Christ; and that the moment we do believe, we live, and have a plenary title to all Christ's benefits.'[5]

I had learned, at Cuckfield Baptist Chapel, that some non-conformist denominations did not baptize or christen babies but baptized those who had made a personal commitment to Jesus Christ. I had no desire to belittle infant baptism and confirmation but felt strongly that I wanted to witness to my new faith by being baptized by immersion. Jesus Christ, himself, had been baptized by immersion in the river Jordan by John the Baptist. The Holy Spirit like a dove had descended and rested on Jesus while his Father had spoken from heaven and said, 'This is my Son, whom I love; with him I am well pleased' (Matthew 3:17).

Believer's Baptism is symbolic, signifying union with Christ: Going down into the water signifies death and burial with Christ; coming up out of the water signifies that the Christian lives a new life based on Christ's resurrection from the dead. I was baptized by immersion at Cuckfield Baptist Chapel on Sunday evening, 19 November 1967, by Pastor Erroll Hulse.

At Guy's Hospital, there was a long tradition of the Christian Union holding *15-minute ward services* on a Sunday evening in twenty of the medical and surgical wards. We had four teams that took these, covering five wards each. The hospital chaplain, Rev. Beevers, led one team and three students led the other teams. Each ward had a piano and hymn books for all the patients. The wards were informed in advance of the time of the services on Sunday evenings after the patients had had their evening meal. A last-minute check was made on arrival at each ward with the senior member of staff, in case there was any emergency happening; if so, we might go elsewhere and return later, if the situation allowed. We would sing a hymn, read a passage from the Bible, say a prayer and have a short five-minute talk.

In 1968, Liz Hogwood and I began dating and we started to help with the ward services. After a while, I began to take my turn at leading a team. I remember one very moving occasion in November 1970, when I spoke from Revelation 21 on the new heaven and new earth, as a young man was dying of leukaemia. We sang a hymn that he chose. It is difficult for people who are very ill to engage with big issues, which reminds me of what 2 Corinthians 6:2 (KJV) states: 'Behold, now is the day of salvation'. Good health is certainly to be enjoyed and appreciated but should not become a reason to put off getting right with God.

In chapter 6, about physiology, I discussed the issue of purpose. In becoming a Christian, it became clear to me that God certainly had a purpose in creating the Earth and each of our lives. This made me realize that God had a purpose for my life, which not only involved training and working as a doctor but, also, how I treated and related to my family and fellow human beings on a day-to-day basis. This would involve using the gifts which God had given me and endeavouring to develop them. I was learning to read the Bible regularly and to pray to God for direction for my life.

I believed that God would show me his will for my life and that I could trust the promises of God found in the Bible. To modernize the opening question of *The Westminster Shorter Catechism* we can ask, 'What is the main purpose of mankind?' The answer: 'To glorify God and to enjoy him for ever.' The second question, again modernized, asks, 'What rule or guidance has God given to us?' The answer: 'The word of God given in the Old and New Testaments is the only rule showing us how we can glorify and enjoy him.'[6]

As I moved onwards in my life journey and search for a rational worldview, there remained an unresolved question: 'What about Adam and Eve and the Genesis account, if evolution is true?' If Genesis chapters 1 to 3 are poetic descriptions, as the Inter-Varsity Fellowship Travelling Secretary had said, and not real history, what does that mean for the authority of the rest of the Bible?

In the next chapter I will begin to examine the 'evidence' for evolution.

NOTES

1 *Book of Common Prayer*, (Oxford University Press, 1928 edition), pp. 350–358.
2 Ibid., p. 353.
3 Iain H Murray, *David Martyn Lloyd-Jones; The Fight of Faith 1939–1981*, (Edinburgh: The Banner of Truth Trust, 1990), p. 186.
4 R.S. Lee, *Freud and Christianity*, (London: Pelican Books, 1967).
5 Bishop J. C. Ryle, *Christian Leaders of the 18th Century*, (Edinburgh: The Banner of Truth Trust, 2017), pp. 11–18.
6 Kevin Bidwell (Ed.) *Westminster Shorter Catechism*, (Welwyn Garden City, UK: Evangelical Press, 2019).

10 Examining the evidence for biblical Creation and evolution

When we come to consider the cosmological question of how the universe began (or even if it had a beginning at all) and the question of how mankind originated, we, of course, examine the available evidence. This informs and helps us as we consider the possible and likely explanations. When someone studies law at university or trains to be a barrister, they spend a lot of time learning about the different sorts of evidence, what is admissible in a court of law and the relative merits of one sort of evidence over against another.

When a witness, such as an eyewitness, gives testimony to having actual knowledge of a fact, that witness's testimony is *direct evidence*. On the other hand, evidence of facts and circumstances from which reasonable inferences may be drawn is *circumstantial evidence*.

Testimonial evidence is viewed by the court to be the simplest type of evidence. It does not require any other piece of evidence to support it or make it legitimate. Certainly, the court will have to decide whether the witness's testimony is truthful, but it is inherently admissible evidence and must be respected and carefully examined as among the strongest sort of evidence. The testimony of one claiming to be an eyewitness cannot be lightly ignored and discarded. The judge and the jury, in the case of a jury trial, must consider such evidence.

In trying to develop a rational worldview, I had to consider the evidence for evolution and that for Biblical Creation. I am taking evolution to mean neo-Darwinism, where the influence of genetic mutations is added to the mechanism of natural selection. Biblical Creation, as I understand it, is a literal interpretation of Genesis chapters 1 to 3, being a historical account and, by using the chronologies listed in Genesis, concludes that the Earth is close to 6,000 years old.

Bishop James Ussher, Anglican Archbishop of Armagh, published *The Annals of the World* in 1650, originally in Latin with the first English edition appearing in 1658.[1] He included a chronology of world history based on a literal reading of the Bible chronologies. His proposed date of 4004 BC for Creation was close to other biblically based estimates, such as those of Bede (3952 BC), Johannes Kepler (3992 BC) or Sir Isaac Newton (about 4000 BC).[2]

There are many Christians who believe in Biblical Creation but also believe that the Earth is old, holding to a view described as theistic evolution. In this chapter, I will present evidence for believing in the Bible's record of world history but not discuss the *young versus old* age of the Earth. I will leave that debate until chapters 29 and 30. Here, I will present the main headings of *evidence* for evolution, though I will deal with these in greater detail in chapter 11, as I continue to explain my journey to a settled worldview about our origins and those of the Earth.

Before considering the evidence for believing the Bible—and particularly for believing that the account of Creation in Genesis chapters 1 and 2 and 'The Fall' in Genesis chapter 3 are historical records given to us through God's own testimony—I would like to give an example of the confusion which can arise when someone only has circumstantial evidence available as they endeavour to interpret facts set before them. When an eyewitness is able to explain exactly how the facts came to be, then suddenly an apparent mystery can be solved.

The account I want to describe is fictional. However, Winnie the Pooh and Piglet faced a really difficult question and they were quite fearful about the facts as they saw them. In chapter 3 of *Winnie the Pooh*, published in October 1926, we find Piglet was brushing some snow from outside his house when he saw Pooh, who was walking around in a circle. Pooh explained to Piglet that he was hunting and tracking something, although he did not know what it was. Piglet joined in and, on seeing the paw marks in the snow, he was very excited. Piglet thought that they might be tracking a Woozle and Pooh agreed.

After a little while, Pooh stopped because there were now two sets of paw prints. They continued their walk around a clump of larch trees but were taken by surprise when they found that there were three sets of prints and soon four sets, meaning there might actually be four Woozles. This was all too much for Piglet who remembered he needed to go home to do something important. Fortunately for Pooh, Christopher Robin arrived just at that moment. He had been sitting up in a big oak tree watching Pooh and Piglet as they walked round in circles. He explained to Pooh that he had watched him walk round the trees twice alone, and then twice with Piglet. This revelation caused Pooh to sit down and put his paw

Examining the evidence

into one of the tracks. 'I see now; I have been foolish and deluded and am a bear of no brain at all,'[3] said Winnie the Pooh. Just in case there is any doubt, Christopher Robin, the eyewitness, was able to explain they were following their own tracks and there never was a Woozle.

In A. A. Milne's story, Christopher Robin had a great advantage of being able to see what actually happened. The claim in the Bible in 2 Timothy 3:16–17, that God breathed out the Scriptures as a record of the history of the Earth, is a claim that God has been an eyewitness of everything that has taken place in the history of the Universe and particularly here on the Earth. The evidence of God, the eyewitness, cannot be dismissed.

The Bible claims that this scriptural record has been written by men who were carried along by the Holy Spirit of God as they wrote the sixty-six books of the Holy Bible. The Bible was written in three languages: Hebrew, Greek and Aramaic—the language which Jesus would have spoken. It describes events on three continents: Asia, Africa and Europe. It is written by thirty-five to forty authors over a period of 1600 years.

At this point in discussing evidence, I want to acknowledge a very helpful lecture, which I heard in October 2019 at the UK Creation Mega Conference held in the West Midlands. The speaker, Dr Voddie Baucham, who is a black American, spoke on, 'Why I Believe the Bible'.[4]

Dr Baucham was brought up by a single mother, who was a Buddhist. He did not hear the Christian gospel until he was in college. His journey to faith was unusual and so he understands what it means to be a sceptic and knows what it is like to try to figure

The Something Delusion **97**

out the Christian life, without relying on church traditions. He is married to Bridget and father of nine children, seven of whom are adopted. A former pastor, author, and church planter, he currently serves as Dean of Theology at The African Christian University in Lusaka, Zambia.

Dr Baucham began by introducing us to the concept of *falsifiability*. In the practice of science, to say that a theory, hypothesis or statement can be contradicted by evidence is to say that it is falsifiable. The philosopher, Karl Popper[5], proposed this principle in science and, while he had several critics, the principle is useful when applied to the Bible as a historical document being sequentially written down by eyewitnesses. I will summarize Dr Baucham's lecture.

(1) The Bible is a reliable collection of historical documents. *Reference:* 2 Peter 1:16–17. 'For we did not follow cleverly devised stories when we told you about the coming of our Lord Jesus Christ in power, but we were eyewitnesses of his majesty. He received honour and glory from God the Father when the voice came to him from the Majestic Glory, saying, "This is my Son, whom I love; with him I am well pleased."'

Comment: Muhammed had no witnesses to his receiving the *Quran* from Gabriel (Jibril) over a period of some twenty-three years.

(2) It was written by eyewitnesses during the lifetime of other eyewitnesses. *Reference:* 1 John 1:1–3. 'That which was from the beginning, which we have heard, which we have seen with our eyes, which we have looked at and our hands have touched—this we proclaim concerning the Word of life. The life appeared; we have seen it and testify to it, and we proclaim to you the eternal life,

which was with the Father and has appeared to us. We proclaim to you what we have seen and heard.'

Comment: These witnesses would be the apostles, disciples, his half-brothers—particularly James and Jude—and his half-sisters. Also, there were perhaps 300 witnesses still alive (referred to in 1 Corinthians 15:6 by Paul as, 'five hundred of the brothers and sisters ... most of whom are still living, though some have fallen asleep'). Paul wrote in 1 Corinthians 15:8, 'and last of all he appeared to me also, as to one abnormally born'. This referred to Paul's meeting with Jesus on the Damascus Road, when he was known as Saul, and led to his repeated claim of being a witness of the risen Lord Jesus Christ.

All these witnesses could have been cross examined, and if their statements were false, they could have been exposed as frauds. Bible facts were falsifiable at the time, if indeed they had been false!

Comment: Joseph Smith claimed, in 1823, that an angel showed him a book of golden plates. In 1830, Smith published his translation, called the *Book of Mormon.*[6] There were no witnesses to the angel's visit and nobody else saw the plates, which were not preserved.

(3) They report supernatural events—some of which took place in fulfilment of specific prophecies.

The *Transfiguration was a significant supernatural event* when Moses and Elijah appeared with Christ in front of the three disciples, Peter, James and John. They were witnesses of this event, recorded in Luke 9:28–36.

Isaiah, in chapter 35:5–6, prophesied that 'the eyes of the blind be opened and the ears of the deaf unstopped. Then will the lame leap like a deer and the mute tongue shout for joy.' This was fulfilled by

Jesus, recorded in Matthew 11:4–5, and John the Baptist's disciples and many others witnessed it.

Isaiah, in chapter 53, prophesied in verse 5: 'But he was pierced for our transgressions,' *and in verse 9*: 'He was assigned a grave with the wicked, and with the rich in his death.'

King David, in Psalm 22, prophesied in verse 16: 'they have pierced my hands and my feet,' *and in verse 18*: 'They divide my garments among them and cast lots for my garment.'

David was writing Psalm 22 a thousand years before Christ and, thus, well before the practice of crucifixion had been introduced by the Romans. Isaiah was, likewise, writing about 700 years before Christ. Jesus Christ died by crucifixion with two wicked criminals but was buried in the grave of a rich man, Joseph of Arimathea.

About a quarter (220 scrolls) of the Dead Sea Scrolls[7] are books of the Hebrew Bible, which we know as the Old Testament. They have essentially the same content as the books in our Holy Bible. All the Old Testament books are represented, except for Esther and Nehemiah. The most common books found are Psalms and Deuteronomy. The prophecies, mentioned above, are impressive evidence, encouraging belief in the truth of the whole Bible.

(4) They claim that their writings are divine rather than of human origin. 2 Timothy 3:16–17 states: 'All Scripture is God-breathed and is useful for teaching, rebuking, correcting and training in righteousness, so that the man of God may be thoroughly equipped for every good work.'

As stated above, God inspired up to forty different authors to write the Bible. We do not know who wrote Judges or Hebrews, but 2 Timothy 3:16–17 explains that God himself directed them and the other known authors in what they wrote, including their own different experiences. Their individual characters are often evident from the text.

If you take Dr Baucham's four headings and read them one after the other, you will, I believe, have a substantial and reasonable testimony of many eyewitnesses that make a compelling body of direct evidence which will stand up to intellectual scrutiny.

The writer of the book, *Who Moved the Stone?*[8], Albert Henry Ross (pseudonym Frank Morison), thought that the evidence for the resurrection of Jesus Christ was poor and decided to investigate the Gospels and write an analysis with the title, 'Jesus—the Last Phase', showing that the resurrection was untrue. However, his research led him to be convinced that the resurrection of Jesus Christ really happened. He submitted his book to Faber and Faber, the publishers where T. S. Eliot was a board member. Eliot was very enthusiastic about the book, which was published in 1930. Eliot sent G.K. Chesterton a copy of the book, who was also very complimentary about the logical and apparently legal way Albert Ross had set out the case for the resurrection.

A misconception over the years was that Albert Ross was a lawyer, but he was in fact an advertising agent. One of Ross's colleagues during that employment was Dorothy L. Sayers, who relied on details from *Who Moved the Stone?* when she wrote her play, *The Man born to be King.*[9] *Who Moved the Stone?* has been reprinted at least ten times and translated into other languages. Ross's challenge is that there is a large amount of evidence for the resurrection of Jesus Christ and the truth of the Holy Bible. But how many people are prepared to examine this evidence or even read one book such as *Who Moved the Stone?*

Josh McDowell B.A., M.Div. is an author and evangelist who wrote the book, *Evidence That Demands a Verdict*[10], published in 1972. This is another scholarly book that gives proper time to exploring the Biblical evidence.

I have looked generally at the nature of direct evidence and circumstantial evidence and the evidence that Dr Baucham, a theologian, has presented for belief in the Bible and I have suggested two helpful books which examine the evidence.

Having looked at some of the evidence for biblical Creation, I will now examine *evidence* for evolution. What would someone believing in neo-Darwinian evolution consider to be the evidence for their belief? In general terms, the evidence would be naturalistic explanations about the cosmos, the origin of life and of human life particularly.

For an evolutionary explanation of origins to be true, there is need for at least two things: firstly, long ages (deep time) and secondly, for there to be a mechanism that can produce matter and energy from nothing! Assuming that one can get simple non-living chemicals from nothing, a mechanism is needed to turn them into a living organism. Then, there needs to be a mechanism for the simplest organism to turn into more complex creatures and finally into man, who can reason, memorize, speak and experience relationships.

Charles Darwin, in his book, *The Origin of the Species*, suggested that geology, which we see all around us, provided evidence of very long ages[11] and that natural selection was the mechanism by which change occurred. The scientific community later acknowledged that natural selection alone would be inadequate to fulfil Darwin's ideas. So, by adding the understanding gained from Gregor Mendel's laws of genetics,[12] Darwinism became Neo-Darwinism.

Mutations were seen to be a necessary tool of evolution, but such mutations would have to be beneficial; there is, in fact, serious doubt as to whether any beneficial mutation can be named. To illustrate this difficulty, I draw your attention to a recording of a 1997 interview.

On 16 September 1997, Professor Richard Dawkins was interviewed at his home in England by Gillian Brown and Philip Hohnen and a video recording was made. This was subsequently published as a DVD, *From a Frog to a Prince.* [13] During the recording, Dawkins realized that he was being interviewed by biblical creationists. In the interview, he was asked a question by Gillian Brown: 'Can you give an example of a genetic mutation or an evolutionary process which can be seen to increase the information in the genome?' Dawkins was silent for a total of nineteen seconds before asking for a break in the recording. Later, the recording restarted and Dawkins continued to speak but did not answer the question. He had the opportunity to describe a beneficial mutation but did not. The reference gives full details of the recording and timing of questions and answers.[13]

I turn now to a popular modern author, Bill Bryson, who published *A Short History of Nearly Everything* in 2003. Bryson writes: 'This is a book about how it happened—in particular, how we went from there being nothing at all to there being something, and then how little of that something turned into us, and also some of what happened in between and since.'[14] I respect Bryson for being clear about the challenge which lies at the heart of cosmology: I would ask, '*How did we get from nothing to something?*' This is really important because if one dismisses an Almighty Creator as the first cause of the Universe, then one must be honest and explain how evolution works starting with nothing. You cannot have 'nearly nothing' or 'something' or 'energy' without explaining where they came from!

Bill Bryson has an easy-to-read style. His book opens with his congratulations that the reader 'could make it'. The sixth sentence of the book reads, 'To begin with, for you to be here now trillions of drifting atoms had somehow to assemble in an intricate and curiously obliging manner to create you.'[15]

The paragraph which you just read, contains a fallacy of 'begging the question'.[16] By assuming that drifting atoms have the ability to assemble in an intricate way to create human beings, Bill Bryson has made an invalid assumption.

Arguments for evolution often use fallacies of 'reification'.[17] This means attributing a concrete characteristic to something that is abstract. An example of such a fallacy is, 'Mother Nature designed amazing creatures.' In fact, nature does not have a mind (or gender) and cannot design or create anything. The phrase, 'The evidence speaks for itself', when used in an argument is also a fallacy of reification. Evidence cannot speak; it is a body of facts which people can draw conclusions from.

The third paragraph of Bryson's book begins with a fallacy of reification and makes this frank admission: 'Why atoms take this trouble is a bit of a puzzle. Being you is not a gratifying experience at the atomic level. For all their devoted attention, your atoms don't actually care about you—indeed, don't even know that you are there. They don't even know that *they* are there. They are mindless particles, after all, and not even themselves alive.'[18] Bryson fails to see how this undermines most of his book.

In chapter 19, I will draw attention to a question attributed to the German philosopher, Gottfried Leibniz of there being something there 'rather than nothing being there'[19]—or as Bryson puts it, 'Why do atoms take this trouble?' This question reminds me of the following issue: 'Why would amino acids want to be proteins?'

Bill Bryson ends his book reflecting on the central message of the book: 'If this book has a lesson, it is that we are awfully lucky to be here—and by "we" I mean every living thing. ... As humans we are doubly lucky, of course. We enjoy not only the privilege of existence, but also the singular ability to appreciate it. ... Modern humans have been around for no more than about 0.0001 per cent of Earth's history—almost nothing, really—but even existing for that little while has required a nearly endless string of good fortune.'[20]

Contrary to my school motto, '*Deo, non Fortuna*' (by God not by luck), evolution does seem to need and claim a continuous stream of good luck!

So, what are some of the most common headings used to document *evidence* for evolution? The following headings are those in my Epsom College, Grove & Newell textbook *Animal Biology*[21], over 20 pages. Surprisingly, at Epsom, we learned a lot about the study of fossils (palaeontology) but nothing much about geology, which is claimed as a significant area of evidence and included in the list here. In the next chapter of this book, I will deal in greater detail with fossil evidence, vestigial organs and embryology.

(1) The Fossil Record. Palaeontologists explain the fossil record as having been laid down slowly over millions of years. The sedimentary rocks that the fossils are found in, are also considered to have been formed over millions of years. Such an interpretation of the origin of fossils is controversial and some modern experts are prepared to concede that catastrophic, rapid processes are needed to explain many fossils. For example, there are thousands of beautiful fish fossils. Consider when a fish dies, it may be scavenged as it floats on the surface and, if it falls to the sea bottom, further scavenging or bacterial decay takes place. Many fish fossils show one fish eating another fish! There is also an ichthyosaur fossil in the process of giving birth to three babies. Surely a catastrophe must have occurred. Palaeontologists consider that millions of years were needed to produce the fossil record. (The Bible account of the catastrophe of Noah's flood offers a very different explanation of the large fossil graveyards which are found or of the fossils described in this paragraph.)

(2) Homology. This means similarity due to 'shared ancestry' between a pair of structures or genes in different groups (taxa). For example, the human arm, a bird or bat's wing, a dog's leg and a dolphin's flipper are 'homologous structures'. The common design is believed to indicate a common ancestor.

(3) Vestigial Organs. Some body parts are currently thought to be useless. It is suggested that these are remnants of organs which have lost their function as evolution progressed from ancestor to the present day. The thymus, appendix and coccyx have at various times been labelled as vestigial.

(4) Embryology. The fact that the embryos of creatures which

possess a spinal cord look similar was believed to indicate that they are closely related and share a common evolutionary ancestor. Darwin claimed this.

(5) Genetics. Gregor Mendel published the laws of genetic inheritance in 1866. People had always recognized that a child had traits from each of their parents. For example, I might have mother's eye colour and father's hair colour. Mendel showed that each parent contributed a single allele, or variant form of a gene, to their child for each trait. Each gene sits at a particular place on a chromosome in two copies—one copy of the gene inherited from each parent.

The changes which occur in populations of organisms over generations are believed to be due to genetic variations. Examples of genetic variation are eye colour or blood group. This variation is caused by the difference in DNA among individuals. Genetic variation can be caused by mutations, genetic recombination and other factors. If a trait improves survival, then that genetic variation is more likely to be passed on to the next generation. This is known as *natural selection*.

Mutations are the source of new alleles in the gene pool. The vast majority of mutations are harmful, reducing genetic information and do not add or produce beneficial information. Genetic drift means that the relative frequency of alleles in a population can increase or decrease by chance over time. This most often happens in small populations where uncommon alleles have a greater chance of being lost. Gene flow is what happens when one population migrates to live in the area of another population and their alleles or gametes are transferred to the other population during reproduction. In any given population, natural selection, mutations, genetic drift and gene flow are claimed as forces altering allele frequencies and driving evolution.

(6) Biogeography. There are striking differences between the animal populations of the world's different continents. Species which inhabit different islands or landmasses have found suitable environments in which to multiply and a lack of predators may have helped. Giraffes live in Africa and llamas in South America but not vice versa. Thirteen species of finches have diversified on the Galapagos Islands, sometimes in different niches on different islands. They are thought to have come from South America from one ancestral species.

(7) Geology. The concept of long periods of geological time was suggested by James Hutton in the 18th century. In June 1788, when looking at the strata of the angular unconformity at Siccar Point in Scotland, his friend John Playfair remarked, 'The mind seemed to grow giddy by looking so far into the abyss of time.'[22] Later, Charles Lyell in his *Principles of Geology*[23] (1830–1833) developed Hutton's understanding of endless deep time and very slow processes into a theory called *uniformitarianism*. He and Hutton believed that 'the present is the key to the past'. The possibility of catastrophic events in the formation of the geological record was rejected. Darwin, as a young man, studied the successive volumes of Lyell's book during his voyage on the Beagle in the 1830s. Lyell thought the earth was 2 to 8 billion years old. The current estimate of 4.56 billion years for the age of the Earth and 13.79 billion years for the age of the Universe helps to sustain the theory of evolution which certainly needs a lot of time.

There are three particular geological issues which I will address in chapters 34 and 35 of this book:

(a) The Geological Timescale; (b) Radiometric Dating; (c) The formation of the Grand Canyon and the eruption of Mount St Helens in 1980.

NOTES

1   James Ussher, *The Annals of the World*, (printed by E. Tyler for J Crook at the Sign of the Ship in St Paul's Churchyard, 1658) p. 1.

2   Ussher chronology, https://en.wikipedia.org/wiki/Ussher_chronology

3   A. A. Milne, *Winnie the Pooh*, illustrated E. H. Shepard, (London: Methuen, 1926) chapter 3.

4   Voddie Baucham, *Why I Believe the Bible*, 28th January 2014. https://www.youtube.com/watch?v=15EoR6O-rUA

5   Karl R. Popper, *The Logic of Scientific Discovery*, (Abingdon-on-Thames: Routledge Classics, 2nd Ed, 2002), pp. 10, 20, 56, 61, 63.

6   Joseph Smith, *Book of Mormon*, (Palmyra, USA: E. B. Grandin, 1830).

7   Dr Geza Vermes, *The Complete Dead Sea Scrolls in English*, 7th Ed, (London: Penguin Classics, 2011).

8   Frank Morison, *Who Moved the Stone?* (Milton Keynes: Authentic Lifestyle, 1983).

9   Dorothy L. Sayers, *The Man Born to be King*, (San Francisco: Ignatius Press, 1999).

10 Josh McDowell, *Evidence That Demands a Verdict, Volume 1: Historical Evidences for the Christian Faith*, (Orlando: Campus Crusade for Christ, 1972).

11 Charles Darwin, *The Origin of Species, First Edition*, (Albemarle Street, London: John Murray, 1859), pp. 293-294.

12 Mendel as the Father of Genetics, DNA from the beginning. http://www.dnaftb.org/1/bio.html

13 Creation Ministries International, *From a Frog to a Prince*, (DVD, Creation.com). 'Was Dawkins Stumped? Frog to a Prince critics refuted again', 12 April 2008. https://creation.com/was-richard-dawkins-really-stumped-by-a-question-about-genetic-information

14 Bill Bryson, *A Short History of Nearly Everything*, (London: Black Swan, 2004) p. 20.

15 Ibid., p17.
16 Jason Lisle, *Logic & Faith—discerning truth in logical arguments*, (Petersburg, Kentucky: Answers in Genesis, 2016), p. 19.
17 Ibid., p. 11.
18 Bill Bryson, *A Short History of Nearly Everything*, p. 17.
19 Francis Schaeffer, *He Is There and He Is Not Silent, Trilogy*, (Leicester: Inter-Varsity Press, 1990), p. 277.
20 Bill Bryson, *A Short History of Nearly Everything*, pp. 573–574.
21 Grove & Newell, *Animal Biology*, (London: University Tutorial Press Ltd, 1964, 6th edition reprint), pp. 731–751.
22 John Playfair, *Illustrations of the Huttonian Theory of the Earth,* (Cambridge University Press, 2011), cited from: 'Siccar Point, Hutton's Unconformity', (Edinburgh: Lothian and Borders GeoConservation Group, 2018), p. 1.
23 Charles Lyell, *Principles of Geology*, (London: Penguin Classics, 1997).

11 Evolution – the evidence given at Epsom College revisited: fossil evidence, vestigial organs and embryology

In considering the question of our origins and the meaning of life, Charles Darwin believed that, in natural selection, he had found a working mechanism to drive his theory of 'Descent with Modification' which, for him, explained the development of all living things. Darwin preferred using this title for his theory rather than the word, *evolution*, which he used only once in the final paragraph of his book, *The Origin of Species*.

The word, 'origin', in the title of his book is rather misleading as he did not claim to know how life originated. He speculated that 'All organic beings that have lived on Earth could be descended from some primordial form,' maybe in a 'warm little pond'.[1]

In texts he wrote and in correspondence with friends we read that he assumed the natural emergence of the first life forms. He said that 'Laws of chemical combination, and the universality of latter render spontaneous generation not improbable.'[2] He knew that, at the time, no one could design an experiment to study the emergence of life, nor can we now!

He wrote to his friend, Ernst Haeckel, 'I will at the same time send a paper which has interested me; it need not be returned. It contains a singular statement bearing on so-called Spontaneous Generation. I much wish that this latter question could be settled, but I see no prospect of it. If it could be proved true this would be most important to us.'[3]

The *survival of the fittest* was an observation Darwin made about nature and seemed confirmed in his own family when, very sadly, three of his ten children died before the age of 11. Darwin had married his first cousin, Emma Wedgwood, and later became concerned about the dangers of inbreeding, leading to weak offspring. He requested that questions about this should be included in national censuses.

Now, I turn to the evidence presented to me in A-level biology at Epsom College.

(1) Fossil evidence

Two examples were given. The first is a type of sea urchin called *micraster*, now extinct, found fossilized in chalk. The second was the evolution of the modern horse. Grove and Newell declared that the fossilized remains, in a few instances, present a moderately complete series of the changes during the evolution of one animal from another—the evolution of the modern horse being cited as such an example.[4]

Considering *micraster* first, my school notes say that, in lower depths of chalk, the 'mouth' is slit-like and the grooves for the arms are in an asymmetrical position. In higher levels, the mouth has 'become' curved to scoop up food from the bottom and the arms are in a 'more efficient' symmetrical position. I would comment that, we may see morphological changes in sea urchins over time, but a different creature has not developed. Natural selection is at work, but that it is not the same as evolution.

Micraster is far from being dead and buried! A 2016 scientific article[5] stated *micraster* is one of the most famous examples of a continuous evolutionary lineage in invertebrate palaeontology! Populations of *micraster*, found in Germany, were compared with those found in Spain. It concluded that differences in structure were because the Spanish *micraster* lived at a greater burrowing depth than the German population and the sand was coarser in Spain. But the German and Spanish *micraster* were still *micraster*.

You may think that 'sea urchin evolution' is a trivial matter. However, *micraster* was used by H. G. Wells, Julian Huxley and G. P. Wells (son of H.G. Wells) in their 1,515-page-long book, *The Science of Life* (1931)[6] to show a fossil whose evolution could be traced over some 10 million years in chalk beds. They wrote that thousands of fossil *micrasters* can be collected showing a change in shape of the sea urchin and of the position of the mouth as you moved from lower depths to higher in the chalk. Julian Huxley was the grandson of T.H. Huxley—Darwin's associate—who had taught H.G. Wells biology at the Royal College of Science in South Kensington. These three trained biologists, with their prior commitment to naturalism, could not see that for a sea urchin to still be a sea urchin after 10 million years is a problem for the theory of evolution, not a proof!

The Science of Life was published in thirty-one fortnightly parts from 1929 to 1930 and appeared in one volume in 1931, sub-divided into nine 'books'. Book three had the uncompromising title, 'The

Incontrovertible Fact of Evolution'. Book eight contained a section titled, 'Modern Ideas of Conduct', in which H.G. Wells emphasized that he did not believe in personal immortality but urged readers to realize that we are part of a greater being whether that be 'the Deity' or 'Man'.[7] This sounds rather like Hinduism, where the individual soul is identified with, and united to, the all-pervading 'god', also known as the 'Ultimate Reality'.[8]

H. G. Wells's worldview, was strongly influenced by Darwinism. In later life, he said of Christianity: 'It is not now true for me.'[9] Of other world religions he said, 'They have served a purpose, … only they are not true for me to live in them.' He saw all the main religions as a 'jostling and mutually destructive movement'.[10]

H. G. Wells was not the last to dismiss Christianity. Fred Hoyle, in his Pelican book, *The Nature of the Universe*, spent much of the last chapter dismissing Christianity.[11] In his later book, *The Intelligent Universe*, he discussed the meaning and origin of life and began his penultimate paragraph saying, 'I am not a Christian, nor am I likely to become one as far as I can tell.'[12] Richard Dawkins continues to rail against the God of the Bible.

H. G. Wells's phrase, 'It is not now true for me,' is a profoundly modern remark, reflecting today's moral relativism, when something can be true for you but not true for me. Many believe that each individual can choose what *truth* they will believe for their life. So, every person thinks and does what is right in their own eyes.

It is not surprising that, with no belief in personal immortality, H. G. Wells should write in his last 34-page book, *Mind at the End of Its Tether* (1945), that if humanity was replaced by another species, that might not be a bad idea.[13] He wrote, 'Man's mind accepted the secular process as rational and it could not do otherwise, because it has evolved as part and parcel of it.'[14] Wells' secular Darwinian worldview was pessimistic and without hope.

Turning to *horse evolution*, we are told that the origin of horses is believed to date from about 50 to 55 million years ago. Initially, a linear story of horse evolution was proposed but newer research suggests that there are several bushy branches of horse evolution. Changes in the size of the horses, of their foot and leg structure and of their teeth are involved. Nowhere in the world can the evolutionary succession of the horse be seen. Fossils have been found in different continents and then used to explain horse evolution.

Consider a 2009 paper, 'Evolutionary Transitions in the Fossil Record of Terrestrial Hoofed Mammals'[15] by Donald R. Prothero. His abstract begins, 'In the past few decades, many new discoveries have provided numerous transitional fossils that show the evolution of hoofed mammals from their primitive ancestors.' His paper was in a special edition of *Evolution: Education and Outreach* describing transitional fossils. Clearly, if one kind of animal evolved into another, you would expect there to be transitional fossils— exhibiting traits common to the ancestral group and the derived descendant group.

Donald Prothero, in the final paragraph of his conclusions, is dismissive of people who are unconvinced by his *transitional fossils*. He wrote that they, 'have no training in anatomy or palaeontology and cannot tell one bone from another'. He refers to the 'complete intellectual and scientific bankruptcy of creationists' whose 'arguments are worthless.'[15] This chapter will go on to explain that eminent palaeontologists at the American Museum of Natural History, Harvard University and the Natural History Museum in London all believed that there are no transitional fossils.

Living horses vary greatly in size; the English Clydesdale Shire horse measures as much as twenty hands, while the Fallabella is just over four hands when fully grown (one hand is 10cms). Variation within a kind is often presented as evidence for evolution. The Natural History Museum in London suggests that Darwin's pigeons for the breeding of dogs show evolution. But pigeons are still pigeons; dogs are still dogs; and horses are still horses.

While variation within a kind occurs, the variation is limited by the genes which are already present within the kind and there has never been scientific evidence of genes being added. *Horse evolution* has serious genetic problems. Modern horses can have seventeen to nineteen pairs of ribs, but some fossilized forms have as few as fifteen pairs. The small extinct horse, Eohippus, had five digits in the forelimbs and four digits in the hind limbs. Other extinct horses had fewer digits and the modern horse is said to have only one digit. Some three-toed horses are known today and some scientists actually say the hoof of the modern horse represents five toes! The number of lumbar vertebrae varies between six and eight among the different horse fossils. The modern horse has six lumbar vertebrae while the Arabian horse has five.

Horse evolution tells of horses becoming larger and stronger with fewer toes and a change in structure. These changes were supposedly dictated by a cooling and drying climate. The greater number of toes adapted to marshy ground where the horses browsed on shrubs and trees and, later, fewer toes for running on grassy plains where they grazed on grass.

Teeth on leaf-eating horses were low crowned with rounded cusps and wore down as the animal ages. In grass-eating horses, the teeth continued to grow throughout the life of the horse and these are high crowned. This difference is a complete change in design. There is no evidence of a halfway type of tooth or a transformation of one kind to the other. The current bushy-branched tree of horse evolution is complex but, despite appearances suggesting that change and adaptation to environment may have happened, the first horses and the modern horses, and all those in between, are all still horses.

According to Julian Huxley, at least 1 million positive mutations were needed for the modern horse to evolve. But he believed that only 1 mutation in a total of 1,000 mutations was beneficial. That would mean that 999 mutations would be harmful, blocking evolution. He calculated that the probability for the horse to have evolved from one single unicellular organism was 1 in 103,000,000. These statistics suggest that *horse evolution* is impossible, though Julian Huxley still believed natural selection could solve the problem.[16]

Dr Niles Eldredge, a believer in evolution and curator at the American Museum of Natural History, in a recorded interview with Luther Sunderland, 1984, in *Darwin's Enigma: Fossils and Other Problems*, said, 'I admit that an awful lot of that has gotten into the textbooks as though it were true. For instance, the most famous example still on exhibit downstairs (in the American Museum) is the exhibit on horse evolution prepared perhaps 50 years ago. That has been presented as literal truth in textbook after textbook. Now I think that that is lamentable, particularly because the people who propose these kinds of stories themselves may be aware of the speculative nature of some of the stuff. But by the time it filters down to the textbooks, we've got science as truth and we've got a problem.'[17]

I have discussed *micraster* and *horse evolution* as taught in my sixth form. But does the overall fossil record demonstrate evolution of new *kinds* of creatures, or does it simply show changes of natural selection? Darwin himself said that a lack of fossil evidence of transitional forms would reduce him to an embarrassing footnote in history. In chapter nine of *The Origin of Species*, Darwin writes about the imperfection of the geological record. He commented that enormous numbers of intermediate or transitional forms had been exterminated by natural selection. *(Or there never were any—my comment.)* He asked, 'Why then is not every geological formation and every stratum full of such intermediate links? Geology assuredly does not reveal any such finally graduated organic chain; and this, perhaps, is the most obvious and gross objection which can be urged against my theory. The explanation lies, as I believe, in the extreme imperfection of the geological record.'[18]

Two eminent, now deceased, palaeontologists, Dr Colin Patterson of London and Professor Stephen Jay Gould of Harvard University, both agreed that there was no firm fossil evidence of transitional forms. This testimony was obtained by Luther Sunderland who was asked by the New York State Education Department, in 1978, to do a detailed study of how theories on origins should be treated in a revised version of the state's Regents Biology Syllabus.

During 1979, Sunderland conducted taped interviews with officials in five natural history museums that contained some of the largest fossil collections in the world. Among those interviewed were Dr Niles Eldredge in New York City and Dr Colin Patterson in London. Written transcripts of the interviews were given to the New York State Education Department for use in their study on origins. I have already referred to the interview with Dr Eldredge in the discussion of horse evolution, above.

Luther Sunderland corresponded with the late Dr Colin Patterson, Senior Palaeontologist at the Natural History Museum in London. Dr Patterson had authored a book called *Evolution*.[19] Mr Sunderland asked why there was no photograph of a transitional fossil in the book. Dr Patterson replied: 'I fully agree with your comments on the lack of direct illustration of evolutionary transitions in my book. If I knew of any, fossil or living, I would certainly have included them. You suggest that an artist should be used to visualise such transformations, but where would he get the information from? I could not, honestly, provide it, and if I were to leave it to artistic licence, would that not mislead the reader?'

Dr Patterson also went on to say of the now deceased Professor of Palaeontology at Harvard University, 'Stephen Jay Gould and the American Museum people are hard to contradict when they say there are no transitional fossils. ... You say that I should at least "show a photo of the fossil from which each type of organism was derived." I will lay it on the line—there is not one such fossil for which one could make a watertight argument.'[20]

Dr Patterson's comments have proved controversial with a pro-evolution writer, Lionel Theunissen, contesting in 1997, that

Mr Sunderland had misrepresented what Dr Patterson meant in his answer. Theunissen wrote to Dr Patterson about the quotation and received a reply dated 16 August 1993. Dr Patterson said the point he was making is that from the geological record one cannot make a confident watertight argument that any particular fossil is a transitional form. He continued by saying, 'Statements about ancestry and descent are not applicable in the fossil record. It is easy enough to make up stories of how one form gave rise to another, and to find reasons why the stages should be favoured by natural selection. But such stories are not part of science, for there is no way to put them to the test.'[21]

It does seem a dramatic admission that one cannot use the fossil record to draw conclusions about ancestry and descent. A taped recording of an informal talk which Dr Patterson gave to the Systematics Discussion Group at the American Museum of Natural History, on 5th November 1981, also led to controversy. He did not know that he was being taped and Theunissen quite reasonably thought that was wrong. Rightly or wrongly, there can be no argument about what he said and we have to conclude that the Senior Palaeontologist of the Natural History Museum in London had serious misgivings about the 'truth' of evolution.

Dr Patterson, writing about this meeting, said, 'I had been asked to talk to them on "Evolutionism and Creationism", fired up by a paper by Ernst Mayr published in *Science* just the week before. I gave a fairly rumbustious talk, arguing that the theory of evolution had done more harm than good to biological systematics (classification).[21]

I'm speaking on two subjects, evolutionism and creationism,

and I believe it's true to say that I know nothing whatever about either. ... One of the reasons I started taking this anti-evolutionary view, well, let's call it non-evolutionary, was last year I had a sudden realization. ... One morning I woke up ... and it struck me that I had been working on this stuff (evolution) for twenty years, and there was not one thing I knew about it.

He added:

That was quite a shock that one could be misled for so long. ... I've tried putting a simple question to various people and groups of people: 'Can you tell me anything you know about evolution; any one thing that you think is true?' I tried that question on the geology staff in the Field Museum of Natural History (*Chicago*—my italics), and the only answer I got was silence. I tried it on the members of the Evolutionary Morphology Seminar in the University of Chicago ... and all I got there was silence for a long time, and then eventually one person said: 'Yes, I do know one thing. It ought not to be taught in high school.'[22]

Theunissen contested that Dr Patterson had been misrepresented. You are left to judge what Dr Patterson meant when he said, 'If I knew of any, fossil or living, I would certainly have included them.' The record of his comments in a professional discussion group shows that Dr Patterson's personal experience of 'this stuff (evolution)' was that 'there was not one thing I knew about it.' Does the fossil record support evolution?

Dr. Niles Eldredge and Professor Stephen Jay Gould responded to the lack of transitional fossils by proposing their Theory of Punctuated Equilibrium, in 1972. This proposes that evolutionary changes happened in rapid, hectic phases in small, isolated populations and therefore would not be shown up in the fossil record. Some have called this 'Evolution by Jerks.' Today, *Gradualism* (Darwin) and *Punctuated Equilibrium* (Eldredge and Gould) remain favoured mechanisms.

(2) Vestigial organs

Returning to the second heading from my Epsom College notes, these 'useless body parts' are considered to be remnants of lost functions that our evolutionary ancestors possessed. Robert Wiedersheim listed eighty-six vestigial human organs in *The Structure of Man: An Index to His Past History*[23], in 1895, but today very few are still claimed. Muscles on our ears and the coccyx may still be claimed but my notes listed the appendix, Darwinian points on our ears, and pelvic bones in whales. The appendix and the tonsils contain lymphoid tissue and are now thought to play a part in immunity. The thymus, previously thought to be vestigial, produces cells which develop into T-cells that help destroy infected or cancerous cells.

The Darwinian tubercle on the posterior helix of the human ear is a small protuberance of cartilage under the skin. In Darwin's book, *The Descent of Man*, the second figure in the book was of this projecting point, whose function was unclear.[24] Wikipedia's entry on Darwin's tubercle shows a photograph of a human ear and the *homologous* point on a Macaque monkey's ear. The word, *homologous*, implies this similarity between man and monkey is due to shared ancestry.

Wikipedia explains that 10.4 per cent of the Spanish adult population and 58 per cent of Swedish school children have the point.[25] The condition can be bilateral or unilateral. When we were taught about this in our biology lesson, we all examined our ears and I have one on the left side.

Both whales and dolphins have pelvic (hip) bones, said to be evolutionary remnants from when their ancestors walked on land more than 40 million years ago. It did seem to me as a 16-year-old that the whale pelvis was quite difficult to explain. These bones are still often declared to be vestigial, slowly withering away like tailbones (coccyx) on humans.

In 2014, researchers Matthew Dean and Jim Dines, at the University of South California, found that whale and dolphin pelvic bones serve a purpose, during a four-year project. They examined more than 10,000 boxes of unsorted bones of whales and dolphins at the Natural History Museum of Los Angeles, finding hundreds of pelvic bones. They found that the muscles controlling the penis of these creatures are attached to their pelvic bones.

While they dismissed the idea that the bones were vestigial, they proposed that the pelvic bones might offer an evolutionary advantage in reproduction by giving greater mobility to the penis of a particular whale. They concluded: 'Our research really changes the way we think about the evolution of whale pelvic bones in particular, but more generally about structures we call "vestigial". As a parallel, we are now learning that our appendix is actually quite important in several immune processes, not a functionally useless structure.'[26]

Visiting the Natural History Museum, London, in September 2019, I saw in the main hall the very large skeleton of a blue whale. Usually pride of place belongs to Dippy, the cast of the original large dinosaur discovered in Wyoming in 1898. This 'copy' of a Diplodocus skeleton graced the main hall from 1905 until 2017, when Dippy went on a three-year, nationwide tour. I saw Dippy in October 2019, at the National Museum, Cardiff.

A sign explaining the blue whale skeleton declares: 'Evolving from sea to land and back again, whales present one of the greatest evolutionary puzzles.' The sign continues, 'In the first edition of *The Origin of Species*, Charles Darwin proposed that whales might have evolved from bears after he had heard of black bears swimming in rivers catching fish. Although heavily criticized, Darwin had the right idea albeit the wrong animal.

> Whales actually evolved around 45 million years ago from an order of land-living mammals called Artiodactyla, which includes pigs, hippopotamuses and giraffes. Whales have undergone a series of adaptations for their marine mode of life, including the front legs evolving into large flippers used to aid steering, and the hind legs and pelvis reducing to just two small bones towards the enormous tail.

At a genetic level, the supposed mutations helping flippers turn into legs and then reversing this to help legs turn into flippers does sound like 'Just so Stories' again.

(3) Embryology

Evidence for evolution, in the embryological development of animals, was referred to by Charles Darwin in *The Origin of Species* published in 1859. Darwin wrote, 'In two groups of animal, however much they may at present differ from each other in structure and habits, if they pass through the same or similar embryonic stages, we may feel assured that they have both descended from the same or nearly similar parents and are therefore in that degree closely related.'[27] While Darwin may have been sure, science today is not.

Darwin's ideas about embryos were popularized by Ernst Haeckel (1834–1919) in drawings which he published in 1868. The *Recapitulation Theory* proposed that all the developmental stages of an organism (ontogeny), from embryo to adult, express the intermediate forms of its ancestors throughout evolution (phylogeny). Grove & Newell declared, 'There is a remarkable similarity between all early chordate embryos, which is cogent evidence of their common evolutionary origin.'[28]

Grove & Newell perhaps did not know that Haeckel's illustrations were fraudulent or, perhaps, they chose to use apparent embryological similarities to bolster the evolutionary story. His drawings misrepresented the clear differences between the early stages of vertebrate embryos. As a 16-year-old, I had no reason to doubt my textbook of Biology.

Haeckel in fact wanted to prove that all vertebrates share a common ancestor, so made inaccurate drawings. Nick Hopwood, Professor of History of Science and Medicine at the University of Cambridge, in his book, *Haeckel's Embryos-Images, Evolution, and Fraud*,[29] explains that he discovered the original drawings and the wood blocks of the drawings.

The website of Evolution News, in April 2015, declared, 'Haeckel's Fraudulent Embryo Drawings Are Still Present in Biology Textbooks.'[30] I was surprised in 1998 to see Haeckel's drawings in *Molecular Biology of the Cell 3rd Ed*[31] by authors including James Watson, of DNA fame, which my daughter was using while reading Natural Sciences at University.

Truth seems to be sacrificed in order to maintain the propaganda of the reigning paradigm. The most recent publication of a serious science textbook containing Haeckel's drawings, *Bringing Fossils to Life: An Introduction to Paleobiology*, [32] was in 2013 written by Donald Prothero, the expert on horse evolution mentioned above!

I was beginning to see that fossil evidence is often evidence for natural selection, or variation within a kind, but it does not show new kinds of creatures evolving. We must conclude that pigeons, finches, sea urchins and horses are all still pigeons, finches, sea urchins and horses. Vestigial organs are a shrinking body of evidence for evolution. Embryology is no longer a credible source of evidence for evolution.

NOTES

1 Juli Peretó et al, 'Charles Darwin and the Origin of Life', *Origins of Life and Evolution of Biospheres* (39), 2009, p. 395.
2 Ibid., p. 395.
3 ibid., p. 398.
4 Grove & Newell, *Animal Biology*, (London: University Tutorial Press Ltd, 1964, 6th edition reprint), p. 736.
5 Nils Schlüter, 'Ecophenotypic Variation and Developmental Instability in the Late Cretaceous Echinoid *Micraster brevis* (Irregularia; Spatangoida)', *PLOS ONE*, 11(2): e0148341. https://doi.org/10.1371/journal.pone.0148341 2016.
6 H. G. Wells, Julian Huxley and G. P. Wells, *The Science of Life, 3 vols*, (Glasgow: The Waverley Publishing Company Ltd, 1931).
7 Ibid., p. 1475.
8 Colin Chapman, *The Case for Christianity*, (Chicago Illinois: Lion Publishing Ltd, 1981), pp. 143–144.
9 H. G. Wells, *First & Last Things: A Confession of Faith and Rule of Life*, (London: Cassell & Co Ltd, 1917), pp. 77–80.
10 H. G. Wells, *The Fate of Homo Sapiens*, (London: Secker & Warburg, 1939), p. 291.

11 Fred Hoyle, *The Nature of the Universe*, (London: Pelican Books, 1963), pp. 122–125.

12 Fred Hoyle, *The Intelligent Universe*, (London: Michael Joseph, 1983), p. 251.

13 H. G. Wells, *Mind at the End of Its Tether*, (Portsmouth, New Hampshire: William Heinemann Ltd, 1945), pp. 18–19.

14 Ibid., p. 3.

15 Donald R. Prothero, 'Evolutionary Transitions in the Fossil Record of Terrestrial Hoofed Mammals', *Evolution: Education and Outreach*, vol 2, 2009, pp. 289–302.

16 Julian Huxley, *Evolution in Action*, (London: Chatto and Windus, 1953), pp. 47–48.

17 Luther Sunderland, *Darwin's Enigma: fossils and other problems*, (El Cajon, CA: Master Books, 1988), p. 89.

18 Charles Darwin, *The Origin of Species 1st Ed.*, (Albemarle Street, London: John Murray, 1859), p. 292.

19 Colin Patterson, *Evolution*, (London: British Museum, Natural History, 1978).

20 Luther Sunderland, *Darwin's Enigma: fossils and other problems*, pp. 101–102.

21 Lionel Theunissen, *Patterson Misquoted; A Tale of Two 'Cites'*, © 1997. http://www.talkorigins.org/faqs/patterson.html

22 Colin Patterson, 'Evolutionism and Creationism', Transcript of Address at the American Museum of Natural History, New York NY, 5 November 1981, p. 1.

23 Robert Wiedersheim, *The Structure of Man: An Index to His Past History*, 2nd Ed Translated by H. and M. Bernard, (London: Macmillan and Co, 1895).

24 Charles Darwin, *The Descent of Man*, (Albemarle Street, London: John Murray, 1871), pp. 22–23.

25 https://en.wikipedia.org/wiki/Darwin%27s_tubercle

26 James P. Dines et al., 'Sexual selection targets cetacean pelvic bones', *Evolution: International Journal of Organic Evolution*. https://doi.org/10.1111/evo.12516 2014

27 Charles Darwin: *The Origin of Species* 1st Ed., p. 427.

28 Grove & Newell, *Animal Biology*, p. 742.

29 Nick Hopwood, *Haeckel's Embryos—Images, Evolution, and Fraud*, (University of Chicago Press, 2015).

30 Casey Luskin, 'Haeckel's Fraudulent Embryo Drawings Are Still Present in Biology Textbooks—Here's a List', *Evolution News*, 2015. https://evolutionnews.org/2015/04/haeckels_fraudu/

31 Bruce Alberts et al., *Molecular Biology of the cell* 3rd Ed., (New York and London: Garland Publishing, 1994).

32 Donald Prothero, *Bringing Fossils to Life: An Introduction to Paleobiology*, (Columbia University Press, 2013).

12 Marriage, junior doctor posts and working abroad

Towards the end of chapter 9, I wrote that Liz and I began dating in 1968. I turned twenty that year and Liz was fifteen months older than me. Liz had already been at Guy's Hospital for one year studying 1st MB when we met for the first time in October 1966. The students were divided into tutorial groups based on our surnames. Our group were surnames H to L. To my embarrassment, I remember her asking me my name, to which I replied, 'Jones'! She showed no surprise and said, 'Mine's Liz'. At boarding schools, Christian names were not often used.

Erroll Hulse, who had baptised me in 1967, once said that there were two important questions in life: 'What will you do with Jesus Christ?' and 'Who will you marry?' I do recognize that the second question can be a clumsy question under certain circumstances. Some choose not to or are unable to get married for various reasons. For some, this might be in order to devote oneself to a particular service of others, where marriage may be too serious a responsibility. This may be in military service or in another dangerous occupation. Many, particularly ladies, have served on the Christian mission field as single people.

My developing worldview, having become a Christian, saw marriage as it is described in Genesis chapter 2: A lifelong commitment to wife or husband 'until death do us part'. This commitment is to the exclusion of all other persons and is the only context for a sexual relationship and, if God so blessed, for the raising of children.

If you look at the Office of National Statistics data since 1937, the peak year for marriage rates in England and Wales was 1972. In that year, 78.4 unmarried males per 1000 and 60.5 unmarried females per 1000 married. The figures for 2019, the most recent year of published data, were 18.6 unmarried males and 17.2 unmarried females per 1000 married.[1] The average age of marriage for men in 2018 was 34.3 years old and for women was 32.3 years old. In 1970, when Liz and I married, the average age for both men and women was 11 years younger! In 1970, there were 415,487 marriages and, in 2019, there were 219,850 marriages in England and Wales.

One might ask, 'What is happening?' The Office of National Statistics' statistician, Dr James Tucker, offers his opinion: 'This long-term decline is a likely consequence of increasing numbers of men and women delaying marriage, or couples choosing to cohabit rather than marry, either as a precursor to marriage or as an alternative.'[2] As a Christian, I would have to answer that people are ignoring God's design for the family of one man married to one woman and any children with which they are blessed. The creation mandate, Genesis 1:28, to be fruitful and increase in number, is also overlooked, with consequences for our demography.

If one wishes to be married the question, 'Who will you marry?', is clearly very important. In the West, marriage has, in the 20th century, been based on love, mutual respect, companionship and shared values and interests. This is often good and, clearly, it is helpful if a couple have a common and shared worldview. This will have a bearing on the division of tasks in running a home, how leisure time is spent and how children are reared.

Liz and I shared mutual romantic love but also shared a common worldview in Biblical Christianity. In common, we had trusted Jesus Christ as our personal Saviour. For Liz, this had happened when she was about 11 years old and she had also witnessed to her faith at that age by being baptised by immersion. We shared a common interest as medical students and, later, qualified doctors. We both had the aspiration to have children. We believed that, if we became a married couple, God would have a plan for our lives that we could together discover as we followed his providential guidance. We found this prospect exciting and I was thrilled when Liz accepted my proposal of marriage.

Liz and I were approximately halfway through our three clinical years at Guy's Hospital. Faced with the prospect of marrying as newly qualified doctors and very possibly working in different hospitals—on a one-in-two rota—for twelve months, we decided to get married as students! We were not alone in our student year as several other couples married.

We were married on 2nd May 1970, at Cuckfield Baptist Chapel, Sussex, on a beautiful sunny day, by Pastor Erroll Hulse. My best man was a fellow medical student, John, who had been my flatmate and we had three bridesmaids. Another close friend, Lionel Ball, said the closing prayers at the wedding. Lionel was a London City Missionary based in a mission hall off Drury Lane where he served with his wife, Joan. Liz and I used to visit with Lionel in the blocks of flats around the theatres one evening each week.

Many family members, fellow students and other friends

attended. Then, we had a wonderful two-week holiday on the Greek island of Rhodes. We took medical books with us, as we were studying for our final medical exams! It was also the first and last time that we hired a Vespa motor scooter! When I stalled on a hill in Lindos, I caused the scooter to rear up, throwing Liz off the back and I landed on top of her. She suffered a bad bruise on her shin and I had learned a lesson—motor scooters were not for us!

After qualification in May 1971, Liz worked at St Olave's Hospital in Rotherhithe for twelve months and I worked at Guy's Hospital and the Miller Hospital in Greenwich for six months each. Fortunately, during those twelve months, we managed to synchronize our off duties and would meet up alternate evenings at our flat in Forest Hill for a meal and sleep. Weekends off duty were precious. Both St Olave's and the Miller Hospital have since been knocked down.

After these jobs, Liz gained a 12-month Senior House Officer position at the Whittington Hospital in North London, passing the Membership of the Royal College of Physicians (UK) during that time. I spent six months in Guildford working again as a House Surgeon in General Surgery. My first post had been in Orthopaedics and I wanted to be a General Surgeon. Part of this six-month period was difficult as our off-duties did not match. To see each other, I would drive from Guildford alternate evenings to North London where my evening meal would be in the oven in the doctor's mess and I might see Liz at some stage between her admitting emergencies.

Sleep in a single bed was not too comfortable and the early start in the morning to get back to Guildford for the morning ward round could be stressful. Liz was called out one memorable night to a cardiac arrest and put her white coat over her nightie. The patient was successfully resuscitated but had to be transferred by ambulance to the National Heart Hospital, with Liz in attendance. The ambulance crew could not take her back to the Whittington, so she returned in a taxi!

For the second six months of this year, I did two months of locums in General Practice at Lansdowne Medical Mission and Bermondsey Medical Mission. At Lansdowne, I helped Dr Doris Oxford, a committed Christian, who was a remarkable, single-handed GP. I remember sitting in medical outpatients as a student at Guy's Hospital when she referred a young girl to Dr R. K. Knight, whose firm we were attached to. The letter indicated her schoolteachers had commented that she would not keep still in PE and asked for the doctor's help. Dr Oxford wrote a short letter asking Dr Knight to see her because she had Sydenham's Chorea. This neurological disorder, which is, of course, rare today, is caused by a streptococcal infection (the same bacteria that causes rheumatic fever). The patient had rapid, aimless, involuntary movements of the arms, legs and facial muscles. Dr Knight praised Dr Oxford's clinical skills and the little girl was admitted to our ward.

At Bermondsey Medical Mission, I worked for Dr Margaret Jenkins, who had worked for the China Inland Mission and who had been expelled from China by the communists. There was an old-people's home attached to the mission and I can remember leading the Sunday morning service there. Dr Jenkins visited every patient older than 65 years in her practice every three months in their home. There were usually about six to eight visits each weekday in her diary. These were all close, geographically, and, having made the visit, we then wrote their name in the diary for the next visit three months later. I remember in a block of flats being attacked by a lady's budgie which would not let go of my hair. I used to sleep in the surgery at night when I was on-call on a camp bed. Interesting times!

These locums allowed me to study for the Primary Fellowship of the Royal College of Surgeons (FRCS) exam. I, then, attended a full-time Basic Medical Sciences course, in Anatomy, Physiology and Pathology, at the Royal College of Surgeons of England in Lincoln's Inn Fields for three months. Fortunately, I passed the Primary Fellowship.

I have said that Liz and I shared the belief that God had a plan for our lives together. We wondered about overseas medical missionary work and received some magazines regularly about such work. In early 1973, we read in two different places about the need of a replacement for Dr David Masters, who was working at Pimu Hospital in the Republic of Zaire, now known as the Democratic Republic of the Congo. David had trained at Guy's Hospital and had worked at Pimu, with his wife Irene, for four years without a furlough. He had established a training school for auxiliary nurses, which had national recognition, but required a doctor to be present and supervising it, for this recognition to continue. This, of course, was in addition to the medical and surgical care which he offered. The hospital was described as serving an area the size of Wales with one doctor and three English nurses plus the local nurses, who were all male. The training school had, by then, admitted girls who wanted to be nurses.

We felt led to offer to serve for a short-term to allow Dr Masters (who had recently suffered with hepatitis) to come home to the UK for a rest. In mid-July 1973, we flew to Zaire. We took a lot of materials for the hospital laboratory; many washed disposable surgical gloves; and various other pieces of equipment which were needed in the hospital. Baptist Missionary Society staff met us in Kinshasa, where we spent one night, and then travelled to Lisala by air. We were taken to the banks of the Zaire River, where a long dugout canoe fitted with an outboard motor awaited us. On the far side, we were met by Norman in the hospital Land Rover.

Our nursing colleagues were Ruth, Brenda and Katie from the UK. David was a trainee accountant who was serving for two years, helping to teach administration. Norman, from South Dakota, USA, helped the hospital workmen paint, repair and build facilities for the hospital.

We lived in a bungalow with mud-brick walls and a corrugated, tin roof. A surprise on arrival was to find a large ant hill in the spare bedroom. This did not trouble the hospital workmen who simply poured diesel fuel into it and then, later, removed the remnants. We slept under a mosquito net, took our antimalarials and avoided malaria, which was common locally. Rainwater was collected off the roof and boiled and filtered for drinking. If you wanted a bath, a large metal bucket of water was heated. The fridge in our home and in the hospital pharmacy was powered by petrol. We had to check that the flame under the fridge had not gone out each day. If the flame went out, then the vaccines stored in those fridges would be ruined.

As we both worked full-time in the hospital, we had a houseboy called Daniel (*Mokwambe* in the *Lingala* language). Daniel lived about 4 miles away and walked each day. If it rained, he arrived with a large banana leaf keeping him dry. Before he started to work for us, the authorities, hearing of his employment, locked him up and demanded seven-months tax in advance! I still have the letter. He baked bread in a wood-fired oven at the back of our house and used a charcoal iron for our clothes. We were very fond of Daniel.

We overlapped with David Masters for a week, during which he taught us many things. He left us a small notebook with all the various drug regimens for treating different worm infestations. We did an outpatient's clinic each afternoon, when one of the senior male nurses translated for us. We spoke to the nurses in French, and they translated into *Lingala*, the regional language, or *Lingombe*, the local tribal language. We shared the morning ward rounds on a large male and female ward. The beds had no mattresses and the patient simply laid their rush mats on the beds. The families who cooked for the patients usually slept under the bed on the concrete floor. In the *Nouvelle Salle*, a new ward supported by Oxfam, we had a better standard of bedding to teach the trainee nurses good clinical skills. Sicker patients were looked after in the Nouvelle Salle.

Liz oversaw the paediatrics and looked after patients with tuberculosis (TB), who lived in a dedicated building offsite. When TB patients started their drug treatment, they often felt better within a week or two and occasionally, despite being warned, they would disappear back to their villages, miles away. This would lead to drug resistance and a poor outcome. I was responsible for the surgery and obstetrics and visited the Leprosy village each week by bicycle.

Each morning we were called by the large 'talking drum' to a short service in the church, which was a massive wooden building with a thatched roof. We had colourful Sunday services with a very competent choir who rehearsed regularly under the direction of one of the secondary school teachers. The young minister of the church, Pastor Bombimbo, was a wise and helpful friend and the chief man in the village.

To hear the 'talking drum' was a special experience. The drum was a section of a large tree trunk about five feet long. This lay on its side with a longitudinal slit, the length of the 'log' in the middle of the top, like in a letter box. The trunk was hollowed out, with the wood on each side of the slit being of different thicknesses which made different tones. It would come to just below the waist of the drummer. Two wooden mallets, about half the size of a cricket bat, were used to strike the drum in a rhythmical fashion and different notes were made. There was a language based on the local tribal language and messages could be sent over long distances by a series of drummers in each village. Dr John Carrington, who worked for many years at Yakusu Hospital in Zaire, not only learned the local languages but also how to use the drums. The local people considered him to be a member of their tribe!

During the seven and a half months, we had to deal with some sad and challenging medical problems. Dealing with a lady whose lower leg had been bitten through by a hippopotamus, thankfully, had a good outcome. A man, whose ear was incompletely cut off in a fight with a machete, also healed well. Sadly, an 11-year-old boy, who arrived with paraplegia because of a tuberculous abscess pressing on his thoracic spinal cord, did not walk again despite appropriate anti-tuberculous drugs and our successfully draining the spinal abscess. Snake bites, malaria, amoebic dysentery, sickle cell crises, many worm infections and babies with malnutrition filled our days. We also dealt with an outbreak of meningococcal meningitis.

In the Auxiliary Nurses' Training School, we taught thirty students about the medical conditions they would meet and trained them to do vaccinations and give health education in the surrounding villages. The young people studied a two-year course with an option of a third year. We were responsible for feeding them and pastorally caring for them.

Pimu, the name of the hospital and village, meant, 'hole in the forest'. We did go out on public health trips in the Land Rover with nurses and students about every two weeks. We were rarely idle. Sleep could be disturbed by a nurse at the bedroom window calling us to the Obstetric building to help with a lady in difficult labour. There were amusing moments, such as young people coming to the door to sell us a pineapple out of our own garden. A large avocado pear tree overshadowed part of our roof. From time to time, an avocado could be heard hitting the tin roof but we never once saw one to eat! On one occasion, when we were short of certain medicines to treat children's worm infections, we travelled to a Portuguese palm oil plantation to purchase the medicines and some food. After a night away (our one day off), we returned with tomato ketchup and piccalilli to share with colleagues!

Towards the end of our time in Zaire, we were able to apply for medical posts back in the UK. Thankfully, these applications proved successful and, on 1 March 1974, we both started work back at Guy's Hospital.

NOTES

1 Marriages in England and Wales: 2019, Office of National Statistics
2 Ibid., Main point 1 – Statistician's comment

13 The surgical ladder—the apprenticeship model

Less than a week after returning to the UK, after our time in Zaire, starting at Guy's was a mild culture shock. From being the primary decision-makers in the various medical problems we had met, we were now, again, on the lower rungs of the paediatric and surgical training ladders. In Zaire, at times, our knowledge was seriously stretched by the conditions which we dealt with but now, we were again in a junior position, where the all-important principle of 'always pass the buck upwards when you don't know what to do' was drilled into us. This, of course, is most reassuring and helps the development of good and safe medical practice.

We were back in our flat in Forest Hill, which had been let while we were away, again working on a one-in-two rota. On duty nights, Liz had a room in the doctor's mess and I was required to sleep in a room close to the Cardiothoracic ITU (Intensive Therapy Unit). Liz passed the Diploma in Child Health (DCH) during the job at Guy's.

The reason that I had applied to do six months in Cardiothoracic surgery was not because I wanted to be a heart surgeon but to learn about the extreme challenges to patients needing massive surgery and intensive care. Heart surgery had been pioneered at Guy's Hospital by Sir Russell Brock, later Lord Brock. He was the first to describe the anatomical segments of the human lung. My father, when a junior anaesthetist at Guy's Hospital, had helped to give anaesthetics for him.

Soon after qualifying, I had done a locum on the unit and was the second assistant during a private operation that Lord Brock performed to close an atrial septal defect with the patient not on cardio-pulmonary bypass. I had to hold a sucker to remove blood from inside the heart without letting air through the septal defect, which would have then passed catastrophically up to the patient's brain. Appearing somewhat timid about this responsibility, he asked if I wanted to be a surgeon. Replying in the affirmative he told me to 'get that sucker in there boy!' The patient did well. A week later I received through the post a letter from Lord Brock's secretary with a cheque for 10 guineas made out to Dr Nigel Jones. This was a dilemma—did I keep the cheque uncashed with Brock's autograph on it or cash it? I photocopied it and cashed it!

I worked for three consultants, Mr G. Brain, Mr A. Yates and Mr D. Ross. Mr Ross was a pioneer who developed the switch operation to deal with a diseased aortic valve. This involved taking the patient's own pulmonary valve (exposed to lower pressures than the aortic valve) and using this to replace the diseased aortic valve. A cadaveric (from a dead person) aortic valve was then put in the pulmonary position. Some of these procedures could take all day and were physically demanding on the surgeons.

To progress in surgical training, I needed to pass the Final FRCS examination. Surgery is obviously a practical subject, so you had to fulfil several, different, six-month posts in certain specialities and thereby learn the hands-on aspect of a surgeon's job. In order to sit the exam, which had both written and oral components to it, you had to spend six months in Casualty (now known as Accident and Emergency), twelve months in General Surgery and six months in a surgical speciality—I did Urology. Such positions were put together in Surgical Rotations. These were usually of two years duration. I applied for four Junior Registrar Rotations and was offered interviews at Leeds General Infirmary, Manchester Royal Infirmary, Westminster Hospital and St Bartholomew's Hospital. The first interview was in Leeds which pleased my boss, Mr Yates, who said if I could not get a job in Sheffield (where he came from), Leeds was the next best place.

My developing Christian worldview gave me some reassurance that God would lead me to the right place for further training. As it says in Jeremiah 29:11, 'For I know the plans I have for you,' declares the Lord, 'plans to prosper you and not to harm you, plans to give you hope and a future.' Believing that God has a plan for your life does not guarantee perfect health, success or the absence of trials and difficulties. The Christian is as subject to the difficulties of life in this broken world as anybody else.

So, in 1974, I went by train to Leeds for the interview. The Postgraduate Dean, Professor Lynch, chaired the interview with three other surgeons including Mr David Wilson, the surgeon in charge of the Accident and Emergency Department. I had never met any of the surgeons before. The questions seemed straightforward until Mr Wilson cross-examined me about orthopaedic conditions, which I had had to deal with in Zaire.

He then asked if I had done much public speaking! This was hardly a question I had anticipated. I had to answer truthfully and say 'yes,' as during my student years at Guy's Hospital, I had led five fifteen-minute ward services on many Sunday evenings. Mr Wilson left the matter there, but I had publicly declared my allegiance to Jesus Christ in front of the interview panel.

I was delighted to be called back in after the interview and was offered the job. Mr Wilson then kindly led me to the Accident and Emergency Department to introduce me to his consultant colleague, Mr Michael Flowers, with whom I would also be working. To my great surprise, Mr Wilson explained that he had worked for the Baptist Missionary Society in Pimu Hospital, Zaire, from 1954 and, later, at Kimpese Hospital near the Angolan border, finally returning to the UK in 1968. During the Congo uprising, he sent his wife and four children back to the UK and remained in Kimpese, where he treated many horrific injuries owing to the civil war.[1]

Mr Michael Flowers had also worked for the Baptist Missionary Society for several years in Bangladesh at the Christian Hospital, Chandraghona. Before I departed for the station, Mr Wilson and Mr Flowers prayed with me and then I telephoned Liz to tell her the good news. This interview confirmed our view that we could trust God with our future.

Liz was appointed to a position as Tutor in Paediatrics, organizing medical student teaching in Leeds and as Professor Meadow's registrar with a 1 in 3 resident on-call commitment as Neonatal Registrar at Leeds Maternity Hospital.

We were able to sell our flat in London quite quickly and buy a newly built house in Leeds. We both got very good training in our respective specialities. My first publication in the *British Journal of Surgery*[2] was co-authored with Mr David Wilson. Among other bosses that I worked for, was Professor J. C. Goligher, who was renowned as a colonic surgeon. He was a workaholic, but I got on well with him and he gave me references for future jobs.

Our first daughter was born in January 1976 at Leeds Maternity Hospital (LMH), a source of great joy to us and our parents. I managed to get away from work to be present at the delivery and then went back to work. Liz had been looking after the neonates at LMH only ten days prior to our daughter's birth. It was a kind gesture when the Consultant Neonatal Paediatrician arrived about two hours after the delivery with a bottle of champagne in an ice bucket and checked the new baby! When I returned in the evening Liz was well rested, with both sets of grandparents in attendance.

Having passed the Final FRCS in late 1975, the next requirement in surgical training was either to spend a period in research, working towards a higher degree, or to get post-Fellowship surgical training with more hands-on surgical experience. After unsuccessful interviews in Bristol and Birmingham, I was appointed at St Thomas' Hospital in London as a Post-Fellowship Surgical Registrar. The first year of this post was spent at St Peter's Hospital, Chertsey, in Surrey, and the second year at St Thomas'. We moved home to West Byfleet near St Peter's.

There can be a tension when husband and wife are both pursuing training in a medical career. For different couples, different solutions will be found. For us, after the birth of our daughter, Liz had worked part-time. When we moved south to West Byfleet, Liz was offered a part-time position at Guy's Hospital for further training in Paediatrics but, with a nine-month-old daughter and another baby expected, she chose not to take up this position.

I began working at St Peter's Hospital, Chertsey, in October 1976.

There were three general surgical consultants and I worked very happily for Mr Chris Anders on a 1 in 2 emergency rota. Driving to work in my old MG Midget, through roads lined by sweet chestnut and oak trees, was a happy experience. Mr Anders ensured that I had a good training. I gained significant elective surgical experience and much emergency experience. I organized all the admissions and planned the operating lists. We operated in parallel theatres. I also did an operating list each week at one of the local cottage hospitals in Woking and Weybridge. Mr Anders was very supportive and my fourth publication in the *Annals of the Royal College of Surgeons* was written with him.[3]

I remember one amusing event in an outpatient clinic when a patient, for whom I had prescribed Fybogel, declared that it was ruining her saucepans. The medication, a powder, should be mixed with water and drunk quickly before it turned into a gel. She seemed to be using it like gravy thickener!

Our second daughter was born in July 1977 at St Peter's. We were very content in a lovely home and as members of Send Evangelical Church, near Woking. The American pastor, Eric Olson and his wife Edith, with their four daughters, were close and supportive friends.

On one memorable occasion, we invited a Christian surgeon, Mr Denis Burkitt[4] CMG, MD, FRCSEd, FRS, to speak at a summer evening barbecue at our home. Mr Burkitt was well-known, having described the tumour, in 1958, often affecting children in Africa, which was later named Burkitt's Lymphoma. As a medical student, I had visited Uganda in 1969 for my student elective. I had stayed for five days in the North-West Nile District, at Kuluva Hospital, with Dr Ted Williams, who had shared with Mr Burkitt and Dr Cliff Nelson a journey of 10,000 miles to visit fifty-six hospitals in Africa, detailing information about the lymphoma in an attempt to find the cause. I still have many black-and-white photographs which Dr Williams gave me of children with Burkitt's Lymphoma, affecting their faces. In 1964, the Epstein-Barr virus was shown to be involved in the pathogenesis of Burkitt's Lymphoma—this being the first time that a virus had been incriminated in causing a human tumour. Mr Burkitt, later, engaged in other research which confirmed the need for a high fibre intake and changed the diet of the Western world. He was nicknamed, 'The Bran Man' or the 'Fibre Man'.

Mr Burkitt lost an eye, at the age of 11, during an incident at school. When he volunteered for the Colonial Medical Service in West Africa in 1941, he was turned down without interview because he only had one eye! He later commented, 'When I eventually reached Africa, God, in his mercy, enabled me with one eye to see things which my predecessors had missed with two.'

Mr Burkitt lived in Gloucestershire at the time and, initially, quite reasonably, felt it was rather a long distance to travel to speak at our summer barbecue. However, he kindly came and we enjoyed good weather with a catering officer from the RAF (a member of our church) supervising the cooking. Ninety people attended as he spoke, addressing the question, 'Where are you going?'

His talk, 'Where are you going?',[5] was later published in 1982 by the Christian Medical Fellowship. The first section questioned, 'Where have we come from?' He quoted Sir Ernst Chain, Nobel prize recipient for his work on penicillin, as saying that the origin of DNA molecules by sheer chance, cannot be seriously considered. Mr Burkitt drew attention to Sir Fred Hoyle's opinion of it being extremely improbable that the development of complicated structures which form the basis of life could have happened by chance.

His second section asked, 'What are we?' He described man as fundamentally a spiritual being, resident in a body which he likened to a 'carton' with our eternal souls as 'contents'. He, then, focused on life being a journey with our destination depending inevitably on the path chosen. Mr Burkitt spoke of Jesus' parable about 'The rich man and Lazarus', the beggar (Luke 16:19–31). The rich man, during his life's journey, had neglected the spiritual component of his life and at death could not join Lazarus in heaven.

In October 1977, I began working on the Professorial Surgical Unit, at St Thomas' Hospital, for Professor J. B. Kinmonth and Professor Norman Browse. I commuted by train from West Byfleet to Waterloo and walked to the hospital for the 8 o'clock ward round. JBK, as we called him, was a pioneer in understanding the investigation and diseases of the body's lymphatic system.

I worked more closely with Professor Browse, who patiently trained me in vascular surgical technique. The Royal College of Physicians website says he 'was also renowned for his superlative operative technique'.[6] He would assist me in abdominal aortic graft surgery and in femoro-popliteal bypass grafts using reversed long saphenous vein. The abdominal aorta can be dangerously dilated (an aneurysm) or narrowed so that a prosthetic woven or knitted dacron tube graft can be stitched in place to resolve the problem. Likewise, blockage of the femoral or popliteal artery causes poor arterial blood supply to the leg leading to restrictive pain on walking or gangrene.

Being a surgical trainer requires patience and being prepared for things to go more slowly. It may mean that operating time can be used up and later cases on the operating list might risk been cancelled. Perhaps because of those pressures, it was not that common for consultants to train as he did. It was a privilege to work for him. The sixth edition of his excellent book, *Symptoms and Signs of Surgical Disease*, was published in 2020.[7] Professor Sir Norman Browse later became the President of the Royal College of Surgeons of England.[8]

By now, I needed to embark on research, which would lead to a higher degree to progress my climb up the surgical ladder. There were rather a lot of hopeful trainees in the queue at St Thomas' and I began looking elsewhere. In God's providence, a vacancy came up in the Thrombosis Research Unit at King's College Hospital, in Camberwell. I applied for this position and was appointed by Professor V. V. Kakkar,[9] the Director, as an MRC (Medical Research Council) Research Fellow with Honorary Senior Registrar status.

My move to King's College Hospital added a bus journey to my train journey. During my research period, I was the resident emergency general surgeon at Dulwich Hospital one night a week, to maintain my surgical skills. I also worked in Professor Kakkar's surgical outpatient clinic.

The Thrombosis Research Unit was a hive of activity and many publications. We ran many trials in the prevention of deep-vein thrombosis in the calf, thigh and arm veins and the development of safer types of anticoagulants. I did research on elastic compression stockings, used in the treatment of venous disease, but my main focus was on platelets! Platelets are solid components of blood, as are red and white blood cells; they are about a fifth of the diameter of red blood cells and do not have a cell nucleus. Platelets are found only in mammals. Their function is to block blood leaking through a break in the wall of blood vessels and are vital in the process of clotting. They change shape from a biconvex disc and clump together to form a haemostatic plug, which then stops bleeding from a hole in the blood vessel. In addition to this beneficial role, platelets participate in the pathological development of arteriosclerosis, which can narrow our arteries. An example of this is the narrowing of coronary arteries to the heart, which can lead to a heart attack.

Platelets live for eight to ten days and a healthy platelet count is 150,000 to 450,000 per cubic millimetre. A low platelet count increases the chances of bleeding. The haemostatic effect (stopping bleeding) of platelets is blocked by taking aspirin or non-steroidal anti-inflammatory drugs. Thus, aspirin is used in the prevention of coronary thrombosis. Since the days of my research, 1978 to 1980, the role of platelets in immune responses has also been recognized.

My personal research involved a drug trial of an anti-platelet drug which we hoped might help patients with peripheral arterial disease to walk further with less pain in their leg muscles. I also designed an animal model of arterial thrombosis to investigate novel antiplatelet drugs. I learnt to use a scanning electron microscope. I also did initial work on new platelet function tests in people with arterial disease, diabetes mellitus and raised lipids (fats) in their blood. My thesis, of 263 pages, was submitted for the higher degree of Master of Surgery (London University) with the title: 'The Role of Platelets in Peripheral Arterial Disease'. I spent two years and five months in the unit. After an oral examination with two Professors of Surgery and one Professor of Haematology, who had read my thesis, I was awarded this degree in 1981.

My search for scientific understanding of the Genesis account of Creation continued throughout this time of surgical training. I purchased two helpful books in 1977 and will explain their contents in the next two chapters. Books and lectures on matters related to human origins were important to me. As a family, we were very happy where we were living and had many friends, especially in our church. However, the next step up the surgical ladder might well mean having to move anywhere in the UK.

My focus now turned to obtaining a General Surgical Senior Registrar post. At that time there were 196 such posts in England and Wales. The training requirement was to stay in the post for a minimum of four years to obtain a Certificate of Higher Surgical Training. Thus, one might expect 50 positions a year to be advertised—it did not always work out like that. There were 960 general surgical consultant posts in England and Wales and one became available only if someone retired or died. During my last year in the Thrombosis Research Unit, I applied for all the senior registrar positions advertised. After eight unsuccessful interviews, I was appointed to the rotation based at Leeds General Infirmary, St James' University Hospital, and Leeds and Bradford Royal Infirmary.

General Surgery was a competitive speciality, so many of us, at that time, experienced unsuccessful interviews and disappointments. Having phoned Liz to tell her the outcome of an interview, I would get into my car to drive home and repeat to myself the first verse of this hymn:

God holds the key of all unknown,
And I am glad;
If other hands should hold the key,
Or if He trusted it to me,
I might be sad, I might be sad.

The fourth verse continues:

I cannot read His future plans;
But this I know;
I have the smiling of His face,
And all the refuge of His grace,
While here below, while here below.[10]

The first year of my Senior Registrar training would begin at Bradford Royal Infirmary on 1 October 1980. Liz and I would have to find a new home in Leeds (our fourth) and Liz was also expecting our third child, due in mid-November!

From the time of our graduation in 1971, I had spent nine years in training and had gained experience by working for many consultant surgeons for six- or twelve-month periods. This time-honoured, long apprenticeship would continue until the Calman Report[11] in 1993 and, later, Modernizing Medical Careers[12] in 2005 introduced shorter, competency-based training programs. Training would begin to focus on a narrower area of surgical skills as specialization increased, and the introduction of the European Working Time Directive[13] into the UK reduced the working week to forty-eight hours.

NOTES

1 David Hedley Wilson, 1928–2015. *Plarr's Lives of the Fellows, Royal College of Surgeons* https://livesonline.rcseng.ac.uk. Resource Identifier: "rcs: E009038"

2 N. A. Jones and D. H. Wilson, 'The treatment of acute abscesses by incision, curettage and primary suture under antibiotic cover', *British Journal of Surgery* 63, 1976, pp. 499–501.

3 N. A. Jones and C. J. Anders, 'A new approach to the surgical treatment of reflux oesophagitis', *Annals of the Royal College of Surgeons of England* 61, 1979, pp. 48–50.

4 Denis P. Burkitt, 'Obituary', *British Medical Journal* 306, 1993, p. 996.

5 Denis Burkitt, 'Where Are You Going?' (London: Christian Medical Fellowship, 1982), pp. 3–11.

6 Sir Norman Leslie Browse, Sir Barry Jackson, *Royal College of Physicians* https://history.rcplondon.ac.uk/inspiring-physicians/sir-norman-leslie-browse

7 Norman L. Browse, Symptoms and Signs of Surgical Disease, (41, Bedford Square, London: Edward Arnold Ltd, 1978).

8 Sir Norman Browse, K. Burnand and D. Alderson, *RCS Bulletin* Vol 101, 2019 pp. 276.

9 Vijay Kakkar, 'Obituary', *The Times* Nov. 11, 2016.

10 'God holds the keys of all unknown', John Parker 1825–1911.

11 S. Hunter and P. McLaren, 'Specialist medical training and the Calman report', *British Medical Journal* 306, 1993, pp. 1281–1282.

12 Tony Delamothe, 'Modernising Medical Careers: final report', *British Medical Journal* 336, 2008, p. 54.

13 'European Working Time Directive', *European Parliament and Council of the EU Art.* 137(2), 4 November 2003.

14 Ape-men – fact or fallacy

When, as a young medical student, I first heard an evangelistic address by an InterVarsity Fellowship Travelling Secretary at Guy's Hospital, you may remember, in chapter 9, that a really important question for me was, 'What about Adam and Eve and the Genesis account if evolution is true?' I ended that chapter by indicating that the issue of evolution, when I became a Christian in late 1967, remained unresolved. In chapters 10 and 11, I discussed the nature of direct witness evidence and of circumstantial evidence and described the evidence for evolution that had been presented to me at Epsom College.

At that time, I was unaware of books which tackled the *Creation versus Evolution* debate. They did exist, for example *Genes, Genesis and Evolution*[1] by John W Klotz, published in 1955. Later, in 1976, Henry M. Morris would publish his book, *The Genesis Record*[2] which was the first commentary written on the complete book of Genesis by a creationist scientist.

There were organizations devoted to apologetics for a Biblical Creation position (approximately 6,000-year-old earth), such as the *Creation Science Movement* (CSM)[3] – founded in the UK in 1932 as, *The Evolution Protest Movement,* by a small group of Christians concerned about the propaganda that was promoting the theory of evolution as if scientifically proven. I was not, at the time, however, aware of such organizations. In the early years of our marriage, I was involved in surgical training, taking and passing examinations, our time in Zaire, and the birth of our first two daughters in 1976 and 1977. I was convinced of the infallibility of the Bible from 1967 onwards, but I was not, at that time, able to give reasoned scientific arguments for a literal understanding of Genesis chapters 1 to 11.

The founders of CSM, in 1932, were Douglas Dewar, a barrister and Auditor General of the Indian Civil Service, and Captain Bernard Acworth RN, DSO, who was a submariner in the First World War. *The Times* reported on the first public meeting, in February 1935, when Sir Ambrose Fleming, the first president of the movement, spoke. Fleming, a physicist, had designed the transmitter used by Marconi to send radio waves 2,000 miles across the Atlantic in 1901. He was the inventor of the Thermionic Valve in 1904, said by the Institute of Electrical and Electronics Engineers to be 'one of the most important developments in the history of electronics'.[4] Fleming's valves were used in early radio receivers and were also used as a *rectifier*—a device for converting alternating current into direct current.

Fleming, in his 1935 address[5], referred to those convinced of Darwin's *Origin of The Species* as 'Darwinian anthropologists'. He said that numerous books had created a public belief that the theory of evolution was settled, scientific truth. The fact that many scientists did not believe evolution was proven, was being publicly overlooked. He feared that, to the delight of many, the foundations of Christianity were being shaken by public opinion, popular fictional literature and contemporary scientific thought, leaving what was simply a humanistic social construct. Fleming and his colleagues felt it was of national importance to counteract a philosophy that man was simply a highly developed ape. Evolution, they believed, could not account for the altruistic, aesthetic, intellectual, spiritual and religious faculties of man that are never seen in animals.

Between 1962 and 1979, Sir Cecil Wakeley DSc, FRCS, FRS Ed[6], who was a consultant surgeon at King's College Hospital and President of the Royal College of Surgeons of England, was the President of CSM. He was a remarkable man who edited the *British Journal of Surgery* for twenty-five years and founded and then edited the *Annals of the Royal College of Surgeons* for twenty-two years. It was said that he never forgot a face or name and encouraged younger surgeons. Sir Cecil also presided over The Lord's Day Observance Society for many years. He was a devout Christian.

The President of the CSM, who followed from 1979 to 1997, was Professor Verna Wright MD, FRCP, Professor of Rheumatology at the University of Leeds and co-founder of United Beach Missions. Verna wrote, *Relevance of Christianity in a Scientific Age*[7], in 1981, published by the Christian Medical Fellowship. I reference this 18-page booklet as he would wish to be remembered by the gospel message, not a personal biography. I knew Verna personally and he encouraged my involvement with United Beach Missions for fourteen years. Verna was a professor for twenty-four years in Leeds and co-authored over 1000 scientific papers and wrote 21 books. This extraordinarily prolific output was confirmed to me (on 23rd November 2020) in a telephone conversation with Stephen Wright, his son—indeed there were over 1,100 other published communications as well.

Verna was involved, not only in medical research but, also, in engineering and pharmacological research into human joint disease, and was partly responsible for establishing rehabilitation medicine as a separate speciality. He predicted genetic links in rheumatic disease before tests could prove this was true. He served as chairman of the Arthritis and Rheumatism Council. He was also president of the Lord's Day Observance Society. I attended his remarkable memorial service in 1998, in Leeds Town Hall, along with many hundreds of others who wished to honour him.

I have related short biographies of Ambrose Fleming, Cecil Wakeley and Verna Wright to indicate that these men, with postgraduate degrees and enormous contributions in the scientific world, all believed the Genesis account of God's creation in six days and of Adam and Eve, our first ancestors. In understanding our currently broken world, they argued that we would go seriously astray if we denied the clear record of God's creation, the fall of mankind and of God's promise of redemption. Promises of a coming Saviour, who would be one of Abraham's descendants and therefore a Jew, are recorded throughout the Old Testament. We remember these promises in the readings of *Nine Lessons and Carols* each Christmas Day service.

In the USA, the Creation Research Society[8] was founded in 1963 and now has worldwide membership. The original ten founding scientists had found that they were unable to publish scientific information favourable to the creation viewpoint in established journals. They, therefore, decided to form the society in order to publish a scientific journal, *The Creation Research Society Quarterly*, first published in July 1964. While Wikipedia paints a picture of division and purges in the early years of the society, when people with different beliefs joined, the current board of directors are united, holding to a clear statement of faith as follows:

1. *The Bible is the written Word of God,* and because it is inspired throughout, all its assertions are historically and scientifically true in the original autographs. To the student of nature, this means that the account of origins in Genesis is a factual presentation of simple historical truths.

2. *All basic types of living things,* including man, were made by direct creative acts of God during the Creation Week described in Genesis. Whatever biological changes have occurred since Creation Week, have accomplished only changes within the original created kinds.

3. *The great flood described in Genesis,* commonly referred to as the Noachian Flood, was a historic event worldwide in its extent and effect.

4. *We are an organization of Christian men and women* of science, who accept Jesus Christ as our Lord and Saviour. The account of the special creation of Adam and Eve as one man and one woman, and their subsequent fall into sin, is the basis for our belief in the necessity of a Saviour for all mankind. Therefore, salvation can come only through accepting Jesus Christ as our Saviour.

In 1977, I bought two books which helped my understanding of how the Bible's account of the origin of man and the universe can be believed as real history. These books showed me that the evidence for the *theory of evolution* was weak and it appeared that unreasonable assumptions had been made. They showed me that the facts of science and history fit far better with the Bible account of a literal six-day creation dated only thousands of years ago, followed by a worldwide flood, than with the changing hypotheses and billions of years of evolution. The first was written by Malcolm Bowden, *Ape-Men—Fact or Fallacy*.[9] I heard Mr Bowden give a talk on this subject in Woking, Surrey, where I bought his book.

His book is a thorough examination of the circumstances surrounding the discovery of the most important, ape-men fossils up to that time. The book first deals with the *Piltdown Forgery* and then with the 'discoveries' of *Peking man, Java man, Neanderthal man* and various African Ape-Men found in East and South Africa.

Peking Man

Bowden comments on the meagre fossil evidence for ape-men links with *Homo Sapiens*. At the time of writing his book, in 1977, these apparent fossil links were fragments of jaws, broken skull bits, parts of long bones or bones of the foot. For example, *Peking man* was identified as a member of the human lineage by Professor Davidson Black, in 1927, on the basis of a single tooth.[10] Later excavations at Zhoukoudian, near Beijing in China, did yield several skull caps and mandibles, limb bones and teeth. These were found in several deep caves where there was evidence of a very large-scale industry being carried on. There were layers of chipped quartz and great heaps of ash and many skulls, which Bowden suggests are those of monkeys, killed for their brains. After Davidson Black's death in 1934, Teilhard de Chardin took over leading these excavations. Today there is a large museum at Zhoukoudian dedicated to *Peking man*.

Nebraska Man

Bowden makes a passing reference to *Nebraska man* who was, again, based on the finding of a single tooth. A Mr Cook had found the tooth in Pliocene deposits in Nebraska and sent it to H. F. Osborn, head of the American Museum of Natural History. He concluded, because the tooth had characteristics of the teeth of humans, chimpanzees and of *Java man*, that *Nebraska man* was a further missing link. He said, 'The tooth is like the still, small voice. Its sound is by no means easy to hear .... This little tooth speaks volumes of truth, in that it affords evidence of man's descent from the ape.'[11]

Osborn's allusion to the 'still small voice' borders on blasphemous as it refers to the voice of God in 1 Kings 19:12 (NKJV), when God is speaking to the prophet Elijah. Osborn seemed to suggest that a single tooth, found in Nebraska, was evolutionary evidence of how God created man. The tooth actually belonged to an extinct pig![11]

Piltdown Man

Another interesting aspect of Bowden's book is that it explores the various characters involved with the Piltdown find and the possible identity of the hoaxer. The three main excavators at Piltdown were: Charles Dawson, a solicitor, living at Uckfield, who was an amateur archaeologist and historian; his friend, Sir Arthur Smith Woodward FRS, keeper of the Geological Department at the British Museum; and Pierre Teilhard de Chardin, student at the Jesuit College, Ore Place, Hastings from 1908 and ordained in 1911.[12]

Sir Arthur Keith FRCS, FRS[13], Hunterian Professor and Conservator of the Hunterian Museum at the Royal College of Surgeons of England, worked extensively on the Piltdown fossils. He had obtained a Bachelor of Medicine degree from Aberdeen

University in 1888 and, later, studied anatomy at University College, London and in Aberdeen. He edited the *Journal of Anatomy* for twenty-one years. He was made a fellow of the Royal College of Surgeons in 1908 and of the Royal Society in 1913. He was known as a leading anthropologist and was president of the Royal Anthropological Institute.

Sir Arthur was involved in the discovery of the sinoatrial node[14] in the wall of the right atrium of the heart. The node produces an electrical impulse, causing the heart to contract approximately 80 times a minute in humans. His co-worker was a young medical student, Martin Flack, who had found the sinoatrial node in the heart of a mole in 1906.

The Piltdown fossils were found originally in a trench in the drive leading to Barkham Manor, owned by a friend of Charles Dawson. In 1908, workmen struck and shattered what turned out to be part of a skull. A piece was handed to Charles Dawson who continued excavating in the trench with various friends until 1911, when he found another piece of skull. This fitted the first piece and he, thereafter, recruited his friend, Sir Arthur Smith Woodward from the British Museum. These two men began excavating the trench in June 1912, assisted by Teilhard de Chardin. Teilhard de Chardin had considerable knowledge of chemistry, having lectured in Chemistry at Cairo University for three years.[15]

Their excavations found nine pieces of a skull, a jaw, flint tools and teeth of a hippopotamus and an elephant. Teeth of a beaver and mastodon (an extinct elephant like creature from North and Central America) and, particularly, a missing canine tooth from the jaw were also found. The findings were presented, in December 1912, to a packed meeting of The Geological Society in London. Strangely, no one seemed to be troubled by the finding of a tooth of an extinct creature from North or Central America.

The Piltdown Hoax or Fraud was not fully exposed until 1953, when it was concluded that the skull remains were those of a modern man and the jaw, that of an orangutan with its teeth filed down. Various chemical stains had been applied to some of the bones.[15] Publication of the discovery of the fraud caused embarrassment in scientific circles because of sweeping claims made on the basis of the Piltdown finds. A motion was tabled in the House of Commons: 'That the House has no confidence in the trustees of the British Museum ... because of the tardiness of their discovery that the skull of the *Piltdown man* is a partial fake.'[16]

Initially, Charles Dawson was suspected of the hoax but his lack of expertise in anatomy, palaeontology and chemistry led to his being exonerated by many investigators. Malcolm Bowden, in his book, felt that Teilhard de Chardin was the culprit. Indeed, Dr L. S. B. Leaky, the famous palaeontologist who excavated at Olduvai Gorge in modern Tanzania, seemed to agree with this conclusion. He was writing a book at the time of his death about the hoax that his wife prevented from being published as she felt it would damage her husband's reputation. In another book, *Leakey's Luck*[17], published in 1975, Sonia Cole, the author, states Teilhard de Chardin actually told Leakey that Dawson was not responsible but refused to elaborate.

Others have pointed the finger of suspicion at Sir Arthur Keith. I have a cutting from a free medical journal called *Hospital Doctor*, dated 11 October 1990, with the front-page article, about Sir Arthur

Keith, headed, 'Surgeon accused in Piltdown Man hoax'.[18] The article reports that experts at the Natural History Museum (in London) say the bones were carefully broken so that their improbable joints could not be matched—a feat requiring a deep knowledge of anatomy. The article was prompted by the publication of a new book by Dr Frank Spencer, a professor and chairman of the Anthropology Department, Queens College, City University of New York. The book, published in 1990, is about Spencer's own investigation called, *Piltdown. A Scientific Forgery.*[19] Spencer died in 1999.

His book documented his own investigations and those of Dr Ian Langham, an Australian historian, whose research became available to Dr Spencer when Dr Langham died in 1984. They both had, independently, reached similar conclusions that Sir Arthur Keith was the leading hoaxer. Before the Piltdown finds were made public in 1912, Keith was speaking publicly about his opinion that the earliest humans evolved earlier than had been supposed and that the first sign of this evolution was present in a large brain. The finding of a skull big enough to contain a human brain, but with the jaw of an ape, suited his theory.

Dr Spencer was able to establish that Mr Dawson and Sir Arthur Keith had held meetings dating back to a year before the supposed 'discovery'. Spencer reckoned that Keith was the scientist with the most to gain from the Piltdown discovery. Spencer wrote that the hoax had been 'a deliberate use of fraud to alter the entire course of palaeontology'. Spencer believed that Keith provided technical expertise and possibly the bones, which were stained to look prehistoric. Mr Dawson then planted them in the gravel pit where he then led others, including Teilhard de Chardin, on fossil hunts. Spencer said, when interviewed about his new book, 'We don't have the smoking gun. But I think the interpretation we've made is a reasonable one and in harmony with the facts.'[20]

You might ask what did such a highly respected scientist think he would gain by perpetrating such a fraud? Keith was obviously a very bright man and devoted his life to evolutionary theory. I believe that he had come to a settled, 'scientific' worldview that man had evolved and all his energy was devoted to proving this. When faced with the frustration that the fossil evidence for the theory was very poor, he (if indeed he was the hoaxer) resorted to making the evidence up. While others may not go to such lengths to 'manufacture' evidence in fossils that can be handled, there are numerous 'Just So Stories' which have been fabricated to try and prove evolution. In some ways, these are even more powerful when written by 'scientists in white coats', who write in a language that the general public cannot understand and who could not possibly be involved in a conspiracy of dishonesty!

The temptation to deceive people, in defending the theory of evolution, is not simply to prove the theory but also to enhance personal reputation and standing in the scientific community. Speaking up about the paucity of evidence, or our reasonable personal doubts, can lead to exclusion and dismissal from scientific academia and from teaching positions at every level. Cancel culture is no new thing!

Bowden explains that the Dutch physician, Eugene Dubois, 'discovered' *Java man* (also known as *Pithecanthropus*) in 1891. Dubois had long been ambitious to discover the missing link in man's evolution. Ernst Haeckel, who was responsible for the fraudulent drawings of embryos, also invented a hypothetical, ape-like man, which he named *Pithecanthropus Alalus* (speechless ape-man). He commissioned a painting of what he imagined this evolutionary intermediary would look like. Haeckel, in fact, taught Dubois at Jena University in Germany.[21]

You may feel it is excessive to suggest that people are wanting to deceive others. G. K. Chesterton, when writing about *Java man* in his book, *This Everlasting Man*, first published in 1925, said, 'A detailed drawing was reproduced, carefully shaded to show the very hairs of his head were all numbered. No uninformed person, looking at its carefully lined face, would imagine for a moment that this was a portrait of a thighbone, a few teeth and a fragment of a cranium.'[22] Incidentally, C. S. Lewis credited Chesterton's *The Everlasting Man* with 'baptising' his intellect[23] as much as George MacDonald's writings had baptised his imagination, so as to make him more than half-converted well before he could bring himself to embrace Christianity.

Dubois concealed much of what he found, as it contradicted the message of human evolution that he wanted to report. He released it later, without giving a satisfactory explanation of why he had concealed it. Before his death in 1940, he admitted that the skullcap he found was that of a large gibbon.[24] Haeckel, for his endeavours, was charged with fraud by five professors and, when convicted by a university court at Jena, admitted that he had altered his drawings of the embryos. A report of his verbal defence recorded, 'I should feel utterly condemned and annihilated by the admission, were it not that hundreds of the best observers and biologists lie under the same charge.'[25] In his defence he was saying many other experts were cheating so he did not feel bad to be doing the same thing!

You may feel that lumping Sir Arthur Keith (or Teilhard de Chardin), Ernst Haeckel and Eugene Dubois together as deceivers of the general public is unkind. While Haeckel was proven to be a dishonest witness, could there actually be some truth in his statement that hundreds of the best observers and biologists were also guilty of concocting evidence for evolution. Misinformation from the past is still often perpetuated in the present. I have commented on Haeckel's drawings in my daughter's book, *Molecular Biology of the Cell*[26], published in 1994 and recommended at her university.

The issue of scientific dishonesty is real and was highlighted in the introduction to the 1956 republication of Darwin's *The Origin of Species*, by the publishers J. M. Dent[27], who invited the Canadian Professor, W. R. Thompson PhD, DSc, FRS, to write the introduction to this 100th anniversary publication. Thompson warned them that his words would not be flattering but the publishers raised no objection.

He began his introduction by noting, 'I am not satisfied that Darwin proved his point or that his influence in scientific and public thinking has been beneficial.' Thompson also wrote, 'The success of Darwinism was accompanied by a decline in scientific integrity. This is already evident in the reckless statement of Haeckel and in the shifting, devious, and histrionic argumentation of T. H. Huxley.' Thompson then mentions the Piltdown skull fraud, revealed in 1953, and continues, '... but even before this, a similar instance of tinkering with evidence was finally revealed by the discoverer of

Pithecanthropus, who admitted, many years after his sensational report, that he had found in the same deposits bones that are definitely human. Though these facts are now well-known, a work published in 1943 still accepts the diagnosis of Pithecanthropus given by Dubois, as a creature with a femur of human form permitting an erect posture.'[28]

NOTES

1 John W. Klotz, *Genes, Genesis and Evolution*, (St Louis, Missouri: Concordia Publishing House, 1955).
2 Henry M. Morris, *The Genesis Record*, (Ada, Michigan: Baker Books, 1976).
3 Creation Science Movement, 17–18, The Hard, Portsmouth PO1 3DT, United Kingdom.
4 Milestones: Fleming Valve, 1904. IEEE Global History Network 2015. https://ethw.org/Milestones:Fleming_Valve,_1904
5 'Evolution Protest Meeting—first public meeting addressed by Sir Ambrose Fleming', *The Times*, 12 February 1935.
6 Sir Cecil Wakeley, *Plarr's Lives of the Fellows, Royal College of Surgeons of England*, 2006. Resource Identifier: "rcs: E000231".
7 Verna Wright, *Relevance of Christianity in a Scientific Age*, (Christian Medical Fellowship, 1981).
8 Creation Research Society, 1 W. Firestorm Way #145 Glendale, AZ 85306 USA.
9 Malcolm Bowden, *Ape-Men—Fact or Fallacy?* (Kent: Sovereign Publications, 1977).
10 'Peking man', *Encyclopedia Britannica*, 24 March 2009, https://www.britannica.com/topic/Peking-man. Accessed: 9 November 2021.
11 Malcolm Bowden: Ape-Men—Fact or Fallacy? p. 46.
12 Ibid., pp. 3–5.
13 Sir Arthur Keith, *Plarr's Lives of the Fellows*, 2014. Resource Identifier: "rcs: E005084".
14 Mark Silverman et al., 'Discovery of the sinus node by Keith and Flack: on the centennial of their 1907 publication', *Heart* 93 (10): 2007, pp. 1184–1187.
15 Malcolm Bowden, *Ape-Men—Fact or Fallacy?* p. 28.

16 Ibid., p. 8.

17 Sonia Cole, *Leakey's Luck*, (Glasgow: Collins, 1975), p. 339.

18 'Surgeon accused in Piltdown Man hoax', *Hospital Doctor*, October 11, 1990.

19 Frank Spencer, *Piltdown. A Scientific Forgery*, (New York: Natural History Museum Publications and Oxford University Press, 1990).

20 Michael T. Kaufman, 'Frank Spencer is Dead at 58; Anthropologist Studied a Hoax', *New York Times*, 3 June 1999, Section B, p. 11.

21 Malcolm Bowden, *Ape-Men—Fact or Fallacy?* p. 124.

22 G. K. Chesterton, *The Everlasting Man*, (Connecticut: Martino Fine Books, 2010), Part 1 Chapter 2—'Professors and Prehistoric Men', pp. 15–22.

23 G. K. Chesterton, The Everlasting Man, https://en.wikipedia.org/wiki/The_Everlasting_Man

24 Malcolm Bowden, *Ape-Men—Fact or Fallacy?* p. 133.

25 Ibid., p. 128.

26 Bruce Alberts et al., *Molecular Biology of the cell*. 3rd Ed., (New York and London: Garland Publishing, 1994).

27 W. R. Thompson, *Introduction to The Origin of Species*, 6th Edition, (London: J. M. Dent, 1956).

28 Ibid., pp. xx–xxi.

15 Myths and miracles

In this chapter, I want to turn to the second book that I bought in 1977: *Myths and Miracles—A new approach to Genesis 1–11.*[1] This was written by David C. C. Watson, who was an English schoolteacher, born in India in 1920. He was educated at Cambridge University, where he graduated with first class honours in Classics and was, later, a senior scholar at Trinity College.

Watson went to India as a missionary, teaching in a Christian school near Chennai. There, he met and was influenced by Professor Hannington Enoch, who was a Zoologist and author of two books: *Where Did Man Come From?*[2] and *Evolution or Creation.*[3] Watson wrote a short appreciation of Professor Enoch in the magazine, *Creation*, in December 1990, where he said that Enoch's books and friendship 'got me hunting down evolution!'[4] Watson himself later became a member of the Evolution Protest Movement.

Professor Enoch taught University science students for more than thirty years. Enoch travelled widely and visited various parts of the world, acquainting himself with some of the original materials and arguments on which the theory of evolution is founded. The professor finally concluded that the theory of evolution was a colossal mistake—a 'grand illusion', he said.[4]

Enoch was a Christian who, for a time, was President of the Union of Evangelical Students of India and was one of the Vice Presidents of the International Fellowship of Evangelical Students. An unnamed student, writing on the *Courage to Tremble*[5] website, reproduced the following information from Professor Enoch's book, *Where Did Man Come From?* which he had used in a debating society talk. He quoted Prof. Enoch who said, 'Now it is true that some similarity exists between the blood of mammals which may even admit of their being arranged in a graded system. But this chemical similarity cannot prove evolution. Further research along the same lines has shown that the tiger and the whale are closer of kin. But such inconvenient facts are ignored by evolutionists.

'Blood analysis has revealed other interesting facts. The specific gravity of human blood is 1059; of the pig and hare, 1060; of frog 1055–56; of the snake 1055; and the monkey's is 1054.9. From this table we can see that the frog and snake are closer to man than the monkey, while our nearest relation is the pig!' Enoch's reasoning that similarity or increased complexity does not prove evolution, is similar to the point that I made about 'the evolution of bile salts' in chapter 8.

David Watson's first book, *The Great Brain Robbery*[6], was published in 1975, though I did not obtain a copy until some years later. Dr Martyn Lloyd-Jones was quoted on the back cover: '... an excellent piece of work. I think that coming at this time it would be of very great help to many Christians who are in a state of great confusion on this subject ... I shall certainly make it known as I travel round the country. I cannot think of a better introduction to this subject.'

Watson's next book, *Myths and Miracles-A new approach to Genesis 1-11*, was published in 1976 and I bought this the following year. His book was later translated into other languages including German, Spanish and Finnish. He logically deals with the first eleven chapters of Genesis in his own eleven chapters, with a verse-by-verse approach. The foundational basis of the Bible, in the first three chapters, is dealt with in 72 pages, with chapters 4 to 11 requiring 40 pages. I think he must have hoped that his book would be used in the classroom. The opening words of his introduction are, 'What shall we teach the children about Genesis 1-11?'[7] In a later paragraph he states, 'In a school textbook it is pointless to give detailed references to source material, but RE Teachers would be well advised to study and stock their libraries with five or six of the books listed in the Bibliography.'[7]

I found his book extremely helpful but now only draw attention to his epilogue,[8] where he explains 'why I wrote this book'. He describes the experience of switching on the television in the middle of a play as being confusing sometimes. While the conclusion of the play may seem satisfactory, how do we recover the first scenes of the play? He answers, 'Buy the book, of course, and read what happened in the beginning.' Born at our own particular moment in history, we see others in many lands living their lives out in many conflicting ways. 'Why are so many things wrong? How and when, if ever, will they be put right?' The answer: Genesis shows how things went wrong in the first 'scene'; Revelation shows how everything will be put right in the last scene.

> If the first chapters of God's Book were wrong about the first things, you might safely disregard what the last 'chapter' say about the last things. ... But if in fact Genesis gives a true account of real events at the beginning of the world, you may be quite sure that Revelation gives a true account of real events at the end of the world. Only a fool would ignore them.[8]

Watson continued: 'I want you to read and believe Revelation.

That is why I have written a book on Genesis. He then closes his book with a quote from Revelation 1:6–7: 'Unto Him who loves us and freed us from our sins by His blood ... to Him be the glory and power for ever and ever, Amen. Behold, He comes with the clouds, and every eye shall see Him!'[8]

In the same year, 1976, that Watson published his book, *Myths and Miracles*, he lost his job teaching religious education at a state school in the United Kingdom. Perhaps, the publication brought controversy and too much scrutiny to the school where he taught or, perhaps, it was felt he strayed from the RE syllabus. In more modern times, I co-signed a letter with twenty-nine others (including many PhD holders and professors) to the Secretary of State for Education, in 2014, about the Government's opposition to teaching 'creationism' in state-funded schools. To quote the reply of Nick Gibb MP, Minister of State for School Reform, 5th January 2015, 'The Department's policy on schools is that public money should not be used to fund providers to promote matters of belief as evidence-based scientific theory.'[9] This represents the usual implication that belief in Genesis is a matter of faith (religion), whereas science is all about evidence-based facts. I trust, as you continue reading this book, you will see that evolutionary science is as much about faith and is an arena where facts and 'truth' change all the time!

Dr Martyn Lloyd-Jones wrote in his 1958 book, *Authority*[10], 'If you study the history of science, you will have much less respect for its supposed supreme authority than you had when you began. ... Without arguing in detail about scientific matters ... it is not only lacking in faith and unscriptural, but it is ignorant to accord

"Science", "Modern Knowledge" or "Learning" an authority which they really do not possess.'

I have commented on the claimed authority of my Professor of Anatomy, Jack Joseph, in his description of the evolution of man's ability to walk with an upright posture or the claimed authority of Sir Arthur Keith, involved with the Piltdown finds. We must decide whether the claims of evolutionary science, particularly for billions of years, are supported by credible evidence or whether Genesis's account of world history has more evidence to support it.

Teaching the Genesis account of Creation to young people, is becoming more challenging. Nick Gibb MP, in his final paragraph, sounded somewhat reassuring in his phraseology until we read his final caveat, which trumps a literal belief in Genesis. He wrote:

> These changes do not threaten the Christian ethos of church-faith schools; nor do they require teachers to promote or endorse views which go against their beliefs. Teachers will continue to have the clear right to express their own beliefs, and schools will be able to continue to include fundamental tenets of Christian faith in the curriculum, so long as they do not undermine the teaching of the established scientific consensus around evolution.[11]

The minister does give a mandate for Christians to express their own beliefs so that, as Jesus taught in Matthew 10:16, they must be 'as shrewd as snakes and as innocent as doves,' and as bold as the apostle Paul recommends in 2 Timothy 1:8: 'Do not be ashamed to testify about our Lord.'

An influential book, written to describe individuals who take an anti-evolution position, did pass comment on David C. C. Watson's dismissal, quoting 'The Times Educational Supplement' as reporting that students interrupted Watson's class with shouts of 'rubbish'. This book, *The Creationists: From Scientific Creationism to Intelligent Design*[12], written by Ronald Numbers , a Professor of the History of Science at the University of Wisconsin–Madison, has been described as 'probably the most definitive history of anti-evolutionism'[13] and runs to 624 pages. The author describes himself as an agnostic and no longer believing in creationism of any kind, though his father was a Seventh-day Adventist preacher.

Without knowing the exact reasons for David C. C. Watson's dismissal from that school, we can at least be sure that he did help the worldwide cause of Young Earth Creationism in two further, much quoted ways. In 1984, he wrote to Professor James Barr of the Oriental Institute of Oxford University, who later became Professor of the Interpretation of Holy Scripture and then Regius Professor of Hebrew, 1978–1989, at Oxford University. Watson's enquiry concerned the Hebrew word, y*om*, translated as, 'day', in Genesis 1.

Watson wanted the opinion of an expert and James Barr certainly fitted the bill. At Edinburgh University, he had gained a first-class MA in Classics and a BD with distinction in Old Testament. After his ordination, he served for two years as the Church of Scotland minister in Tiberias, Israel, where he became fluent in modern Hebrew and Arabic.

Barr was described as a liberal theologian, who did not hold to a literal belief in Genesis, opposing scriptural inerrancy and was an outspoken critic of evangelicalism. Despite these facts, Barr clearly understood what the Hebrew meant in its context and said that *a day*, in Genesis chapter 1, meant 'a day'. It was only the need of some to stretch the length of the days to fit with an old age for the Earth, that led people to think anything different. Professor Barr wrote to David C. C. Watson on 23 April 1984:

> Dear Mr Watson, Thank you for your letter. I have thought about your question and would say that probably, so far as I know, there is no professor of Hebrew or Old Testament at any world-class university who does not believe that the writer(s) of Genesis 1–11 intended to convey to their readers the ideas that (a) creation took place in a series of six days which were the same as the days of twenty-four hours we now experience, (b) the figures contained in the Genesis genealogies provided by simple addition a chronology from the beginning of the world up to later stages in the biblical history, (c) Noah's flood was understood to be world-wide and extinguish all human and animal life except for those in the ark.

Barr continued:

> Or, to put it negatively, the apologetic arguments which suppose the 'days' of creation to be long eras of time, the figures of years not to be chronological, and the flood to be a merely local Mesopotamian flood, are not taken seriously by any such professors, as far as I know.'[14]

Barr was not a creationist, but he was an expert Hebrew scholar. Barr closes his letter by mentioning, 'but I have another book coming out soon'. This book, he was referring to, first appeared in 1985—*Escaping from Fundamentalism*[15]—so he was by no means sympathetic to Watson's 'creationist' viewpoint.

David C. C. Watson's other claim to fame was that, in 1986, he suggested to the president of the Oxford Union Debating Society that the Huxley Memorial Debate should be on creation versus evolution. This debate took place on 14 February 1986, between Professor A. E. Wilder-Smith (Professor of Pharmacology) and

Professor Edgar Andrews (Materials Scientist & President of the Biblical Creation Society) speaking for Creation, and Dr Richard Dawkins (Zoologist, Oxford University) and Professor John Maynard-Smith (Professor of Biology, University of Sussex), for evolution. The motion they debated was, *'That the Doctrine of Creation is more valid than the Theory of Evolution.'*

David C. C. Watson actually later bought the audiotapes and the copyright of the Oxford Debate from the Oxford Union. The content of these tapes is available to purchase as a CD from Renton Maclachlan[16] in New Zealand. He purchased a copy of the audiotape direct from David C. C. Watson. Information about this is available on his website: worldviewsonline.com.

It was agreed prior to the debate, in the Oxford Union's President's office, that no religious or non-scientific material could be presented in the debate. Only repeatable, falsifiable, scientific facts could be presented.

Richard Dawkins, in his reply for evolution, proceeded to attack Wilder-Smith's religious beliefs describing him as a Christian fundamentalist. Edgar Andrews intervened to remind Dawkins that all four of the debaters had agreed to present scientific arguments not religious ones. The President of the Oxford Union agreed and Richard Dawkins had to sit down.

I am unable to find a written record of Edgar Andrews' contribution but Professor Maynard- Smith described Wilder-Smith's science as 'impeccable'! Maynard-Smith then also strayed from the debating rules by claiming that Wilder-Smith believed in a small tribal god, which was not acceptable in today's enlightened society. He claimed that he and his friends believed the whole big universe was *God*, which was a superior belief to Wilder-Smith's belief. On reflection, he might have realized that he was claiming Hinduism is superior to Christianity! (In my next chapter, about Professor Fred Hoyle, we will learn that Hoyle discussed Hinduism and similarities to his own beliefs.)

Richard Dawkins, perhaps perceiving that on the basis of debate he and Maynard-Smith were losing, implored (the very word that Dawkins used) the audience not to give a single vote for the creationist's position as this 'would be a blot on the escutcheon of ancient University of Oxford'.[16] (Escutcheon means a shield or emblem bearing a coat of arms.)

The debate lasted over three and a half hours. All written records of the debate at Oxford University have been lost, but Professor Wilder-Smith's opening speech can be listened to on YouTube.[17] There is considerable controversy about the votes cast at the end of the debate. In 2003, the American Association for the Advancement of Science had the evolutionists winning the debate by 198 votes to 15 votes. On the audiotapes, the chairman of the Oxford Union (a lady) is clearly heard reading out the figure 150 (with no objection by the tellers, those counting the votes, or the speakers). The figure of 150 votes for the motion means that 43 per cent voted for the creationists.

Such debates were usually given prominent publicity in the press, or on radio and television. This did not happen. An enquiry by Paul Humber of the Creation Research Society in Australia to the Oxford Union obtained the following information from Jeremy Worth: 'The only records kept of debates are the title, speakers' names and result. ... Unfortunately, I can't even give you the result for this debate. The results are noted in a large minute book which spans several years. I'm sorry to say that the minute book in question was either lost or stolen many years ago, which is a great pity.'[18]

A further incident involving Professor Wilder-Smith, which I am unable to date, relates to a talk that he gave at a media conference, during which he stated that the BBC presented the biggest barrier of all broadcasting corporations to creationist topics. Two senior executives of the BBC, in the audience, were annoyed by this and offered to make a program on the subject of evolution and creation which he promptly accepted, but the programme was never transmitted-due to 'technical problems'![19]

It is for you to decide whether University academics actively suppress creationist arguments and whether the BBC, which presents David Attenborough's programs regularly, is also guilty of censorship. The book, *The Noble Liar*, by Robin Aitken with the subtitle, 'How and why the BBC distorts the news to promote a liberal agenda' is illuminating. I quote:

> There is a solemn covenant that lies at the heart of the BBC's relationship with the country, and it is this: in return for the licence fee revenue (a valuable privilege), it promises to tell the truth and to be impartial on all matters of public debate. This promise is broken on a daily basis and, over time, its performance is worsening. The BBC's worldview, its composite 'noble lie', if you will, has become more pronounced, more dogmatic, more entrenched. On certain topics it barely tries to disguise its own prejudices any longer. Whether through carelessness or hubris it hardly even attempts to maintain the pretence of impartiality.[20]

I am thankful for David C. C. Watson's writings which helped my developing worldview. He died in 2004.

NOTES

1 David C. C. Watson, *Myths and Miracles—A new approach to Genesis 1–11*, (Worthing: H. E. Walter Ltd, 1976).

2 Hannington Enoch, *Where Did Man Come From?* (Republished Union of Evangelical Students of India, 2004).

3 Hannington Enoch, *Evolution or Creation*, (Welwyn Garden City: Evangelical Press, 1966).

4 https://creation.com/the-man-who-got-me-hunting-down-evolution

5 https://couragetotremble.blog/.../where-did-man-come-from-and-prof-enoch 2008

6 David C. C. Watson, *The Great Brain Robbery*, (Worthing: H. E. Walter Ltd, 1975).

7 David C. C. Watson, *Myths and Miracles—A new approach to Genesis 1–11*, p. vii.

8 Ibid., p. 116.

9 Letter of Nick Gibb MP, Minister of State for School Reform, to Professors McIntosh and Taylor, 5 January 2015.

10 David Martyn Lloyd-Jones, *Authority*, (Westmont, Illinois: Inter-Varsity Press, 1958) p. 40.

11 Letter of Nick Gibb MP, Minister of State for School Reform, to Professors McIntosh and Taylor, 5 January 2015.

12 Ronald L. Numbers, *The Creationists: From Scientific Creationism to Intelligent Design*, (Harvard University Press, 2006), pp. 300, 521–522.

13 Steve Paulson, 'Seeing the light -- of science, Salon, 2 January 2007. https://www.salon.com/2007/01/02/numbers_12/

14 Letter from Professor James Barr to David C. C. Watson, 23 April 1984. 'Should Genesis be taken literally?' *Russell Grigg Creation* 16(1) 1993, pp. 38–41.

15 James Barr, *Escaping from Fundamentalism*, (London: SCM Press, 2012).

16 Oxford Union Debate CD, The Huxley Memorial Debate: 'That the Doctrine of Creation is more valid than the Theory of Evolution', *Oxford Union*, 14th February 1986, available from: worldviewsonline.com, Renton Maclachlan

17 https://www.youtube.com/watch?v=lh_SdprE5lg Sourced: 26/05/23

18 Oxford Union Debate CD, The Huxley Memorial Debate: 'That the Doctrine of Creation is more valid than the Theory of Evolution', *Oxford Union*, 14th February 1986, available from: worldviewsonline.com, Renton Maclachlan

19 Malcolm Bowden, *True Science Agrees With The Bible*, (Bromley: Sovereign Publications, 1991), p. 257.

20 Robin Aitken, *The Noble Liar*, (London: Biteback Publishing Ltd, 2018), pp. 249–250.

16 Chemical evolution—an impossibility!

I would now like to consider what may be termed 'chemical evolution'. This deals with the issue of how living organisms could have originated on earth from simple, inorganic chemicals. For evolution to be true, a mechanism for simple, inorganic chemicals to become complex proteins and nucleic acids by spontaneous generation, without intelligence, must be found. If life was unable to start by itself, then Darwinian evolution is without foundation.

The origin of life is supposed to have happened around 4.2 billion years ago[1] and is referred to scientifically as *abiogenesis*, meaning 'spontaneous generation of life'. Living organisms are made up of carbon, oxygen, hydrogen, nitrogen, phosphorus and other elements. There is a need for evolutionists to show how these elements have been combined through chemical evolution to produce a living organism. Charles Darwin himself speculated, in a letter to Joseph Hooker on February 1st, 1871, 'If (and oh what a big if) we could conceive in some warm little pond with all sorts of ammonia and phosphoric salts, light, heat, electricity present, that a protein compound was chemically formed, ready to undergo still more complex changes.'[2]

This idea of a primordial soup (prebiotic soup) was encouraged by the biologist J. B. S. Haldane FRS in an eight-page article titled, 'The

Origin of Life'[3] in the Rationalist Annual in 1929. He described the primitive oceans as a 'vast chemical factory'. He wrote, 'When ultra-violet light acts on a mixture of water, carbon dioxide, and ammonia, a vast variety of organic substances are made, including sugars and *apparently* (my italics) some of the materials from which proteins are built up.' He goes on to say, 'Before the origin of life *they must have accumulated* (my italics) till the primitive oceans reached the consistency of hot dilute soup.' Haldane's use of 'apparently' and 'must have accumulated' are wishful speculation that is not supported by scientific facts.

Haldane thought that viruses were intermediate between the prebiotic soup and the first cells. He made this assertion about prebiotic life: 'But for all that, life may have remained in the virus stage for many millions of years before a suitable assemblage of elementary units was brought together in the first cell. There must have been many failures, but the first successful cell had plenty of food, and an immense advantage over its competitors.'

Modern science indicates that viruses could not remain viable for millions of years. Viruses may persist on stainless steel, plastic or in a refrigerator for days. A report from Australia suggested that the Covid-19 virus can remain infectious on banknotes, phone screens and stainless steel for twenty-eight days when the research was conducted in the dark.[4]

My school biology textbook (see chapter 4) had picked up this idea that viruses were intermediaries in the evolution of life. Viruses are complex, made up of proteins, nucleic acids, lipids, and carbohydrates. Viruses are not really alive because they cannot reproduce by themselves. They have to invade a living cell and hijack its genetic machinery in order to reproduce. This is an egg–chicken situation—you can only have a virus if cells are already in existence!

Experiments have tried to model a primordial soup. The Miller–Urey experiment was designed to produce amino acids, by two USA chemists in 1952.[5] Water, methane, ammonia and hydrogen were all sealed inside a sterile glass flask from which oxygen was excluded (a so-called 'reducing atmosphere'). Electrical sparks were fired inside the flask to simulate lightning, continuously, for a week. Stanley Miller and Harold Urey found a small amount of red tar in the trap. This was mostly an insoluble, toxic, and carcinogenic mixture called *tar*. In the tar they identified five amino acids, predominantly the simplest amino acids, glycine and alanine, in tiny amounts. When Miller repeated the experiment in 1983 with a slightly different mixture of gases, he only got trace amounts of glycine. Such a highly artificial experiment designed by intelligent scientists (Harold Urey had won the 1934 Nobel Prize for Chemistry for discovering deuterium, heavy hydrogen), produced tiny amounts of a few amino acids and did not produce life in any sense!

Amino acids are three-dimensional and, just as our hands are mirror images of each other, so for each amino acid two distinct forms could exist which are mirror images of each other; for simplicity we call them 'left' or 'right-handed'. One of the great mysteries of all life forms on earth, is that their amino acids are always 'left-handed' and all their sugars are 'right-handed'. If it had been possible that Miller's amino acids spontaneously joined together to make a protein, then the insertion of one of the 'right-handed ones' would have wrecked the process. In the Miller–Urey experiment, although some of the correct amino acids for life were made (left-handed ones), some of the 'wrecking' types of amino acids (right-handed ones) were also produced.

In a 2011 paper, Jeffrey Bada carried out a new analysis of the old products produced in Miller and Urey's experiment, using modern techniques, and found twenty-three different amino acids in the tar. The yields of even simple glycine remained very low. Most life forms use only twenty amino acids. Seven of Bada's twenty-three amino acids are not found in proteins. He was unable to detect the proteinaceous amino acids, phenylalanine, proline, histidine, tyrosine, lysine, asparagine, arginine, or glutamine.[6] (Proteinaceous amino acids are considered as those incorporated into proteins during protein synthesis.)

Some of the proteinaceous amino acids are in fact destroyed by the very conditions that produced them. In addition, the intelligent design of a trap at the bottom of the apparatus, to isolate the products before the energy source destroyed them or they were oxidized, hardly represented a natural process. Protein synthesis requires highly concentrated amounts of amino acids and so, finding tiny amounts is unhelpful.

A factor in the design of experiments seeking to mimic a primordial soup, is that they were performed in a 'reducing atmosphere' containing hydrogen-rich compounds like methane ($CH4$) and ammonia ($NH3$), but with oxygen excluded. This is because scientists generally believe that there was no free oxygen in the atmosphere and seas of the early Earth.

Speculation about chemical evolution being possible is dependent on a reducing atmosphere. Evolutionists believe that, on the early earth, organisms existed which did not rely on oxygen to live. Our current atmosphere, containing approximately 21 per cent oxygen, would have destroyed the so-called 'building blocks of life' and indeed prevented their formation in the first place. Evolutionists believe that early organisms were later superseded by cyanobacteria—blue-green algae—which produces oxygen as a by-product of its photosynthesis. Current oxygen levels in the atmosphere sustain life and prevent fires beginning spontaneously! It is of interest that the earth's crust is made up of 46 per cent oxygen, mostly as silicates which are oxygen and silicon combined.

Scientists believe that about 2.4 billion years ago, oxygen in the atmosphere suddenly increased by about 10,000 times. This period, known as the *Great Oxidation Event*, completely changed chemical reactions on the surface of the Earth. It is claimed that a later build-up of oxygen enabled the development of multicellular life forms. Arizona State geochemist, Ariel Anbar says, '(this event) is probably the most fundamental transformation in the history of the planet, aside from the origin of life itself. ... But we still don't really understand fully how it happened.'[7]

Scientists at the New York Center for Astrobiology at Rensselaer Polytechnic Institute published research, funded by NASA in 2011, which analyzed, what they called, the oldest minerals on Earth: zircons, 'dated' at 4.35 billion years old.[8] These contain a grey metal called cerium. They expected to confirm that the atmosphere of the early earth did not contain oxygen. If oxygen was present in the past, then more cerium would be found in the highly oxidized form, $Ce4+$, with less in the more reduced form, $Ce3+$.

They examined zircons in rocks (magmatic melts) from two periods in 'the evolutionary Big Bang timeline of Earth history': the *Hadean* period 'began' with the formation of the Earth about 4.6 billion years ago, 'followed by' the *Archean* period which 'began' 4 billion years ago. They found significant levels of cerium in the highly oxidised form in both *Hadean* and *Archean* zircons, which were consistent with an oxidation state similar to present-day atmospheric conditions. These findings suggest that there never was a reducing atmosphere and that conditions on the early earth were never suitable for chemical evolution.

Discussing the results of this research, *ScienceDaily*, an online site, suggested, 'Despite being the atmosphere that life currently breathes, lives, and thrives on, our current oxidized atmosphere is not currently understood to be a great starting point for life. Methane and its oxygen-poor counterparts have much more biologic potential to jump from inorganic compounds to life-supporting amino acids and DNA. As such, Watson (the second *author*) thinks the discovery of his group may reinvigorate theories that perhaps those building blocks for life were not created on Earth but delivered from elsewhere in the galaxy.'[9] In other words, the authors resorted to the theory of panspermia (the idea that seeds of life are present throughout the Universe and can be dispersed from one place to another—this was advocated by Fred Hoyle and Francis Crick) to cope with the shock of their findings.

The evolutionary mechanism of natural selection cannot be responsible for chemical evolution because natural selection depends upon the prior existence of entities capable of self-replication. An amino acid making a further copy of itself (self-replication) is not possible. D. Kenyon and G. Steinman proposed in their 1969 book, *Biochemical Predestination*, that amino acids might have inherent properties predisposing them to self-organize in biologically useful ways.[10] However, experiments showed that the affinity of one amino acid for another particular amino acid did not lead to sequences found in known proteins. Kenyon later repudiated the theory. Likewise, the four nucleotides which are part of DNA—adenine, thymine, guanine, and cytosine—have no special affinities to assemble in specific sequences. No inherent mechanisms have been identified leading to the formation of proteins.

What advantage would an amino acid have in becoming a protein? Natural selection selects advantageous features and passes them on to the next generation. Being unable to self-replicate, an amino acid cannot produce a protein on its own. Most proteins consist of linear structures built from twenty different types of amino acids, which are usually directed by genes to fold into specific 3D structures that determine the protein's activity. Some proteins provide structure for cells and others can allow the body to move. Antibodies are proteins, as are some types of hormones. Many proteins are enzymes which speed up chemical reactions occurring within the cell.

Before the 1982 discovery of ribozymes (ribonucleic acid (RNA) enzymes), it was thought that the only catalytic (speed-up) proteins in the cell were protein enzymes. However, a ribozyme is an RNA enzyme which can catalyse specific reactions in a similar way to protein enzymes. The idea gained ground that a molecule of RNA was capable of copying itself after it had, itself, arisen by chance as ribose, phosphate and heterocyclic bases, combined in a prebiotic soup. A new theory, 'the RNA-world hypothesis', was born. It is postulated that, within the soup, complexity increased as a consequence of natural selection. The RNA molecules began to make proteins and eventually, we are told, DNA emerged, which 'gained genetic information' and stored this information.

Molecular biologists have been able to make and study novel ribozymes, capable of metabolic tasks. However, it is evident that this process is under the direction of intelligent scientists and is not evolution. The story of a self-assembling RNA molecule remains implausible and as ribozyme engineering has grown due to the input of human intelligence, so the evidence all points to intelligent design being the driving force for replication and the origin of life.

Robert Shapiro was a professor of chemistry at New York University, who died in 2011. He wrote a popular book, *Origins: A Skeptic's Guide to the Creation of Life on the Earth*, in 1986, where he opposed many origin-of-life suggestions but maintained that there had to be a naturalistic explanation for the origin of life. He proposed that reactions between simple molecules would inevitably lead to more complex molecules, such as RNA, as a natural consequence of the laws of nature. He did not say where these laws came from and failed to produce any evidence for his theory.

Robert Shapiro wrote:

> Some future day may yet arrive when all reasonable chemical experiments run to discover a probable origin of life have failed unequivocally. Further, new geological evidence may yet indicate a sudden appearance of life on the earth. Finally, we may have explored the universe and found no trace of life, or processes leading to life, elsewhere. Some scientists might choose to turn to religion for an answer. Others, however, me

included, would attempt to sort out the surviving, less-probable scientific explanations in the hope of selecting one that was still more likely than the remainder.[11]

There is a determination, by many scientists, to keep a creator out of explaining the origin of life. Louis Pasteur's conclusion, that the spontaneous generation of life (abiogenesis) is impossible, remains valid. Chemical evolution, as a first step in this imaginary process, is impossible.

NOTES

1 'The origin of life: The conditions that sparked life on Earth, Research Outreach.' 23 December 2019. https://researchoutreach.org/articles/the-origin-of-life-the-conditions-that-sparked-life-on-earth/: Accessed 26/02/2022.

2 Francis Darwin (Ed.), *The life and letters of Charles Darwin, including an autobiographical chapter, Vol 3*, (London: John Murray, 1887), pp. 168–169.

3 J. B. S Haldane, 'The Origin of Life', *The Rationalist Annual*, 1929, (republished: Breadtag Sagas: Author Tony, 18 December 2015, pp. 1–8.

4 'Virus that causes Covid-19 can survive up to 28 days on surfaces, scientists find', Monday 12 Oct 2020, Australian Associated Press, *The Guardian*.

5 'The Miller–Urey experiment revisited', *Creation.com*, 15 March 2015. https://creation.com/miller-urey-revisited-oxidizing-atmosphere

6 Parker, E.T. et al., 'Primordial synthesis of amines and amino acids in a 1958 Miller H2S-rich spark discharge experiment', *Proceedings of the National Academy of Sciences* 108(14) 2011, pp. 5526–5531.

7 Richard Blaustein, 'The Great Oxidation Event: Evolving understandings of how oxygenic life on Earth began', *BioScience* Vol 66, (3) 2016, pp. 189–195.

8 Dustin Trail et al., 'The oxidation state of Hadean magmas and implications for early Earth's atmosphere', *Nature* (480) 2011, pp. 79–82.

9 'Setting the stage for life: Scientists make key discovery about the atmosphere of early earth', *sciencedaily.com*. 30 November 2011. https://www.sciencedaily.com/releases/2011/11/111130141855.htm

10 Dean H. Kenyon & Gary Steinman, *Biochemical Predestination*, (New York: McGraw-Hill, 1969).

11 Robert Shapiro, *Origins: A Skeptic's Guide to the Creation of Life on the Earth*, (Portsmouth, New Hampshire: William Heinemann Ltd, 1986), p. 130.

17 Senior registrar in Leeds and Bradford

My senior registrar training involved my rotating between Bradford Royal Infirmary; St Luke's Hospital, Bradford; St James's University Hospital, Leeds; and Leeds General Infirmary. I commenced at Bradford in October 1980. There were two surgical firms: one with three consultants and the other with two. I and my fellow senior registrar were on a 1 in 2 rota for emergencies, unless our colleague was on holiday (or vice versa) when we were on call all the time.

The most important event of our time living in Leeds was the birth of our third daughter in November 1980. We settled into happy family life with our three young girls, who made new friends at their school and in our church. My work was busy and I gained a lot of elective and emergency surgical experience. My drive to work was 14 miles each way and I do remember making this journey three times one evening and night! While we were in Surrey, Liz had done some sessions as a Staff Grade Community Paediatrician and in Leeds, again, she did similar work. After twelve months, I rotated to St James's University Hospital *(Jimmys)* in Leeds, working for two consultants for the next year.

Mr Wilson, a Yorkshireman, and Mr Brennan, who trained in Dublin, could not have been more different. On my first morning, I did an outpatient's clinic with Mr Wilson and we then walked along the corridor to the surgical block. The ward was on a higher level than the corridor and so we stopped in front of two lifts. I pressed the button for each lift and Mr Wilson asked, 'Why do you need two?' I thought silence was the best response. He was good fun to work for, but I never let on that I was a Lancastrian.

Mr Brennan was a hive of activity and quite an innovator. I learned diagnostic laparoscopy with him and an unusual approach to exploring the bile duct for stones, through the duodenum. This skill was often helpful in later life. One of my biggest responsibilities working for Mr Brennan was finding beds for patients who he had seen on the many domiciliary visits that he made. I explained earlier that surgical training was an apprenticeship and one could not complain about Mr Brennan's workload.

In October 1982, I moved across to Leeds General Infirmary (LGI) where I had previously worked for two years from 1974 to 1976. I worked for Mr Shoesmith and Mr Doig, getting more training in vascular surgery and thyroid surgery. At both Jimmy's and LGI, the emergency rota was 1 in 3, which was less onerous than in Bradford. In October 1983, I returned to Jimmy's to work for Mr Pratt and Mr Kester, who both had an interest in vascular surgery. Mr Kester did some of the larger, more modern vascular operations and, again, was a good trainer in surgical technique. He, also, has a claim to fame in our family in removing one of our daughter's inflamed appendix.

I rotated, in October 1984, back to Bradford and was on duty on Saturday, 11 May 1985, when the Bradford City stadium fire occurred. Fifty-six spectators died and at least two hundred sixty-five people were injured. Many, of course, suffered burns to the back of their head, ears and hands. The football match, against Lincoln City, was the final game of the season and Bradford had received the Third Division trophy at the beginning of the match. The wooden roof of the main stand had been officially condemned and was due to be replaced with a steel structure after the end of the season.

It took four minutes for the whole stand to be engulfed in flames. Many, trying to escape, were blocked by locked doors at the back of the stand. Adults threw children over the wall at the back and there were many heroic acts, with over fifty people receiving bravery awards. I remember a special story I was told, of a father who thought he was leading three children to a place of safety, when he found that his daughter had become separated. Actually, she had seen an elderly man at the front of the stand paralysed with fear and not moving, and had gone to take his hand and lead him to safety on the pitch. She had bad burns to the back of her head and was looked after in the children's ward at St Luke's where Mrs Thatcher, then Prime Minister, visited her and others the following day.[1]

As a general surgeon, I was not involved on the day of the fire with patients who had burns but I did have a fireman under my care for head injury observations. He had a large dent in his yellow helmet, which rested on his bedside locker. The plastic surgeon on duty at St Luke's Hospital that day was Mr David Sharpe. He was able to organize consultant plastic surgeons from centres all over the UK to come to St Luke's, during the following days, to treat the injuries of over two hundred individuals. All general surgery at St Luke's was cancelled, and I and my senior registrar colleague became assistants at operations to treat these burns. During this time, the 'Bradford

Sling', for elevating hands and arms, was developed in order to reduce swelling. 'Tissue expanders' were used to cover large defects in the skin. If a burn causes a large defect in the skin, a tissue expander (a balloon) can be put under the skin of an adjacent area and, by regularly inflating this over several days, the skin is stretched and can then be rotated over the adjacent defect. The University of Bradford, later, established a large academic research centre for skin sciences, for plastic surgery and for burns research.

I had arranged for a landline telephone to be put in our church so that, if my pager went off while I was at church, I could answer the phone. This was before the days of mobiles. One Sunday morning, I was called for advice by my registrar and was speaking to him while at church. As I stood there, to my surprise and horror, the wooden floorboards, below me, gave way and I fell through into an under-space which came up to my armpits! I struck the right side of my chest, where I almost certainly broke a couple of ribs. Breathing was painful but I managed to finish the conversation. Having called for help, I was lifted out of the hole. The church building at that time was made of wood and was soon replaced by a nice brick building!

In October 1985, I rotated back to Leeds General Infirmary to work for Mr Smiddy and Mr Benson. Mr Smiddy was a senior surgeon and a charismatic character who was, again, keen to train and particularly exposed me to more thyroid and parathyroid surgery. He was always writing books and giving me chapters to proofread. In those days, these were handwritten in pencil!

On one occasion during the Friday morning outpatients, he offered a patient with a thyroid swelling an operation on the afternoon operating list, reassuringly telling the patient that we would contact the family! She declined. He would dictate very humorous letters to GPs that would not pass the censor today. After he had some difficulty swallowing a piece of steak, he decided that he needed an endoscopy to check that he did not have an oesophageal stricture. He asked me to do this at the end of one of his operating lists. I, of course, obliged with a reassuring outcome. By October 1986, I had completed six years as a senior registrar.

Higher Surgical Training (HST) as a senior registrar was planned to last for four years. A certificate of HST was then awarded, assuming that annual reviews and an interview by a committee of the Consultant Surgeons of Leeds and Bradford had been satisfactory. As the four-year milestone passed, I began applying for consultant posts all over England. Posts were advertised in the weekly *British Medical Journal*. As I have said, there would be about 35–50 consultant general surgeon retirements each year.

In chapter 13, I said that my ninth senior registrar interview had been successful, but it was not until my thirteenth consultant interview that I was the successful candidate. I had repeated the lines, 'God holds the keys of all unknown', many times. Liz and I believed that God had a plan for our life, which included leading us to the right destination for my consultant post.

During the last year of our time in Leeds, our two older daughters were baptised (by immersion) accompanied by a lady in her 80s! They had both made personal commitments to Jesus Christ and it was a joy to see them baptised and hear their short testimonies.

In wanting to demonstrate the providence of God in our life, I would mention two places where I was interviewed. My first interview was at St Peter's Hospital, Chertsey, which in a way was my 'dream job'. Having worked there very happily, knowing the hospital and colleagues and many friends at the local church, it seemed ideal. I was up against more senior candidates, including my Senior Registrar colleague at St Thomas' Hospital. He was appointed and justice was done.

Another interview was at Haywards Heath Hospital in Sussex. This was close to Liz's parent's home and to Cuckfield Chapel where we had been married and I had been baptised. I, again, knew the successful candidate from St Thomas' Hospital, who was slightly older than me. My point in mentioning these two places is that I believe God was kindly helping us to let go of the places we would have chosen and keeping us looking to Him for guidance.

Among the consultant posts advertised was a position in Newcastle upon Tyne. However, I was aware that the interview in Newcastle would take place before a consultant interview in Leeds, where our family were happily settled. I had, therefore, not applied. In the event, I was not appointed in Leeds and, amazingly, none of the candidates at the Newcastle interview had been appointed, which was unusual. The job was re-advertised, and I applied and was appointed! Humorously, this was despite there being the Professor of Latin on the committee. He clearly had not checked up on my O-level results.

Not to be appointed in Leeds, was a surprise to my referees; but then to be appointed in Newcastle, where I had not initially applied, was a big surprise to me. We continued to believe that God held the keys of all unknown and we were glad. We embarked on a new adventure: moving to a new city which, thirty-five years later, we have come to love and to a post at the Freeman Hospital, which, in retrospect, was the best job I ever applied for!

At the Leeds General Infirmary consultant interview to replace Mr Smiddy, a panel member suggested that I would not pursue his thyroid and parathyroid interest, but instead concentrate on vascular surgery. In the event, at the Freeman Hospital, I played my full part as a Vascular Surgeon but also did over 1,150 Thyroid and Parathyroid operations during twenty-two years as a consultant.

I received two kind letters when I got the job in Newcastle upon Tyne. One was from Mr Smiddy in Leeds, who offered his congratulations and said he recognized that I had been sustained by my Christian faith as I waited for the right consultant post. The other letter was from a Christian friend, Alan Johnson, Professor of Surgery in Sheffield who reminded me that, as Joseph in the Bible found, it had been worth waiting patiently. I will return to our life in Newcastle upon Tyne and my experience as a consultant in a later chapter.

NOTES

1 D. T. Sharpe et al., 'Treatment of burns casualties after fire at Bradford City football ground', *British Medical Journal* (Clin Res Ed) 1985; 291, pp. 945–948.

18 Professor Hoyle: 'A super-intellect has monkeyed with physics.'

P rofessor Fred Hoyle FRS, my guide in developing a rational worldview back in 1965, was out of step with most cosmologists because he did not believe the universe had a beginning. Professor Hoyle proposed the 'steady-state theory' in the 1940s. Professor Hoyle said, 'Every cluster of galaxies, every star, every atom had a beginning, but the universe itself did not.'[1] To clarify, he was saying that the universe itself was eternal, but galaxies, stars and atoms formed later. He coined the term, 'Big Bang'[2] in 1949, during a broadcast lecture, to describe the alternative view that the universe had a beginning.

Fred Hoyle was born in 1915, in Bingley, Yorkshire. It is reported that he often skipped school but enjoyed reading chemistry books at home. He made gunpowder and enjoyed small explosions. He went to Bingley Grammar School, and then read mathematics at Cambridge University, graduating in 1939. During the Second World War, he led a team that developed radar for the British Admiralty. On his team, he met Hermann Bondi and Thomas Gold, both gifted physicists and astronomers. These three, later, proposed the 'steady-state theory'.[3,4]

Professor Hoyle rejected Darwin's theory of evolution, advocating the Panspermia Theory[5], which suggested that the building blocks of life could be carried to planets by comets or drifting interstellar dust. Professor Hoyle believed that evolution occurred because mutating life forms continually fall from space and this was no accident. It was deliberately arranged long ago by a super-intelligent civilization who wished to 'seed' our planet.

In 1981, Professor Hoyle published *Evolution from Space*[6], written with Professor Chandra Wickramasinghe. In this book, the authors propose that the biological makeup of the living things on our planet was and is radically changed by the arrival of pristine genes from outer space. They believed that a thin layer of graphite would protect bacteria and viruses from the damage of solar radiation or ultraviolet light. They suggested that large flu epidemics, such as the Spanish flu epidemic of 1918, came from outer space. They concluded their book by stating that, 'God is the Universe'[7], and emphasized this by writing 'God ≡ Universe'. This sign in algebra means 'equivalent to' or 'identical to'.

Professor Hoyle next published *The Intelligent Universe,*[8] in 1983—a beautifully illustrated book, with this remark on the flyleaf: 'A component has evidently been missing from cosmological studies, a component involving intelligent design ....' He wrote, 'The intelligence responsible for the creation of carbon-based life in the cosmic theory is firmly within the universe and is subservient to it. Because the creator of carbon-based life was not all powerful, there is consequently no paradox in the fact that terrestrial life is far from ideal.'[9]

It seems very muddled to suggest that an intelligence, capable of creating carbon-based life, would be subservient to the universe that intelligence had created! Professor Hoyle was facing up to the problem that, 'terrestrial life is far from ideal'. The Bible explains that this was not due to any inferiority or subservience of the creative intelligence but due to the rebellion of created mankind, after which death, disease and decay entered our world. Professor Hoyle, perhaps, failed to explore the Genesis account because of personal bias.

Professor Hoyle wrote, 'The creation of carbon-based life was motivated by a harsh necessity, after which the present situation may well be the best that could be managed.'[9]

As my worldview continued to develop, I learned that some people believe God used evolution (Theistic Evolution) to create the universe and man. This is problematic because death, disease and decay would have been present before Adam and Eve walked in the Garden of Eden. If this was the case, then Professor Hoyle's comment that *terrestrial life is far from ideal* would be true. Theistic evolution and Professor Hoyle describe a created world very different from the description in Genesis Chapter 1, which repeatedly states that God saw what he had made and it was 'good' or 'very good'.

Later in *The Intelligent Universe*, Professor Hoyle's leaning towards Hinduism is revealed.[10] Hinduism embraces a vast range of traditions and diversity of beliefs, with many gods being worshipped. A cycle of birth, life, death and rebirth is called, *saṃsara*. The Hindu gods or god are present within all that exists. Professor Hoyle did recognize that, in contrast, for Christians, God exists 'outside space and time'.[11]

Professor Hoyle, in his forward to the book, is actually deeply disturbed by the conclusions of Darwinian evolution. The opening sentence asks, 'if there is any real purpose in life?'

It continues, 'What of a long-range purpose? For what reason do we live our lives at all?' Professor Hoyle points out that biology 'answers that the purpose is to produce the next generation'. But if we protest that there must be more meaning to life, biology replies, 'There is nothing except continuity.'[12]

Professor Hoyle asked, 'What is the use of that unique feature of our species, *the moral code*, present in all human societies?' The biologist replies, 'Humans achieve more by working together in groups,' as this promotes survival. Professor Hoyle describes 'man's moral sense as a fragile affair'. He has 'to bolster it with a tangle of laws because in itself virtuous behaviour is not predominantly advantageous to survival. In many cases in our daily lives cheating is more profitable than truthfulness, while brutality and aggression are all too often profitable to the survival of nations.'[12]

Professor Hoyle entered into an emotional description of his father's experiences as a machine gunner in the First World War. His father was plagued by the thought of meeting a lone German and the fact that, without the possibility of verbal communication, they would be committed to armed combat. If they took their helmets off and realized they were both members of the same species, then they might have chosen to drop their weapons.[13] Professor Hoyle criticizes Darwin's theory of biological evolution through natural selection as it allows for any opportunistic behaviour, including cheating or murder.[14]

Professor Hoyle states, 'Frankly, I am haunted by a conviction that the nihilistic philosophy which so-called educated opinion chose to adopt following the publication of the *Origin of Species* committed mankind to a course of automatic self-destruction.' He concludes with the following: 'The number of people who nowadays sense that something is fundamentally amiss with society is not small, but sadly they dissipate their energies in protesting against one inconsequential matter after another. The correct thing to protest, as I propose to do here with something approaching mathematical precision, is the cosmic origin and nature of man.'[14]

Professor Hoyle believed that, by proving where man came from *(his cosmic origin)* and understanding the nature of man, he would have the answer to mankind's serious condition which, in his opinion, was heading for self-destruction. This observation is astute and is exactly what God's revelation in the Bible explains. God created man in his image (his origin); man rebelled by falling into sin; but Jesus Christ, the Saviour, has been sent to save man from self-destruction. 'The Father has sent his Son to be the Saviour of the world' (1 John 4:14).

The scientific community reckoned that Professor Hoyle's greatest scientific achievement was his theory of *Stellar Nucleosynthesis*. He published research papers in 1946,[15] and 1954,[16] about the synthesis of the chemical elements, heavier than helium, by nuclear reactions in stars. A further landmark publication, known as the B2FH paper, published in 1957,[17] suggested that oxygen and the elements between carbon and iron in the periodic table were forged in the nuclear furnaces of giant stars, which later exploded and from whose relics the solar system was born. The authors were Margaret Burbidge, Geoffrey Burbidge, William A. Fowler, and Fred Hoyle—hence the B2FH paper. This is the accepted paradigm today for the supernova nucleosynthesis of these primary elements.

The joint discovery was strangely rewarded. In 1983, Fowler won a share of the Nobel Prize for Physics for his work, but shared the prize with Subramanyan Chandrasekhar, who published different work on the structure and evolution of the stars. Unfortunately, Professor Hoyle, who had in the past criticized the Nobel committee, was overlooked!

Professor Hoyle believed that a superb, calculating intellect had designed the carbon atom! He calculated that one particular nuclear reaction, the triple-alpha process, which generates carbon from helium, would require the carbon nucleus to have a very specific resonance energy and spin for it to work. The large amount of carbon in the universe, which makes it possible for carbon-based life-forms of any kind to exist, demonstrated to Professor Hoyle that this nuclear reaction must work in a particular way.

Based on this notion, Professor Hoyle predicted the values of the energy, the nuclear spin and the parity of the compound state in the carbon nucleus formed by three alpha particles (helium nuclei), which was later borne out as true by experiment.[18] He believed that this energy level, while needed to produce carbon in large quantities, was statistically very unlikely to fall where it does in the scheme of carbon energy levels. Professor Hoyle later wrote:

> Would you not say to yourself, some super-calculating intellect must have designed the properties of the carbon atom, otherwise the chance of my finding such an atom through the blind forces of nature would be utterly minuscule. A common-sense interpretation of the facts suggests that a super-intellect has monkeyed with physics, as well as with

chemistry and biology, and that there are no blind forces worth speaking about in nature. The numbers one calculates from the facts seem to me so overwhelming as to put this conclusion almost beyond question.[19]

In the final chapter of *The Intelligent Universe*, Professor Hoyle states, 'We have seen that life could not have originated here on this Earth. Nor does it look as though biological evolution can be explained from within an Earthbound theory of life. Genes from outside the Earth are needed to drive the evolutionary process.' He continues, 'We must still return to the same problem that opened this book—the vast unlikelihood that life, even on a cosmic scale, arose from non-living matter.'[20]

Professor Hoyle's long-term collaborator, Professor Chandra Wickramasinghe, when testifying in a trial in Arkansas, USA, stated:

> My own philosophical preference is for an essentially eternal, boundless Universe, wherein a creator of life somehow emerges in a natural way. My colleague, Sir Fred Hoyle, has also expressed a similar preference. In the present state of our knowledge about life and about the Universe, an emphatic denial of some form of creation as an explanation for the origin of life implies a blindness to fact and an arrogance that cannot be condoned.[21]

Professors Hoyle and Chandra Wickramasinghe have been ridiculed by many for believing that the 'building blocks of life' have arrived from outer space, but they were not alone. Francis Crick, co-discoverer of the double helix of DNA, had his own slightly different version of panspermia theory called *Directed Panspermia*. He felt it would be unlikely that 'viable spores' could have arrived on the earth after a long journey through space, without being damaged by radiation. In 1973, with the biochemist Leslie Orgel, he published a suggestion that microorganisms travelled in the head of an unmanned spaceship, sent to Earth by a higher civilization which had developed elsewhere some billions of years ago. The spaceship was unmanned so that the range of its journey could be as great as possible. Life started on Earth when these microorganisms dropped into the primitive ocean and began to multiply.[22]

Either version of panspermia, effectively, puts the search for the origin of life beyond the earth. One element of panspermia that has been tested, is the ability of microorganisms to arrive alive on the earth on or in a meteorite. French scientists at the Centre of Molecular Biophysics in Orleans, France, managed to simulate a meteorite entry by attaching rocks to the heat shield of a returning Russian space-capsule, in September 2008. These rocks were smeared with a hardy bacterium, *Chroococcidiopsis*, to resemble a 'germ from Mars'. *Chroococcidiopsis* is known for its ability to survive harsh environmental conditions, including both high and low temperatures, ionizing radiation, and high salinity. The rocks also contained microfossils. After the spacecraft was retrieved, the microfossils survived, but the *Chroococcidiopsis* was burned black, though their outlines remained.[23,24]

Professor Hoyle stated the extreme improbability of life forming on its own, or even a single functional biopolymer, such as a protein, being formed by chance. He said, 'Now imagine 1050 blind persons (standing shoulder to shoulder, they would more than fill our entire planetary system), each with a scrambled Rubik cube, and try to conceive of the chance of them all simultaneously arriving at the solved form. You then have the chance of arriving by random shuffling of just one of the many biopolymers on which life depends. The notion that not only the biopolymers but the operating program of a living cell could be arrived at by chance in a primordial soup here on earth is evidently nonsense of a high order. Life must plainly be a cosmic phenomenon.'[25]

His science-fiction novel, *The Black Cloud*, which I bought and read in September 1965, and recently re-read, describes an intelligent cloud of dust interposing itself between the Sun and Earth, absorbing the Sun's energy and creating an Ice Age on Earth. The main character, Chris Kingsley, Professor of Astronomy at Cambridge, tries to understand and reason with the Black Cloud to save the Earth. However, at the end of the book, in dialogue with the Black Cloud, Chris Kingsley fits and dies over a two-day period as his temperature rises to 104°F. His brain had been filled with information which was too much for him to absorb. Professor Hoyle, of course, was himself the Professor of Astronomy at Cambridge and perhaps saw himself as the man able to speak with the super intelligence out there. *The Times Literary Supplement* review stated, 'The imagination is touched by this desperate effort by man to regain control of his environment by using his knowledge and his wits.'[26]

At one level, scientists realize that information and intelligence are needed for there to be an origin of life. Because of this, they continue an extremely expensive search for extra-terrestrial intelligence to support the idea that life could begin spontaneously on the earth, or elsewhere in the universe, as the theory of evolution claims. Paradoxically, such scientists refuse to acknowledge the signs of God's intelligence written all over the Earth, from the complexity of a single cell to the complexity of the human brain—which they are using to reason—or the amazing development of the human embryo in a mother's womb. They prefer to believe that *something* can be intelligent.

That a 'super intelligence out there' might communicate with us, as in Hoyle's book, *The Black Cloud*, is intriguing and Christians would affirm that the God of the Bible has done just that. He has communicated through His Word, the Bible, and by His Son Jesus Christ, through Creation and by speaking through our consciences. Sadly, man naturally does not listen. Romans 1:19–20 declares, 'What may be known about God is plain to them, because God has made it plain to them. For since the creation of the world God's invisible qualities—his eternal power and divine nature—have been clearly seen, being understood from what has been made, so that men are without excuse.'

I have a soft spot for Professor Fred Hoyle, who I found quite helpful in my journey to a Christian worldview. I think the way he questioned the ruling paradigms of science was healthy and his comments about the impossibility of life starting spontaneously on the Earth contain significant truth! Writers suggest that his being a Yorkshireman was a reason that he was argumentative about the theories of others. I think that is a disrespectful caricature. Professor Hoyle was on a personal journey to find the truth but, like many, refused to accept the revelation that Biblical Christianity offered him.

Tragically, he wrote in *The Nature of the Universe*:

> If I were given the choice of how long I should like to live with
> my present physical and mental equipment, I should decide on

a good deal more than 70 years. But I doubt I should be wise to decide on more than 300 years. Already, I am very much aware of my own limitations, and I think that 300 years is as long as I should like to put up with them. Now, what the Christians offer me is an eternity of frustration. And it is no good there trying to mitigate the situation by saying that sooner or later my limitations would be removed, because this could not be done without altering me.[27]

The apostle Paul, in 1 Corinthians 15, makes it clear that, in heaven, Christians will have new bodies and there will be no sense of frustration. In 2 Corinthians 5:17 we read, 'Therefore, if anyone is in Christ, he is a new creation; the old has gone, the new has come!' Professor Hoyle correctly stated that he needed to be altered. If Professor Hoyle had never heard of the conversation between Jesus and Nicodemus (John 3:7) containing the radical statement, 'You must be born again,' that is sad.

After being forced to resign as Professor of Astronomy in Cambridge for political reasons, in 1973, he lived in the Lake District and then in Bournemouth, authoring many books. Very sadly, in November 1997, while trekking across the moors, he fell into a steep ravine in West Yorkshire and was not found for twelve hours. After two months in hospital his health had deteriorated. Later, after a series of strokes, he died in August 2001. Wikipedia gives a full account of Fred Hoyle's life and the *Daily Telegraph* obituary[28] is informative.

NOTES

1   Sir Fred Hoyle; Coined 'Big Bang.' *Los Angeles Times Archives*, 23 Aug 2001. https://www.latimes.com/archives/la-xpm-2001-aug-23-me-37483-story.html

2   Helge Kragh, 'Big Bang: the etymology of a name', *Astronomy & Geophysics*, Vol 54(2) 2013, pp. 2.28–2.30.

3   H. Bondi & T. Gold, 'The Steady-State Theory Of The Expanding Universe', *Monthly Notices of the Royal Astronomical Society*, Vol 108, No3 1948, pp. 252–270.

4   Fred Hoyle, 'A New Model for the Expanding Universe', *Monthly Notices of the Royal Astronomical Society*, Vol 108, No5 1948, pp. 372-382.

5   https://www.telegraph.co.uk/news/obituaries/1338125/Professor-Sir-Fred-Hoyle.html

6   Fred Hoyle & Chandra Wickramasinghe, *Evolution from Space*, (London: J.M. Dent, 1981) ISBN 978-0-460-04535-3.

7   Ibid., p. 143.

8   Fred Hoyle, *The Intelligent Universe*, (London: Michael Joseph Ltd, 1983).

9   Ibid., p. 236.

10 Ibid., p. 236; pp. 248–249.

11 Ibid., p. 249.

12 Ibid., p. 6.

13 Ibid., p. 7.

14 Ibid., p. 8.

15 Fred Hoyle, 'The synthesis of the elements from hydrogen', *Monthly Notices of the Royal Astronomical Society* Vol 106, No5 1946' pp. '343–383.

16 Fred Hoyle, 'On Nuclear Reactions Occurring in Very Hot STARS. I. The Synthesis of Elements from Carbon to Nickel', *The Astrophysical Journal Supplement* Series 1:5, 1954, pp. 121–146.

17 Margaret Burbidge et al., 'Synthesis of the Elements in Stars', *Reviews of Modern Physics*, 29 (4): 1957, pp. 547–651.

18 C. W. Cook et al., 'B12, C12, and the Red Giants', *Physical Review*, 1957, Vol 107, p. 508.

19 Fred Hoyle, 'The Universe: Past and Present Reflections', *Annual Review of Astronomy and Astrophysics*, Vol 20, 1982, p. 16.

20 Fred Hoyle, *The Intelligent Universe*, p. 242.

21 'Chandra Wickramasinghe's Testimony in Arkansas', 1981 https://www.panspermia.org/chandra.htm

22 F. Crick & L. Orgel, 'Directed panspermia', *Icarus* Vol 19 Issue 3 1973, pp. 341–346.

23 'Meteorite experiment deals blow to bugs from space theory', 2008. https://www.

abc.net.au/news/2008-09-25/meteorite-experiment-deals-blow-to-bugs-from-space

24 F. Westall et al., 'STONE 6: Sedimentary meteors from Mars', *European Planetary Science Congress* Abstracts 3, EPSC2008-A-00407, 2008.

25 Fred Hoyle, 'The Big Bang in Astronomy', *New Scientist* 92, 1981, pp. 521–527.

26 Fred Hoyle, *The Black Cloud*, (London: Penguin Books, reprint 1964), the back cover.

27 Fred Hoyle, *The Nature of the Universe*, (London: Pelican Books, 1963), p. 123.

28 https://www.telegraph.co.uk/news/obituaries/1338125/Professor-Sir-Fred-Hoyle.html

19 Professor Dawkins: 'The universe was made out of nearly nothing.'

I
n April 2006, I attended a public lecture at the Centre for Life, Newcastle upon Tyne, when Professor Richard Dawkins and his wife, Lalla Ward, presented readings from his books. He had laryngitis so his wife helped by reading the excerpts. Following this, Professor Dawkins took questions from the audience.

I took careful notes of his address and was surprised by his comment that, 'The universe was made out of nearly nothing.' Apart from the imprecise concept of 'nearly nothing', I was struck by his personal confidence about the beginning of the universe. Professor Dawkins did not explain what was there at the beginning, either in his talk or when answering questions. Did Professor Dawkins think that 'nearly nothing' might slip under the radar as being plausible, as it was not much?

Christian teacher, Francis Schaeffer, taught that if we exclude God from the debate about the origin of the universe, we must start with nothing. Francis Schaeffer strongly insisted that nothing must mean 'absolutely nothing'. He coined the phrase, 'nothing nothing', to emphasize this: 'There must be no energy, no mass, no motion and no personality.'[1]

Francis Schaeffer first published, *He Is There and He Is Not Silent*, in

1972. It was later republished with two other books as a trilogy. The book shows how God has revealed himself to mankind. The first chapter is entitled, 'The Metaphysical Necessity'. Metaphysics is the study of Being—that is *the problem of existence*. He stated, 'that the existence of man is no greater problem than is the fact that anything exists at all'.[2] Francis Schaeffer quoted Gottfried Leibniz, German philosopher and mathematician, who said, 'The basic philosophic question is that something is there rather than nothing being there.'[2] I refer to Schaeffer's books in chapter 32.

Professor Dawkins seemed to invent 'nearly nothing' as a halfway house between something and nothing. Professor Dawkins, I presume, needed some energy, some mass and some motion to start the universe, though where they come from is left to imagination. Professor Fred Hoyle also imagined that 'the Galaxy started its life as a rotating flat disc of gas with no stars in it.'[3]

Many scientists believe they know how the universe began and believe that something, including information, can arise by chance, but are unable to answer the question, 'Why did the universe begin?' The best that Professor Dawkins or Stephen Hawking, confidently, assert is, because there are laws of physics, the universe can and will create itself from nothing.[4] This of course begs the question as to where those laws came from.

Given that intelligence is needed to understand the whole subject of physics and its laws, surely Professor Dawkins and Stephen Hawking would consider that an intelligent designer must have initiated those laws. It is only because of the laws of nature that we can 'do science'. Newton, Kepler, Copernicus, Faraday and Clerk Maxwell, all well-known scientists, appreciated that the laws of nature did not happen by chance and based their scientific investigations on the continuity of these laws. Professor Fred Hoyle accepted that concept when he said, 'A super-intellect has monkeyed with physics.'[5]

The Christian would repeat Francis Schaeffer's assertion that, if one excludes God from the origin of the universe, one must start with nothing. In reading the eyewitness testimony of the Bible, a Christian understands why the universe was made. Here are two reasons: *firstly*, to manifest the glory of God: 'The heavens declare the glory of God; the skies proclaim the work of his hands' (Psalm 19:1); and *secondly*, that when God made mankind in his own image, he was creating Adam and Eve and their descendants to be his family. Malachi 2:10 asks, 'Do we not all have one Father? Did not one God create us?'

The Bible tells us that man is made in the image of God (Genesis 1:26–27). The family likeness passes down through the generations of mankind, though, because of the Fall, man inherits the sinful nature of Adam and Eve. In Genesis 5:3 we read, 'When Adam had lived 130 years, he had a son in his own likeness, in his own image; and he named him Seth.'

Having created Adam and Eve, Genesis 1:28 tells us that God blessed them and said to them, 'Be fruitful and increase in number; fill the earth and subdue it.' This theme of God's plan for mankind is clear. For example, we read in Psalm 115:14–16:

> May the Lord make you increase, both you and your children.
> May you be blessed by the Lord, the Maker of heaven and earth.
> The highest heavens belong to the Lord, but the earth he has given to man.'

God, in his kindness, has given the earth to men and women as his stewards. The mandate given to Adam and Eve in Genesis 1:28–29 continues: 'Rule over the fish in the sea and the birds in the sky and over every living creature that moves on the ground.' Then God said, 'I give you every seed-bearing plant on the face of the whole earth and every tree that has fruit with seed in it. They will be yours for food.' The creator's instructions include looking after the 'Blue Planet'. God gave us these instructions because he is a good God who wants our best.

Returning to Professor Dawkins and his lecture, I was eager to ask my question: 'Professor, isn't your job to explain how the universe was made out of nothing?'

He replied, 'Don't be so silly, there had to be something there to start with.' Professor Dawkins is always at pains to compare the truth of science with the faith of religion. Science, he states, is based on facts, whereas faith is based on what we want to believe without facts to support it. He has made comments about people of faith believing in the 'tooth fairy' and tells us that real scientists only deal with facts. Professor Dawkins' answer demonstrated his personal faith—'There had to be something there to start with.'

I replied, 'You give the impression, Professor Dawkins, that you were an eyewitness.' To his credit, he came back with the riposte that in a court of law there were two sorts of evidence: that of an eyewitness and that of circumstantial evidence. In the case of the origin of the universe, he claimed the circumstantial evidence was very strong. He ignored the eyewitness record in Genesis and elsewhere in the Bible.

The seeds of this book and its title were sown that afternoon. Professor Dawkins' blunt claim that there had to be something there to start with, reflects a naturalistic worldview, which claims that there are natural processes by which humans and all other living beings have come into existence from non-living matter or chemicals, without a creator. *Naturalism* is the ruling scientific paradigm today.

A naturalistic worldview believes that all knowledge of the properties of the universe falls *only* within the reach of scientific investigation. By implication, no truth about the origin of the universe can come from anywhere else. There is no chance that 'Someone', who witnessed the beginning of the Universe, could have left an account or testimony of that event.

Christians argue that God is an eyewitness. In Genesis, he records what he did when he created the Universe. The Bible explains that God gave the Earth to mankind to enjoy and by it to be blessed. Walking in the Lake District recently, my wife and I witnessed the beauty of autumnal colours, two red squirrels, a heron, a wren and a dipper swimming under the water, all declaring the glory of God. At the same time many of us were experiencing various degrees of 'lockdown' because of the Covid-19 virus. This reminded us of the terrible consequences of Adam and Eve's fall into sin, as death, disease and decay have spoiled God's creation.

Professor Dawkins' view, that we live in a naturalistic universe, had its origins in the Age of Enlightenment,[6] an intellectual and philosophical movement, which dominated thought in Europe during the 17th to 19th centuries. Reason was the god of the Enlightenment and the evidence of the senses was the primary source of knowledge. René Descartes, wrongly, believed, 'the way to find truth was to strip the mind of everything that can possibly be doubted until we finally reach a bedrock of truths that cannot possibly be doubted. He believed that he, himself, had dug deep enough to hit that infallible bedrock in his famous cogito: "I think, therefore I am."[7] Experience tells us that is simply untrue. The outcome of these views was, and continues to be, a complete trust in an unknown something as the origin of the universe and of life, and the rejection of a Someone who is an intelligent creator. Professor Dawkins would view those who hold a belief in a supreme, intelligent, spiritual being, and any religious doctrines associated with that being, as having a belief based on faith rather than on facts.

The Age of Enlightenment threw scorn on the scholastic endeavour of previous centuries and coined the phrase, 'The Dark Ages',[8] strongly targeting the church as a maleficent influence keeping people in darkness. This false analysis is brilliantly exposed by Professor Rodney Stark in his book, *The Triumph of Christianity*, in which he documents the many scientific contributions made well before the 17th century by Christian believers.[9]

Professor Dawkins indicated that there was a beginning to the universe when he said, 'at the start', and would subscribe to this being due to a 'Big Bang'. I will not go into detail, but if you were to look at the phrase, the 'Chronology of the Universe', in Wikipedia[10], you would be amazed to see what apparently happened at the beginning of time in the first second after the Big Bang! We are told that by one second, a radius of ten light years of observable universe was visible. Six epochs of time had occurred during that one second.

Professor Dawkins claims that this idea is beautiful. In February 2012, while debating with the, then, Archbishop of Canterbury, Rowan Williams, at Oxford University, he said, 'What I can't understand is why you can't see the extraordinary beauty of the idea that life started from nothing—that is such a staggering, elegant, beautiful thing, why would you want to clutter it up with something so messy as a God?'[11]

Professor Dawkins was being very casual with words that day. He reverted to, 'everything started from nothing'. He had told me that I was silly making such a suggestion! The archbishop should have asked, 'Let us be clear; do you mean no matter, no energy and no motion?' Dawkins would have struggled to give an answer.

I find it difficult to see the beauty in the idea that life started from nothing, without a designer. It is like looking at a Rembrandt painting or Christopher Wren church and saying how wonderful that nobody painted that picture or designed that church. I believe that the youngest child would understand that it is not possible for *nobody to make anything out of nothing!*

The story is told of a scientist who said to God, 'We don't need you anymore; scientists have figured out a way to create life out of nothing.' 'Well, show me,' said God—and the scientist bent down to pick up some dust. 'No, no,' said God. 'Get your own dust.'[12]

Top of form

When Professor Dawkins authored his book, *The God Delusion*[13], he was claiming that belief in God was contradicted by reality and rational argument and amounted to a mental disorder. So, the believer in God was deluded. Interestingly, in 2009, Professor Andrew Sims, a Christian and former President of the Royal College of Psychiatrists, published his book, *Is Faith Delusion? Why religion is good for your health.*[14]

He defines a delusion as 'a false, unshakeable idea or belief, which is out of keeping with the patient's educational, cultural and social background; it is held with extraordinary conviction and subjective certainty'.[15] In the last chapter of *Is Faith Delusion?* Professor Sims summarizes that delusion is a psychiatric symptom and the contents of that delusion may indeed be religious, but the whole of belief, of itself, is not and cannot be delusion.[16]

He provided substantial evidence that religion is in fact good for your health. For example, Andrew Sims quotes, *The Handbook of Religion and Health*, by Koenig et al., which surveyed 1200 studies and 400 reviews and concluded,

> In the majority of studies, religious involvement is correlated with well-being, happiness and life satisfaction; hope and optimism; purpose and meaning in life; higher self-esteem; better adaptation to bereavement; greater social support and less loneliness; lower rates of depression and faster recovery from depression; lower rates of suicide and fewer positive attitudes towards suicide; less anxiety; less psychosis and fewer psychotic tendencies; lower rates of alcohol and drug use and abuse; less delinquency and criminal activity; greater marital stability and satisfaction.[17]

Professor Sims commented in the preface to his book: 'If the findings of the huge volume of research on this topic had gone in the opposite direction and it had found that religion damages your mental health, it would have been front-page news in every newspaper in the land!'[18]

If God is to be dismissed, as Professor Dawkins recommends, how does he believe we should view our lives in this world. He is very keen to tell us in several frank and well-publicized remarks. For example: 'Nature is not cruel, only pitilessly indifferent. This is one of the hardest lessons for humans to learn.'[19]

Of course, if the mechanism of human origins is evolution, then the survival of the fittest would entail cruelty and indifference. If there is no giver of a moral law, then Richard Dawkins is right to say, 'We cannot admit that things might be neither good nor evil, neither cruel nor kind, but simply callous—indifferent to all suffering, lacking all purpose.'[19] By his thinking, the love that parents have for their children is only chemicals and electricity, and moral judgements are neither right nor wrong.

When asked the question, 'Why are we here?', Professor Dawkins answered, 'We are machines built by DNA whose purpose is to make more copies of the same DNA. ... This is exactly what we are for. We are machines for propagating DNA, and the propagation of DNA is a self-sustaining process. It is every living object's sole reason for living.'[20] To be consistent, this worldview is obliged to explain all non-scientific aspects of human experience. Is Beethoven's music just meaningless vibrations or the Mona Lisa just a collection of blobs of paint?

When our first daughter was born, Liz and I saw her as a unique, beautiful baby, made in our image, with the potential for a future filled with purpose and happy times. We did not look upon her as a machine, built by our DNA, who perhaps would one day make further copies of her DNA. We were aware as doctors of potential medical conditions which could afflict her in the future and the harshness of some of life's experiences. However, as we faced our new responsibilities as parents and having learned God's good purposes for our own lives, we trusted Him for her future.

Professor Dawkins holds to the universal applicability of the scientific method and approach, and the view that empirical science constitutes the most authoritative worldview and the most valuable part of human learning, to the exclusion of other viewpoints. The word, *Scientism*, has been used to describe this view.

During an interview with Freddie Sayers on LockdownTV, 18th June 2021, Professor Dawkins said that Scientism is a 'dirty word used by people who are critical of scientists'. [21]

Scientism, I suggest, means having an excessive trust in the power of the methods of natural science to discover truth in all areas of investigation, including philosophy and the humanities.

The scientific method has five steps: Observation—Hypothesis—Prediction—Experiment—Conclusion. An experiment is the tool designed to answer a scientific question. Can an experiment be designed to prove how the Universe began, either by Biblical Creation or by Evolution? The answer, of course, is NO! So, we must make a choice as to which worldview is best supported by the evidence we have? Which worldview explains the Universe around us and the laws of nature that we observe?

Professor Dawkins concedes that scientific theories are being disproved and replaced all the time by new theories. This is not wrong; the scientific method sets up hypotheses or theories and then seeks to falsify them. However, he is wrong to say that 'anyone advocating a creator God is scientifically illiterate'[22] or, 'No qualified scientist doubts that evolution is a fact.'[23] Professor Dawkins holds that only those believing in evolution are real scientists.

However, to quote from, *Doubts about Darwin: A History of Intelligent Design*, by Thomas Woodward, many respected professors are 'arguing that Darwinism is woefully lacking in factual evidence and is rather based on philosophical assumptions'.[24] For example, Dr Jonathan Wells, a biologist at the University of California at Berkeley has said, 'The Darwinian paradigm is in serious trouble, of the kind that matters most in science: it doesn't fit the evidence.'[25]

Francis Crick, DNA discoverer and Nobel Prize winner, in *What Mad Pursuit*,[26] advised that when we see design in creation all around us, 'Biologists must constantly keep in mind that what they see was not designed but rather evolved.' Professor Dawkins wrote in, *The Blind Watchmaker*, 'Biology is the study of complicated things that give the appearance of having been designed for a purpose.'[27] But then he argued in the book that they were not. The position which these men both defended is that evolution must be a non-directed process. To accept design in the world argues for a designer and is incompatible with evolution.

Crick and Dawkins urge us to ignore complicated design features in our study of biology. But does that make sense? If we study an example of design in nature, we learn so much and may be able to mimic the design features. Take for example the flippers of a thirty-five-ton humpback whale. These flippers have large, irregular-looking bumps called tubercles along their leading edges. The whale's flippers, augmented by tubercles, help it to jump out of the water—known as breaching—despite its massive weight. The whale while catching krill—its shrimp-like food—can swim in a tight circle because of these specialized flippers producing a 'net of bubbles' only five feet across. Normally, sheets of water flowing over smooth flippers break up into turbulent vortices as they cross the flipper, which would reduce the efficiency of the whale's hunt for food. The design feature of tubercles has been added to the leading edge of wind-turbine blades and tested in wind tunnels by *Whalepower*, a company based in Toronto.[28] They now have turbines which are 20 per cent more efficient in making electricity from wind. There are many other potential applications of this design feature. Who designed the tubercles? Genesis 1:21 tells us: 'So God created the great creatures of the sea and every living thing with which the water teems and that moves about in it.' It is right that we should recognize design.

A little boy, admiring a chair in a stately home, might say to his father, 'Daddy who made that beautiful chair?' His father would possibly reply, 'I don't know, my boy, but I know the designer was called Thomas Chippendale. This sign tells us that he was born in Otley, Yorkshire, and died in 1779 of tuberculosis and is buried in St Martin-in-the-Fields in London.' In 1754, Chippendale published a book of his designs, titled, The Gentleman and Cabinet-Maker's Director[29], which led to him and his designs becoming very famous. Surely Francis Crick and Richard Dawkins would agree that a Chippendale chair had been designed! The worth of that design was recognized in December 2010, when a piece of Chippendale furniture sold for £3.79 million at Sotheby's![30]

Peter S. Williams, Christian philosopher and author of, *The Case for God*, has written,

> When Dawkins affirms that 'God is dead' because 'science reveals a world without purpose or design,' he certainly says something that 'sounds important'. So perhaps we should take Dawkins' advice and ask ourselves, 'Is this the kind of thing that Dawkins knows because of the evidence?' When we do, we find that Dawkins believes in evolution as a philosophically

certain deduction from his atheistic worldview (a deduction that elsewhere he presents as if it disproves belief in design!).[31]

Richard Dawkins urged me, in 2006, to believe his statement that, 'The universe was made out of nearly nothing,' and, in 2012, encouraged the, then, Archbishop of Canterbury, Rowan Williams, to celebrate 'the extraordinary beauty of the idea that life started from nothing'.

Alternatively, we might believe King David, writing in Psalm 19:1, 'The heavens declare the glory of God; the skies proclaim the work of his hands.'

NOTES

1 Francis Schaeffer, *He Is There and He Is Not Silent, Trilogy*, (Leicester: Inter-Varsity Press, 1990), p. 282.

2 Ibid., p. 277.

3 Fred Hoyle, *The Nature of the Universe*, (London: Pelican Books, 1963), p. 60.

4 Graham Lawton with introduction by Stephen Hawking, *New Scientist: The Origin of (almost) Everything: from the Big Bang to Belly-button Fluff*, (London: John Murray, 2016), pp. 1–3.

5 Fred Hoyle, 'The Universe: Past and Present Reflections', *Annual Review of Astronomy and Astrophysics*, Vol 20, 1982, p. 16.

6 Rodney Stark, *The Triumph of Christianity*, (New York: HarperCollins, 2011), p. 252.

7 Nancy Pearcey, *Total Truth, Liberating Christianity from its Cultural Captivity*, (Wheaton, Illinois: Crossway Books, 2005), p. 39.

8 Rodney Stark, *The Triumph of Christianity*, p. 239.

9 Ibid., pp. 241–244.

10 https://en.wikipedia.org/wiki/Chronology_of_the_universe

11 BBC—Will & Testament: Richard Dawkins v Rowan Williams https://www.bbc.co.uk/blogs/ni/2012/02/richard_dawkins_v_rowan_willia.html

12 'Scientists decide to tell God that we no longer need him.' aumamen.com/joke/scientists-decide-to-tell-god-that-we-no-longer-need-him

13 Richard Dawkins, *The God Delusion*, (London: Transworld Publishers Ltd, 2006).

14 Andrew Sims, *Is Faith Delusion? Why religion is good for your health*, (London: Bloomsbury Publishing, 2009).

15 Sims, A., *Symptoms in the Mind: An Introduction to Descriptive Psychopathology*, 3rd Edition, (Edinburgh: Saunders, 2003).

16 Andrew Sims, *Is Faith Delusion? Why religion is good for your health*, p. 230.

17 Ibid., p. 100.

18 Ibid., p. xi.

19 Richard Dawkins, *River Out of Eden: A Darwinian View of Life*, (New York: Basic Books, 1995), p. 96.

20 https://www.azquotes.com/quote/573352

21 https://unherd.com/thepost/richard-dawkins-scientism-is-a-dirty-word

22 Julia Hinde, 'Does God Exist?' *Big Questions in Science*, Ed., Harriet Swain, (London: Jonathan Cape, 2002,) p. 2.

23 Richard Dawkins, *A Devil's Chaplain, Selected Essays*, (London: Orion, 2003) p. 220.

24 Thomas Woodward, *Doubts about Darwin: A History of Intelligent Design*, (Ada, Michigan: Revell, a division of Baker Publishing Group, 2003), p. 196.

25 P.E. Johnson et al. (Ed.), *Darwinism Defeated?* (Vancouver: Regent College Publishing, 1999), p. 137.

26 Francis Crick, *What Mad Pursuit: A Personal View of Scientific Discovery*, (New York: Basic Books, 1988), p. 138.

27 Richard Dawkins, *The Blind Watchmaker*, (New York: W. W. Norton & Company, 1986), p. 1.

28 Tyler Hamilton, 'Whale-Inspired Wind Turbines; Mimicking the bumps on humpback-whale fins could lead to more efficient wind turbines', *MIT Technology Review*, March 6, 2008).

29 Thomas Chippendale, *The Gentleman and Cabinet-Maker's Director*, (New York: Dover Publications, 1754). https://search.library.wisc.edu/digital/A4EUDQX4ZS33VG8F

30 https://moneyinc.com/the-most-expensive-antique-furniture-pieces-ever-sold

31 Peter S. Williams, 'Darwin's Rottweiler and the Public Understanding of Scientism', 2004, arn.org/docs/williams/pw_dawkinsfallacies.htm

20　Irreducible complexity

In my journey to a Christian worldview, I learned about the idea of *irreducible complexity*. Biochemist, Michael J. Behe, although an evolutionist, popularized the concept in his 1996 book, *Darwin's Black Box: The Biochemical Challenge to Evolution*. In the book, he defined *irreducible complexity* as, '… a single system which is composed of several well-matched, interacting parts that contribute to the basic function, and where the removal of any one of the parts causes the system to effectively cease functioning.'[1]

The bacterial flagellum. Michael Behe's book, introduces us to the bacterial flagellum, a whiplike cellular organelle used for propulsion, rather like an outboard motor. The proteins making up a flagellum are arranged into motor components, a universal joint and other structures, like those that a human engineer might specify. Michael Behe argued that this intricate design, of about forty protein components, could not have arisen through stepwise evolutionary modification. Even if the components already existed, they must be assembled into a working motor; the right organization is just as important as the right components.

Michael Behe[2] is a devout Catholic. His motivation for teaching irreducible complexity is to prove that all creation is intelligently designed, though he agrees that evolution may have been used. The 'scientific community' denies his premise of irreducible complexity, claiming that it is pseudoscience.

Charles Darwin was aware of the concept of irreducible

complexity. In *The Origin of Species*, he wrote, 'If it could be demonstrated that any complex organ existed, which could not possibly have been formed by numerous, successive, slight modifications, my theory would absolutely break down. But I can find out no such case.'[3]

Michael Behe's advocacy of irreducible complexity suffered a setback in 2005, when he was a witness in the *Kitzmiller v. Dover Area School District* trial.[4] An attempt was being made to mandate the teaching of intelligent design as legitimate science. Behe had to concede that there were no peer-reviewed papers supporting his claims that complex molecular systems or structures are 'irreducibly complex'. We should of course note that publication of such an idea, in mainstream scientific literature, is difficult because it is a threat to conventional evolutionary theory.

Michael Behe used the mousetrap as an illustrative example of irreducible complexity. A mousetrap has five interacting pieces: the base, the catch, the spring, the hammer, and the hold-down bar. All must be in place, as the removal of any one piece stops the mousetrap working. He claimed that biological systems require multiple parts to be assembled correctly and work together in the same way as the mousetrap.

Biologist, Kenneth R. Miller, in, *Only A Theory*, published in 2008, challenged the claim that the mousetrap is irreducibly complex.[5] Miller observed that mixing less than five of the mousetrap components can produce something with a different function than the mousetrap. A school classmate had removed the hold-down bar and catch from a mousetrap and produced a spit-ball catapult. He claimed that, in a biological system, it was similarly possible for a function to have been developed along the evolutionary pathway before the final different function.

A further objection, by secular evolutionists, states it is a false assumption to assume intelligent design when a naturalistic explanation for a biological phenomenon is unknown. They argue that further investigation is needed. In addition, they claim it is wrong to assume that current evolutionary theory and intelligent design are the only two valid models to explain life.

Cilium and intraflagellar transport

So, where does irreducible complexity stand today? Actually, the evidence is getting stronger! Evolution News (EN), an online 'journal' of the Discovery Institute which advocates intelligent design, posted an article on 30 June 2021, with the title 'Cilium and Intraflagellar Transport: More Irreducibly Complex than Ever.'[6] The article begins with these words: 'Michael Behe's introduction of irreducibly complex (IC) molecular machines in *Darwin's Black Box* is a gift that keeps on giving.'

It continues:

> Many readers probably had never heard of cilia or flagella back in 1996. The fact that those machines still make useful illustrations of irreducible complexity now, even more powerfully than they did 25 years ago, is a strong affirmation of his thesis that irreducible complexity gives evidence of intelligent design. The bacterial flagellum tends to get more mentions because it is such a cool outboard motor that laypersons can immediately relate to. No less wondrous, though a little more obscure, is the cilium.
>
> The cilium nails the case for intelligent design more than ever, especially when considering how the organelle is built.

Inside those tiny hairlike projections is an advanced transportation system that looks for all the world like a motorized two-way railcar inside a mine shaft!

The EN article was prompted by a 2021 article, 'Intraflagellar transport',[7] in *Current Biology* by Dr Gaia Pigino, in which she describes the extraordinary complexity and make-up of a cilium and how it functions. The author never mentions evolution in her article. Dr Pigino has a PhD in Evolutionary Biology from the University of Siena, Italy. She currently leads a research group at the Max Planck Institute of Molecular Cell Biology and Genetics, Dresden, Germany.

The EN article claims that the cilium provides very strong evidence for intelligent design. Cells need to recognize different signals, such as chemical and mechanical stimuli, from the extracellular environment to function properly. Most eukaryotic cells (those consisting of a cell in which the genetic material is DNA, in the form of chromosomes contained within a distinct nucleus) sense these signals, in part, through a specialized hair-like organelle, the cilium, which extends from the cell body as a sort of antenna.

Cilia are fundamental during early embryonic development, coordinating the asymmetry of the vertebrate body e.g., in man a liver on the right and a spleen on the left. Cilia are required for the development and functioning of organs such as the brain, heart and kidneys. We can see because of connecting cilia of photoreceptors in our retina; we smell because of sensory cilia at the tip of olfactory neurones and we hear because of the kinocilia of our sensory hair cells. Cilia propel sperm cells and contribute to cognition by facilitating the flow of cerebrospinal fluid in the ventricles of our brains. Not surprisingly, defects in the assembly and function of these tiny organelles result in devastating pathologies, collectively known as ciliopathies. Dr Pigino lists fourteen known ciliopathies causing named syndromes. Retinitis Pigmentosa is a ciliopathy causing blindness. Ciliar defects can harm the skeleton, eyes, kidneys, brain, or multiple systems in the body at once. The harmful effects of ciliopathies support Michael Behe's definition of irreducible complexity, 'where the removal of any one of the parts causes the system to effectively cease functioning'. Cilia clearly show irreducible complexity; their proper function is fundamental to human health.

The blood clotting cascade

I now wish to draw your attention to the irreducible complexity of coagulation (blood clotting). This was very important in my work as a Vascular Surgeon. I was often involved in treating abdominal aortic aneurysms—a condition involving the main artery in the abdomen. The aorta may dilate from its usual diameter of approximately 2 cm to diameters of more than 5 cm. A life-threatening event, with a mortality of approximately 50 per cent, occurs if the aneurysm bursts causing catastrophic bleeding. The operation to repair the aneurysm classically involves clamping the aorta above the burst and replacing the affected segment by suturing a prosthetic, fabric, tube graft in place.

One night, my anaesthetic colleagues transfused fifty-six units of blood into a patient with a ruptured aneurysm, who I was operating on, and who survived to go home. I set myself the future target of donating fifty-six units, which I recently achieved! In more recent times, ruptured aneurysms have been stented through the femoral arteries in the groin.

Understanding the amazing mechanism of blood clotting, and the part that blood has in the healing of wounds, speaks to me and others of the awesome God who created us. There are twelve clotting factors in the coagulation cascade, numbered with Roman numerals and given a common name as well. They are numbered according to when they were discovered; not according to the order in which they react. There is extraordinary design complexity in the coagulation cascade. Platelets, which have clumped together, along with other factors, initiate coagulation to produce a clot which fills the break in a blood vessel. In addition, the walls of arteries have circular muscle within them which helps to close the end of a severed artery.

Platelets do not normally adhere to the inner lining of arteries but, when they meet an injured area of blood vessel wall, they start to swell, change shape from discs and develop lots of irregular arms (pseudopods); at the same time, they release granules ('the release reaction') containing multiple active factors and become sticky (aggregation). The release reaction helps the conversion of soluble fibrinogen into a solid fibrin mesh so that a haemostatic plug can develop within twenty seconds of a blood vessel break. After an hour, clot retraction closes the vessel further.

Platelets also initiate the healing process. A few hours after clot formation, platelets release a growth factor which promotes the invasion of the clot by fibroblasts so that fibrous tissue is formed within two weeks. The two sides of the wound are brought together, leaving a contracted scar which is smaller than the original wound. A special soluble blood substance trapped in a clot, plasminogen, is turned into plasmin by *tissue plasminogen activator* (tPA), which is released from the injured tissues. Plasmin digests the fibrin mesh and allows removal of the clot. Genetically engineered tPA can be used to dissolve the blockage in a coronary artery during a heart attack.

The view that the clotting cascade is an example of irreducible complexity has of course been opposed by advocates of evolution, such as Russell F. Doolittle, who earned a Ph.D. in Biochemistry at Harvard University in 1962 for research into blood clotting. He authored *The Evolution of Vertebrate Blood Clotting*[8] in 2012.

In opposing Michael Behe's views, Russell Doolittle cited a paper, Bugge *et al.* 1996,[9] claiming that mice could survive with two of the components of the blood clotting cascade eliminated. When the gene for plasminogen was knocked out of mice, they had thrombotic complications. When the gene for fibrinogen was knocked out, predictably, haemorrhage followed. By crossing the two lines of mice, both genes could be knocked out. Russell Doolittle claimed these mice were normal, proving that the clotting cascade was actually *reducibly complex*, so contradicting Michael Behe's claim. But in fact, they were not healthy as Doolittle implied—they had no clotting, haemorrhaged and died in pregnancy! Michael Behe has written a robust defence at the Discovery Institute, 31 July 2000: 'In Defence Of The Irreducibility Of The Blood Clotting Cascade. Response to R. Doolitte, K. Miller and K. Robison.'[10]

Blood and forgiveness

While writing about blood and the clotting cascade, we should note that blood has a particular function in the Bible, of washing sin away. Hebrews 9:22 tells us that, 'Without the shedding of blood there is no forgiveness.' The Old Testament animal sacrifices looked forward to the sacrifice of Christ and the shedding of His blood. Hebrews 9:28 continues explaining the redeeming power of the blood of Christ: 'So Christ was sacrificed once to take away the sins of many people; and he will appear a second time, not to bear sin, but to bring salvation to those who are waiting for him.' The apostle Peter writes, 'For you know that it was not with perishable things such as silver or gold that you were redeemed from the empty way of life handed down to you from your forefathers, but with the precious blood of Christ, a lamb without blemish or defect' (1 Peter 1:18–19).

You may find this preoccupation with blood unpleasant. God our Creator, the Bible explains, is a just God who will not overlook sin and requires that the lawbreaker be punished. The sinner is in debt to God and a price must be paid to redeem (buy back) the sinner. God loves mankind in the way the father loved the prodigal son. Psalm 145:9 tells us, 'The Lord is good to all; he has compassion on all he has made.' Jesus Christ chose to pay the price to save anyone who will repent of (turn away from) their sin and trust him for forgiveness.

The New Testament Epistles, in various verses, indicate that we can be justified by his blood; redeemed through his blood; brought near through his blood; experience peace through his blood; be purified from all sin by his blood; be freed from our sins by his blood;

be purchased for God with his blood. Leviticus 17:11 states, 'It is the blood that makes atonement for one's life.'

A Christian has been cleansed and drawn back to God by Jesus' precious blood. The estrangement, caused by sin, has been healed by the blood, spiritually drawing the two sides together again. We have peace with God. In heaven, Jesus' hands, feet, side and head bear the fibrosed scars as historical evidence of human redemption. Jesus says to the Christian believer, 'See, I have engraved you on the palms of my hands' (Isaiah 49:16).

Insights of two PhD scientists

Finally, I will mention two scientists who have also written about irreducible complexity. Michael Denton qualified as a doctor and also has a PhD in Biochemistry from King's College, London. In, *Evolution: A Theory in Crisis*, he wrote, 'Although the tiniest bacterial cells are incredibly small, weighing less than 10–12 grams, each is in effect a veritable microminiaturized factory containing thousands of exquisitely designed pieces of intricate molecular machinery, made up altogether of one hundred thousand million atoms, far more complicated than any machine built by man and absolutely without parallel in the non-living world.'[11]

The second is biologist, Michael J. Katz, who states in the book, *Templets and the explanation of complex patterns*:

> In the natural world, there are many pattern-assembly systems for which there is no simple explanation. There are useful scientific explanations for these complex systems, but the final patterns that they produce are so heterogeneous that they cannot effectively be reduced to smaller or less intricate

predecessor components. As I will argue ... these patterns are, in a fundamental sense, irreducibly complex ...

He continues:

Cells ... do not self-assemble. One cannot stir together the parts of a cell or of an organism and spontaneously assemble a neuron or a walrus: to create a cell or an organism one needs a pre-existing cell or a pre-existing organism, with its attendant complex templets. A fundamental characteristic of the biological realm is that organisms are complex patterns, and, for its creation, life requires extensive, and essentially maximal, templets.[12]

Irreducible complexity poses a significant threat to Darwin's theory of evolution.

NOTES

1 Michael Behe, *Darwin's Black Box: The Biochemical Challenge to Evolution*, (New York: Free Press, 2006), p. 39.
2 D. Klinghoffer, *Michael Behe: A Biography*, (Discovery Institute, 2009). https://www.discovery.org/a/10501
3 Charles Darwin, *The Origin of Species, 1st ed*, (Albemarle Street: John Murray, 1859), p. 189.
4 https://rationalwiki.org/wiki/Kitzmiller_v._Dover_Area_School_District
5 K.R. Miller, *Only a Theory: Evolution and the Battle for America's Soul*, (New York: Viking Penguin, 2008) pp. 54–55.
6 'Cilium and Intraflagellar Transport: More Irreducibly Complex than Ever', *Evolution News* @DiscoveryCSC June 30, 2021. https://evolutionnews.org/2021/06/cilium-and-intraflagellar-transport-more-irreducibly-complex-than-ever/
7 Gaia Pigino, 'Intraflagellar transport', *Current Biology* Vol 31, (10) 2021.
8 Russell F. Doolittle, *The Evolution of Vertebrate Blood Clotting*, (University Science Books, 2012).

9 Thomas Bugge et al., 'Loss of fibrinogen rescues mice from the pleiotropic effects of plasminogen deficiency', *Cell* 87 (4), 1996, pp. 709–719.

10 Michael J. Behe, 'In Defence of the Irreducibility of the Blood Clotting Cascade: Response to Russell Doolittle et al', *Discovery Institute*, July 31, 2000. https://www.discovery.org/a/442/

11 Michael Denton: *Evolution: A Theory in Crisis*, (Burnett Books, 1985), p. 250.

12 Michael J. Katz, *Templets and the explanation of complex patterns*, (Cambridge University Press, 1986), pp. 26–27.

21 Consultant general surgeon, clinical teacher, retirement and ethics lecturer

I began my consultant post at Newcastle General Hospital and Freeman Hospital on 1 February 1987. For the first two years, my job was split between these two hospitals. There were four consultants at each hospital in two firms. I was on a 1 in 4 emergency rota for General and Vascular surgery. In 1989, I moved completely to Freeman Hospital with four operating lists a week.

Initially, I lived in hospital accommodation, but soon we were able to purchase an Edwardian, three-storey, semi-detached house. This suited our family because Liz's father had died in 1986 and her mother, later, came to live with us for fifteen years, rather than remaining alone.

The house we bought had been surveyed and, unfortunately, significant dry rot was missed, but found later during some essential renovations. For thirty-three weeks our lives were impacted by builders, engineers and plumbers. It was not an easy start in our new home. Providentially, a Rentokil insurance policy had been transferred to us and this proved extremely helpful!

We settled at Welbeck Road Evangelical Church, where we are still members thirty-five years later. Toward the end of our time in Leeds, our girls had attended a Christian youth group, called

Crusaders, which both our fathers had attended during their youth. We wondered about starting a group in Newcastle.

Imagine my thoughts when, in the first group of medical students I had to teach, there was a young man wearing a Crusader tie! He was definitely interested in helping to start a group and was a gifted pianist. Soon, a recently qualified doctor also agreed to help us. Because of our building work, the launch of Newcastle Central Crusaders was delayed until October 1988. Children were invited by our daughters at school, through our church and in the immediate neighbourhood of our home. On the first Sunday afternoon, we had eighteen children in our lounge and conservatory.

When numbers grew to sixty-five children, we moved to a nearby church hall. In addition to the four original leaders, over the years we recruited more than ten other student leaders to help. The class continued for sixteen years. During our time in both Leeds and Newcastle, in the summer, I was involved with United Beach Missions for fourteen years. I helped in St Ives, Broadstairs and Whitby. Later, I was a team leader in Benllech on Anglesey, in Llandudno, in Scarborough and in Bridlington.

Relevant to my journey to a Christian worldview, I remember an evening, in 1998, on the promenade in Llandudno after I had been speaking at the evening open-air meeting. I was approached by a man who introduced himself as Professor Sam Berry, a Christian geneticist from University College, London. I do not know why he spoke with me, though perhaps it was in response to something I had said. He led the conversation to the origin of man and explained his view of that.

He said that there was no scriptural reason for disbelieving that

God worked through biologically understood mechanisms of evolution by natural selection to produce the world as we see it today. He described the earth being populated by hominids[1] and that God 'placed his image' in an already existing animal. Given that the account in Genesis of the origin of Eve was different from that of Adam, I asked him how Eve was 'born'. He said in the same manner as Adam—she was an 'ensouled hominid'.

I remember being slightly surprised and came out with the question, 'How did all the other hominids feel about this?' I do not remember his answer. I think in retrospect that it was not an unreasonable question. These other hominids presumably had brains which moved their limbs, felt pain and helped them to search for food. I had always thought that evolution was a slow process and wondered how God's 'ensoulment' of Adam and Eve, as he described it, could in evolutionary terms suddenly give them the ability to reason and speak. I will discuss evolutionary theories about the slow origins of consciousness, the mind and speech in chapter 24.

To be sure of what Professor Berry said, I later bought his book, *Science, Life and Christian Belief* by Malcolm A. Jeeves and R.J. Berry. The authors state what I have written above about the ensoulment of hominids. They continue: 'The controversy over the Bible and evolution is intrinsically sterile.' By which, I think, they mean it is not fruitful and wish that those believing that the earth is approximately 6,000 years old would give up talking about it. They also strangely claimed, 'God is relevant, active and powerful, completely distinct from the transcendent watchmaker of some creationists or the woolly imminent urge of the liberals.'[2] This theory about God 'ensouling' hominids has been embraced by many Christian leaders.

I need to mention the help given to me as a surgeon by three medical secretaries: Judith, Jean and Alison. Many hospital consultants recognize their secretaries as the most important member of their team. This is because the planning and safe organisation of one's workload is critical. Results of important investigations need to be chased up, and urgent operations planned. The only letter that I have succeeded in having published in the *Daily Telegraph* was about the need to pay medical secretaries more! Jean, my secretary for about seventeen years, worked for the NHS for forty years!

Medical students attended my two ward rounds and two out-patient clinics each week. The apprenticeship model, with bedside teaching and training young people in how to take a medical history and examine patients, was similar to my own student experience. Students could come to the operating theatres and scrub up. I also had sixth formers from schools on work experience. Teaching operative surgery to my juniors was an important responsibility and I would spend a lot of time on the 'other side of the operating table'. Examining students in their final exams was a further duty.

I had various administrative duties—the most significant was being chairman of the Medical Staff Committee at the Freeman Hospital for three years.

During twenty-two years as a consultant, there was increasing specialization and each surgeon performed a smaller variety of operations. This allowed the duration of training to be shortened.

Latterly, I focused on vascular, thyroid and parathyroid surgery. From four consultant general surgeons, we expanded to fifteen!

There were changes in how nursing was managed. In previous times, the focus was on 'task-orientated nursing' led and supervised by the ward sister and senior staff nurses. This changed to 'patient-orientated nursing', where each nurse did tasks for their own designated patients. Given that shifts normally totalled 37.5 hours each week, the patient still had several different nurses!

The discipline of research, of the writing of scientific papers and the presentation of research work at national or international meetings, is a valuable part of training and helps to develop a critical faculty in the surgeon. It is important to understand statistical methods used in analysis of results and to recognize good scientific work and, indeed, poor work making inappropriate conclusions. Unfortunately, there have been many examples of non-intentional and intentional scientific falsehoods in the literature.

When a scientific paper is written, previous publications about the same subject are reviewed in the discussion and the new work often builds on conclusions made by earlier researchers. A poor publication, lacking good evidence, can be requoted positively and mislead many, including the wider public, into believing there is good evidence for a particular conclusion. This repeated quotation of poor research is labelled the 'Woozle effect' or, 'evidence by citation'! (I refer you back to Chapter 10 where Christopher Robin corrected the confusion during the search for the Woozle.)

The views or conclusions of the original author can be corrupted by firming up the language from a qualified, 'it may', 'it might', 'it could', to an absolute, 'it is'. This constitutes a 'woozle' remark. When deliberate propaganda phrases such as, 'everyone knows', 'It is clear that', 'It is obvious that', 'It is generally agreed that', are used, this is a 'woozle' line of reasoning!

Lives can be harmed or lost by false conclusions and intentional exaggeration. A short letter to the editor of the *New England Journal of Medicine* (NEJM) in 1980, by Jane Porter and Hershel Jick, reported an analysis of medical records concerning the use of pain-killers in hospital patients. They concluded that, 'Despite widespread use of narcotic drugs *in hospitals*, the development of addiction is rare in patients with no history of addiction.'[3] For clarification, I point out that narcotic drugs, used for pain relief in hospital, would not generally lead to a prescription continuing after discharge.

Unfortunately, as time went on, the letter was misquoted to support the claim that addiction was also uncommon when narcotics were prescribed to patients *at home*. A journalist, Sam Quinones, documents in his book, *Dreamland: The True Tale of America's Opiate Epidemic*,[4] that *Scientific American*, in 1990, incorrectly described the 1980 letter as an 'extensive study' and *Time* magazine, in 2001, called it a 'landmark study', so that fears of addiction to narcotics were 'basically unwarranted'. A 2017 letter to the NEJM suggested the inappropriate citations of this 1980 letter contributed to the North American opioid (a narcotic) epidemic by giving false reassurance about the risk of addiction.[5]

Peer review of potential surgical and medical publications, by those who are experts in the field, endeavours to ensure that truthful results and conclusions are published. This hopefully prevents distortions of the truth. I wonder whether evolutionary scientific publications are subject to similar rigorous review?

In the media, the dogma of evolution sails on like an invincible Titanic, growing ever more belligerent as it draws generations of the unthinking on-board. Despite the White Star Line saying, 'She is an unsinkable ship,' the Titanic hit an iceberg and sank on her maiden voyage. Evolution may be the biggest 'woozle' of all and evidence against the theory is growing all the time, like an iceberg.

Is Lawrence Krauss, a North American theoretical physicist and cosmologist, guilty of a 'woozle' remark when he states, 'One of the things about quantum mechanics is not only can nothing become something, nothing always becomes something. Nothing is unstable. Nothing will always produce something in quantum mechanics.'[6]

In his 2012 book, *A Universe from Nothing: Why There is Something Rather than Nothing*, Krauss argues that the laws of physics enable the universe to be created from nothing. He asks, 'What would be the characteristics of a universe that was created from nothing, just with the laws of physics and without any supernatural shenanigans? The characteristics of the universe would be precisely those of the one we live in.'[7]

Surely that is a 'woozle' remark? His argument deceives. He is not beginning with *nothing nothing* (*Francis Schaeffer*) but has sneaked in 'the laws of physics' which represent information, order, intelligence and design. In fact, the laws of physics would be impotent if they were acting on nothing! Lawrence Krauss's argument inadvertently concedes that to *create a universe* (his words) one does need information, order, intelligence and design (the laws of physics), which the God of the Bible has in abundance while *'nothing nothing'* does not.

Stephen Hawking, also, overlooked the question of 'W*here did the laws of physics come from?'* when he wrote in his book, *The Grand Design*, published in 2010, 'Because there is a law like gravity, the universe can and will create itself from nothing in the manner described in Chapter 6. Spontaneous creation is the reason there is something rather than nothing, why the universe exists, why we exist. It is not necessary to invoke God to light the blue touch paper and set the universe going.'[8] He needed to explain, 'Where did gravity come from?' and 'On what does it act?'

As Professor Fred Hoyle acknowledged, when he wrote, 'a super-intellect has monkeyed with physics',[9] the laws and their reliability must have come from somewhere. Likewise, Sir James Jeans, physicist, astronomer, and mathematician, who died in 1946, commented, 'From the intrinsic evidence of his creation, the Great Architect of the Universe now begins to appear as a pure mathematician.'[10]

Both Francis Crick and Richard Dawkins declared that the Universe appears to have been designed but that we must all remember, that is not the case. Richard Dawkins has written, 'Darwinian natural selection can produce an uncanny illusion of design. An engineer would be hard put to decide whether a bird or a plane was the more aerodynamically elegant. So powerful is the illusion of design, it took humanity until the mid-19th century to realize that it is an illusion.'[11] He has also written, 'One thing all real scientists agree upon is the *fact* of evolution itself. It is a fact that we are cousins of gorillas, kangaroos, starfish, and bacteria. Evolution is as much a fact as the heat of the sun. It is not a theory, and for pity's sake, let's stop confusing the philosophically naive by calling it so.'[12]

Richard Dawkins asked his six-year-old daughter what the purpose was of a field of wonderful flowers.[13] She replied, 'to make the world pretty and help the bees make honey for us'. Dawkins replied that was not true, because evolution excludes purpose and design. Flowers were in the world to copy their DNA.

In 1998, I was invited to be a member of *The Moynihan Chirurgical Club*.[14] Lord Berkeley Moynihan of Leeds formed the club in 1909 to encourage surgeons outside London to share in clinical meetings and to travel to other centres in the UK and abroad for mutual education. There are thirty-six active surgeons and, on retirement, all members become honorary members. We have made lifelong friends. Over the years I have presented papers in Brussels, in Oman and in Padua.

In Padua, Italy, I spoke in the Morgagni Lecture Theatre, on the ethical subject of, 'Is Hippocratic Medicine dying?' Hippocrates of Kos (460–377 BC) had an enormous influence on the good practice of medicine, a high view of the sanctity of human life and the special, confidential relationship between doctor and patient. The prevailing culture in Greece at the time of Hippocrates, and later in Rome, saw abortion and infanticide being widely practised.[15] The Hippocratic Oath had four elements: a covenant to the Greek gods of medicine (Apollo, Asclepius, Hygeia and Panacea); a duty to the teachers of medicine; duties to the patient; and, finally, a sanction if these promises were broken.[16]

Christianity and Islam embraced this oath and, for over 2,000 years, medicine was blessed by its influence. The terrible events in Nazi Germany in the 1920s, until the end of the war, found doctors complicit in experimentation and destruction of human lives considered not worth living.

The expression, *'not worth living'*, appeared in the title of a 1920 book, *Die Freigabe der Vernichtung Lebensunwerten Lebens (The Freedom To Destroy Lives Not Worth Living)*, by Professor of Law, Karl Binding, 1841–1920, University of Leipzig, and Professor of Psychiatry, Alfred Hoche, 1865–1943, University of Freiberg. They described some living people who were brain damaged, mentally retarded or psychiatrically ill as, *'human ballast and empty human husks'*, and said their destruction was not only tolerable but downright humane.[17] This had a profound effect on medical & social attitudes in Germany.

Because of the Nazi doctors' involvement in atrocities, after the war, the Declaration of Geneva, 1948, tried to re-establish Hippocratic medicine as the norm, but sadly omitted reference to gods or God.[18] The declaration did refer to life beginning at *'conception'* but in subsequent years this was modified to *'the beginning'* and, later, any reference to unborn life in the womb was removed. Sadly today, the unborn are regularly killed and the human embryo is used as a research commodity. Hippocratic medicine is dying!

I enjoyed my work as a surgeon and my relationships with the medical and nursing staff. I had many strong bonds with patients. In March 2009, I retired as a consultant surgeon.

I, then, taught ethics, part time, to medical students for ten years. Second year medical students debated among other matters, 'Active Euthanasia should be legalized.' Two proposed the motion and two opposed. In 2011, a total of 50 students debated this, as I chaired. Before the debate, 29 students voted in support of the motion (58 per cent) and, after the debate, 23 students still voted for the motion (46 per cent). I noted that young people beginning at a UK medical school in the 21st century have already, wrongly, imbibed that personal autonomy is the most important principle in making such decisions, when in fact the four ethical principles of beneficence, non-maleficence, justice and personal autonomy should be balanced. Some students said they would carry out euthanasia as their medical duty! That is exactly what some German doctors did under the Nazi regime.

Statistics from the Netherlands are relevant to the debates, which I shared with the students. In the Netherlands, in 2008, there were 2,731 cases of legal euthanasia or assisted suicide, while, in 550 cases, lives were terminated without request.[18] In an interview, the late Dutch politician, Els Borst, who successfully promoted the legalization of euthanasia, admitted too late that the government's action was a mistake and should have first focused on palliative care.[19] The current situation in the Netherlands is surprising given that, during the Second World War, 100 Dutch physicians refused to sign transportation orders to the death camps and they themselves were sent to, and died, in concentration camps.[20]

In 2020, Netherlands Regional Euthanasia Review Committees reported 6,938 patients died by euthanasia and assisted suicide. Approximately 150,000 deaths occur each year in the Netherlands so, 1 in 22 deaths were by euthanasia or assisted suicide. The law already allows euthanasia in the first year of life and from the age of 12, with plans to extend this to all ages.[21]

Ethics teaching is important in preparing young people to be doctors, nurses or other health care professionals. Wrong ethics lead to bad practices. How can we be confident about what is right and wrong in medical ethics? My journey to a Christian worldview taught me that in God's Word, the Bible, and in the person and teaching of Jesus Christ, one can be confident of finding the Way, the Truth and the Life which we have all been designed to walk in, believe in and live out.

NOTES

1 M. Jeeves & R. Berry, *Science, Life and Christian Belief*, (Westmont, Illinois: Apollos, imprint of IVP, 1998), pp. 115–116.

2 The family of hominids includes the great apes and humans.

3 J. Porter & H. Jick, 'Addiction rare in patients treated with narcotics', *N Engl J Med* 1980; 302, p. 123.

4 Sam Quinones, *Dreamland: The True Tale of America's Opiate Epidemic*, (London: Bloomsbury Press, 2015), p. 107.

5 P. Leung et al., 'A 1980 Letter on the Risk of Opioid Addiction', *N Engl J Med* 2017; 376, pp. 2194–2195.

6 Opening statement of Lawrence Krauss in his debate with Dr William Lane Craig, http://www.reasonablefaith.org/the-craig-krauss-debate-at-north-carolina-state-university#ixzz2bwKlOhe1.

7 Lawrence Krauss, *A Universe from Nothing: Why There is Something Rather than Nothing*, (New York: Atria Books, 2012), pp. 174–175.

8 S. Hawking & L. Mlodinow, *The Grand Design*, (New York: Bantam Books, 2010), p. 180.

9 Fred Hoyle, 'The Universe: Past and Present Reflections', *Annual Review of Astronomy and Astrophysics*, Vol 20, 1982, p. 16.

10 James Jeans, *The Mysterious Universe*, (Cambridge University Press, 1930), p. 134.

11 Richard Dawkins, 'Big ideas: Evolution', *New Scientist*, 14 September 2005.

12 Richard Dawkins, 'The Illusion of Design', *Natural History* 114 (9) 2005, pp. 35–37.

13 Richard Dawkins, *Climbing Mount Improbable*, (New York: WW Norton & Co, 2006), pp. 256–268.

14 www.moynihanclub.co.uk

15 Alvin Schmidt, *How Christianity Changed the World*, (Grand Rapids, Michigan: Zondervan Publishing House, 2001), p. 56.

16 Nigel M. de S. Cameron, *The New Medicine–the Revolution in Technology and Ethics*, (London: Hodder and Stoughton, 1991), pp. 24–34.

17 Karl Binding & Alfred Hoche, *Die Freigabe der Vernichtung Lebensunwerten Lebens*, (The Project Gutenberg eBook, 1920), p. 32.

18 Nigel M. de S. Cameron, *The New Medicine–the Revolution in Technology and Ethics*, pp. 84–89.

19 Patrick Craine, 'Former Dutch Health Minister admits error of legalising Euthanasia', LifeSiteNews.com, 2 December 2009.

20 Leo Alexander, 'Medical Science under Dictatorship', *N Engl J Med* 241:2 1949, pp. 39–47.

21 Brandon Showalter, 'Record number of people died by physician-assisted suicide in the Netherlands in 2020', *Christian Post World*, 4 May 2021.

22 Medical ethics – the sanctity of human life

In this chapter, I wish to discuss the foundational principle of Christian medical ethics, which is *the sanctity of human life.* I will explain in the following chapter why an alternative view, *respect for human life,* is a dangerous and unsafe principle for medical ethics. The sanctity of human life is enshrined in the will of God who said, 'Let us make man in our image, in our likeness. ... So, God created man in his own image, in the image of God he created him; male and female he created them' (Genesis 1:26–27).

There is a profound meaning in the phrase, *'the sanctity of human life'*, which I think is captured by God's words to Moses in Exodus 3:5: 'Do not come any closer. ... Take off your sandals, for the place where you are standing is holy ground.' As we approach all the tough questions raised in the practice of medicine, and these problems may require significant multidisciplinary discussion, we should recognize that we approach 'holy ground'. God has laid the foundation for medical ethics.

God went further in establishing the sanctity, or sacredness, of every individual human life. When speaking to Noah in Genesis 9:6, God states, 'Whoever sheds the blood of man, by man shall his blood be shed; for in the image of God has God made man.' God emphasized the unique preciousness of each human being by declaring capital punishment for the crime of intentionally killing a man. I will not digress to discuss capital punishment, self-defence or justified war, but have quoted this verse to show God's commitment to the absolute principle that man is made in God's image.

In this chapter, I will also raise the issue of 'personhood'. While it is obvious to most biologists that when human conception takes place (fertilization of an ovum by a spermatozoa) a new genetic being has come into existence, there are those who would deny that this is 'a person' and deprive that human being of the rights and protection they would give to a child or an adult.

In claiming that the sanctity of human life is the correct and safe foundation for medical ethics, I logically look to Almighty God, who laid that foundation for the rules of morality on which I base my medical ethics. It is a sad reflection on modern civilization that the previous consensus of morality, built on the Ten Commandments is being discarded and, today, as described in the Bible at the end of the book of Judges, 'everyone did what was right in his own eyes' (Judges 21:25, ESV). This can be described as moral relativism.

Turning to my own experience when working as a surgeon, on Wednesday evenings, the general surgical teams in the three Newcastle Hospitals gathered for a postgraduate meeting. On one of these occasions, the director of the undergraduate medical ethics teaching, gave a talk in which he defined medical ethics as, 'a moral restraint on the abuse of power'.

In our later discussion, I asked a question: 'Your definition has merits, but how do you define what a moral is?' He replied that a moral is defined as what is right and proper behaviour over against that which is a wrong or improper behaviour. That may be, but we still have to decide on whose authority we, and society, decide what is right and wrong.

Some participants in the discussion suggested that the view of a majority might decide what is right and wrong. However, recent history when Germany was controlled by Nazis, suggests that this was not a safe basis for morality or medical ethics. An elite minority coerced others into behaving in inhuman ways. Here, in the UK, it appears that an elite minority has also changed the 'morality' of a nation within the space of a few decades. This is relevant to both medical ethics and, particularly, sexual ethics.

Over 2,000 years ago, the prevailing public morality of Greece caused Hippocrates of Kos and his fellow physicians to formulate and vow allegiance to the Hippocratic Oath. They were not happy with the ethics and practice of their leaders and philosophers. Plato (424–348 BC), in his 'Republic', stated that women over the age of forty, who fell pregnant, should have an abortion and that infanticide was essential to maintain the quality of the citizens. Aristotle (384–322 BC), in his 'Politics', added that infanticide and abortion should be used if there were an excess number of children in a family and that compulsory exposure of any deformed baby should be practised.[1]

We do well to note the enormous benefits of medicine practised according to the Hippocratic Oath right up to the 20th century. Margaret Mead, an anthropologist, commented that there was a paradigm shift in medical values with the advent of Hippocratic medicine: 'the Hippocratic oath marked one of the turning points in the history of man.'[2] We find ourselves now in a post-Hippocratic age, unsure of whether the democratic process in the UK will make just and right laws regarding medical ethics?

In 1967, The Abortion Act, introduced by David Steel, was passed and, since then, over 9.67 million unborn babies[3] have been aborted in England, Scotland and Wales and their potential progeny lost. This Act ignores the sanctity of human life. In October 2007, forty years after abortion became legal in Great Britain (that excludes Northern Ireland), Patrick Carroll, an actuary and statistician, published a report with the title, 'Assessing the Damage'[4], in which he asked important questions: What is the population impact of losing millions of lives through legal abortion? What is the impact of abortion on pension and National Insurance contributions? Can we explain the dramatic increase in breast cancer observed over the past decades, at least partially, with the increase in abortion? What is the implication of abortion on family structure and on fertility?

His report gave detailed answers—some of which were disturbing. At the time of his report, 2007, the UK working age population had been reduced by nearly 7 per cent. He estimated that this would rise to 11 per cent in 2017. This would represent 7.5 million missing from the working age population in 2017. By April 2021, after 53 years of abortion in the UK, 9,675,153 babies had been lost—an unborn baby every 3 minutes.[5] The impact on the working age population continues to grow and impacts on the availability of carers for increasing numbers of elderly people.

I, like many Christians, believe the only definite ground for abortion would be to save the life of a mother, who is in peril during pregnancy because of another medical condition. When I was a medical student, heart valve damage, caused by Rheumatic Fever, could lead to heart failure because of the extra blood volume of pregnancy. The lives of both mother and baby were threatened. This risk would be rare in the UK today.

A cancer diagnosis, made during pregnancy, might lead to a similar difficult ethical decision. The rare occurrence of pregnancy following rape[6] could be considered as potential grounds for an abortion. However, the reality is that approximately 75 per cent of such pregnancies are carried to term. Sandra Mahkorn, in a survey of counselling agencies assisting women with problem pregnancies, identified 37 women who had reported a rape-related pregnancy. Of them, 28 continued their pregnancy (75 per cent), 5 chose abortion and four were lost to follow up.[6]

The book, *Victims and Victors*, contains the testimonies of 192 women who became pregnant after rape or incest, as well as the moving testimonies of grown children who were conceived that way.[7] Of the 164 women who became pregnant as the result of rape, 73 per cent carried the pregnancy to term; 26 per cent had abortions and 2 per cent had miscarriages. Of the 28 women who became pregnant as a result of incest, 50 per cent carried the pregnancy to term and 50 per cent had abortions.[8] Of the 50 women (88 per cent) who expressed an opinion about their abortions, 44 explicitly regretted them, which they reported had increased their trauma, and they stated abortion had been the wrong solution to their pregnancies. (Six women did not provide any information on how they felt about their abortions.)[9] Notably, not one of the 133 women (119 rape and 14 incest) who carried their pregnancies to term, expressed regret over having given birth to their children, or a wish that they had chosen abortion instead.[10]

A moving testimony, in a 1985 book, *Birthright?* by Maureen Long, tells of a lady, conceived because of rape, whose mother and adoptive father refused to abort her, *an innocent child*. The lady said, 'I don't know how many times, as I lay secure in the loving arms of my husband, I have thanked God for my wonderful Christian father.'[11]

How did it come about that the 1967 Abortion Act[12] was passed? On the statute books at that time was a law, passed in 1929, which condemned such action. The Infant Life (Preservation) Act of 1929 was passed to protect the unborn child. The subtitle of the law was 'Punishment for child destruction'. Those framing the 1929 Act recognized that during pregnancy a child is present.

In the 1929 Act, the qualifying phrase about the unborn child was, 'the life of a child capable of being born alive'.[13] At that time, a pregnancy of twenty-eight weeks or more was proof the child was capable of being born alive. Modern neonatal care has lowered the age at which a premature baby can survive to twenty-four weeks gestation and even earlier.

The 1929 legislation allowed that it would not be an offence to cause the death of the child if abortion was performed in good faith for the purpose only of preserving the life of the mother. But it stated that, 'Any person who, with intent to destroy, by any wilful act causes a child to die before it has an existence independent of its mother, shall be guilty of felony, to wit, of child destruction, and shall be liable on conviction thereof on indictment to penal servitude for life.'[13]

Something changed between 1929 and 1967. Morality changed for many, including the majority of members of Parliament, who believed it was no longer wrong to kill an unborn child or that the pregnancy did not reflect the presence of a new human being. They no longer believed that the unborn child had a right to life. After 1967, a woman could request an abortion on certain grounds and this would be granted if two doctors agreed.

Peter Singer, the Australian philosopher of Princeton and Melbourne Universities, would deny that the unborn child has the same rights as a live rational member of the human race.[14] Singer argues that foetuses are neither rational nor self-aware, and therefore cannot hold a preference. As a result, the preference of the mother to have an abortion automatically takes precedence.[15] It is often said that a woman has the right to do with her body as she wishes, despite the unborn child clearly being a different genetic being.

My Christian worldview recognizes that we live in a broken world where sickness, disease, death and difficult ethical issues have existed since the Fall of Adam and Eve into sin. Modern medicine raises ethical issues which are increasingly complex and the Bible does not precisely address every scenario. However, the ethical principle of the *Sanctity of Human Life* is the best place to start. In dialogue with an expert in the law, Jesus declared, 'Love the Lord your God with all your heart and with all your soul and with all your strength and with all your mind'; and 'Love your neighbour as yourself' (Luke 10:27).

But the expert continued, 'And who is my neighbour?' Jesus told *the parable of the good Samaritan* in response. Jesus indicated that the man who fell into the hands of robbers (in spite of the prevailing discrimination against Samaritans) was made in the image of God and, hence, precious and deserving of love and care. All our patients are deserving of the same love and protection. Sadly, many ethicists, philosophers and doctors have constructed their own arbitrary quality of 'personhood' as a tool to facilitate their ethical decisions. Instead of asking, 'Who is my neighbour?' they ask, 'What is a person?'

Josiah Wedgwood designed a medallion, in 1787, of a kneeling slave, with his hands in chains surrounded by the words, 'AM I NOT A MAN AND A BROTHER?'[16] The black African was treated as a slave—a nonperson—while a small minority petitioned for his and her recognition as a fellow human being, to be loved as a neighbour.

There is no universal agreement about who is a person or what personhood means. Some would see that certain capacities or attributes are necessary to be a person. Mary Midgley, late senior lecturer in philosophy at Newcastle University, in a book edited by Peter Singer, defined a 'person' as being 'a conscious, thinking being, which knows that it is a person (self-awareness)'.[17] Using such a definition puts the unborn, the newborn, the demented, those under an anaesthetic and those in persistent vegetative state at risk of destruction.

I believe the concept of personhood—trying to define if someone is a person—is unhelpful and wrong.

It is significant that the Warnock Report (commissioned to consider recent and potential developments in medicine and science related to human fertilization and embryology), published in July 1984,[18] demonstrated that a carefully selected committee of sixteen experts were unable to agree an answer to the question, '*But is this human being a person?*' To quote: 'Although the questions of when life or personhood begin appear to be questions of fact susceptible of straightforward answers, we hold that the answers to such questions are complex amalgams of factual and moral judgements.' The report continues, 'Instead of trying to answer these questions directly we have therefore gone straight to the question of how is it right to treat the human embryo.'[19]

The committee recognized that the embryo being discussed was human. If they had embraced the truth that the embryo was made in the image of God, they would have concluded that the embryo was entitled to protection, from conception to grave.

When Peter Singer denies certain members of the human race their right to life, he does so using different criteria than the image of God or the principle of the sanctity of human life. I mentioned his views on the unborn child, but he would go further and say that newborn babies lack the essential characteristics of personhood—that is rationality, autonomy, and self-consciousness. Therefore, 'killing a new-born baby is never equivalent to killing a person, that is, a being who wants to go on living.'[20] He is at least clear that this is *killing* a newborn baby.

Francis Crick, of DNA fame, said, 'No new-born infant should be declared human until it has passed certain tests regarding its genetic endowment and that, if it fails these tests, it forfeits the right to live.'[21] James Watson, who shared the Nobel Prize with Crick, wrote in *Prism Magazine*, 'If a child were not declared alive until 3 days after birth, then all parents could be allowed the choice only a few have under the present system. The doctor could allow the child to die if the parents so choose and save a lot of misery and suffering. I believe this view is the only rational, compassionate attitude to have.'[22] How could a scientist, who discovered the truth about DNA, lie about the biological life in a neonate?

In contrast to these views, the Bible never judges anyone based on qualities or abilities. This applies equally to the unborn child; the young person; someone with spina bifida or Down's syndrome; the disabled; an adult or elderly person. A belief in the Biblical principle of the 'sanctity of human life' protects our fellow human beings (neighbours).

Francis Crick viewed the mind and personality purely as a function of brain activity, so that, after death, there is no eternal soul. Crick made strong suggestions about limiting reproduction of the sickly and less intelligent and advocated euthanasia. Peter Lawrence, in a book review of *Francis Crick. Hunter of Life's Secrets*, written by Robert Olby, commented, 'More dangerous was his flirtation with eugenics, which began with the famous lecture he gave to the Cambridge Humanist Society in 1968; there he broached a number of tricky subjects, including overpopulation, the right to bear children and euthanasia.'[23] Crick died aged 88 years.

Some years ago, an article about Peter Singer with the title, 'The Dangerous Philosopher', appeared in *The New Yorker*. The author, Michael Specter, reflected on Singer's own mother, who, sadly, slowly developed debilitating Alzheimer's disease. Singer had regularly argued against families and society expending time and resources on 'those who are no longer useful',[24] which is consistent with his ethic known as *utilitarianism*. This theory of morality advocates that decisions should be based on the pursuit of happiness and well-being for the greatest number of people. As a consequence, society as a whole becomes more important than the individual. Singer and his sister refused to carry out their mother's request, that she should not be cared for in old age if her life was no longer useful, choosing to provide care for her. When asked about the inconsistency between his philosophical teaching and his actions, he said, 'Perhaps it is more difficult than I thought before, because it is different when it's your mother.'[24]

I find the concept of *person* or *personhood* unhelpful and see it as a 'Trojan Horse'. In seeking to define *person* or *personhood*, any definition looks to find attributes or qualities which are open to debate and for which there is no final authority. Dame Mary Warnock's committee spent two years considering such matters and sidestepped the issue as being too difficult. We must ask, 'How can one possibly decide how to treat the human embryo when you are unable to define what "it" is?' (Please note that I have put 'it' in inverted commas. The embryo is not an 'it' but is genetically a male or female member of the human race.)

The Warnock Committee made a flawed decision. Nigel M. de S. Cameron, in *Embryos and Ethics*, has helpfully written:

> They have deliberately chosen not to address the single question on which all the other, lesser questions depend. Moreover, the manner in which the question of the nature of the embryo is dismissed is itself deceptive. It implies that those who hold that the question is susceptible of an answer implicitly deny that 'complex amalgams of factual and moral judgements' may be necessary in order to arrive at it. In other words, their approach to the subject lacks the sophistication which an adequate assessment requires. Yet, of course, it is entirely possible to come to a 'straightforward' answer by means of a complex argument, and Warnock received evidence from some distinguished persons who did just that.[25]

The issue of embryo research is part of a wider issue: 'How do we view the experimental use of human subjects?' When talking about the morality of all human research, it is agreed that research without informed consent, which could harm and not benefit its human subject, is ethically indefensible.

The main purpose of Mary Warnock's committee was to tackle the complex issue of *in vitro fertilization* as a treatment for infertility. Members of her committee had different opinions, with three members arguing that embryos should never be used in research, while others believed experiments were essential. Warnock decided that compromise was needed (this she later outlined in a 1986 lecture) so that 'calculated benefits for society were possible while nevertheless offending and horrifying people as little as possible'.[26] By her own admission, she appeared to take a route under the radar of public scrutiny to allow experimentation. The benefits to society were the driving principle rather than the care of the unborn human embryo.

A developmental biologist, Anne McLaren[27], was a member of the committee. She advised the committee to adopt *14 days* as a cut-off for embryo experimentation. This being the time in embryonic development when the 'primitive streak' differentiates and later becomes the spinal-cord and nervous system. McLaren claimed the embryo could not feel pain before 14 days of development and suggested the beginning of individual development of a person should be recognized at that time and not at fertilization. She supported this by commenting that this was the last point at which the embryo could develop into identical twins.

In July 2017, at an event hosted at the British Library entitled,

'Anne McLaren: Science, Ethics and the Archive', Baroness Mary Warnock gave a keynote speech in which she said, 'The effect that Anne had on the production of the (Warnock) report was incalculable.' She paid tribute to McLaren for sorting out their difficult ethical problem! She continued, 'that since Anne had been the only embryologist on the Warnock committee, she had contributed most of the science underpinning of the report's recommendations. In addition to her scientific knowledge, Anne McLaren had the "clearest head" and her ability to think through problems "kept me in a healthy mind", during difficult times.' Baroness Warnock 'saw herself and Anne as a "powerful pair of persuaders", who talked to people, and explained the science and ethics.'[27]

The committee had recognized that the embryo was human, but their conclusion did not support the sanctity of human life from conception to the grave. You can see that if everything revolves around 'when or what is a person?' then all sorts of ideas and practices can follow. The Bible teaches that we do not have to possess specific qualities or abilities to be considered human.

This principle was emphasized by Simon Isaacs, the 4th Marquess of Reading, when the Warnock report was debated in the House of Lords on 31 October 1984. He said:

> Although the report denies the embryo the status of a human person or human being, nowhere does it define what a human person or a human being is. Nearly everyone accepts the biological fact that the embryo is a human being. After the fertilization process has been successfully completed, we have a genetically distinct individual which may continue its path of development to maturity. In the whole human life cycle, there

is no moment of comparable significance to that of fertilization. However, some have argued that not every human being is a human person and that the embryo, by reason of its immaturity, is not a human person with a right to life.[28]

The Marquess referred to the New Testament descriptions of the intrauterine personalities of John the Baptist and the Lord Jesus Christ, who were recognized by their mothers, Elizabeth and Mary.[28] The question, which the Warnock committee sidestepped, is compellingly answered in the incarnation of Jesus Christ. Luke, the doctor, described the angel Gabriel's announcement and how he answered Mary's question, 'How will this be since I am a virgin?' (Luke 1:34). Mary learned that God himself would become incarnate as an embryo, in the supernatural fertilization of her ovum by the Holy Spirit. If Jesus Christ's human life began with conception, the same must be true of each one of us.

The importance of the incarnation of Christ to understanding that human life begins at conception was illustrated when the Archbishop of York, John Habgood, who was sympathetic to embryo experimentation, cried out during a debate in the Church of England's General Synod, 'I don't want to hear anything more about the incarnation.'[29] Habgood, described as a scientist and philosopher, had a double first in natural sciences from Cambridge University.

Peter Singer agrees that the human embryo is a living human being from conception onwards, but states that only means the embryo is a living member of the species, *Homo sapiens*, which does not itself confer the 'right to life'.[30] Singer believes that human beings are just one of many evolved animal species. They should not be given priority or supremacy over all other animals. This is a logical consequence of belief in evolution. But is man just an evolved 'naked ape'[31], with no greater value or rights than other primates? Singer requires that there must be some 'morally relevant characteristics' for humans to be granted rights as 'a person'. He suggests consciousness, autonomy, rationality, but not race or species.[32]

Jesus Christ took upon himself flesh—he lived from his conception to his crucifixion without sinning. In Hebrews 2:14–15 we read the reason for his incarnation: 'Since the children have flesh and blood, he too shared in their humanity so that by his death he might destroy him who holds the power of death—that is, the devil—and free those who all their lives were held in slavery by their fear of death.'

NOTES

1 Alvin Schmidt, How Christianity Changed the World, (Grand Rapids, Michigan: Zondervan Publishing House, 2001), p. 56.

2 Nigel M. de S. Cameron, *The New Medicine—the Revolution in Technology and Ethics*, (London: Hodder and Stoughton, 1991), pp. 161–163.

3 '53 years of abortion: 9,675,153 lives lost since 1967—one unborn baby every 3 minutes', *Right to Life News*, 27th April 2021.

4 Patrick Carroll, *Assessing the Damage*, (London: Pension and Population Research Institute, 25 October 2007).

5 '53 years of abortion: 9,675,153 lives lost since 1967—one unborn baby every 3 minutes', *Right to Life News*, 27th April 2021.

6 S. Mahkorn, 'Pregnancy and Sexual Assault', in: *The Psychological Aspects of Abortion*, (Washington, DC: University Publication of America, 1979), p. 55–69.

7 David Reardon et al (Ed.), *Victims and Victors: Speaking Out About Their Pregnancies, Abortions, and Children Resulting from Sexual Assault*, (San Diego: Acorn Publishing, January 2000).

8 Ibid., p. 19.

9 Ibid., p. 20.

10 Ibid., p. 22.

11 Maureen Long, *Birthright? A Christian woman looks at abortion*, (London: Triangle SPCK, 1985), p. 73.

12 *Abortion Act 1967*—Legislation.gov.uk https://www.legislation.gov.uk/ukpga/1967/87/contents

13 *Infant Life (Preservation) Act 1929*—Legislation.gov.uk https://www.legislation.gov.uk/ukpga/Geo5/19-20/34/section/1

14 Genericmum, 'Peter Singer: The Ethics of Infanticide', Light up the Darkness blog, 7 May 2015. https://lightupthedarkness.net/peter-singer-the-ethics-of-infanticide/

15 Peter Singer, *Practical Ethics*, (New York: Cambridge University Press, Third Edition, 2011), pp. 151–152.

16 'Am I Still Not a Man and a Brother?' *Historians Against Slavery* www.historiansagainstslavery.org/main/2014/08/am-i-still-not-a-man-and-a-brother/

17 Peter Singer (Ed.), *'Persons and non-persons', in Defence of Animals*, (Oxford: Basil Blackwell, 1985), pp. 52–62.

18 *Warnock Report of the Committee of Inquiry into Human Fertilisation and Embryology*, July 1984. https://www.hfea.gov.uk/media/2608/warnock-report-of-the-committe

19 Ibid., para 11.9.

20 Genericmum, 'Peter Singer: The Ethics of Infanticide', Light up the Darkness blog, 7 May 2015. https://lightupthedarkness.net/peter-singer-the-ethics-of-infanticide/

21 'Murder of Newborn Babies in Infanticide as Bad as Abortion'. https://www.lifenews.com/2012/03/08/murder-of-newborn-babies-in-infanticide-as-bad-as-abortion/

22 James Watson, 'Children from the Laboratory', *Interview Prism Magazine*, May 1973, 1:13 https://citaty.net/autori/james-dewey-watson/

23 Peter Lawrence, 'A scientist unparalleled', *Current Biology*, Vol 19 No 22, pp. 1015–1018.

24 Michael Specter, 'The Dangerous Philosopher', *The New Yorker*. https://www.michaelspecter.com/1999/09/the-dangerous-philosopher

25 Nigel M. de S. Cameron (Ed.), Embryos and Ethics: Warnock Report in Debate, (Edinburgh: Rutherford House Books, 1987), pp. 4–5.

26 Mary Warnock, 'Do human cells have rights?', *Bioethics*, 1987a;1:1–14.

27 Lea Goetz, 'The Event Review: Anne McLaren—Science, Ethics and The Archive', *BioNews* 912, 7 August 2017.

28 'Human Fertilisation: Warnock Report', *Hansard, HL Debate*. The Marquess of Reading 31 October 1984, vol 456, pp. 535–536

29 Nigel M. de S. Cameron, *Creation and the Christian response to Warnock, a symposium*, (Rugby: Biblical Creation Society, 1985). Image in Embryo, p. 11.

30 Peter Singer, *Practical Ethics*, (New York: Cambridge University Press, Third Edition, 2011), p. 50.

31 Desmond Morris, *The Naked Ape: A Zoologist's Study of the Human Animal*, (London: Jonathan Cape, 1967).

32 Singer, *Practical Ethics*.

23 Medical ethics—respect is not enough!

In chapter 22, I explained that the sanctity of human life should be the foundational principle of medical ethics and discussed the dangers of the concept of *personhood*, when applied to ethical decisions relating to human beings. A further real danger exists when healthcare professionals and ethicists replace the word, *sanctity*, with the word, *respect*. These words are not equivalent. I will explain why *respect for human life* is both a dangerous and an unsafe principle for formulating medical ethics.

In chapter 21, I drew attention to the 1920 book, *The Freedom To Destroy Lives Not Worth Living*[1], that introduced the idea of 'life unworthy of life' which, in the opinion of the authors, meant that for some 'living people ... their destruction was not only tolerable but downright humane.' The lawyer and psychiatrist who authored the book were convinced that this showed *respect for human life*.

Since 1971, when Liz and I qualified as doctors, we have been members of the Christian Medical Fellowship (CMF).[2] We have benefited from the mutual support of Christian doctors at many national and regional conferences and our girls have enjoyed the children's programme run by a Scripture Union team. Christians have had different opinions about some aspects of medical ethics, though, by believing in the sanctity of human life, a degree of Christian unity has been achieved.

In 1984, CMF published a Symposium with the title, 'Respect for life',[3] which was a collection of four papers—the first two of which I believe were unhelpful. The first paper was an address given to the British Medical Association, in 1972, by the late Bishop of Durham, Ian T. Ramsey. The second paper was by Mr David R. Millar, a consultant obstetrician and gynaecologist in Sheffield. I will not comment on the other two papers.

The title of the booklet was unhelpful! The preface told me, 'The title has been chosen after some considerable thought and discussion.'[4] The title was acceptable because 'modern modifications of the old Hippocratic Code mainly speak of "respect" for life'. This downgrading of the Hippocratic Code, or Oath, was exactly why the title was wrong. *Respect for life* means different things to different people: respect can be qualified whereas sanctity of life cannot.

The Hippocratic Oath[5] stood as the ethical standard for medical practice for over 2,000 years and was adopted by the Christian church, and later by Islamic medicine as well. There are many positive promises, relating to the art and science of healing but, you may be surprised to learn, no mention of the relief of suffering![6] This does not deny that a duty of a doctor is to relieve pain and suffering. However, suffering is a relative matter, not only affecting the patient but also relatives and dependents. Often the patient's suffering can be relieved by their being healed or by compassion and pain relief. Pain relief is important to God: we read, in Revelation 21:4, that in heaven death, pain and suffering are abolished.

'Respect for life' may lead to Physician Assisted Suicide (PAS) or euthanasia. This may be with the agreement of the patient but, as The Remmelink Report[7] of 1991 showed, Dutch physicians, during

1990, deliberately and intentionally ended the lives of many patients without their request or consent. Professor John Keown, of Georgetown University USA, estimated, by reading The Remmelink Report, that 10,558 patients[8] died by lethal overdoses or injections in the Netherlands in 1990, while another estimate, by the Patients' Rights Council USA, suggested the figure was 11,840 patients[9]. The difference in these figures reflects difficulties in interpreting what The Remmelink Report means. The higher figure would mean that, in 1990, 9.1 per cent of the annual overall death rate of 130,000 that year, died by euthanasia, PAS, involuntary euthanasia or deliberate overdose of medication. Such behaviour by physicians is alarming.

Changes in the law in the Netherlands have legalized such practice, since 1991, and have led to lower numbers of euthanasia and PAS being recorded; however, the numbers of euthanasia cases as a percentage of the total number of deaths per year is rising every year. Regional Euthanasia Review Committees give authorized figures showing an increase from an estimated 1.9 per cent of all deaths in 1990 to 4.2 per cent in 2019.[10]

The 100 Dutch physicians who refused to sign transportation orders for euthanasia in the Nazi death camps are in stark contrast to many Dutch physicians today. The British journalist, Malcolm Muggeridge, writing in his 1984 essay, 'The Humane Holocaust', commented that it only took three decades 'to transform a war crime into an act of compassion'.[11]

The Declaration of Geneva[12], adopted after the Second World War, instead of embracing the sanctity of human life used the words, 'I will maintain the *utmost respect* for human life from the time of conception; even under threat.' It is good that conception was seen as the beginning of human life but, even with the adjective utmost, respect is not the absolute of 'the sanctity of human life'.

In the original Hippocratic Oath, the physician made his promises under the eye of four Greek gods of medicine; he knew that he was being watched! The Christian, of course, is answerable to the God of the Bible and, in truth, so is everybody else! Richard Dawkins concedes that believing 'God is watching us' is a restraint on people doing bad things.[13]

The World Medical Association unfortunately weakened the declaration by omitting any reference to God, allowing further weakening in later years. In 1983, in Venice, the Declaration of Geneva was weakened when 'from conception' was altered to 'from the beginning'. In 2006, any mention of unborn life was removed completely.[14] The gate was opened to terminating unborn human life as a matter of convenience. Today, babies are aborted in the same hospital as Special Care Baby Units fight for the lives of premature babies, sometimes of the same gestation or age!

In the CMF symposium, 'Respect for life', Ian Ramsey's contribution ended with the hope that multidisciplinary teams would make good medical decisions. His last two sentences appear naive. He said, 'Indeed, it is through such multiple, transdisciplinary groups as these, of which medical-moral groups are a particular case, that there will emerge the new culture, the new era of which all these problems, and many others like them, are, in the author's confident view but the travail and the birth pangs of a new culture and a new civilisation.'[15]

How can this be, if members of multidisciplinary teams are divided in their opinions and basis for medical ethics? Thirty-seven years later, there is no ethical unity; moral relativism and evolutionary dogma reign over the sanctity of human life.

Before discussing Mr David R. Millar's contribution to the CMF symposium, I wish to draw attention to the views of another Christian obstetrician and gynaecologist, Mr Rex Gardner of Sunderland, who David Millar quotes in his paper.

Rex Gardner worked in a mission hospital in northern Nigeria, where he was ordained as a minister of the United Free Church of Scotland. He was appointed as a consultant in Sunderland in 1965, two years before the 1967 Abortion Act. In 1972, he published his book, *Abortion, the personal dilemma*.[16]

In his book, he made two suggestions which confused and muddied the waters, particularly for Christians. The first related to foetuses which are lost during early pregnancy, often before the time of implantation. Rex Gardner concluded that, if full value as a human being is to be attributed at the moment of fertilization (conception), then the majority of beings in the afterlife will not be recognizably human.[17]

I would not deny that there is a theological/philosophical question to be asked about the future of miscarried foetuses. However, I suggest that question is best left to God, along with what happens to children who die in infancy? King David declared that he would go to be with his newborn child, who had just died, in 2 Samuel 12:22–23, and rested in that conviction. We should leave the secret things, which belong to God, in his hands and trust Him.

The second matter raised by Rex Gardner was this: 'While the foetus is to be cherished increasingly as it develops, we should regard its first breath at birth as the moment when God gives it, not only life, but the offer of Life.'[18] If this unusual view is placed alongside the incarnation of Christ and His intrauterine life as foetus and embryo, it appears indefensible. Consequently, Rex Gardner believed abortion at full-term could be morally acceptable in some circumstances.

A fair review of Rex Gardner's book is given by John Frame in, *The Doctrine of the Christian Life*.[19] John Frame is a Professor of Systematic Theology and Philosophy in Orlando, USA and has also published the book, *Medical Ethics*.[20] John Frame complements Rex Gardner on the breadth, detail and compassion of his book but describes a *tragic flaw* in his inadequate treatment of the Bible's teaching on the subject. He describes treatment of the biblical texts as superficial— for example, in discussing the passage in Exodus 21:22–25. Rex Gardner said there are three interpretations of the passage, one of which implies there is a difference in the eyes of the law between the foetus and a person! John Frame indicates that is precisely the opposite of what the verses say: verse 23 says that if, following a fight, a pregnant woman is struck and gives birth prematurely, then, if there is serious injury, a severe and serious penalty is due. The verse does not discriminate between mother and child; both we should presume could be affected by the serious injury.[21]

After 1967, many doctors simply followed the new abortion law as their ethical guide. I was present at a debate which took place at a CMF National Conference, in Swanwick, when it was clear that, among professing Christians, there were significant differences of opinion. Christian junior doctors were largely opposed to abortion. The CMF published a survey of 'Members Attitudes to Abortion'[22], in July 1996. It commented: 'There are indications that the present generation of students and junior doctors is more *conservative* than its predecessors.'[23] It also stated, 'There are perhaps worrying suggestions too that this new generation may vote with their feet and not go into areas of work that raise the threat of abortion.'[24]

Mr David R. Millar wrote, in his contribution to the CMF symposium, which quoted Rex Gardner, 'I sometimes wish that I could agree that there are no moral grounds for abortion, other than a strict saving of the mother's life—a very rare situation in real clinical practice. But it is my testimony that prayer helps in my more difficult decisions, and that my gracious Lord seems to take my guilt away.'[25] He appeared to admit the wrongness of his actions.

David Millar ended his paper by saying:

> Legal abortion will never increase our respect for life. Despite selectively destroying many thousands of babies thought to be 'at risk' socially, the incidence of 'baby battering' continues to rise. The need for induced abortion is a social evil, but what is wrong for the community may not always be so wrong for the individual. I have concentrated, perhaps too much, on the diminished value of foetal life in relation to child destruction. Perhaps I should have emphasized how modern medicine has made equally dramatic advances in, and is vitally concerned with, treating infertility, preventing miscarriage and premature labour and keeping tiny neonates alive. The efforts of our paediatric colleagues in intensive care units, and the immense cost of such treatment, in some measure act as a balance to legal abortion in the assessment of how today's experts in perinatal medicine value the baby.[25]

For the sake of truth, the personal views of Ian Ramsey, David Millar and Rex Gardner needed to be examined and I suggest fall short of the Bible's teaching. How can abortion be a social evil and wrong for the community and at the same time 'not always be so wrong for the individual', as David Miller suggested.

Having looked, firstly, at the issue of 'personhood', I will now focus on a second 'Trojan Horse' of medical ethics. I draw your attention to an unbalanced view of 'personal autonomy'. While an important ethical principle, personal autonomy must not be seen as a 'stand-alone' principle which trumps all other ethical principles.

A danger in ethical decision-making arises if *the personal autonomy of a patient* is allowed to rule all decisions. If a patient concludes that they wish to end their own life, they may seek for physician-assisted suicide (PAS) or euthanasia. This choice will impact on relatives, who may be unhappy about the request, and on the wider public. If PAS or euthanasia were legalized, then pressure would be brought on those in society who are vulnerable, lonely or depressed. Some doctors would consider that *respect for human life* in these circumstances would mean they should assist a patient's suicide or actually kill the patient. The physician committed to the Hippocratic Oath, vowed never to do either of those things, and always sought a better way to care.

Medical care becomes unbalanced and dangerous if *personal autonomy* is not balanced by other ethical principles. The outcome for the patient and for the rest of society will be poor. John Donne, the poet, wrote in 1624, 'No man is an island entire of itself; every man is a piece of the continent, a part of the main; ... any man's death diminishes me, because I am involved in mankind.'[26] Donne describes that no one is self-sufficient but that we all depend upon others for support and comfort. If man is in an isolated place, Donne said, he does badly. If a patient finds themselves in a painful, lonely experience and all options of support and treatment are not clarified, they will look for the easiest way out at the hands of a doctor!

A little background will be helpful as I continue to describe the Christian worldview. I have been privileged to be an Associate Lecturer in Newcastle University, teaching medical ethics to undergraduate medical students for ten years, since I retired from clinical practice. There are different frameworks for the teaching and practice of ethics which have been debated for more than 2,000 years. Different approaches have different outcomes.

One system, which focuses on the needs of society in healthcare decisions, is the *Utilitarian* approach.[27] It is based on the idea that the right thing to do is to create the greatest good for the greatest number of people. There are 'victims' of this approach if it leads to the needs of an individual patient being relegated. Rather like a mathematical formula, the *utility calculus* calculates the sum of all pleasure that results from an action, minus the suffering of anyone involved in the action, as the basis of ethical decision-making. Philosophers, such as Epicurus, around 300 BC, believed that happiness is the highest good and should be the driver and the goal of all our actions.

The Utilitarian approach thinks of people in categories. Conversely, the God of the Bible does not categorize people but requires that the personal circumstances of every individual patient, made in His image, should be considered when decisions are made. This does not mean that we strive officiously to preserve life when such action is futile or inappropriate.

Another ethical system, *Deontology*[28] is based on rules or morals which determine whether an action is right or wrong. But we may rightly ask, who makes those rules or defines those morals. In the face of moral relativism within a society, there is no guarantee that medical decisions will be based on the absolute of the *sanctity of human life*. Deontology requires us to do 'the right thing' without regard to the consequences of that action. In contrast to utilitarianism, deontology is patient centred, claiming to do what is in the best interest of the patient.

I have mentioned two ethical systems to show the tensions which can occur in medical decision-making. The favoured system usually taught to medical students is the four ethical principles of US philosophers, Beauchamp and Childress. The first edition of their book, *Principles of Biomedical Ethics*[29], appeared in 1979.

The four principles are:

- *Beneficence*—The principle of acting with the best interest of the patient in mind and with substantial benefit.
- *Non-maleficence*—The principle 'above all, do no harm', as implied in the Hippocratic Oath (Latin: *Primum non nocere*).
- *Personal Autonomy*—An individual has the right to make his or her own choice; assuming that he or she is competent to do so.
- *Justice*—A concept that emphasizes fairness and equality in the distribution and availability of healthcare among individuals.

Beauchamp and Childress have sought to address criticisms over the years. Their principles remain a helpful theoretical framework from which to analyse ethical situations in medicine. I found that, when discussing ethical issues with medical students, the strength of using these four principles lies in using *all of them* in analysing any problem. It is wrong, for example, to say that *personal autonomy* is a principle of greater importance than others.

The word, 'autonomy', derives from the Greek roots, *auto*, meaning, 'self', and *nomos*, meaning, 'custom' or 'law'. So, autonomy means, 'self-law'. A thief robbing a house may have his self-law but that does not make his actions right. Our autonomy (personal wishes) has an effect on others. I will discuss the campaign to legalize *physician assisted suicide* to show how an unbalanced view of personal autonomy will lead to harmful consequences.

Despite several campaigns to legalize Physician Assisted Suicide (PAS), this has not been allowed in the UK. The *British Medical Journal* (BMJ), published by the British Medical Association (BMA), has editorial freedom to express opinions which may not necessarily agree with BMA policy. BMJ editors have campaigned for the legalization of euthanasia and PAS for at least eighteen years.[30]

In the BMJ of 2 July 2014, three editors, Tony Delamothe, Rosamund Snow and Fiona Godlee, wrote an editorial on 'Why the Assisted Dying Bill should become law in England and Wales.' The bill referred to, had been introduced in the House of Lords by Lord Falconer but did not become law. They wrote:

> People should be able to exercise choice over their lives, which should include how and when they die, when death is imminent. In recent decades, respect for autonomy has emerged as the cardinal principle in medical ethics and underpins developments in informed consent, patient confidentiality, and advance directives. Recognition of an individual's right to determine his or her best interests lies at the heart of efforts to advance patient partnership.[31]

I have used italics to highlight an untrue statement made by these editors as they endeavoured to impose their worldview upon patients and the nursing and medical professions. *Personal autonomy is not the cardinal principle in medical ethics.* The other three principles are equally important. In countries where PAS has been legalized, initial restrictions have been softened, indications widened and the principal of doing no harm, *non-maleficence,* has been eroded. To illustrate what was wrong with the BMJ editors' view, I will quote from two Rapid Responses published by the BMJ and still available online.

The first response, dated 7 July 2014, was by Dr Marina E Malthouse. At that time, she was a consultant in palliative care in a hospice in Wiltshire. She opposed the argument that autonomy is the cardinal principle in medical ethics. She wrote:

> But they forget that autonomy is relational and that medical ethics does not stand apart from social ethics in which individuals within society (who may lack or have less autonomy) are protected by laws in the interest of societal welfare as a whole. Many dying individuals who had autonomy become vulnerable and less autonomous often through fear, loneliness and a loss of independence as they become weaker. With financial pressures in and outside the NHS they also can be victims of subtle coercion that they may be wasting resources. If society, including the medical profession, took notice of and attended to the vulnerabilities of individuals who are dying, more could be gained at a societal level rather than offer a path of elimination from society through assisting death by suicide.

She continued: 'We must not pretend it is compassionate to give patients the message that they would be better off dead and to normalize medical foreshortening of life. The truly compassionate response is for our society to improve both care provision and consider our attitudes on what it is to be human.'[32]

The second response, dated 5 August 2014, was from Dr David Jeffrey, an Honorary Lecturer in Palliative Medicine, University of Edinburgh. He wrote:

> However, autonomy is a relational concept that involves people considering the effect of their choices on the autonomy of others. Respect for autonomy has to be balanced against other ethical principles, such as the duty of beneficence and the primacy of not causing harm and of being fair to others. The 'four principle approach' is only one of many ways of looking at ethical dilemmas. Virtue ethics considers what the good doctor would choose to do. Currently, doctors are in no doubt of the absolute prohibition on helping to hasten a patient's death. The editorial takes no account of the reality and complexity of end-of-life care at the bedside. It is naive to assume that it is straightforward to assess mental capacity in a dying patient. Depression can be difficult to identify, and if the diagnosis is missed all 'safeguards' disappear. In 2013, of the 71 patients who committed suicide under the Death with Dignity Act in Oregon, only two were referred for formal psychological or psychiatric assessment. The prescribing doctor was present at the death in only 11.4% of the patients who committed suicide—a lonely choice indeed.[33]

When I was discussing assisted suicide with medical students, they often correctly pointed out that the 1961 Suicide Act[34] had decriminalized suicide and so, every individual has the autonomous right to commit suicide. Two observations need to be made. Firstly, that the motivation for decriminalizing suicide in England and Wales, in 1961, was not a toleration of suicide but a desire to be understanding, helpful and sympathetic towards the 'failed suicide patient' and to the families of the 'successful suicides'. Secondly, suicide almost always has devastating consequences on those left behind.[35]

Each year, since 2003, World Suicide Prevention Day[36] is celebrated on 10 September. The aim is to reduce the, approximately, one million suicides each year. But, paradoxically, a campaign continues to introduce legislation which would allow doctors and nurses to help patients to kill themselves in the UK!

We must recognize that the so-called 'right to die' in reality can become the 'duty to die' in the minds of vulnerable people. The phrase, 'I do not want to be a burden on anyone,' is frequently said by the elderly. The fact that God put us in families to care for each other, is a truth overlooked by many in our society. I assume that people would be shocked to hear a little child say, 'I don't want to be a burden on anyone,' and work to reverse such an emotion.

Infants need feeding, protection and care. The elderly, because of frailty, may also need feeding, protection and care. Because of the desire to be 'in control', adults may find it difficult to accept help. However, the need for care in infancy and old age is a reality which a caring and loving family offers. For those vulnerable individuals who lack family support, adoption for the young and care homes for the elderly are norms in civilized society. In a caring family, grandchildren love and enjoy grandparents' company and storytelling, and those grandparents realize they have much to offer their loved ones.

Under the title, 'Dementia sufferers may have a duty to die',[37] philosopher, Mary Warnock, wrote in the *Daily Telegraph* on 18 September 2008, 'If you're demented, you're wasting people's lives—your family's lives—and you're wasting the resources of the National

Health Service.' Later, on 15 January 2011, Mary Warnock debated with Os Guinness, Christian author and apologist, in the robing chamber of the House of Lords.[38] Their conversation was recorded. Os Guinness was due to speak at the House of Lords on how Christian religious freedoms should be treated in a pluralistic society. Mary Warnock insisted that she was a Christian but, when asked if she actually believed in the historical truth of the biblical accounts, she replied that she did not. She said the stories were man-made.

She and Os Guinness were in agreement about the positive impact of Christianity on the United Kingdom and she indicated that she wished that impact to continue. However, she said that the historical truthfulness of Christianity has nothing to do with public policy and should be strictly kept out of any public policy discussion. Her book, *Dishonest to God*,[39] argues that religious and theological issues should have no place in issues of public morality, particularly euthanasia, assisted suicide, and abortion. As a cross bench peer in the House of Lords, she was an influential voice arguing for liberalization of euthanasia laws.

The protagonists of 'the right to die', focus on PAS rather than euthanasia. They understand that if PAS were legalized, then the case for euthanasia would be impossible to resist. However, there is a significant failure rate to PAS and, in such circumstances, the doctor, who we have noted in the US state of Oregon was rarely present, must be called to administer euthanasia, which was not legalized in 'The Oregon Death with Dignity Act, 1967.'[40]

A paper, 'Clinical Problems with the Performance of Euthanasia and Physician-Assisted Suicide in the Netherlands,'[41] by Hanny Groenewoud et al., was published in 2000. This analysed 114 cases of PAS, showing that it was necessary for the physician to administer a lethal medication in 21 of the cases (18 percent) which, thus, became cases of euthanasia. The main reasons given for this were *failures of completion* (twelve of the patients did not die) and the inability of five patients to take all the medication.

Finally, I quote what Lord Ian McColl, former Professor of Surgery at Guy's Hospital, said in a speech in the House of Lords, in 2003, after a visit to the Netherlands:[42]

> Noble Lords will be aware that the Select Committee visited Holland. When we inquired of a doctor what it was like doing the first case of euthanasia, he said, 'We agonised all day. It was terrible.' But he said that the second case was much easier and the third case—I quote—'was a piece of cake'. We found that very chilling indeed. What is even more alarming is that euthanasia is being given to depressed and disabled people, which has to be uncivilized behaviour.

Respect is not enough—our family, loved ones, patients, fellow humans made in God's image, should not be put down like injured animals. Our consciences must remain alert to the sanctity of human life.

NOTES

1 Karl Binding & Alfred Hoche, *Die Freigabe der Vernichtung Lebensunwerten Lebens*, 1920, The Project Gutenberg eBook, p. 32.

2 Christian Medical Fellowship https://www.cmf.org.uk.

3 *Respect for life—A Symposium*, (London: Christian Medical Fellowship Publications, 1984).

4 Ibid., p. 5.

5 Nigel M. de S. Cameron, *The New Medicine—the Revolution in Technology and Ethics*, (London: Hodder and Stoughton, 1991), pp. 24–34.

6   Ibid., pp. 131–139.

7   *Remmelink report*: Dutch government,—Remmelink 1991 https://archive.org/details/RemmelinkReport

8   John Keown, *Euthanasia in the Netherlands: sliding down the slippery slope?* (London: Centre for Bioethics and Public Policy, 1995), p. 15.

9   *Background about Euthanasia in The Netherlands* https://www.patientsrightscouncil.org/site/holland-background

10 A. S. Groenewoud et al., 'Euthanasia in the Netherlands: a claims data cross-sectional study of geographical variation', *BMJ Supportive & Palliative Care* 2021;0: pp. 1–11.

11 Malcolm Muggeridge, 'The humane holocaust', Cited in: Ronald Reagan, *Abortion and the conscience of the nation*, (Nashville, Tennessee: Thomas Nelson Publishers, 1984), pp. 75–94.

12 *Declaration of Geneva—The World Medical Association* https://www.wma.net/what-we-do/medical-ethics/declaration-of-geneva

13 Richard Dawkins, 'Ending religion is a bad idea', *The Times*, 5 October 2019. https://www.thetimes.co.uk/article/ending-religion-is-a-bad-idea-says-richard-dawkins-sqqdbmcpq

14 *Declaration of Geneva—The World Medical Association* https://www.wma.net/what-we-do/medical-ethics/declaration-of-geneva

15 *Respect for life—A Symposium*, p. 22.

16 Rex Gardner, *Abortion—the personal dilemma*, (Milton Keynes: The Paternoster Press, 1972).

17 Ibid., p. 123.

18 Rex Gardner, *Abortion—the personal dilemma*, p. 126.

19 John Frame, *The Doctrine of the Christian Life*, (New Jersey: P&R Publishing Co, 2008).

20 John Frame, *Medical Ethics—Principles, Persons and Problems*, (New Jersey: P&R Publishing Co, 1988).

21 John Frame, *The Doctrine of the Christian Life*, pp. 994–997.

22 *Members Attitudes to Abortion: a survey of reported views and practice*, (London: Christian Medical Fellowship, July 1996).

23 Ibid., p. 18.

24 Ibid., p. 18.

25 *Respect for life—A Symposium*, p. 30.

26 John Donne, MEDITATION XVII *Devotions upon Emergent Occasions*, 1624. https://www.luminarium.org/sevenlit/donne/meditation17.php

27 Carla Tardi, 'Utilitarianism', *Investopedia*, updated 20 September 2021. www.investopedia.com/terms/u/utilitarianism.asp

28 *Deontology—Ethics Unwrapped*, ethicsunwrapped.utexas.edu/glossary/deontology.

29 Beauchamp T. L., Childress J. F., *Principles of Biomedical Ethics, 8th ed.*, (Oxford University Press USA, 2019).

30 'What is a good death? Editor's choice: Death, come closer', *British Medical Journal* Vol 327 No:7408, 26 July 2003.

31 Delamothe T., Snow R., Godlee F., 'Why the Assisted Dying Bill should become law in England and Wales', *British Medical Journal* 2014; 349: g4349, p. 10.

32 Marina Malthouse, *Rapid Responses*: 7th July 2014, Hospice Consultant in Palliative Care BA1 2XJ

33 David Jeffrey, Rapid Responses: 5th August 2014, Honorary Lecturer in Palliative Medicine, University of Edinburgh.

34 *Suicide Act 1961*—Legislation.gov.uk https://www.legislation.gov.uk/ukpga/Eliz2/9-10/60

35 Jeremy Bouma, '9 Ways Suicide Affects Others', *Zondervan Academic*, 11 May 2018. https://zondervanacademic.com/blog/how-suicide-affects-others

36 *World Suicide Prevention Day—Samaritans*, https://www.samaritans.org/support-us/campaign/world-suicide-prevention-day

37 Mary Warnock, 'Dementia sufferers may have a duty to die', *Daily Telegraph*, 18 September 2008.

38 'Unbelievable?—Os Guinness & Mary Warnock debate religious freedoms.' *Premier Christian Radio*, Saturday 15th January 2011.

39 Mary Warnock, *Dishonest to God: On Keeping Religion Out of Politics*, (Bloomsbury Continuum, 2010).

40 'Oregon's Death With Dignity Act', 1997. *Oregon Health Authority*: https://www.oregon.gov/.../deathwithdignityact/pages/faqs.aspx

41 Hanny Groenewoud et al., 'Clinical Problems with the Performance of Euthanasia and Physician-Assisted Suicide in the Netherlands', *The N Engl J Med* 342:8 2000, pp. 551–556.

42 'Hansard contribution by Lord McColl of Dulwich on Friday 6 June 2003', Column

1682. https://hansard.parliament.uk/Lords/2003-06-06/debates/bf190b92-0209-402e-904d-807cdbaee6b0/Patient(AssistedDying)BillHl

24 Consciousness and the mind

In chapter 10, I referred to the book, *A Short History of Nearly Everything*, written by Bill Bryson. You may remember he asked the question, 'How did we get from nothing to something?'[1] Early in his book, he expressed wonder at how trillions of drifting atoms had somehow assembled into an intricate being, which is you and me. He also posed the question, 'Why do atoms take the trouble to do this?'[2] In this chapter I want to consider the origin of the human brain, our minds and consciousness that lead to logic, memory and rational thought. Bryson's questions are difficult to answer, if we look to the non-directed process of evolution for answers.

Martin Rees, the Astronomer Royal since 1995, was lecturing at the Royal Irish Academy, in Dublin, in 2002, when he said, 'Every atom we are made of has an origin that can be traced back to before the solar system was formed. We are literally the ashes of dead stars or the nuclear waste left behind.'[3] Stephen Jay Gould said, in 1984, on American TV, 'If the history of life teaches us any lesson, it is that human beings arose as a kind of glorious accident ... surely a kind of glorious cosmic accident resulting from the catenation (linking) of thousands of improbable events.'[4] He was claiming that our minds and consciousness have arisen from stardust, by accident.

Whenever did cars, trains or aeroplanes, that have been in a bad accident, look like anything other than a heap of scrap metal? Gould's suggestion that a *cosmic accident* could produce a good outcome is illogical. Accidents usually produce disorder and the *Second Law of Thermodynamics* states that there is a natural tendency for any isolated system to degenerate into a more disordered state. 'Stardust to man' is as improbable as Darwin's 'warm little pond to man'.

Professor V. S. Ramachandran is the Director of the Centre for Brain and Cognition at the University of California, San Diego, United States. He is a popular public lecturer on the functioning of the human brain and diseases which can affect the brain. In 2003, he gave five Reith lectures, broadcast on BBC radio, entitled, *The Emerging Mind*.[5] In my own area of surgery, he has made helpful contributions in the management of *phantom limbs*—when a patient, who has experienced amputation of a limb, not only continues to feel the limb, but often feels extreme pain mimicking the limb before it was amputated.

Professor Ramachandran, holding to the evolutionary worldview, asks, 'How can a three-pound mass of jelly, that you can hold in your palm imagine angels, contemplate the meaning of infinity, and even question its own place in the cosmos? Especially awe-inspiring is the fact that any single brain, including yours, is made up of atoms that were forged in the hearts of countless, far-flung stars billions of years ago. These particles drifted for eons and light-years until gravity and change brought them together here, now. These atoms now form a conglomerate—your brain—that can not only ponder the very stars that gave it birth but can also think about its own ability to think and wonder about its own ability to wonder. With the arrival of humans, it has been said, the universe has suddenly become conscious of itself. This, truly, is the greatest mystery of all.'[6]

Professor Ramachandran describes the mind and consciousness as the greatest mystery of all. But, because he is convinced that our brains are made from stardust, he is stuck in an intellectual dead-end. His bias is impeding his journey to the truth. Ken Ham, an Australian Biblical creationist, living in the USA, has said that we are all biased—we come with a pre-existing worldview to every situation. The question that we need to answer, he says, is, 'Which bias is the best bias with which to be biased?'[7] Bryson, Rees, Gould and Ramachandran all appear star-struck by the Victorian celebrity, Charles Darwin, but I suggest that Darwin's theory sheds very little starlight on this great mystery!

Moving on, it will be helpful to describe what the mind is. In simple terms, the mind is that part of a person which generates thoughts, memories, emotions, logic and awareness. One view of the mind is that it is the product of brain activity. Consciousness is a property of the mind through which thoughts, memories and experiences have their existence. So, we find ourselves asking, 'Is the mind simply the physical workings of the brain? Indeed, are the mind and brain identical?'

A subtly different view is that the mind (something distinct and different from the brain) is generated when the different components of the brain combine in activity. If the different components of the brain were significantly damaged or the person dies, the mind would no longer exist. A third view, which may be a little more difficult to understand, is that the mind is beyond the brain. According to this view the mind and brain can interact but also operate independently of each other. There are also other theories about the mind and the brain which are very complex and, for that reason, I will not be discussing those.

It is important that neuroscientists endeavour by research to understand these matters. The treatment of mental disease is increasingly important, particularly among young people. Psychiatrists treating mental illness often prescribe medication or other physical therapies to help their patients. Knowing how and where in the brain these drugs work is helpful in understanding mental illness. Psychologists also collaborate with patients suffering from anxiety, stress in particular situations, or other conditions and help to train the mind of their patients to deal with their problems in a more positive way.

Magnetic Resonance Imaging (MRI) and Positron Emission Tomography (PET) scanning have allowed new insights into brain function and particularly in such conditions as Persistent Vegetative State (PVS). This condition, caused by severe brain injury due to trauma or a severe lack of oxygen to the brain, means that the higher cortical functions of the brain (movement, sensation, conversation, attention etc.) are destroyed, while brainstem function (breathing and heart function) is preserved. Such patients appear unresponsive to questioning. A research project between the Universities of Liège and Cambridge studied fifty-four patients with suspected PVS, who underwent functional MRI scanning. Their paper, 'Wilful Modulation of Brain Activity in Disorders of Consciousness',[8] was published in the *New England Journal of Medicine*, in 2010. If patients wanted to answer, 'Yes', to a question, they were asked to think of playing tennis strokes while in the scanner. If they wanted to answer, 'No', they were asked to think of walking around the rooms of their home. Obeying this command in normal controls causes particular areas of the brain to 'light up'. When five of the fifty-four patients were able to wilfully modulate their brain activity in response to these questions by their 'brain lighting up', this was inconsistent with a diagnosis of PVS. Three of the five patients, on closer clinical examination, did show some sign of awareness, though the remaining two patients did not.

The literature indicates that scientists are searching for the answer to, 'How did consciousness emerge?' Almost all conclude that this is a very difficult question to answer. Another question which is asked is, 'When did consciousness emerge?' To begin to address these two questions, I want to give you a taste of how a modern textbook of physiology describes *how* consciousness emerged and then a leading anthropologist's opinion about *how and when* cognition emerged.

This extract is from a textbook currently available to medical students in Newcastle University's Medical School Library. In *Human Physiology: An Integrated Approach*[9], by Dee Unglaub Silverthorn, we can read:

> Earliest emergence of consciousness in evolution probably started with tenuous and feeble self-reflective bodily feelings, e.g., of pressure, tension, duration, etc. (Herrick, 1949). Primitive consciousness may have gained some evolutionary advantage when it generated tenuous, self-protective influences, e.g., biasing of kinetics, relaxing of tensions, altering of rhythms, etc. In any case, a fuller blown consciousness is available to us now and obviously involves both reflective and directive functions, including consciously directed behaviours—culminating, for example, in social

altruism which can confer exemplary evolutionary advantages (Herrick, 1956).

Throughout its evolutionary development, consciousness, along with other nervous improvements, contributes to improving internal satisfactions. Now we need desperately to sustain human survival. For that, it is necessary that we cultivate self-conscious thinking about our collective long-range interests, and cooperative strategies that will ensure an increasingly satisfying future for all humankind. Collective evolutionary advantages that are achievable through consciously directed constructive adaptations are essentially unlimited.

When I read this, the words, *'In any case'*, stood out. Having talked about something probably happening and then maybe having gained some evolutionary advantage, the author suddenly takes a leap of faith to full-blown consciousness. What do I mean? The author might just as well have said, 'We don't really know how full-blown consciousness arose but because it is available to us, it must have evolved!' The second paragraph drifts into philosophical remarks about 'internal satisfactions'. An appeal is made for self-conscious thinking about how we all can ensure an increasingly satisfying future for all humankind. Why these are described as, 'collective evolutionary advantages', is unclear.

Ian Tattersall M.A., M.Phil., Ph.D. is the Curator Emeritus of Human Origins at the American Museum of Natural History in New York.[10] His C.V. lists research interests including human and nonhuman primate evolution, as well as the anatomical and cognitive origin of *Homo sapiens*. So, some of his research focuses on how we became thinking primates! In November 2015, he gave an address to the American Philosophical Society, explaining how *cognition* emerged in humans. *Cognition* means the mental process of gaining knowledge or understanding through thinking, experience and our senses.

A written record of his address, 'The Thinking Primate: Establishing a Context for the Emergence of Modern Human Cognition'[11], can be found online. I quote from his opening paragraph:

> Of course, even after many years of neurobiological investigation and extravagant hypothesizing, the neuroanatomical basis of our unusual cognitive style still stubbornly resists reductionist explanation; and it consequently remains true, remarkably enough, that the only reason we have for believing that an ancestor broadly equivalent cognitively to today's great apes could ever have given rise to a descendant that reasons as we do, is that it so self-evidently did.

I drew attention in the earlier paragraph to the phrase, *'in any case'*. Ian Tattersall has given us an honest appraisal of what was known in 2015. Does the phrase, *'it so self-evidently did'*, sound like a scientific proof? He thinks that the only way this could have come about is by evolution. Ian Tattersall is confident that the evolutionary tree of life affirms this: 'There can be no rational doubt whatever that we living *Homo sapiens* are fully integrated into the great Tree of Life that unites all living organisms on this planet.'

For the sake of brevity and to try and do justice to Ian Tattersall's address, I will summarize some of the main steps in his thinking, though quotes are in italics. He said, *'What seems to have happened is that Homo sapiens appeared as a distinctive anatomical entity in Africa at about 200,000 years ago.'* While they were anatomically different from other hominids for 100,000 years, they did not behave any differently. Then, they began to produce symbolic objects (a sign of cognition). *'Very soon after that, populations descended from those first symbolic humans, exited Africa and rapidly took over the world.'* ('Symbolic objects' means tools etc.)

At the 200,000-years milestone in human evolution, it is postulated that *'the genetic innovation involved'* had wider consequences than just anatomical changes.

> It evidently had cascading developmental consequences throughout the body; and there is no reason to believe that those consequences should necessarily have been confined to the skeletal and dental systems, which are all that the fossil record preserves. They could well have affected the internal organization of the brain, creating or allowing the formation of the physical pathways that permit the complex mental associations that are the hallmark of humankind today.

He then describes this new potential for cognition being unused for a *'short but significant lapse of time'*. This is deduced from *'the unremarkable archaeological record associated with the earliest Homo sapiens. ... Eventually, at around 100,000 years ago',* he suggests a new stimulus appeared which allowed *Homo sapiens* to use the latent potential in his brain; *'the most plausible candidate we have for it was the invention of language'.* He describes how *'language and thought are so closely intertwined that they appear to be functionally, if not conceptually, inseparable. ... From the linguistic perspective, there is no compelling reason to believe that the invention of language by a biologically predisposed hominid could not have been a more or less instantaneous event,'* he said. He comments that *'language is an externalized attribute that would have been poised to spread rapidly within a species that was already biologically enabled for it.'*

Having read these two implausible paragraphs in which Tattersall has accounted for the development of the brain and language, you might ask, 'How is the *Homo sapiens* going to speak?' The surprise answer is that the *Homo sapiens* is a species that was already biologically enabled for it. This may seem strange, but it is important to understand where belief in evolution leads. I will continue to quote from Tattersall's address:

> Exaptation is the routine evolutionary process whereby novelties arise in contexts entirely other than the ones in which they will eventually be co-opted, much as bony limbs were initially acquired by the marine ancestors of the terrestrial tetrapods (See chapter 7 of this book, where "fins were modified into limbs"). This same evolutionary mechanism also neatly explains how the highly derived modern vocal tract was in place at precisely the point when it was needed for the expression of language. The proportions of the upper vocal tract that permit articulate speech are very different from those of more primitive hominids, such as the Neanderthals; but they may, in fact, be no more than incidental by-products of the retraction of the face beneath the braincase, that is the most fundamental cranial specialization of Homo sapiens. If that is true, the long-running argument over the condition of the larynx and other structures of the upper vocal tract in various fossil hominids is actually irrelevant to the precise point in human history at which language was acquired. The modern vocal tract was there first, as it had to be.[11]

The debate between Science and Religion (or particularly Christianity) is caricatured by Richard Dawkins as a debate between Facts and Faith. The previous paragraph shows that the debate is between Faith and Faith. Tattersall believes that the human larynx (the modern vocal tract) was fully developed and present in the hominid, just waiting to be used when the hominid decided to start talking. This belief is an act of faith; he has not provided us with facts to support his claim, other than the fact that '*exaptation ... neatly explains it.*' He tells us that the modern vocal tract had to be there first, so man could talk.

In this chapter I have drawn attention to drifting atoms which, it is claimed, became you and me, though how along the way inorganic chemicals became proteins or where genetic information came from has never been explained. Ian Tattersall's address seems to undermine the theory of evolution and reads like another Kipling story.

As I consider consciousness and the mind, I think back to a remark made by Professor Fred Hoyle in *The Nature of the Universe*, where he poses what he calls, 'perhaps the most inscrutable question of all: do our minds have any continued existence after death?' He said:

> Mind is an intricate organisation of matter. In so far as the organisation can be remembered and reproduced there is no such thing as death. If ordinary atoms of carbon, oxygen, hydrogen, nitrogen, etc., could be fitted together into exactly the structural organisation of Homer, or of Titus Oates, then these individuals would come alive again exactly as they were originally. The whole issue therefore turns on whether our particular organisation is remembered in some fashion. If it is, there is no death. If it is not, there is complete oblivion.[12]

Was Hoyle out of his mind? Presumably, Hoyle is thinking of a material object, the brain, when he describes fitting together the exact structural organization of Homer, or of Titus Oates. Homer is described by Herodotus as having been born in 850 BC. He was the presumed author of, *The Iliad*, and, *The Odyssey*. Titus Oates is known for fabricating the Popish plot—a supposed Catholic plot to assassinate Charles II. He was found guilty of perjury and spent three years in prison.

The men whose views I have been describing in this chapter have been, and are, highly intelligent. Their minds could be described as bright and fertile. But are their descriptions of the origin of the human mind plausible? Evolution describes a process occurring over millions of years, though 'real man', *Homo sapiens,* only appears about 200,000 years ago and then does not speak for another 100,000 years. Perhaps Ian Tattersall's most helpful remark was, 'Mankind's ability to think still stubbornly resists reductionist explanation.'

Ian Tattersall's frustration is worth exploring. I believe his desire to understand *mankind's ability to think* is thwarted by his belief in 'reductive materialism'. This view holds that only the material world i.e., 'matter' is truly real. Any process or reality, which we experience, can be reduced to basic scientific components. These will include atoms, molecules and anything else which makes up 'matter'. The view suggests that thought processes, experienced by our minds, are determined entirely by the movement of atoms and action of chemicals in our brains.

In chapters 6 and 16, I introduced J. B. S. Haldane, atheist and evolutionary biologist. In spite of an evolutionary belief consistent with reductive materialism, he made surprising remarks about his mind in his book, *Possible Worlds and Other Essays*, published in 1927. In a chapter entitled, 'When I am Dead', he wrote:

But if death will probably be the end of me as a finite individual mind, that does not mean that it will be the end of me altogether. It seems to me immensely unlikely that mind is a mere by-product of matter. For if my mental processes are determined wholly by the motions of atoms in my brain, I have no reason to suppose that my beliefs are true. They may be sound chemically, but that does not make them sound logically. And hence I have no reason for supposing my brain to be composed of atoms.[13]

Haldane continued: 'Without that body it may perish altogether, but it seems to me quite as probable that it will lose its limitations and be merged into an infinite mind or something analogous to a mind which I have reason to suspect probably exists behind nature. How this might be accomplished I have no idea.'

Haldane's remarks perhaps reflect Pantheism. 'A mind behind nature', might be another way of saying, 'Mother Nature',—a mythical being, to whom many thoughtlessly attribute intelligence and the ability to create. Pantheism believes that 'God' is the world, nature itself, and that all of reality, including the cosmos, is identical with divinity and a supreme supernatural entity. Because the Universe is understood to be still expanding, some see creative activity continuing as it has since the beginning of time. Such is the 'God' of philosopher, Baruch Spinoza, who Albert Einstein believed in. Einstein said that 'Spinoza's God, reveals himself in the lawful harmony of the world, not in a God who concerns himself with the fate and doings of mankind.'[14]

Why should a belief in pantheism be so attractive to the likes of J. B. S. Haldane or Albert Einstein? I believe that it is because the supreme supernatural entity of pantheism makes no moral demands upon those who hold such beliefs. They are free to live their lives as they choose with no reference to the authority of the God of the Bible. No rules for how mankind should live are given by a pantheistic deity.

As quoted in chapter 26, Richard Dawkins wrote in his book, *River Out of Eden*, 'In a universe of blind physical forces and genetic replication, some people are going to get hurt, other people are going to get lucky, and you won't find any rhyme or reason in it, nor any justice. The universe we observe has precisely the properties we should expect if there is, at bottom, no design, no purpose, no evil and no good, nothing but blind, pitiless indifference.'[15] When Richard Dawkins heard an open-air preacher speaking in the Cornmarket in Oxford, in June 2012, he asserted that no one could go along with what the preacher was saying and told him that his brain 'was only a lump of meat!'[16] One presumes that Dawkins' own brain was also a lump of meat and its conclusions cannot be trusted.

C. S. Lewis was converted firstly to theism, and later to Christianity, partly by reflecting on the origin of rational thought and the mind. In his book, *Miracles*, he wrote, 'Nature is quite powerless to produce rational thought … a train of thought loses all rational credentials as soon as it can be shown to be wholly the result of non-rational causes.'[17]

C. S. Lewis talked about the mind, during a series of addresses about Christianity on BBC radio, broadcast between August 1941 to April 1944.[18] He said, 'Supposing there was no intelligence behind the universe, no creative mind. In that case, nobody designed my brain for the purpose of thinking. It is merely that when the atoms inside my skull happen, for physical or chemical reasons, to arrange themselves in a certain way, this gives me, as a by-product, the sensation I call thought.' C. S. Lewis quoted J. B. S. Haldane's remark that the mind is a mere by-product of matter and atoms in his book, *Miracles*.[19]

C. S. Lewis explained where such thinking leads. He continued:

> But, if so, how can I trust my own thinking to be true? It is like upsetting a milk jug and hoping that the way it splashes itself will give you a map of London. But if I can't trust my own thinking, of course I can't trust the arguments leading to Atheism, and therefore have no reason to be an Atheist or anything else. Unless I believe in God, I cannot believe in thought: so, I can never use thought to disbelieve in God.[20]

Thomas Nagel taught philosophy and law at New York University for thirty-six years until his retirement in 2016. As I write he is 85 years old. In his book, *The Last Word*, published in 1997, he wrote,

> I want atheism to be true and I am made uneasy by the fact that some of the most intelligent and well-informed people I know are religious believers. It isn't just that I don't believe in God and, naturally, hope that I'm right in my belief. It's that I hope there is no God! I don't want there to be a God; I don't want the universe to be like that.[21]

His straightforward explanation of his own beliefs is helpful. A further book which he published in 2012, *Mind and Cosmos—Why the Materialist Neo-Darwinian Conception of Nature Is Almost Certainly False*, begins with the statement, 'The aim of this book is to argue that the mind-body problem is not just a local problem, having to do with the relation between mind, brain, and behaviour in living animal organisms, but that it invades our understanding of the entire cosmos and its history.'[22]

He refers to, 'the failure of psychophysical reductionism, a position in the philosophy of mind that is largely motivated by the hope of showing how the physical sciences could in principle provide a theory of everything'. He declared, 'There are independent empirical reasons to be sceptical about the truth of reductionism in biology.'[23]

Nagel wrote,

> But for a long time I have found the materialist account of how we and our fellow organisms came to exist hard to believe, including the standard version of how the evolutionary process works. The more details we learn about the chemical basis of life and the intricacy of the genetic code, the more unbelievable the standard historical account becomes.[23]

Referring specifically to the difficulty which evolution has in explaining the origin of the mind, Nagel wrote,

> The great advances in the physical and biological sciences were made possible by excluding the mind from the physical world. This has permitted a quantitative understanding of that world, expressed in timeless, mathematically formulated, physical laws. But, at some point, it will be necessary to make a new start on a more comprehensive understanding that includes the mind.... Mind, as a development of life, must be included as the most recent stage of this long cosmological history, and its appearance, I believe, casts its shadow back over the entire process and the constituents and principles on which the process depends.[24]

Nagel addressed the conclusions of advocates of *Intelligent Design* when he wrote, 'I confess to an ungrounded assumption of my own, in not finding it possible to regard the design alternative as a real option. I lack the *sensus divinitatis* that enables—indeed compels—

so many people to see in the world the expression of divine purpose as naturally as they see, in a smiling face, the expression of human feeling. He continued: 'I believe the defenders of intelligent design deserve our gratitude for challenging a scientific world view that owes some of the passion displayed by its adherents precisely to the fact that it is thought to liberate us from religion.'[25] (I wonder whether we should understand the phrase, *sensus divinitatis,* as *the work of the Holy Spirit*—a phrase which he preferred not to use.)

In the last chapter of his book, 'Conclusion', he wrote, 'I have argued patiently against the prevailing form of naturalism, a reductive materialism that purports to capture life and mind through its neo-Darwinian extension. But to go back to my introductory remarks, I find this view antecedently unbelievable—a heroic triumph of ideological theory over common sense.'[26]

In contrast we can ask, 'What does the Bible say about how and when human consciousness began?' Enlarging on what the *how* question means—it is asking, 'How did God create man, in his own image, with the immediate ability to think rationally and imaginatively, to behave responsibly, to enjoy relationships with God, his Creator, and with his fellow human being and to be creative, for example in art and music? We read in the ESV translation of Genesis 2:7: 'Then the LORD God formed the man of dust from the ground and breathed into his nostrils the breath of life, and the man became a living creature.' The Hebrew word translated, *formed,* means, 'to mould or form,' and is used to describe the particular care and attention a potter would give to the object being formed.

It is clear that man was made from non-living matter—dust. He was not made from living creatures, as is suggested by evolution. In

Genesis 3:19 (ESV), where God judged Adam for his disobedience, God says, '... till you return to the ground, for out of it you are taken; for you are dust, and to dust you shall return'. The special inbreathing of God to make Adam alive brought him into a close relationship with God at a level enjoyed by no other creature.

The phrase, 'living creature',' in Hebrew, *nephesh chayyah*, is also used to describe the vertebrates God created on days five and six. This word emphasizes possession of life, whether human or animal. The word is not used of plants, which were given as food to man and animals. So, plants were never alive in the *nephesh chayyah* sense like man or the animals. The Bible explains in Genesis 2 and 3, and in Romans 5:12, that man's disobedience caused death, disease and decay to come into the world. Death did not exist before the Fall of man. Romans 5:14 states that 'death reigned from the time of Adam to the time of Moses'; death started with Adam's disobedience and claims about plant life dying cannot be used to prove that animal ancestors existed and died before Adam.

In addressing the 'how question', we are able to describe *what* God did in forming Adam from the dust of the ground, but we cannot explain the details of the mechanism any more than we can explain how God created the heavens and the earth in the beginning, or how by saying, 'Let there be light', there was light. Speaking personally, I recognize that my brain, contained and confined within my skull, has finite abilities. My worldview respects that God knows how he made Adam and he has not revealed to me or any other person how he did it. This does not deny the reasonable pursuit of scientific knowledge or make me agitated or upset that such knowledge is probably beyond my ability to comprehend it.

We read in Deuteronomy 29:29, 'The secret things belong to the Lord our God, but the things revealed belong to us and to our children for ever, that we may follow all the words of this law.' In Ephesians 1:19–20, Paul describes 'his incomparably great power for us who believe. That power is like the working of his mighty strength, which he exerted in Christ when he raised him from the dead and seated him at his right hand in the heavenly realms'. You ask, 'How did Christ rise from the dead or how did God make Adam from dust?' I answer, 'by the working of his great might! God is omnipotent.'

But what of the 'When did human consciousness arise' question? Ian Tattersall, from his evolutionary viewpoint, has suggested that this was about 100,000 years ago. A Christian neuroscientist, Dr Sharon Dirckx, expressing a theistic evolutionary view, wrote a book: *Am I just my brain?* She wrote, 'In anthropological terms, expressing oneself through creativity is a sign of advanced thinking, abstract thought, and, ultimately, human levels of consciousness. This kind of expression was initially absent yet became integral to the life of homo-sapiens during the late Stone Age.'[27] She supports her statement by referencing a chapter, 'Human Evolution: Personhood and Emergence'[28], which Ian Tattersall wrote in a book published in 2015. Sharon Dirckx's expression, 'initially absent' during the early Stone Age, expresses the same idea as Ian Tattersall's, 'potential cognition being unused for a short but significant lapse of time'.

The Stone Age is said to be a prehistoric period during which stone was widely used to make tools with an edge, a point, or a hammer-like surface. The period is dated from roughly 3.4 million years ago to between 8,700 BC and 2,000 BC when metalworking began. This evolutionary view does not match the Biblical description of Adam, who named all the animals in Genesis 2:19, or the musical skill of Jubal and metalcraft of Tubal-Cain, described in Genesis 4:21–22. These accounts in Genesis show that there was advanced *thinking* from the moment God made man in His image in Genesis 1:27. There is no hint that Adam and Eve were simple. Surely, if God made Adam a relational and rational being in his image, it is consistent to believe that consciousness did not *emerge*— it was integral to God's almighty creation of Adam and Eve.

I would suggest that the best way to know the age of something is from an eye-witness account. The Bible, inspired by the Holy Spirit of God, claims to be the best eyewitness account of all history. Using the chronology described in the Biblical text, we can calculate a close approximation to the date when God created Adam with a mind and immediate consciousness. Archbishop James Ussher proposed 4,004 BC for Creation, the Venerable Bede 3,592 BC, and Johannes Kepler 3992 BC. These dates suggest that the Earth is approximately 6,000 years old.

The men who made these calculations were not eccentric biblical creationists. Johannes Kepler[29] is often regarded as the father of modern Astronomy. He wrote, 'The *chief aim of all investigations of the external world should be to discover the rational order and harmony which has been imposed on it by God and which he revealed to us in the language of mathematics.*' Kepler discovered that the planets in our solar system moved in ellipses around the Sun. Kepler published three *Laws of Planetary Motion* between 1609 and 1619. Kepler ascribed glory to God when he wrote: '*Those Laws are within the grasp of the human mind. God wanted us to recognise them by creating us after his own image so that we could share in his own thoughts.'* Note that Kepler refers to the human mind and our sharing in God's thoughts.

The Venerable Bede [30], who died in AD 735, was a monk, author, teacher and scholar at Monkwearmouth-Jarrow Abbey. His most famous book, *The Ecclesiastical History of the English People*, was in five volumes of about 400 pages including beautiful illustrations. After some geographical explanation, it begins with Julius Caesar's invasion in 55 BC. The value of this work gained him the title, 'The Father of English History'. But Bede was more than a historian and theologian; he was extremely interested in time and the cosmos. In his work, 'On the Reckoning of Time', he described how the spherical earth influenced the changing duration of daylight. He explained the changing appearance of the moon and the effect of the moon on tides. He explained why tides occurred twice a day and how at one place on the coast there could be high tide and further along the coast low tide, but at the same time. Bede is considered by many to be one of the greatest Anglo-Saxon scholars. There was no conflict between his many scientific observations and his Christian faith. You can learn more about Bede, who is now buried in Durham Cathedral, at Jarrow Hall where there is an Anglo-Saxon farm, Village and Bede Museum.

So, the answer to that second question, 'When did consciousness arise?', is around 6,000 years ago, plus or minus a few hundred years. I do not believe, according to my Christian worldview, that it was 100,000 years ago, 200,000 years ago or longer!

C. S. Lewis, gifted with a great mind, said, 'It is only when you are asked to believe in reason coming from non-reason, that you must cry, "Halt",... Human minds,... They do not come from nowhere.'[31]

NOTES

1 Bill Bryson, *A Short History of Nearly Everything*, (Cambridge: Black Swan, 2004), p. 20.

2 Ibid., p. 17.

3 Dick Ahlstrom, 'Astronomer says we're all made of stardust', *The Irish Times*, 12 March 2002.

4 Luther Sunderland, 'Can Randomness Produce Ordered Systems?' Chapter 6, *Darwin's Enigma*, (Green Forest, AR: Master Books, 1998), p. 149. Quoting: Stephen J. Gould on American TV: *60 Minutes*, 22 April 1984.

5 Vilayanur Ramachandran, 'The Emerging Mind'; Reith lectures, *BBC Radio*, 2003.

6 Vilayanur Ramachandran, *The Tell-Tale Brain: A Neuroscientist's Quest for What Makes Us Human*, (London: William Heinemann, 2011), p. 4.

7 Ken Ham, *The Lie*, (Green Forest, AR: Master Books, 1996), p. 9.

8 Martin M. Monti et al., 'Wilful Modulation of Brain Activity in Disorders of Consciousness', *N Engl J Med* 362:7 2010, pp. 579–589.

9 D. Silverthorn, *Human Physiology: An Integrated Approach*, (London: Pearson 6th Ed., 2012), p. 1080.

10 Ian Tattersall, https://en.wikipedia.org/wiki/Ian_Tattersall

11 Ian Tattersall, 'The Thinking Primate: Establishing a Context for the Emergence of Modern Human Cognition', *Proceedings of the American Philosophical Society* Vol. 160, No. 3, September 2016, pp. 254–265.

12 Fred Hoyle, The Nature of the Universe, (London: Pelican Books, 1963), p. 123.

13 J. B. S. Haldane, *Possible Worlds and Other Essays*, (London: Chatto and Windus, 1927), p. 209.

14 Albert Einstein, *The Ultimate Quotable Einstein*, Alice Calaprice (Ed.), Freeman Dyson (Foreword), (Princeton, New Jersey: Princeton University Press, 2011), p. 325.

15 Richard Dawkins, *River Out of Eden: A Darwinian View of Life*, (New York: Basic Books, 1995), p. 133.

16 J. Hawley, 'Personal communication: Hawley discussion with Richard Dawkins', Thursday 28 June 2012.

17 C.S. Lewis, *Miracles*, (Glasgow and London: Fontana, 1974), p. 30.

18 Justin Taylor, '75 Years Ago: C.S. Lewis Speaks to Britain about Christianity on the BBC—A Chronology', *TGC—blog*, 5 August 2016.

19 C.S. Lewis, *Miracles*, (Glasgow and London: Fontana, 1974), p. 19.

20 Justin Taylor, '75 Years Ago: C.S. Lewis Speaks to Britain about Christianity on the BBC—A Chronology', *TGC—blog*, 5 August 2016.

21 Thomas Nagel, *The Last Word*, (Oxford University Press, 1997), pp. 130–131.

22 Thomas Nagel, *Mind and Cosmos—Why the Materialist Neo-Darwinian Conception of Nature Is Almost Certainly False*, (Oxford University Press, 2012), p. 11.

23 Ibid., p. 12.

24 Ibid., p. 14.

25 Ibid., p. 16.

26 Ibid., p. 94.

27 Sharon Dirckx, *Am I just my brain?* (Epsom: The Good Book Company, 2019), p. 61.

28 Ian Tattersall, 'Human Evolution: Personhood and Emergence', cited in: M. Jeeves & D. Tutu (Ed.), *The Emergence of Personhood: A Quantum Leap?* (Grand Rapids, Michigan: Eerdmans, 2015), p. 44.

29 Johannes Kepler, https://en.wikipedia.org/wiki/Johannes_Kepler

30 Bede, https://en.wikipedia.org/wiki/Bede

31 C.S. Lewis, *Miracles*, p. 32.

25 Pride, prejudice and bias

You may be able to answer the question of who wrote the following sentence to open her most famous book: 'It is a truth universally acknowledged that a single man in possession of a good fortune must be in want of a wife.' Jane Austen finished writing *Pride and Prejudice* in 1797, though it remained unpublished until 1813.[1] Her plot centres on characters who she describes in great detail and who are often well-to-do people. The main character, in *Pride and Prejudice*, is Miss Elizabeth Bennett who has four sisters; her mother is eager to find a wealthy husband for each of them. When Mr Fitzwilliam Darcy arrives on the scene, it is soon concluded that he is the proudest, most disagreeable man in the world, and everybody hopes that he will never come there again. The story revolves around the pride of Elizabeth and Darcy (as he is called throughout the book) and their strong prejudice against each other. However, in time, a growing affection develops between them as they learn the true facts about each other and Darcy proposes marriage for a second time and is accepted.

Jane Austen initially chose the title, *First Impressions*, for her book, then changed this to *Pride and Prejudice*. I find that interesting because first impressions can be deceiving, particularly if we have pre-conceived ideas about someone or something. Elizabeth and Darcy, on the basis of very little evidence, quickly come to a prejudiced view about each other. Their personal pride—refusing to change their opinion—gets in the way of finding out the truth about each other. They both eventually put their pride and prejudice aside and as a consequence discover happiness in that great relationship of marriage which God designed.

Elizabeth and Darcy's marriage might be a rather romantic parallel to the journey each one of us can make to discover the personal love of God for us. As an unbeliever, when I was exploring the Christian faith at medical school, I was tempted to criticize God for issues in history or the physical world that were difficult or appeared unfair and then, perhaps because of peer pressure, refuse to even read the Bible or listen to a Christian explaining what the Bible said. Pride and prejudice may in this way prevent someone from exploring the Christian faith.

The notion expressed in W. E. Henley's poem, 'Invictus'[2]—'I am the master of my fate: I am the captain of my soul', is not helpful. We cannot save ourselves. God is waiting for us to repent of our sins and turn to him for forgiveness. This forgiveness can be granted because Jesus died on the cross, taking the penalty of our sin upon himself, as it says in 1 Peter 3:18: 'For Christ died for sins once for all, the righteous for the unrighteous, to bring you to God. He was put to death in the body but made alive by the Spirit.'

I quoted Bishop Ryle in chapter 9: he said, 'Before we believe, we are dead, and have no interest in Christ; and that the moment we do believe, we live.'[3] Ephesians 2:1 confirms this: 'As for you, you were dead in your transgressions and sins,' and continues in 2:4–5: 'God, who is rich in mercy, made us alive with Christ even when we were dead in transgressions.' This is a description of our natural spiritual state, inherited from Adam and Eve. It also describes that the principle of physical death, through the process of ageing or other cause, is unavoidable. Jesus explained to Nicodemus, in John chapter 3, that we must be born-again to become a Christian. A transforming work of regeneration (being born again) must be worked by the Holy Spirit of God. The unbeliever who is seeking God must do that wholeheartedly, as it says in Jeremiah 29:13: 'You will seek me and find me when you seek me with all your heart.' Another encouraging verse is found in James 4:8: 'Come near to God and he will come near to you. Wash your hands, you sinners, and purify your hearts, you double-minded.'

The book of Hosea, in the Old Testament, describes the tender heart of God as he seeks to draw his lost children back into a family relationship. The book describes the hurt that their rebellion causes God. The story of the Prodigal Son, in Luke 15:20, tells of the father running to embrace and kiss his lost son. One of the most moving verses in the Bible revealing God's love and urgency is found in Ezekiel 33:11: 'Say to them, "As surely as I live, declares the Sovereign Lord, I take no pleasure in the death of the wicked, but rather that they turn from their ways and live. Turn! Turn from your evil ways! Why will you die, O house of Israel?"'

What is the explanation for our opposition to God? I think it is most clearly stated in Romans 8:7. When I was 21 years old, I learnt this verse in the Authorised Version, which I still feel explains the matter very clearly: 'Because the carnal mind is enmity against God: for it is not subject to the law of God, neither indeed can be.' Chapter 8 of Romans is concerned with life in the flesh (our natural condition) and life in the Spirit (after we have been born-again by the Holy Spirit). 'Carnal' means, 'of the flesh', and is the nature which we have all inherited from Adam and Eve. This nature is like the bias on the bowl, in a game of Bowls, which causes the bowl to travel a curved path on a bowling green.

I quoted in the previous chapter Ken Ham's remark: 'Which bias is the best bias with which to be biased?'[4] In his book, *The Lie*, originally published in 1987, Ham points out that, in discussions about biblical creation and evolution, we are talking about beliefs— that is, religion. The controversy is not religion versus science, as the evolutionists try to make out. It is religion versus religion; the science of one religion versus the science of the other. Ken Ham continues:

> Evolution is a religious position that makes human opinion supreme. As we shall see, its fruits (because of rejection of the Creator and Lawgiver) are lawlessness, immorality, impurity, abortion, racism and a mocking of God. Creation is a religious position based on the Word of God, and its fruits (through God's Spirit) are love, joy, peace, patience, kindness, goodness, faithfulness, gentleness and self-control.[5]

As a Christian, I believe that if we do not get the matter of our Origins, and Adam and Eve's Fall into sin, right, then people will continue to experience great unhappiness, loneliness and despair.

The Enlightenment was a time in our history when human opinion and thought was elevated to a position of supremacy and God's Word was criticized, ridiculed and discarded. Rodney Stark in his book, *The Triumph of Christianity*, brilliantly exposes the 'Myth of Secular Enlightenment.'[6] He explains that those who proclaimed the Enlightenment were literary men such as Voltaire, Rousseau, Diderot, Hume and Gibbon, who were irreligious, whereas the central figures in the scientific achievements of the era were deeply religious. Secularists would have us believe that there were Dark Ages in our past history, caused by the repressive influence of the church and religion. Rodney Stark explains that the progress made in scientific understanding and developments in Europe was because of 'an extraordinary faith in reason and progress that was firmly rooted in Christian theology, in the belief that God is the rational creator of a rational universe.'[7]

I draw your attention to two recent, prejudiced remarks against God, both in 2020. The first occurred on Good Friday, 10th April on the *Today* programme on BBC Radio 4. Mr Hylton Murray-Philipson was interviewed about his experience of the Covid–19 pandemic. He, his mother and his sister had all been infected by the virus, and he himself had come close to death, but survived. He said to his interviewer, Nick Robinson, 'One of the very powerful images I had (while in intensive care) was the image of Jesus calming the storm on the Sea of Galilee and that just came to me and I like to think that it was Jesus Christ coming to me and helping me in my hour of need.'[8] Mr Robinson, perhaps disrespectfully, responded by suggesting that this vision was 'partly because of the drugs you have to be on in order to be on a ventilator machine, which plays tricks with the mind, doesn't it, really?' (Mr Robinson did later apologize.)

The second example of prejudiced remarks was published in *The Daily Telegraph* on 26 May 2020.[9] This was written by Sir Tim Laurence, Chairman of English Heritage and son-in-law of the Queen. He is a retired Vice Admiral in the Royal Navy. He wrote an article with the title 'The Dunkirk evacuation was no "miracle".' The reason for the article was the 80th anniversary of 'Operation Dynamo', the mission to rescue the British army from France. His subtitle emphasized that, above all, human effort brought us success in Operation Dynamo. He drew attention to the tunnels deep under Dover Castle where 'the brilliant Vice Admiral Sir Bertram Ramsay' directed operations. Dover Castle and these tunnels are managed by English Heritage. Laurence remarks that, without the guiding hand of Ramsay and his team, it would have been a shambles.

I disagreed with Sir Tim Laurence's article and wondered what his mother-in-law thought of it. The Dunkirk evacuation was enabled because of three miracles. The Prime Minister and King George VI both recognized that. Winston Churchill, speaking on 4 June 1940 in the House of Commons, referred to a 'miracle of deliverance'. Winston Churchill at another time acknowledged God's place in our national life. He said, 'The more closely we follow the Sermon on the Mount, the more likely we are to succeed in our endeavours.'[10]

King George VI had called the nation on Sunday, 26th May, to a National Day of Prayer. In a broadcast to the nation, he called on the people to commit their cause to God. Three miracles followed. Firstly, Hitler irrationally ordered his generals to halt the advance of his armoured columns towards the west coast of France. Secondly, on Tuesday, 28th May, a furious storm broke over Flanders, grounding the German Luftwaffe and enabling the British Army, now 8 to 12 miles from Dunkirk, to reach the coast with minimal interruption. The third miracle was the great calm which settled over the English Channel during the following days, with low cloud cover. This allowed the armada of little ships to cross the Channel and ferry the waiting soldiers out to the Royal Navy warships, for their return to England. The rest is history with the nation thanking

Almighty God for this deliverance on Sunday, 9th June, a Day of National Thanksgiving. Sir Tim Laurence presumably thinks the Prime Minister, the Queen's father and the nation were all deluded and that the six other National Days of Prayer were also irrelevant. According to him, human effort was all that was needed!

Rev. C. B. Mortlock wrote in the *Daily Telegraph*, 8 June 1940, 'The prayers of the nation were answered,' and 'The God of hosts himself had supported the valiant men of the British Expeditionary Force.'[11]

Sir Tim Laurence's article drew parallels between Dunkirk and the Covid-19 crisis afflicting the United Kingdom during the writing of this book. He suggested that improvisation was the key, for Dunkirk, along with quick decision-making, twenty-four hours a day, often based on very limited information. He is right to celebrate the planning of Ramsay and the bravery of the personnel involved, just as we gave thanks for our frontline NHS and Care Home staff and our Prime Minister, Government and Parliament during the Covid-19 crisis. But we should not forget the miracles that occurred in 1940 and those miracles during the rest of the war following National Days of Prayer. Many Christians pray that we will experience miracles again today, though national repentance for the state of our nation is in short supply.

My letter of 27 May, to the Editor of the *Daily Telegraph*, suggesting that there were three miracles, was not published. A previous letter of 28 March, suggesting the need for the nation to pray, in the light of the Covid-19 crisis, was also not published. In that letter, I quoted the personal testimony of Air Chief Marshall Hugh Dowding who attributed victory in the Battle of Britain to 'the intervention of God',' following another National Day of Prayer.

Sir Hugh Dowding made an important statement of Christian faith: 'I say with absolute conviction that I can trace the intervention of God, not only in the Battle itself, but in the events which led up to it ...'. On another occasion, Dowding noted, 'At the end of the Battle one had the feeling that there had been some special Divine Intervention to alter some sequence of events which would otherwise have occurred. I see that this intervention was no last-minute happening .... It was all part of the mighty plan.'[12]

I am afraid that prejudice against the God of the Bible is strong in the 21st century. It was no different in Jesus' day. He regularly met groups of people who were proud, prejudiced and biased. Some belonged to the strict group of theologians known as the Pharisees. One account of their prejudice is recorded in John chapter 9, when Jesus enabled a man, who was born blind, to see. The Pharisees first declared that Jesus could not be from God because he had healed on the Sabbath. They then asked the healed man what his opinion about Jesus was, to which the man replied, 'He is a prophet' (v. 17).

The Pharisees next tried denying that the man had ever been born blind. So, the interrogation went on until the healed man himself summarized the situation: 'Now that is remarkable! You do not know where he comes from, yet he opened my eyes. We know that God does not listen to sinners. He listens to the godly man who does his will. Nobody has ever heard of opening the eyes of a man born blind. If this man were not from God, he could do nothing' (vv. 30–33). The Pharisees were enraged and said, '"You were steeped in sin at birth; how dare you lecture us!" And they threw him out' (v. 34).

On Palm Sunday, as recorded in Luke 19:28–44, the Pharisees were again wanting to oppose what Jesus was doing. As he rode into

Jerusalem on a colt, spontaneous adoration broke out among the crowd who joyfully praised God, in loud voices. They cried, in v. 38, 'Blessed is the king who comes in the name of the Lord! Peace in heaven and glory in the highest!' The first sentence quotes Psalm 118:26, but changes the word, *he*, to the word, *king*.

Jesus' actions, when riding into Jerusalem on the colt, fulfilled the prophecy of Zechariah 9:9, where we read, 'See your king comes to you ... on a colt.' Jesus was telling the world that he is God and King. The crowd, convinced by the evidence of the miracles and the beauty of Christ's ministry, were acknowledging their King and Messiah. The Pharisees called on Jesus to rebuke his disciples, presumably angry at the triumphal entry fulfilling Zechariah's prophecy or at the crowd for their 'misappropriating' Psalm 118. As Jesus rode down from the Mount of Olives in triumph, the Pharisees, because of their prejudice, refused to believe the evidence, which a recently healed blind man had so clearly seen.

Lazarus had been recently raised from the dead and the blind man made to see but the Pharisees remained spiritually dead and blind. Prejudice often holds humanity in darkness.

NOTES

1 Jane Austen, *Pride and Prejudice*, (Whitehall: T. Egerton, Military Library, 1813).
2 https://www.poetryfoundation.org/poems/51642/invictus
3 Bishop J. C. Ryle, *Christian Leaders of the 18th Century*, (Edinburgh: The Banner of Truth Trust, 2017), pp. 11–18.
4 Ken Ham, *The Lie*, (Green Forest, AR: Master Books, 1996), p. 9.
5 Ibid., pp. 12–13.
6 Rodney Stark, *The Triumph of Christianity*, (New York: HarperCollins, 2011), p. 252.
7 Ibid., p. 253.

8 Catherine Utley, 'When a BBC radio guest mentioned Jesus, the response was telling', *Catholic Herald*, 11 April 2020.

9 Sir Tim Laurence, 'The Dunkirk evacuation was no "miracle"', *The Daily Telegraph*, 26 May 2020.

10 Jonathon Van Maren, 'Winston Churchill: A Surprising Champion of Christian Heritage', *The European Conservative*, 2 March 2022. https://europeanconservative. com/articles/essay/winston-churchill-a-surprising-champion-of-christian-heritage/

11 Rev. C. B. Mortlock, 'The prayers of the nation were answered', *The Daily Telegraph*, 8 June 1940.

12 W. B. Grant, *We Have a Guardian: Some Instances of Divine Intervention in British History*, (County Durham: Covenant Publishing Co. Ltd, 2011), p. 13.

26 Altruism, evolution and forgiveness

I n Bromsgrove Cemetery in Worcestershire, stands the grave of surgeon, Sir Thomas Chavasse MD, FRCS and members of his family. He died in 1913 and his doctor son, Captain Arthur Chavasse RAMC, who died on active service in 1916 in France, is also remembered on the tombstone. Lying flat on the ground in front of the memorial, is a stone plaque in memory of Sir Thomas's nephew, Noel Chavasse, who was engaged to Sir Thomas's daughter.

The Chavasse family produced two Bishops of the Church of England, two Olympic athletes, a Knight Bachelor and one of only three people to be awarded a Victoria Cross (VC), twice. Sir Thomas's brother was Bishop Francis Chavasse (Noel's father), who was instrumental in the building of the Anglican Liverpool Cathedral and founded St Peter's College, Oxford.[1]

Noel's memorial reads as follows: In Memory Capt Noel Chavasse RAMC, VC and bar, MC died of wounds 4th August 1917. Buried at Brandhoek, Nr Ypres Fiancé of Gladys Chavasse 2nd Daughter of Sir Thomas and Lady Chavasse. His last words: 'Tell her duty called and called me to obey.'[2]

Noel Chavasse's actual grave, in Belgium, has two Victoria Crosses engraved on it, with the Bible verse from John 15:13 (KJV): 'Greater love hath no man than this, that a man lay down his life for his friends.' Noel Chavasse is remembered on more war memorials (sixteen) than any other person in the UK. He won his first VC in August 1916, in France, when he rescued twenty wounded soldiers from in front of the enemy's lines, in spite of being wounded himself. A year later at Passchendaele, in spite of serious personal wounds, he continued for two days to treat the wounded and, under heavy enemy fire, searched for more wounded. He saved many lives from harsh weather conditions and enemy fire but died of his wounds on 4 August 1917. A surgeon who cared for Noel and described his terrible wounds, Lieutenant Colonel Arthur Martin-Leake, was also the recipient of two VCs (one in the Boer War and the second in 1914).

Incidentally, there is only one other recipient of the double VC and he was a New Zealander, Captain Charles Upham, for actions during the Battle of Crete in May 1941 and during the First Battle of El Alamein in July 1942. Strangely he was related by marriage to Noel Chavasse!

In this chapter entitled, 'Altruism, Evolution and Forgiveness', I draw your attention to Noel's last words: 'Tell her duty called and called me to obey.' Noel and his brother, Christopher (later Bishop of Rochester), were committed Christians and sons of the second Bishop of Liverpool. They both ran for Great Britain in the 400 metres at the 1908 Olympic Games, though they were eliminated in the heats. Perhaps Noel's sense of duty was due to good military training, his schooling and the Christian upbringing received at home, but he clearly saw that his medical care of others was more important than self-interest and his own survival. He was a courageous man and certainly never driven by selfishness.

Like Noel, many brave men and women have laid down their lives to save others and so may share the verse from John 15:13 as their epitaph. This self-sacrifice in the service of others can be referred to as *altruism*. Individuals from all religions, or none, have been moved by compassion, love and perhaps, in times of war, also by the motivation to defeat the enemy.

Chambers 20th Century Dictionary defines *altruism* as, 'the principle of living and acting for the interests of others'.[3] *Altruism* may be concerned with the needs of others to whom we are not related and even to strangers on the other side of the world but is the concept of altruism compatible with the evolutionary struggle— the survival of the fittest? While caring for members of our own family or tribe might seem of evolutionary benefit, caring for distant famine or natural disaster victims, and even for enemies, is not of evolutionary benefit.

Richard Dawkins, in his 1976 book, *The Selfish Gene*[4], claimed that evolution is not really about the survival of the fittest organism; rather it is about survival of the fittest gene, with genes that are able to make copies of themselves favoured in the next generation. The example is given of worker ants or bees sacrificing themselves in the service of the queen and her offspring, to ensure that her genes are represented in the next generation. This is known as *eusociality*.[5]

One review of *The Selfish Gene* states, 'He believes that evolution happens to genes, not species. He also thinks there is no gene for *altruism* (selfless or kind behaviour). He thinks this is quite a radical view because it implies that we humans are 'lumbering robots', programmed by our genes to help them—the genes—survive. He thinks this is as strange as 'science fiction' but it's actually the truth.'[6]

We might ask, 'Was Noel Chavasse really driven by his genes, which somehow controlled him so that they would be reproduced in a subsequent generation?' On the contrary, his courage, self-sacrifice and his love of his fellow men, meant that Chavasse's genes would soon decay in the soil of a French cemetery.

In *The Selfish Gene*, Richard Dawkins said that there is *no gene for altruism*. But he has actually discussed that a gene for altruism could be favoured by natural selection if the altruism is directed at other individuals who share the same gene. In a BBC interview at the 2018 Hay Festival, he was asked, 'Does your scientific understanding of selfishness and altruism chime with your own personal experience of human behaviour and altruism?'

This was Richard Dawkins' reply verbatim:

> When we do something that we all in this room do, I hope, from time to time, and we think that we truly are behaving altruistically, are we ever? I think we have to explain it as a form of Darwinian selection—we have to say something like this: "We were naturally selected; our genes were naturally selected in ancestral times when we were surrounded by close kin in small villages or roving bands and surrounded by individuals whom we knew personally and who might be expected to reciprocate good turns later." That's no longer true—we are surrounded by strangers. We feel empathy towards strangers although they're never going to reciprocate and they're not kin. I think you have to remember that natural selection .... doesn't well ... selfish genes are not conscious little gremlins that know what's good for them—they are favoured because they build into the body in the process of embryology, they build in rules of thumb which foster their survival under normal natural conditions.[7]

Later he said, 'The rule of thumb is now misfiring because we no longer live in small villages but the rule of thumb is still there in exactly the same way in our ancestral past.'[7] Richard Dawkins implied that altruistic actions are motivated by the expectation that the recipient will later reciprocate the good turn. He admits, in *The Selfish Gene*, 'Much as we may wish to believe otherwise, universal love and welfare of the species as a whole are concepts which simply do not make evolutionary sense.'[8]

During the coronavirus pandemic, which started in 2020, many altruistic acts were done. When the Prime Minister appealed for 150,000 volunteers to help the NHS, 400,000 people responded within twenty-four hours and the number later rose to 750,000. Such altruism is consistent with a Judeo-Christian worldview in which humans are created in the image of God, and though sin has spoiled that image, it has not been erased. The image of God explains why people can be selfless and other person centred, even to those who they have never met or ever will. The parable of the Good Samaritan and the majority of charity work are examples of altruistic behaviour. Supremely, the action of the Lord Jesus Christ in becoming a servant and dying as an atoning sacrifice for our sins, described in Philippians 2:3–8, is the perfect example of altruism.

If we contrast, (a) the altruism which arises from a belief that man is made in the image of God and the commandment of God to love, care for and respect, our neighbour, with (b) behaviour which arises from a belief in evolution, we see a stark difference. Richard Dawkins had written in *River Out of Eden*:

> In a universe of blind physical forces and genetic replication, some people are going to get hurt, other people are going to get

lucky, and you won't find any rhyme or reason in it, nor any justice. The universe we observe has precisely the properties we should expect if there is, at bottom, no design, no purpose, no evil and no good, nothing but blind, pitiless indifference.[9]

Richard Dawkins effectively denies human responsibility and blames pitiless evolution. Sin as a concept is dismissed in his reasoning.

Following the publication of his book, *River Out of Eden*, Richard Dawkins' responses in an interview to *Skeptic* magazine are informative.[10] The interviewer quoted William Shakespeare who wrote, 'a tale told by an idiot, filled with sound and fury, signifying nothing'[11] and went on to ask Richard Dawkins, 'Is that in fact your position?' Richard Dawkins replied:

> Yes, at a sort of cosmic level, it is. But what I want to guard against is people therefore getting nihilistic in their personal lives. I don't see any reason for that at all. You can have a very happy and fulfilled personal life even if you think that the universe at large is a tale told by an idiot. You can still set up goals and have a very worthwhile life and not be nihilistic about it at a personal level.[12]

The interviewer probed Richard Dawkins as to whether evolution can be a reasonable guide as to how the world ought to be run if religion is discarded as a dependable guide? Richard Dawkins answered:

> I'd rather not do that. ... In my opinion, a society run along evolutionary lines would not be a very nice society in which to live. But further, there's no logical reason why we should try to derive our normative standards from evolution. It's perfectly consistent to say this is the way it is—natural selection is out

there and it is a very unpleasant process. Nature is red in tooth and claw. But I don't want to live in that kind of a world. I want to change the world in which I live in such a way that natural selection no longer applies.[12]

Denis Alexander, a Christian who believes in Theistic Evolution, agreed when he wrote, 'But of course evolutionary processes are not there to teach us morality; Christians are called to behave like children of God, according to God's moral law, as revealed in the Bible.'[13] But why should the children of a random undirected evolutionary process, based on the survival of the fittest, obey God's moral law? The Biblical account of creation, where Adam and Eve are made in the image of God as rational, responsible moral beings does explain why they should behave like children of God by keeping His laws.

In Richard Dawkins' worldview, natural selection has produced an advanced humanity with powers of civilization and technology, but this very humanity tends towards a nihilistic outlook on the world and is very often cruel. The humanity he recognizes, actually, has no purpose other than giving birth to more selfish genes and so aiding the onward march of evolution. He is uncomfortable with this reality and so tells us that he wants to change the world in order that natural selection has no further power. His life has been dedicated to the propagation of evolutionary theory, but he disowns natural selection and evolution, as he does not like the consequences.

Richard Dawkins may also wish to disown how evolutionary ideas have led to many cruel and inhuman actions, including those of dictators such as Adolf Hitler. It is helpful to learn a little here from

Winston Churchill who, in Volume 1 of his history of *The Second World War* gives a short biographical account of Adolf Hitler.[14] I summarize some of Churchill's comments from chapter IV:

> Very soon after the end of the First World War, Hitler saw shining before him his duty to save Germany from 'the accursed Bolsheviks in their international conspiracy of Jewish intellectuals'. Hitler believed the path to power lay through aggression and violence—the survival of the fittest. Churchill described Hitler's main thesis as being simple: 'Man is a fighting animal; therefore, the nation, being a community of fighters, is a fighting unit ... The fighting capacity of a race depends on its purity. Hence the need for ridding it of foreign defilements. The Jewish race, owing to its universality, is of necessity pacifist and internationalist.'[15] No alliance with Russia could be tolerated by Hitler because he thought the aim of the Soviets was the triumph of international Judaism.

Between 1907 and 1913, Hitler had been a failed art student in Vienna. A Pelican Book, *A pictorial history of Nazi Germany*, states that, during the time in Vienna, his feelings of inferiority developed into a pathological hatred of the world around him. This hatred was encouraged by a fanatical racist, Jorg Lanz von Liebenfels, whose journal, *Ostara*, contained illustrations of what were claimed as distinctive racial features. Jorg's theories had a powerful influence on Hitler who became a convinced anti-Semite.[16] Hitler viewed Polish people, particularly, as subhuman, with their only function being to serve the Master Race.

Stephen Jay Gould, in his book, *Ontogeny and Phylogeny*[17] (1977), stated that Ernst Haeckel (of the embryo fraud) bolstered National Socialism in Germany by his evolutionary racism. He called for racial purity and unflinching devotion to a 'just' state. Ernst Haeckel believed that harsh, inexorable laws of evolution ruled human civilization and nature alike. This view conferred upon favoured races the right to dominate others, contributing to the rise of Nazism. We see how Hans Frank, the Governor-General of Poland in 1940, could say, 'We too find the Jews exceptionally troublesome animals.'[18]

Hitler also wrote:

> There is only one right that is sacrosanct, and this right is at the same time a most sacred duty. This right and obligation is that the purity of the racial blood should be guarded, so that the best of human values may be preserved and that thus we should render possible a more noble development of humanity itself. ... Finally, it is the duty of their People's State to arrange for the writing of a world history in which the race problem will occupy a dominant position.[19]

We must understand that discarding the principle of the Sanctity of Human Life in favour of evolutionary biology places mankind in a dangerous place. The views of Peter Singer and Francis Crick are based solidly on evolutionary theory. Fortunately, for over 2,000 years, medical ethics have been underpinned by the Hippocratic Oath. Thus, human altruism has been encouraged by Bible-based ethics, protecting people and forming the basis of many of our laws, systems of government and justice.

I want to suggest that whatever the source of an individual's altruism, we can be perplexed at times by an even higher plane of altruism—namely forgiving one's enemies. Richard Dawkins might argue that this is the selfish gene expecting a favour in return! However, forgiveness can be a risky business. My Christian worldview emphasizes that forgiveness is possibly the greatest need of mankind. Many individuals harbour bad feelings towards those who have abused them in various ways. This is understandable but will not lead to healing. Jesus urges us to love our enemies and to forgive those who despitefully treat us. This, ultimately, can lead to healing for the abused individual. I will illustrate this in the lives of two ladies who served others and forgave their enemies.

The first, Edith Cavell[20], was born in 1865, the eldest of four children of a vicar in a village 4 miles from Norwich. Edith was a committed Christian who, after caring for her sick father, at the age of thirty trained as a nurse and worked for ten years in poor parts of London and Manchester. In 1907, she moved to Brussels and started the first Belgian professional nurse training school.

She was actually on holiday, with her widowed mother in England, in the summer of 1914, but chose to return to Brussels to be with her nurses, in spite of the imminence of war. German occupation followed and she hid British and French soldiers, who were often wounded, and then helped their escape into Holland. She did this for nine months, helping at least 200 men. She and her colleagues were aware that, if caught, they would be shot. Sadly, she was betrayed and tried by a German military court which lead to her execution by firing squad at dawn on October 12, 1915. After the war, her body was brought back to the UK and buried at the East end of Norwich Cathedral.

On the night before her execution, an Anglican chaplain, Horace Gahan, was allowed to see her and gave her Holy Communion. He recorded her conversation: 'I am thankful to have had these ten weeks of quiet to get ready. Now I have had them and have been kindly treated here. I expected my sentence and I believe it was just. Standing as I do, in view of God and Eternity, I realize that patriotism is not enough; I must have no hatred or bitterness towards anyone.' These words have been inscribed on her statue in St Martin's Place, close to St Martins in the Fields Church in London. Her final words to the German Lutheran prison chaplain, were recorded as, 'Ask Father Gahan to tell my loved ones later on that my soul, as I believe, is safe, and that I am glad to die for my country.'[21]

Edith's motivation for her care and sacrifice was her Christian faith, which sustained her through twenty years as a nurse. She saw British and French soldiers as her brothers needing shelter, nursing and help to escape. Like Noel Chavasse, she had a sense of duty, whatever the personal cost to herself. At times she walked with the soldiers to a rendezvous, where they met further Belgian guides who would lead them to the Dutch border.

The second lady tells her own story in *The Hiding Place*, written in 1971. A film of the same title was made in 1975. Corrie ten Boom was born in 1892 and lived in Haarlem, in the Netherlands, where her father was a watchmaker. During the war, she and her family hid Jews behind a false wall in Corrie's bedroom. Six people could hide in the *Hiding Place* if the house was searched. The family helped many to escape but were finally betrayed.

Corrie and her sister, Betsie, were sent to the Ravensbrück concentration camp, where Betsie and Corrie discussed plans to open a home for healing and reconciliation after the war. Sadly, Betsie's health was poor and she died in December 1944. Corrie was released twelve days later, apparently because of a clerical error. A week later, all the women in her age group were killed in the gas chambers. Corrie witnessed awful cruelty, including one guard who treated Betsie terribly. The biggest challenge for Corrie in those early post-war years was to forgive her enemies. She describes this in the last two pages of *The Hiding Place*:[22]

> It was in a church service in Munich that I saw him, the former SS man who had stood guard at the shower room door in the processing centre at Ravensbrück. He was the first of our actual jailers that I had seen since that time. And suddenly it was all there—the roomful of mocking men, the heaps of clothing, Betsie's pain-blanched face. He came up to me as the church was emptying, beaming and bowing. 'How grateful I am for your message Fraulein,' he said. 'To think that, as you say, "He has washed my sins away!"'
>
> His hand was thrust out to shake mine. ... I kept my hand at my side.

She realized that Jesus Christ had died for this man and prayed for help to forgive him. She tried to smile but could not raise her hand. She prayed again asking Jesus to give her his forgiveness. But then she took his hand and an incredible thing happened; she felt a current pass from her to him and into her heart sprang a love for the stranger that almost overwhelmed her.

> And so, I discovered that it is not on our forgiveness any more than on our goodness that the world's healing hinges, but on His. When He tells us to love our enemies, He gives along with the command, love itself.

After the war Corrie was granted the use of a fifty-six-room mansion, in Bloemendaal, with beautiful gardens, where many hundreds of damaged people were cared for and rehabilitated. Later, she began to travel to teach reconciliation and talk of the love of

God. She was even given the use of a former concentration camp, Darmstadt, in Germany.

Liz, I and thousands of others, have visited the Ten Boom Museum in Haarlem and seen the *Hiding Place* in Corrie's bedroom, and listened to the story of the love of the Ten Boom family for the despised and rejected, who also were made in the image of God. It is a very moving experience.

I suggested, in passing, that the actions of the Lord Jesus Christ were the perfect example of altruism. In 1 John 4:10–11, we read, 'This is love: not that we loved God, but that he loved us and sent his Son as an atoning sacrifice for our sins. Dear friends, since God so loved us, we also ought to love one another.' Later in verse 19 we read, 'We love because he first loved us.' We also read in John 1:10–13, 'He was in the world, and though the world was made through him, the world did not recognize him. He came to that which was his own, but his own did not receive him. Yet, to all who received him, to those who believed in his name, he gave the right to become children of God—children born not of natural descent, nor of human decision or a husband's will, but born of God.'

We can read, in Luke 22:44, about Jesus praying in the Garden of Gethsemane before his crucifixion: 'And being in anguish, he prayed more earnestly, and his sweat was like drops of blood falling to the ground.' Jesus knew how much he would suffer physically and spiritually over the next few hours. Jesus supremely lived and died for the interests of others (altruism) who needed forgiveness.

'Believe in the Lord Jesus Christ and you will be saved' (Acts 16:31).

NOTES

1 Francis Chavasse, https://en.wikipedia.org/wiki/Francis_Chavasse.

2 Noel Chavasse, https://www.britishlegion.org.uk/stories/the-only-vc-and-bar-of-the-first-world-war.

3 *Chambers 20th Century Dictionary*, (Edinburgh and London: W & R Chambers, 1901, reprinted 1950), p. 25.

4 Richard Dawkins, *The Selfish Gene: 30th Anniversary Edition*, (Oxford University Press, 2006).

5 Heather Brennan, (Jun 3, 2013), *The Selfish Gene Theory and Altruism*. Retrieved: 1 Dec 2021 from: Explorable.com: https://explorable.com/selfish-gene-theory

6 LitCharts study guide on Richard Dawkins's *The Selfish Gene*, 'Plot Summary', 2019. https://www.litcharts.com/lit/the-selfish-gene

7 'Richard Dawkins on the evolution of altruism', BBC Arts–Hay Festival, 2018. https://www.bbc.co.uk/programmes/p05wprkm

8 Richard Dawkins, *The Selfish Gene*, pp. 2–3

9 Richard Dawkins, *River Out of Eden: A Darwinian View of Life*, (New York: Basic Books, 1995), p. 133.

10 Frank Miele, 'Darwin's Dangerous Disciple—an Interview with Richard Dawkins', *Skeptic* vol. 3, no. 4, 1995, pp. 80–85.

11 William Shakespeare, *Macbeth*, Act 5 Scene 5, lines 26–28. https://myshakespeare.com/macbeth/act-5-scene-5

12 Frank Miele, 'Darwin's Dangerous Disciple—an Interview with Richard Dawkins', *Skeptic* vol. 3, no. 4, 1995, pp. 80–85.

13 Denis R. Alexander, 'Can a Christian believe in evolution?' *Evangelical Alliance*, 1 May 2005.

14 Winston S. Churchill, *The Second World War*, Volume 1, chapter IV, (Boston, Massachusetts: Houghton Mifflin, 1948–53).

15 Ibid., p. 50.

16 Erwin Leiser, *A pictorial history of Nazi Germany*, (London: Pelican Books, 1962), p. 25.

17 Stephen Jay Gould, *Ontogeny and Phylogeny*, 'Cambridge, Massachusetts: Harvard University Press, 1977).

18 Erwin Leiser, *A pictorial history of Nazi Germany*, p. 140.

19 Ibid., p. 171.

20 'Who Was Edith Cavell?' Imperial War Museums. https://www.iwm.org.uk/history/who-was-edith-cavell

21 Horace Gahan, 'Account by Reverend H. Stirling Gahan on the Execution of Edith Cavell', 1923, www.firstworldwar.com

22 Corrie Ten Boom, *The Hiding Place*, second impression, (London: Hodder and Stoughton, 1976), pp. 220–221.

27 Miracles and the laws of nature

I wonder what you think about miracles. An adjective often used about such events is that they are *supernatural*. A miracle, or supernatural event, is attributed to some force beyond scientific understanding or the laws of nature. The question of miracles divides opinion. Richard Dawkins has stated that, 'Any belief in miracles is flat contradictory not just to the facts of science but to the spirit of science.'[1] On the other hand, C. S. Lewis states, 'We have not, in fact, proved that science excludes miracles: we have only proved that the question of miracles, like innumerable other questions, excludes laboratory treatment.'[2]

Let me draw your attention to the miracles described in the Bible. These are not confined to the lifetime and ministry of Jesus Christ but, from the first verse of Genesis to the penultimate verse of the book of Revelation, miracles happen. The 'history-writing miracles' *(my phrase)* of God's Creation, the Incarnation of Christ and of Christ's Resurrection are, of course, crucial to a Christian's understanding of the history, meaning and purpose of life. C. S. Lewis has said, 'The central miracle asserted by Christians is the Incarnation. They say that God became Man. Every other miracle prepares for this, or exhibits this, or results from this.'[3] The Bible's promise that Jesus will return in power to judge all mankind who have ever lived and to create a New Heavens and Earth, anticipates a further 'history-writing miracle'.

The four New Testament Gospels record many of the miracles which Jesus performed on this earth. If you have a serious interest to study these, I strongly recommend a book called, *Notes on the Miracles of Our Lord*[4] written by Archbishop Richard Trench and republished by Baker Book House. In his opening six chapters, he discusses the nature of miracles and makes comparison with the laws of nature.

He asks, 'Wherein, it may be asked, does the miracle differ from any event in the ordinary course of nature? For that too is wonderful; the fact that it is a marvel of continual recurrence may rob it, subjectively, of our admiration; yet it does not remain the less a marvel still.'[5] He quaintly quotes Augustine and Gregory the Great as saying, 'The daily miracles of God have grown cheap by repetition.'[6]

Trench indicates that the world is no piece of mechanism that God constructed, with its laws of nature, and then walked away from. Jesus says in John 5:17, 'My Father is always at his work to this very day, and I too am working.' In Hebrews 1:3 we read, 'The Son is the radiance of God's glory and the exact representation of his being, sustaining all things by his powerful word.' So, we see that maintaining the laws of nature is, itself, a miraculous activity of God. Secular scientists would dispute this, assuming that the laws of nature can take care of themselves. Richard Trench very helpfully states, 'The miracle is not a *greater* manifestation of God's power than those ordinary and ever repeated processes; but it is a *different* manifestation.'[7]

Richard Trench writes that God speaks throughout history to humanity by the laws of nature. But a miracle is seen by particular men or women at a particular time claiming their special attention and speaking to them in particular. The miracle speaks directly to them and singles them out from the crowd. God urgently wants them to listen.[8] Trench quotes Romans 1:20 to underline that God has shown himself from the beginning by the things that he has made, including the laws of nature, and these things demonstrate his eternal power so that people are without excuse for denying God's existence and his creative power.

Richard Trench describes 'the unresting activity of God, which at other times hides and conceals itself behind the veil of what we term natural laws, does in the miracle unveil itself; it steps out from its concealment, and the hand which works is laid bare.'[9]

C. S. Lewis, in his book, *Miracles*, has commented, 'It is therefore inaccurate to define a miracle as something that breaks the laws of Nature. It doesn't...'.[10]

One of the attacks that have been made on *miracles* is in finding a natural explanation for what has occurred. Liberal theology has tried to explain away such miracles as the feeding of the 5,000 by suggesting that widespread embarrassment among the crowd, who were hiding their lunchboxes, was overturned when the boy offered his picnic to Jesus.

A more scientific attempt is in saying that some of the plagues of Egypt were natural events known in that land at that time. Atheist, Richard Dawkins, pins his hopes on this line when he says that all legitimate 'miracles', are simply coincidences bound to happen because there are 7 billion people on the planet and thus 7 billion opportunities for coincidence every day![11]

If we examine the claim that the plagues of Egypt were natural events, we must note that the severity and extent of the plagues, the dreadful succession in which they followed one another, their following immediately after the pronouncements of Moses and their all serving God's purpose in delivering Israel from slavery, means we are justified in calling them, 'the signs and wonders of Egypt'. These were not coincidences. God, in Genesis 15:13–14, told Abraham more than four hundred years prior to the Exodus that he would deliver Israel: 'Then the Lord said to him, "Know for certain that your descendants will be strangers in a country not their own, and they will be enslaved and ill-treated for four hundred years. But I will punish the nation they serve as slaves, and afterwards they will come out with great possessions."'

You may ask how God does miracles. I would answer, 'by his almighty power'. Paul describes this in Ephesians 1:19–20: 'and his incomparably great power for us who believe. That power is like the working of his mighty strength, which he exerted in Christ when he raised him from the dead and seated him at his right hand in the heavenly realms.' The following examples will show how God's power is released by his touch and speech.

In Luke 8:46, we read of Jesus miraculously healing a lady who had been subject to bleeding for twelve years. In faith, she touched the hem of his garment and Jesus said, 'Someone touched me; I know that power has gone out from me.' We can read elsewhere in the Gospels, of Jesus healing lepers and blind people by touching them. So, we learn that God's power may be passed by touch. In addition, in Genesis 1:3, we learn that God's power is released when he speaks: 'God said, "Let there be light," and there was light.' When Jesus calmed the storm, he spoke to the wind and waves and they obeyed. In John 18:5–6, we have another record of the power of God's speech: at the time of Jesus's arrest in the Garden of Gethsemane, he asked the soldiers and Jewish officials who they were looking for. When they said, 'Jesus of Nazareth,' he replied, 'I am he,' at which point they fell to the ground!

I want to show how the miracles of Christ teach and confirm who Christ is. In John 14:11, Christ himself said to his disciples, 'Believe me when I say that I am in the Father and the Father is in me; or at least believe on the evidence of the miracles themselves.' Jesus was preparing his worried disciples for his departure and return to heaven. For three years, he had been preparing them to take his message, of forgiveness by God and reconciliation to God, to all nations. What he taught them was substantiated by his miracles. Jesus showed that he had:

- power over nature (the calming of the storm)—Matt 8:23–27; Mark 4:35–41; Luke 8:22–25.
- power to provide (feeding the 5,000)—Matt 14:13–21; Mark 6:30–44; Luke 9:10–17; John 6:1–15.
- power over physical and mental sickness (healing lepers and the demon possessed)—e.g., Matt 8:1–4; Mark 5:1–20.
- power to forgive sins (when he forgave the paralysed man and proved he had the right to do this by instantly healing his paralysis)—Luke 5:17–39.
- power to change lives (Zacchaeus repented and repaid the money he had stolen)—Luke 19:1–10.

- power over death (His own resurrection and the raising of Lazarus, Jairus' daughter and the Widow of Nain's son all from the dead)—Acts 2:22–24; John 11:17–43; Mark 5:35–43; Luke 7:11–15.
- power over sin (living a sinless life and then dying as an atoning sacrifice on the cross, so destroying Satan's evil power)—Hebrews 4:15; Hebrews 2:14–15; 2 Cor 5:21; 1 John 3:5.

Richard Dawkins sets himself up against God when he says, 'The virgin birth, the Resurrection, the raising of Lazarus, even the Old Testament miracles, all are freely used for religious propaganda, and they are very effective with an audience of unsophisticates and children.'[12]

Not all miracles are performed by God. Satan and others can perform miracles. Satan is a master of disguise. He came to Eve as a talking and lying snake. He led her and Adam to disobey God. He arranged for the destruction of all 'righteous' Job's children and his possessions. He appeared bodily to Jesus in the wilderness and tempted Him three times. Ordinary men can be used by Satan as well. Pharaoh's 'magicians' had miraculous powers—they were not doing conjuring tricks. However, Aaron's rod, when transformed into a snake, ate all the snakes which the magicians' rods had become. God's power triumphed over Satan's best efforts. Satan is a loser.

We must remember the war Satan wages against God and not be fooled by miracle workers, motivated by evil. A miracle alone does not prove the authority of the 'miracle worker' or their supposed truth. Archbishop Trench helpfully says of evil miracles, 'They are abrupt, isolated, parts of no organic whole; not the highest harmonies, but the deepest discords of the universe; not the omnipotence of God wielding his own worlds to ends of grace and wisdom and love, but evil permitted to intrude.'[13]

Deuteronomy 13:1–3 deals directly with this issue:

> If a prophet, or one who foretells by dreams, appears among you and announces to you a miraculous sign or wonder, and if the sign or wonder of which he has spoken takes place, and he says, 'Let us follow other gods' (gods you have not known) 'and let us worship them,' you must not listen to the words of that prophet or dreamer. The Lord your God is testing you to find out whether you love him with all your heart and with all your soul.

Moving our attention from miracles to the laws of nature, we see that mankind is able to live in a predictable environment (especially important when designing aeroplanes, ships or buildings) and that man has the intellect (for example, Isaac Newton was able to describe the Laws of Gravitation) to investigate the creation and natural laws all around him. My comments in this chapter are related to what might be called 'physical laws of nature'; these are scientific generalizations based on phenomena which are observed to occur regularly in the world around us. But it is right to comment that there are also 'natural laws' which reflect firm beliefs in moral, legal or political theory as well. According to 'natural law' theory, all people have inherent rights such as owning property and protection from harm.

Considering the *physical laws of nature*, some claim that there are four laws which explain forces or interactions: gravitation, electromagnetism, the weak interaction, and the strong interaction.

Newton, Faraday and Clerk Maxwell are associated with the first two of these laws. The laws of weak and strong interaction are related to the forces which maintain the integrity of atomic structure. The strong nuclear force attracts protons and neutrons to each other, keeping the nucleus of an atom intact, while the weak nuclear force is responsible for the radioactive decay of certain nuclei. There are of course other laws: for example, Newton's laws of motion, Kepler's laws of planetary motion, the three laws of Thermodynamics, Mendel's laws of genetics, the ideal gas laws and others.

A person's worldview affects how they understand the origin of the laws of nature. I will consider three of these, beginning with the Christian worldview based on Biblical truth. Then I will describe the worldview of Albert Einstein and finally that of Stephen Hawking.

The Christian worldview

The Christian worldview motivated great scientists like Isaac Newton, Michael Faraday, Johannes Kepler and James Clerk Maxwell. These Christian men saw order and design in nature all around them. They believed these laws to have been designed by their kind and generous God. Kepler once wrote, 'I was merely thinking God's thoughts after him. Since we astronomers are priests of the highest God in regard to the book of nature, it benefits us to be thoughtful, not of the glory of our minds, but rather, above all else, of the glory of God.'[14] C. S. Lewis said in his book, *Miracles*, 'Men became scientific because they expected Law in Nature, and they expected Law in Nature because they believed in a Legislator' (a lawmaker).[15]

The worldview of Albert Einstein – pantheism

A second worldview was that of the great 20th century physicist, Albert Einstein, who was born into a family of secular Jews. In 1905, he presented his Special Theory of Relativity and received a PhD from the University of Zurich. Clearly Einstein knew a lot about the laws of nature! His own worldview has been much debated but might be best described as very muddled. For example, in 1930, when attending a concert of the Berlin Philharmonic Orchestra, he was so excited at the performance of the soloist, Yehudi Menuhin, that he afterwards embraced Menuhin and said, 'Now I know there is a God in heaven.'[16]

Einstein talked a lot about God in his explanations of physics, receiving a rebuke from his friend, physicist Niels Bohr, for constantly telling God what he could do. Einstein appeared to respect Jesus and felt that the Judeo-Christian religious tradition gave mankind its highest principles. Einstein wrote in his 1949 book, *The World As I See It*, that the 'scientist's religious feelings take the form of rapturous amazement at the harmony of natural law, which reveals an intelligence of such superiority that, compared with it, all the systematic thinking and acting of human beings is an utterly insignificant reflection.'[17] You would think this statement was compatible with Biblical Christianity, but was perhaps closer to Fred Hoyle's opinion.

Einstein did not believe in the God revealed in the Bible. He admired the Jewish philosopher, Baruch Spinoza, and wrote, 'I believe in Spinoza's god, who reveals Himself in the lawful harmony of the world, not in a god who concerns himself with the fate and the doings of mankind.'[18]

Spinoza's god was the god of Pantheism—the belief that all of reality is identical with god. Such a god is said to be infinite, without cause and everything that exists is in this god. But I suggest that such a god is simply a useful intellectual fudge—useful to explain where the laws of nature came from with the attraction that there is no given moral standard or responsibility for mankind to behave in a good way. Pantheism is a convenient way of getting rid of the God of the Bible with His ethical demands.

Einstein had a dismissive view of the Bible. He wrote, 'No interpretation (of the Bible), no matter how subtle, can (for me) change anything' about the fact that the Bible text represented to him 'an incarnation of primitive superstition'.[19] Einstein's personal life, two wives and 'his marriages marred with affairs',[20] was very muddled, in spite of his comments about the Judeo-Christian religious tradition.

The worldview of Stephen Hawking—naturalism

The third worldview is tied up with the title of this book, *The Something Delusion*. This view holds that the laws of nature arose from nothing or nearly nothing. I have already quoted Stephen Hawking and Leonard Mlodinow in their book, *The Grand Design*: 'Because there is a law such as gravity, the universe can and will create itself from nothing. Spontaneous creation is the reason there is something rather than nothing, why the universe exists, why we exist.'[21]

Most of us find physics a challenging subject. However, this quotation is clear and easily understood. The best-known theoretical physicist of the 21st century tells us that spontaneous creation has made SOMETHING from nothing and that the laws of nature have also arisen spontaneously. Spontaneous generation of animal life is necessary for Darwin's theory of evolution to explain biological questions and Hawking now tells us that spontaneous creation has answered the questions of physics by making everything out of nothing! Richard Dawkins welcomed *The Grand Design* and said, 'Darwinism kicked God out of biology but physics remained more uncertain. Hawking is now administering the coup de grace.'[22]

Is that really the case? Not every Oxford professor agrees. John Lennox, a Professor of Mathematics at Oxford University and a Christian, declared about *The Grand Design*, 'Nonsense remains nonsense, even when talked by world-famous scientists.'[23]

I believe that there are only two possible explanations for the origin of the laws of nature. As stated previously, we must decide which model or bias best fits the evidence. Science is limited in not being able to design an experiment to prove which possibility is correct. The two interpretations are: (i) God created these laws and maintains them (John 5:17: 'My Father is always at his work to this very day, and I too am working.') and (ii) Things made themselves (Naturalism or Pantheism).

Science is a tool which we can use to investigate the world around us. However, it deals with repeatable observations in the *present* while evolutionary theory has to make unprovable assumptions about the *past*. The biblical account, explaining the origin of the laws of nature, provides historical evidence based on the testimony of witnesses. We must recognize that the biases of the religions of Christianity and of Evolutionary Humanism interpret the same facts in diametrically opposite ways.

Chapter 27

The apostle Peter makes an interesting comment about the times in which we live. The days since Jesus returned to heaven (his Ascension) are known biblically as the last days. I think for the modern scoffer we would have to reinterpret Peter's phrase, 'the beginning of creation', as being from the beginning of time, if the particular scoffer was happy to accept that there was a beginning! Peter wrote, in 2 Peter 3:3–6:

> You must understand that in the last days scoffers will come, scoffing and following their own evil desires. They will say, 'Where is this "coming" he promised? Ever since our fathers died, everything goes on as it has since the beginning of creation.' But they deliberately forget that long ago by God's word the heavens existed and the earth was formed out of water and by water. By these waters also the world of that time was deluged and destroyed.

The global geological evidence for the worldwide flood at the time of Noah shows us that the world has not continued in a naturalistic way from the beginning until the present. Biblical history tells us that God intervened to deal with the wickedness of mankind in judgement and the scars of that judgement lie all over the surface of the earth in geological testimony. Peter continues in verse 7 to tell us of what will happen in the future when God, in the person of Jesus Christ, judges the world at the Last Day: 'By the same word the present heavens and earth are reserved for fire, being kept for the day of judgement and destruction of the ungodly.'

George Wald, a Jewish Nobel Prize winning biologist, made discoveries about vitamin A and pigments in the human retina. A pacifist and an atheist, he believed that physicalism (everything which exists is no more extensive than its physical properties) was responsible for all that exists. There is no 'programming of life'. He said, 'I will not believe that philosophically because I do not want to believe in God. Therefore, *I choose to believe in that which I know is scientifically impossible*: spontaneous generation arising to evolution.'[24]

Wald said of spontaneous generation, in the August 1964 *Scientific American*, 'However improbable we regard this event, *it will almost certainly happen at least once* (my italics) ... The time ... is of the order of two billion years ... Given so much time, the "impossible" becomes possible, the possible probable, and the probable virtually certain. One only has to wait: time itself performs the miracles.'[25] You may remember, in chapter 4, I remarked that my school Biology textbook, also dated 1964, arrived at the same conclusion: 'Some simple forms of life *certainly must have arisen spontaneously.*'[26] Such unscientific statements are common in defence of the 'just so story of evolution'.

During the 1980s, Wald often talked about how special the elements carbon, hydrogen, oxygen and nitrogen are. Given that he was an atheist and did not believe in 'programming of life', he strangely remarked in an interview that he believed the universe was designed for life. He concluded that the evidence was clearly obvious because the elements carbon, hydrogen, oxygen and nitrogen 'have unique properties that fit the job and are not shared by any element in the periodic system'.[27]

I have suggested that Evolutionists are men and women of faith! George Wald published an article in 1970 with the title, 'The Origin of Death', with this remark in the penultimate paragraph:

> If the germ plasm wants to swim in the ocean, it makes itself a fish; if the germ plasm wants to fly in the air, it makes itself a

bird. If it wants to go to Harvard, it makes itself a man. The strangest thing of all is that the germ plasm that we carry around within us has done all those things. There was a time, hundreds of millions of years ago, when it was making fish. Then ... amphibia ... reptiles ... mammals, and now it's making men. If we only have the restraint and good sense to leave it alone, heaven knows what it will make in ages to come.[28]

I will leave the final word in this chapter to C. S. Lewis, who (perhaps with a twinkle in his eye) said,

Belief in miracles, far from depending on an ignorance of the laws of nature, is only possible in so far as those laws are known. We have already seen that if you begin ruling out the supernatural you will perceive no miracles. We must now add that you will equally perceive no miracles until you believe that nature works according to regular laws. If you have not yet noticed that the sun always rises in the East, you will see nothing miraculous about his rising one morning in the West.[29]

NOTES

1 David Van Biema, 'God vs. Science, TIME convenes a debate with Francis Collins and Richard Dawkins', 5 November 2006. https://content.time.com/time/magazine/article/0,9171,1555132-6,00.html

2 C. S. Lewis Essay Collection: and other short pieces, (New York: Fount/Harper Collins, First Edition, 2000). https://www.amazon.co.uk/C-S-Lewis-Essay-Collection/dp/0006281575

3 C. S. Lewis, *Miracles*, (Oxford: Fount, 1974), p. 112.

4 Richard C. Trench, *Notes on the Miracles of Our Lord—Popular Edition*, (Grand Rapids, Michigan: Baker Book House, 1949).

5 Ibid., p. 9.

6 Ibid., p. 9 footnote.

7 Ibid., p. 10.

8 Ibid., p. 10.

9 Ibid., pp. 10–11.

10 C. S. Lewis, *Miracles*, p. 63.

11 Paul Pavao, 'Miracles and Coincidences—from the Blind Watchmaker', *Proof-of-Evolution.com* 2014.

12 Richard Dawkins, 'The Great Convergence', *The Irish Times*, 17 February 2003. Extracted from: *A Devil's Chaplain*, (London: Weidenfeld and Nicholson, 2003).

13 Richard C. Trench, *Notes on the Miracles of Our Lord—Popular Edition*, p. 16.

14 Johannes Kepler, *New World Encyclopaedia*, 2019. https://www.newworldencyclopedia.org/entry/Johannes_Kepler.

15 C. S. Lewis, *Miracles*, p. 110.

16 Nick Spencer, 'Did Albert Einstein believe in God?', 4 December 2018. https://www.prospectmagazine.co.uk/philosophy/did-albert-einstein-believe-in-god

17 Albert Einstein, *The World As I See It*, (New York: Philosophical Library, 1949), p. 29.

18 Mario Livio, 'Einstein's Famous "God Letter" Is Up for Auction', *Scientific American*, 11 October 2018.

19 Stephen Hawking and Leonard Mlodinow, *The Grand Design*, (New York: Bantam Books, 2011). https://www.reuters.com/article/us-britain-hawking-idUSTRE6811FN20100902

20 Biography.com editors, 'An Inside Look at Albert Einstein's Personal Life', 2 June 2020. https://www.biography.com/news/einstein-love-life-wives-affairs-letters

21 Stephen Hawking and Leonard Mlodinow, *The Grand Design*, (New York: Bantam Books, 2011). https://www.reuters.com/article/us-britain-hawking-idUSTRE6811FN20100902

22 Mukul Sharma, 'A God-forsaken solution', *The Economic Times*, 22 October 2010. https://economictimes.indiatimes.com/opinion/vedanta/a-god-forsaken-solution/articleshow/6790759.cms

23 John Lennox, 'Nonsense Remains Nonsense', *Evolution News @DiscoveryCSC*, 16 August 2011.

24 Donald E. Johnson, *Programming of Life*, (Alabama: Big Mac Publishers, 2010), p. 123.

25 George Wald, 'The Origin of Life', *Scientific American*, August 1954, 191, No. 2, p. 46.

26 Grove & Newell, *Animal Biology*, (London: University Tutorial Press Ltd, 1964 6th edition reprint), pp. 724–726.

27 'Four Simple Facts Behind the Miracle of Life', *Parade Magazine*, 12 June 1998, p. 12.

28 George Wald, 'The Origin of Death', https://www.elijahwald.com/origin.html

29 C. S. Lewis, *Miracles*, p. 51.

28 The periodic table, carbon and water

The Periodic Table of all the known chemical elements, displays the elements according to their atomic number, electron configuration, and recurring chemical properties. The elements are displayed in transverse rows, known as periods, and in columns, known as groups. Russian chemist, Dmitri Mendeleev[1] published his version of the periodic table in March 1869.

To mark the 150th anniversary of this event, BBC News (29 January 2019) interviewed a present-day chemist, Dr Peter Wothers, who teaches Chemistry at the University of Cambridge. He said, 'If aliens came down to Earth, this flag of science would not have escaped their attention.' When asked if aliens would have a periodic table, he replied, 'I think they probably would, because it is something that is absolutely fundamental—*this is not just some creation of humans*, there is something innate and fundamental to this—there's chemical law, physical law behind this.'[2]

In saying that the periodic table was not a creation of humans, I believe that Dr Wothers was recognizing that man did not have the power or the intelligence of a supreme designer who could *create* such a periodic table. That being so, how could nothing or indeed an inanimate something, without a brain, create a periodic table?

When Dr Wothers described that there is chemical law and

physical law behind the periodic table, he has not provided an explanation for the origin of the periodic table; he has simply transferred the discussion from, 'Where did the periodic table come from?' to, 'Where did the chemical and physical laws come from?' One detects echoes of Fred Hoyle and Francis Crick who were unable to tell us where life on earth came from, so, they moved the argument or discussion further away and told us that life came from outer space (by Panspermia).

When I studied A-level Chemistry, I learned about the group 7 elements, known as halogens. The elements in this group have similar properties: they all form acids when combined with hydrogen; they are all fairly toxic and potentially lethal; they readily combine with metals to form salts; they have seven valence electrons in their outer shell; and they are highly reactive and electronegative.

The first 94 elements in the table, from hydrogen to plutonium, all occur naturally, though some are only found in trace amounts. Elements 95 to 118 have only been produced in laboratories, nuclear reactors, or nuclear explosions. I should clarify that elements can exist in more than one form. These different forms are known as isotopes and have different masses; e.g. carbon has two stable isotopes found in nature, one is C–12 (^{12}C) and the other is C–13 (^{13}C). Many synthetic radioisotopes of naturally occurring elements have been produced in laboratories.

Elements such as carbon, sulphur, copper and gold have been known since antiquity. The first element discovered in more recent history was phosphorus. In 1669, a German merchant and pharmacist, Hennig Brandt,[3] had mixed charcoal and sand with a tar-like substance, which he had produced by patiently distilling about 1,200 gallons of urine over a two-week period. He was hoping to create a 'philosophers' stone' which would transform base metals into gold (a false idea). He kept the mixture at a very high temperature for many hours and a white vapour was produced that then condensed into drops which gleamed brightly. This glowing wax-like substance was unknown and Brandt called it, *phosphorus*, after a Latin word meaning that it 'gave off light'.

Like many at that time, Brandt thought that there were only four elements: fire, air, water, and earth, and he assumed that his new compound was formed from these elements. An important development in human understanding occurred when the French chemist, Antoine-Laurent Lavoisier, replaced the ancient view of four elements with a larger number of simple substances that could not be further broken down and described thirty-three elements in his textbook, *Traité* élémentaire *de chimie* [4] (Elements of Chemistry), published in 1789 and translated into English by Robert Kerr in 1790. This book and his other discoveries became the foundation of modern chemistry. Very sadly, this great scientist was guillotined during the French Revolution in 1794.

An English chemist, John Newlands, wrote papers between 1863 and 1866, noting that when the elements were listed in order of increasing atomic weight, similar physical and chemical properties recurred at intervals of eight. He likened this to the octaves of music. This so called, *Law of Octaves* [5], was ridiculed, and the Chemical Society refused to publish his work. After Mendeleev's publication in 1869, they did acknowledge the significance of his work; he was awarded the Davy Medal of the Royal Society in 1887.

Dmitri Mendeleev made two decisions which led to his periodic table of 1869 being internationally recognized. Firstly, he left gaps in the table when it seemed that a missing element had not yet been discovered. His second decision was to occasionally ignore the order suggested by the atomic weights and switch adjacent elements to fit them better into chemical groups. The United Nations declared 2019 as the *International Year of the Periodic Table*—one of the greatest achievements in science.

Dr Wothers also said of the periodic table:

> We now know the 'how it works, why it works', and this is to do with quantum mechanics and the arrangements of electrons in atoms and so on; the periodic table is now a thing of both beauty and practical use. You can understand certain things just by considering the place of an element in this table, or in this arrangement, that's why it's so useful to chemists.[6]

The addition of 4 elements to the periodic table in December 2015, led Dr Wothers to say this made it 'quite whole and beautiful. ... The periodic table is in its most perfect form and probably the most perfect form it will ever be in,' he said.[6]

In chapter 18, I referred to the beauty of Chippendale furniture and the fame of its designer. I wonder if you see beauty and design in the periodic table. In Romans 1:20, Paul has written, 'For since the creation of the world God's invisible qualities—his eternal power and divine nature—have been clearly seen, being understood from what has been made, so that men are without excuse.' Beauty and design logically point to a designer and to deny so has consequences.

We should ask, 'Where did the periodic table come from?' There is regularity, predictability and beauty written all over it, in the opinion of Dr Wothers! I suggest that there are three possible answers: *Firstly,* some naturalistic evolutionary process is responsible; *secondly,* the actions of the Almighty God of the Bible (a supernatural intelligence); or *thirdly,* a mixture of the two.

(1) If we consider *some naturalistic evolutionary process,* there have been modifications in recent years of how scientists think this might have happened. In the late 1940s, many believed that virtually all isotopes were synthesized in conditions which followed in the first twenty minutes after the Big Bang explosion, due to so-called, *Big Bang Nucleosynthesis.*[7] Today, only a few isotopes (e.g., hydrogen, deuterium, helium4 and Lithium7) are thought to have formed in this way while the majority, such as oxygen, carbon and iron, are believed to have formed by nuclear reactions within giant stars— so-called, *Stellar Nucleosynthesis.*[8] The theory, formulated by Professor Fred Hoyle, claims that most of Earth's elements were cooked for billions of years in stars and then released in the universe through super-nova explosions. This process is called *cosmic chemical evolution theory.*

Nuclear astrophysics claims to explain how the isotopes/ elements of the periodic table were made! How the regularity, predictability and organization into groups came about, remains speculative.

When William Fowler gave his 58-page Nobel lecture entitled, 'Experimental and theoretical nuclear astrophysics; the quest for the origin of the elements', on 8 December 1983, he said,

> In spite of the past and current research in experimental and theoretical nuclear astrophysics, ... Hoyle's grand concept of

element synthesis in the stars will not be truly established until we attain a deeper and more precise understanding of many nuclear processes operating in astrophysical environments. It is not just a matter of filling in the details. There are puzzles and problems in each part of the cycle which challenge the basic ideas underlying nucleosynthesis in stars.[9]

He declared that Hoyle's theory was not proven. He continued to explain how they thought the elements were born:

The stars which synthesized the heavy elements in the solar system were formed or born, evolved or aged, and eventually injected the ashes of their nuclear fires into the interstellar medium over the lifetime of the galaxy before the solar system itself formed 4.5 billion years ago. The lifetime of the galaxy is thought to be more than 10 billion years but less than 20 billion years. In any case, the galaxy is much older than the solar system. The injection of the nuclear ashes or newly formed elements took place by slow mass loss during the old age of the star, called the giant stage of stellar evolution, or during the final spectacular stellar explosions called supernovae. Supernovae can be considered to be the death of stars. White dwarfs or neutron stars or black holes which result from stellar evolution may represent a form of stellar purgatory.[9]

As Fowler concluded his lecture he said,

And now permit me to pass along one final thought in concluding my lecture. My major theme has been that all of the heavy elements from carbon to uranium have been synthesized in stars. Let me remind you that your bodies consist for the most part of these heavy elements. Apart from hydrogen you are 65 per cent oxygen and 18 per cent carbon with smaller percentages of nitrogen, sodium, magnesium, phosphorus, sulphur, chlorine, potassium, and traces of still heavier elements. Thus, it is possible to say that you and your neighbour and I, each one of us and all of us, are truly and literally a little bit of stardust.[9]

I mentioned, in chapter 22, that Martin Rees, the Astronomer Royal, affirmed that we are nuclear waste from long-dead stars. Stephen Jay Gould thought that we are a glorious cosmic accident! So, where does love, faithfulness, altruism or self-sacrifice come from?

Professor Stephen Hawking, in his introduction to the 2016 New Scientist book, *The Origin of (Almost) Everything*, wrote,

> The universe started off in the Big Bang and expanded quickly. This is called 'inflation' and it was extremely rapid: the universe doubled in size many times in a tiny fraction of a second. Inflation made the universe very large, very smooth and very flat. However, it was not completely smooth: there were tiny variations from place to place. These variations eventually gave rise to galaxies, stars and solar systems. We owe our existence to these variations. If the early universe had been completely smooth, there would be no stars and so life could not have developed. *We are the product of primordial quantum fluctuations* (my italics). As will become clear many huge mysteries remain. Still, we are steadily edging closer to answering the age-old questions: 'Where did we come from? And are we the only beings in the Universe who can ask these questions?'[10]

Stephen Hawking also explained how, in the 1920s, Edwin Hubble discovered the Universe was expanding. Some were unhappy with this discovery because it suggested that the universe had a beginning. If so, it implied an outside agency, which for convenience one could call 'god', caused the Universe to begin. An expanding Universe put paid to the steady-state theory of the Universe favoured by Fred Hoyle. If the Big Bang is the beginning of the Universe, we are entitled to ask, 'Where did the matter, energy and motion for a Big Bang come from and why do isotopes/elements in groups exhibit similar properties?' Could a naturalistic process give rise to all that we see and experience around us?'

Stephen Hawking argued that God is not necessary to explain the origins of the Universe because the Big Bang is a consequence of the laws of physics alone. He has said, 'One can't prove that God doesn't exist, but science makes God unnecessary.'[10] He clarified that he did not believe in a personal God. The back cover of the 2016 New Scientist book, described above, asks the following, 'Where did we come from? How did it all begin? These are the biggest questions in the Universe and New Scientist has the answers.' Really?

(2) *The creative activity of Almighty God* is the second possible explanation for the origin of the periodic table and Universe. The evidence for this is not primarily scientific. In fact, no scientific experiment can be performed to repeat and prove how the Universe came to be. The evidence for this second possibility is that of an eyewitness, Almighty God. His scribe, Moses, inspired by the Holy Spirit, has recorded in the book of Genesis the historical account of the origin of the Universe and of mankind. The origin of death, disease and decay here on the Earth is explained. The Old Testament writers, from Moses to Malachi, record the history of our planet. After a silence of 400 years, the New Testament records the incarnation of the eternal second person of the Trinity, Jesus Christ. Jesus testified to the Creation, Adam and Eve, the inauguration of the Sabbath, the honourable status of work and of God's design of marriage and the family. Jesus spoke of the worldwide flood of

Noah's day, which has left geological evidence which many choose to misinterpret. During the time that Noah was building the ark, he preached of impending divine judgement on sin. This warning was and is still ignored.

Jesus Christ demonstrated in his miracles that he does have the power to create the Universe. Genesis 1:3 tells us that God spoke light into existence. On each of the following days of creation week, the method of God creating is by his speaking. Hebrews 11:3 reminds us 'that the universe was formed at God's command, so that what is seen was not made out of what was visible'. Romans 4:17b repeats this truth: 'the God who gives life to the dead and calls into being things that were not'. Jesus spoke the truth and lived a perfect life. He is a reliable witness. Colossians 1:15–20 is helpful in answering the question, 'Where did the periodic table come from?'

In that passage, St Paul wrote of Jesus Christ:

> He is the image of the invisible God, the firstborn over all creation. For by him all things were created: things in heaven and on earth, visible and invisible, whether thrones or powers or rulers or authorities; all things were created by him and for him. He is before all things, and in him all things hold together. And he is the head of the body, the church; he is the beginning and the firstborn from among the dead, so that in everything he might have the supremacy. For God was pleased to have all his fullness dwell in him, and through him to reconcile to himself all things, whether things on earth or things in heaven, by making peace through his blood, shed on the cross.

(3) A third possibility is *a mixture of the first two*. Theistic Evolution is the subject of the next two chapters in this book. However, for now, we should note that theistic evolution holds that there is an

intelligence using evolution. This an unsatisfactory position to hold. Why? Because evolution is, by definition, an undirected process. Darwinian evolution depends upon random genetic mutations which are preserved by a blind, undirected process of natural selection that cannot have long-term goals. Indeed, it would be strange to ascribe a goal to something that is mindless.

Richard Dawkins, in describing genes as being 'selfish', in his book, *The Selfish Gene*, explains that this does not mean that they have any motive or goal, but that they can be described metaphorically as if they had! As part of his explanation of the mechanism of evolution he wrote, 'At some point a particularly remarkable molecule was formed by accident. We will call it the *Replicator*. It may not necessarily have been the biggest or the most complex molecule around, but it had the extraordinary property of being able to create copies of itself.'[11] He has not demonstrated that scientifically but imagines it. In truth, the random and undirected process, based on genetic mutations, tends to harm organisms by the loss of genetic material and does not build greater complexity.

I now wish to wish to turn your attention to *carbon* and to *water*. I suggest to you that we will see the Christian worldview strengthened by looking at them.

Carbon (C) is perhaps the most unique of all elements. Carbon certainly caused Fred Hoyle enormous excitement; he declared, 'that some super-calculating intellect must have designed the properties of the carbon atom'.[12] Sir James Jeans, physicist and astronomer, stated, 'Life exists in the Universe only because the carbon atom possesses certain exceptional properties.'[13]

Carbon is a non-metal, having unlimited capacity to participate in every known type of covalent chemical bonding (i.e., pairs of electrons shared between atoms), which unites atoms of the same kind to each other and to other kinds of atoms. This feature, called catenation, is virtually unlimited for the element carbon alone.

Other elements, such as silicon (Si), nitrogen (N), sulphur (S), or phosphorus (P) display limited capacities for catenation, which do not compare to the catenation ability of carbon. This unique feature allows the formation of biomolecules essential for life, such as proteins, DNA, RNA and cellulose. Despite this amazing property, carbon comprises only 9 to 10 percent by weight of the composition of all living things and only 0.017 percent of the Earth's composition. If even one or two carbon atoms were replaced by other elements in biomolecules, the biological integrity of those systems would be destroyed.

Carbon is familiar to us as charred wood, coal, diamonds and as graphite in lead pencils. Carbon occurs naturally in three isotopes: ^{12}C, ^{13}C and ^{14}C. The last of these, ^{14}C, is radioactive and present in very small amounts in the upper atmosphere and down on earth. ^{12}C is found in the carbon dioxide (CO_2) in the air, which is taken up by plants that, in turn, are eaten by animals. Thus, bones, leaves and a wooden chair contain carbon. Carbon dioxide, also, is formed with the ^{14}C isotope. Both forms of carbon dioxide get cycled through the cells of animals and plants.

The radioactive isotope, ^{14}C, has a 'half-life' of 5,730 years. It decays back to ^{14}N (nitrogen) at a constant rate. However, in living animals or plants, carbon dioxide is still exchanged with the surroundings so that the amount of ^{14}C remains about the same as in the atmosphere, despite this decay. Since dead tissue does not absorb any more carbon, the amounts of ^{14}C and ^{12}C in dead material can be used as one of the methods of radiometric dating of biological material. It is important to understand that there is a time limitation of about 50,000 years old on the radiocarbon dating technique.

The 5,730-years 'half-life' of ^{14}C means that in two half-lives, or 11,460 years, only one-quarter of the original ^{14}C will be left in dead material. By looking at the ratio of ^{14}C to ^{12}C in the dead sample and comparing it to the ratio known in living organisms we can calculate the theoretical age of the sample. If, for example, the quantity of ^{14}C was one-quarter of that in living organisms, then it has a theoretical age of 11,460 years. Anything older than about 50,000 years old should theoretically have no detectable ^{14}C left in it. Radiocarbon dating cannot give ages of millions of years. In fact, if a sample contains 14C, it is good evidence that it is not millions of years old. Radiocarbon has been found in fish fossils, 'Palaeozoic wood', coal, diamonds and shells, all supposedly tens or hundreds of millions of years old.[14,15]

By looking at the ^{14}C levels in objects from sites which can be historically dated e.g., seeds in graves, it is possible to estimate the level of ^{14}C in the atmosphere at that time and so, a partial calibration of the '^{14}C clock' is possible, perhaps increasing accuracy. Even with such historical calibration, archaeologists cannot trust ^{14}C dates absolutely because of anomalies. Outside the range of recorded history, calibration of the '^{14}C clock' is not possible.

Coal is a fossil fuel, described by conventional geology as being up to hundreds of millions of years old. In fact, coal contains ^{14}C, suggesting that it is less than 50,000 years old. This is true of all sources of coal and suggests a much younger age than millions of years.[14]

It is generally held that diamonds formed about 1–3 billion years ago. In 2005, geophysicist, Dr John Baumgardner, published his investigation of ^{14}C in a number of diamonds and found radiocarbon was present at over 10 times the detection limit. There should have been none. The radiocarbon age for these diamonds was in thousands of years. Examination of six alluvial diamonds from Namibia found even more radiocarbon.[16]

Dinosaurs are generally held to have become extinct 65 million years ago. Radiometric dating usually supports such a timeframe. However, dinosaur bones have been found to include real bone that has not completely mineralized. In recent years, blood cells, haemoglobin, osteocytes, proteins and soft tissue, such as collagen and nerves, have been found in dinosaur bones, along with ^{14}C radiocarbon and DNA.[17] Short segments of ancient DNA from dinosaur fossils have been reported by Mary Schweitzer, who made the original observations about collagen in dinosaur bones in 2005.[18]

The finding of ^{14}C in collagen within dinosaur bones has been confirmed in the PhD thesis of Brian Thomas at the University of Liverpool.[19] The radiocarbon would suggest the bones are less than 50,000 years old. Interestingly, Dr Mary Schweitzer, who made the original observations, also noticed that a T-Rex skeleton had a distinctly cadaverous odour. The skeleton was from Hell Creek in Montana and another experienced palaeontologist, Jack Horner, commented, 'All Hell Creek bones smell.'[20]

Carbon is of enormous importance in the carbon-based life of the Earth and its ^{14}C isotope provides evidence of a young Earth.

Water (H_2O) is one of the most abundant chemicals upon the Earth. Water has several very special characteristics, making it unique among all other materials. It is made from two atoms of hydrogen with one atom of oxygen. The oxygen strongly attracts the two single electrons of the hydrogen atoms, leaving the positively charged hydrogen nuclei fairly free to attract other negative atoms. This causes the very strong hydrogen bond that is so important between water molecules. The hydrogen nuclei can then attract the oxygen atoms in other water molecules and large frameworks are formed. The angle of 104.5° between the hydrogen and oxygen atoms is almost that of a perfect (though warped three dimensionally) six-sided tetrahedron shape which maintains this shape with little stress on the bonds. The strong tendency of water molecules to bond with others around it results in large three-dimensional tetrahedron frameworks.

On Earth, water exists in three forms: *liquid, solid* (ice) or *gas* (vapour). Oceans and seas hold about 97 percent of the Earth's water; the rest is found in glaciers, ice, rivers and lakes or in clouds.

Water, as a liquid, can dissolve more substances than any other liquid. Plants can use nutrients which are transported throughout the plant dissolved in their sap. The oceans act as a reservoir for gases which are dissolved in them: if carbon dioxide in the air increases, it is absorbed by the sea and, again, it is released if the atmospheric level falls.

There are a huge number of chemical reactions between complex molecules in living organisms which happen successfully because of the powerful solvent properties of water. In addition, the environment can be balanced to ensure that conditions are neither too acidic nor too alkaline by buffering systems.

In the liquid state, water molecules are attracted to each other with a force greater than for all other materials except mercury. On the surface of the water, this attractive force allows the surface to behave like a thin film, on which small loads can be supported. This *surface tension* can support a metal pin placed carefully on the top of water. Insects, such as the water boatman, can walk on the water. Water droplets, perhaps on the tip of a finger, adopt a perfect spherical shape and soap bubbles come in the form of a sphere because of surface tension. Water is also attracted to the side of a vessel or a capillary tube so that water rises within tubes. This is called *capillary action* and is of special importance in the growth of tall trees, where water can be raised to over 100 feet.

The solid state of water happens when the temperature is lowered to 0°C—its freezing point. Almost all materials decrease in volume as they get colder. Water does this down to 4°C but the volume of the water then increases below that level. This property is very important in nature, particularly in a lake containing fish. As the temperature drops, so the surface water gets colder, decreases in volume and becomes denser, so that it sinks to the bottom of the lake. This has the benefit of dragging oxygen to the bottom of the lake, supporting 'lake bottom organisms'. The process continues until the whole depth of the lake has reached 4°C. As the surface water cools below this temperature, it increases in volume and becomes less dense than the water below, so it has no tendency to sink, and the top layer eventually freezes, acting as an insulation layer. Without this amazing property, the whole lake would freeze and all fish and living creatures in the pond would die. The ice floats on the lake with a density 9 per cent less than water. This is the reason that icebergs float with most of their volume below sea level. It is of great interest that the molecular structure of ice does not allow other chemicals to be included, so that, when seawater freezes, the ice on the surface contains no salt! If we take a sample and melt it there will be no salt or other impurities in it.

A water pipe, in winter, can burst because of the expansion of ice. However, expansion as water freezes, can be beneficial when breaking up hard earth into smaller particles. This allows soil to crumble and makes it suitable for seed germination.

The third form of water is vapour. When water is heated, it evaporates, turns into water vapour and expands. At 100°C—the boiling point—it evaporates more rapidly. At this point, the invisible gas of steam is created. If you put your hand by the spout of a boiling kettle in the invisible length before the visible steam vapour, your hand will be burned. The opposite of evaporation is condensation, which is when water vapour condenses back into tiny droplets of water. We see this on the inside of a cold exterior window in the winter from our breathing inside the room. In very cold weather, water vapour forms ice crystals which join and fall as snowflakes. There are millions of patterns of snowflakes all of which are unique! Wilson Bentley, many years ago, took thousands of photographs of snow crystals calling them, 'miracles of beauty'. [21]

Steam, of course, has been a wonderful tool for mankind. Water increases in volume by 1,700 times at standard temperature and pressure when boiled. Engineers, such as James Watt FRS, realized they could use steam to drive machines, like railway engines, or to power machines in factories. Watt's steam engine, in 1776, was fundamental to the Industrial Revolution.

There are more amazing properties of water; I will mention one more. A protein is made up of a very long chain of amino acids. However, this does not remain a long chain but is folded in multiple ways with many different links between adjacent sections of the chain, so that the final shape is convoluted with deep crevasses and bumps. As the protein molecule is formed, these crevices can hold water molecules, which will make up from 27 to 77 percent of the final weight of the protein. These water molecules can move in and out of the grooves at extraordinary speeds of a million times in the fraction of a second. The water itself can link into long chains and influence the shape and function of the protein. The water molecules also act to keep the crevasses open for other chemicals to enter and react with the protein. The importance of water to the whole way in which proteins operate, amazes biochemists and affirms the design abilities of our Creator. These amazing properties are consistent across many species. An enzyme (one sort of protein) can have the same water-related mechanism whether it comes from cows, humans or even yeast!

We cannot imagine a world without water. As the heat of the sun draws water from the surface of the Earth into the clouds, it then falls back to the earth as rain or snow. This is called *The Water Cycle*. In Job 36:27–28, we read, 'He draws up the drops of water, which distil as rain to the streams; the clouds pour down their moisture and abundant showers fall on mankind.'

As I have been drawing your attention to the brilliant design of the water molecule, it is right to mention a very great scientist, James Clerk Maxwell FRS, who spoke and wrote a lot about molecules. He was a Bible-believing Christian, a mathematician and a scientific genius. He showed that magnetism, electricity and light were phenomena which were different manifestations of the same scientific laws. As a young man, he won a prestigious prize for mathematically answering the question, 'Were the rings of Saturn completely solid, were they fluid or made of separate solid particles?' He proved that they must consist of small but separate solid particles; a fact confirmed over 100 years later by the Voyager space probe to Saturn.

The four mathematical equations on electromagnetism, which James Clerk Maxwell described, explained Michael Faraday's experimental results, and are as important as Sir Isaac Newton's laws of motion and Albert Einstein's theory of relativity.

James Clerk Maxwell presented a paper called 'Discourse on Molecules'[22] as an evening lecture, open to the public during the annual weeklong meeting of the British Association for the Advancement of Science held in Bradford in 1873. He declared,

> No theory of evolution can be formed to account for the similarity of molecules, for evolution necessarily implies continuous change.... the exact equality of each molecule to all others of the same kind gives it, as Sir John Herschel has well said, the essential character of a manufactured article, and precludes the idea of its being eternal and self-existent.[23]

James Clerk Maxwell commented on the implications of realizing that, all over the universe, molecules and atoms of a given kind are identical. He wrote, 'A molecule of hydrogen ... whether in Sirius or in Arcturus *(both stars)*, executes its vibrations in precisely the same time. Each molecule, therefore, throughout the universe bears, impressed upon it, the stamp of a metric system as distinctly as does the meter of the Archives at Paris.' Because of this, he stated in 1879, 'We are then forced to look beyond them to some common cause or common origin, i.e., supernatural creation, to explain why this singular relation of quality exists ....'[23]

Charles Petzold, an American freelance writer, in a paper, 'Maxwell, Molecules, and Evolution'[24], has argued that Maxwell was not arguing against evolution in general but only speaking about the nature of molecules in particular. Petzold did agree that 'Maxwell certainly believed that God created the universe'. Petzold quotes from the conclusion of Maxwell's lecture about the permanency of molecules: 'They continue this day as they were created — perfect in number and measure and weight—... they are essential constituents of the image of Him who in the beginning created, not only the heaven and the earth, but the materials of which heaven and earth consist.'[25]

Petzold, who is one of Microsoft's seven 'Windows Pioneers', accepted Herschel and Maxwell were making a theological point that molecules were created, but claimed they were making an argument for design rather than an argument against evolution. If one considers the angle of 104.5° between the hydrogen and oxygen atoms in the water molecule, which maintains its shape with little stress on the bonds, Petzold would concede that this indicates design. It follows that there was a designer. Why would anybody prefer to attribute the origin of man to a non-directed, imaginary process rather than to the designer who fixed the angle between the hydrogen and oxygen atoms of water? Sadly, the majority of mankind commit their past, present and future to the doubtful theory of evolution.

James Clerk Maxwell died in Cambridge of abdominal cancer on 5 November 1879, at the age of 48. The minister who regularly visited him in his last weeks was astonished at his lucidity and the immense power and scope of his memory, and commented,

> His illness drew out the whole heart and soul and spirit of the man: his firm and undoubting faith in the Incarnation and all its results; in the full sufficiency of the Atonement; in the work of the Holy Spirit. He had gauged and fathomed all the schemes and systems of philosophy and had found them utterly empty and unsatisfying — 'unworkable' was his own word about them — and he turned with simple faith to the Gospel of the Saviour.[26]

As death approached, James Clerk Maxwell told a Cambridge colleague, 'I have been thinking how very gently I have always been dealt with. I have never had a violent shove all my life. The only desire which I can have is, like David, to serve my own generation by the will of God, and then fall asleep.'[26]

James Clerk Maxwell was convinced that science and the teachings of the Bible were not only compatible but must be linked. A prayer found among his notes stated,

> Almighty God, Who hast created man in Thine own image, and made him a living soul that he might seek after Thee, and have dominion over Thy creatures, teach us to study the works of Thy hands, that we may subdue the earth to our use, and strengthen the reason for Thy service; so to receive Thy blessed Word, that we may believe on Him Whom Thou hast sent, to give us the knowledge of salvation and the remission of our

sins. All of which we ask in the name of the same Jesus Christ, our Lord.[27]

NOTES

1 Suzanne Deffree, '1st periodic table is presented March 6, 1869', 2019. https://www.edn.com/1st-periodic-table-is-presented-march-6-1869/

2 Helen Briggs, '150 years of the periodic table: Test your knowledge', 29 January 2019. https://www.bbc.co.uk/news/science-environment-47008289

3 Bert Hansen, 'Hennig Brandt and the Discovery of Phosphorus', July 30th, 2019, *Science History Institute* – Distillations.

4 Antoine Laurent Lavoisier, *Traité Élémentaire de Chimie-tome premier*, (Paris: Chez Cuchet, 1789).

5 John Alexander Reina Newlands, https://www.encyclopedia.com, 2018.

6 Helen Briggs, '150 years of the periodic table: Test your knowledge', 29 January 2019. https://www.bbc.co.uk/news/science-environment-47008289

7 'Nucleosynthesis', University of Sheffield. Powerpoint: www.hep. shef.ac.uk/cartwright/phy111/ppt/Nucleosynthesis 2013

8 Fred Hoyle, 'On Nuclear Reactions Occurring in Very Hot Stars. I. the Synthesis of Elements from Carbon to Nickel', *Astrophysical Journal Supplement* vol 1, 1954, p. 121.

9 William A. Fowler, 'Experimental and Theoretical Nuclear Astrophysics; The Quest for the Origin of the Elements' (Nobel Lecture), *Wiley Online Library* 1984. https://onlinelibrary.wiley.com/doi/abs/10.1002/anie.198406453

10 Graham Lawton with introduction by Stephen Hawking, *New Scientist: The Origin of (almost) Everything: from the Big Bang to Belly-button Fluff*, (London: John Murray, 2016), pp. 1 – 3.

11 Richard Dawkins, *The Selfish Gene: 30th Anniversary Edition*, (Oxford University Press, 2006), p. 15.

12 Fred Hoyle, 'The Universe: Past and Present Reflections', *Engineering and Science*, 1981. pp. 8 – 12.

13 James Jeans, *The Mysterious Universe*, (London: Pelican Books, 1938 reprint), p. 19.

14 J. R. Baumgardner et al., 'Measurable 14C in fossilized organic materials: confirming the young earth creation-flood model', www.icr.org/i/pdf/research/RATE_ICC_Baumgardner.pdf 2003

15 Brian Thomas et al., 'Radiocarbon in Dinosaur and Other Fossils', *Creation Research Society Quarterly* 2015 51(4): pp. 299–311.

16 Jonathan Sarfati, 'Diamonds: a creationist's best friend. Radiocarbon in diamonds: enemy of billions of years', *Creation* 28(4) 2006, pp. 26–27, (updated 2020).

17 Mary Schweitzer et al., 'Soft-tissue vessels and cellular preservation in Tyrannosaurus rex', *Science* 307, 2005, pp. 1952–55,

18 Mary Schweitzer et al., 'Molecular analyses of dinosaur osteocytes support the presence of endogenous molecules', *Bone*, 52 (1) 2012, pp. 414–423.

19 Brian Thomas, 'Collagen remnants in ancient bone', PhD thesis, *University of Liverpool*, 2018.

20 Barry Yeoman, 'Schweitzer's Dangerous Discovery', *Discover* 27(4) 2006, pp. 37–41, 77.

21 Wilson Bentley & W. J. Humphreys, *Snow Crystals*, (New York: Dover Publications Inc., First published 1931, Republished 1962).

22 James Clerk Maxwell, 'Molecules', *Nature*, Vol VIII No. 204, 1873, pp. 437–441.

23 'Post-Darwin, James Clerk Maxwell's Views Presaged Modern Arguments for Intelligent Design', *Evolution News,* December 8, 2016. https://evolutionnews.org/2016/12/post-darwin_jam/

24 Charles Petzold, *Maxwell, Molecules, and Evolution*, 2005. http://www.charlespetzold.com/etc/MaxwellMoleculesAndEvolution.html.

25 James Clerk Maxwell, 'Molecules', *Nature*, Vol VIII No. 204, 1873, pp. 437–441.

26 James Clerk Maxwell, Wikipedia. Later years, 1865–1879.

27 B. M. Moritz, 'James Clerk Maxwell: Light in Nature and in Faith', *Science Meets Faith*, 2017. https://sciencemeetsfaith.wordpress.com/2017/06/10/james-clerk-maxwell-light-in-nature-and-in-faith/

29 Theistic evolution, Part 1

I n February 1997, the Evangelical Alliance ran a UK tour of forty-six towns entitled, *Nothing but the Truth*.[1] As I look at the page advertising the tour, I read, 'Are you challenged by questions you find hard to answer? *Nothing but the Truth* will look at key issues which confront us today. Come to this event and you will leave with a deeper understanding of the Christian faith.' One of the five topics to be covered was *The Truth about Science*. I, along with two other Christian surgeons, attended the event on 12 February in the Curtis Auditorium lecture theatre, which is part of Newcastle University.

The presenters were Rev. Robert Frost, National Evangelist with the Methodist Church, and Rev. Dr David Wilkinson, an astrophysicist, Methodist minister and, at that time, chaplain of Liverpool University. Rob Frost put us at ease by confessing that he had struggled with physics at school, but we could be confident that, *The Truth about Science,* would be faithfully addressed by David Wilkinson. His first PhD concerned the study of star formation, the chemical evolution of galaxies and terrestrial mass extinctions. His second PhD had the title, 'Christian Eschatology and the Physical Universe'.

The speakers suggested that there were two views of how Christians understand the opening chapters of Genesis. The older view took Genesis as literal history, leading to belief in a young Earth (approximately 6,000 years old). The modern alternative accepted that God used evolution (theistic evolution) which, we were assured, was compatible with a scientifically informed reading of Genesis. After twenty-five years, my memory of the event and its importance remain clear. I understood that there is a battle for truth and for the minds of men, women and children. I would go so far as to say, that for me, it was a *pivotal moment*.

Approximately five minutes were devoted to the *older view* and the rest of the meeting to the *modern view*. The presenters said that people holding to the older, literal view should be respected, but the presentation was heavily weighted to teaching 'the truth' of evolution. An impressive film began with the microscopic substructure of the human cell, building upwards through the tissues of the human body into a human being, who was then displayed in his environment on earth and then upwards and outwards into the vast expanses of space. It certainly presented the awesomeness of God's creation from the microscopic to the astronomical.

I was struck by the realization that *Nothing but the Truth* was a strange title for the meeting which presented two conflicting views. The presenters were not prepared to say that one view must be wrong, though it was very clear which they believed to be true. Their words and impressive visual presentation seemed designed to carry the audience along and leave those believing in a young Earth to soon join the *dodo* in extinction!

In the question time, I asked the presenters how they viewed Romans 5:12–21, which describes the fall and sin of the one man, Adam, and the salvation and righteousness available through the one man, Jesus Christ. Verse 12 is particularly clear that sin and its consequence, death, entered our world when Adam and Eve sinned: 'Therefore, just as sin entered the world through one man, and death through sin, and in this way death came to all people, because all sinned.'

This teaching is repeated in 1 Corinthians 15:21–22: 'For since death came through a man, the resurrection of the dead comes also through a man. For as in Adam all die, so in Christ all will be made alive.' Neither speaker accepted that these verses contradicted their evolutionary view, which requires death before the sin of Adam and Eve.

The UK tour had been advertised claiming that, 'You will leave with a deeper understanding of the Christian faith.' But the presenters had actually used modern scientific theory to undermine confidence in the historical truth of the Bible. Denis R. Alexander took a similar position, when writing in the Evangelical Alliance magazine, *Idea*, 1 May 2004[2]: 'Christians should not abuse the Bible by trying to treat it as a scientific textbook, when scientific writing as we understand it now did not even get going until thousands of years after the early chapters of Genesis were written.' He repeated this view in his book, *Creation or Evolution—Do We Have to Choose?*[3]

This is a straw-man fallacy. As a Christian, I take the book of Genesis to be a historical record of the Creation of the Universe and mankind. I do not treat it as a scientific textbook. When it comes to origins, true history trumps modern science! The fallacy also reflects a poor view of the authorship of the Bible. If God breathed out all of the Scriptures, as recorded in 2 Timothy 3:16—'All Scripture is God-breathed and is useful for teaching, rebuking, correcting and training in righteousness'—how can anyone suggest that God is not able to write in any genre He pleases? God is not limited to following styles of writing once man has 'invented' them.

It is true that in the writing of Scripture, both God and man were active participants. God dictated the content of Scripture, so it records what God said. The training or personality of the human author may be evident but, because he was carried along by the Holy Spirit (2 Peter 1:21), he wrote what God said. On my journey, I had come to believe that God and Moses were not limited in writing Genesis because scientific literature had not been invented. God, the eyewitness of Creation and of the fall of man, directed a historical account to be written down for our eternal benefit and to introduce us, in Genesis 3:15 (part of the first reading in the Nine Lessons and Carols Service at Christmas), to the promise of redemption through the seed of the woman.

Romans 5:12–21 is central to the debate about our origins. The passage confirms the Genesis 3 record of the disobedience of Adam and Eve in eating from the tree of the knowledge of good and evil and the historical fall of man. There is no room in these Bible passages for theistic evolution's story 'that God "placed his image" in an already existing animal', as Malcolm A. Jeeves and R. J. Berry wrote in *Science, Life and Christian Belief*, published in 1998.[4]

Charles Hodge D.D. published a reliable *Commentary on the Epistle to the Romans*. The preface declares it 'was rewritten and enriched with his mature studies in 1864'. He wrote of Romans 5:

> The dreadful evil of sin is best seen in the fall of Adam, and in the cross of Christ. By the one offence of one man, what a waste of ruin has been spread over the whole world! How far beyond conception the misery that one act occasioned! There was no

adequate remedy for this evil but the death of the Son of God, verses 12, 15, 16, etc. It is the prerogative of God to bring good out of evil, and to make the good triumph over the evil. From the fall has sprung redemption, and from redemption results which eternity alone can disclose, verses 20, 21.[5]

Professor Charles Hodge of Princeton, USA, was a great Christian thinker. His short book, *What is Darwinism?*, [6] was written in 1874, at the height of the controversy over Darwin. The book, which can be read on the internet, has concluding sections titled, 'The Evolution Theory Contrary to Facts and to Scripture'[7] and 'Darwinism Tantamount to Atheism'.[8]

When taken to its logical end, Darwinism equals atheism despite the pleadings of theistic evolutionists. Humanist, Sir Julian Huxley FRS, wrote in 1960, 'Darwinism removed the whole idea of God as the creator of organisms from the sphere of rational discussion. I think we can dismiss entirely all idea of a supernatural overriding mind being responsible for the evolutionary process.'[9]

The Encyclopaedia Britannica states, 'Darwin did two things: he showed that evolution was a fact contradicting scriptural legends of creation and that its cause, natural selection, was automatic with no room for divine guidance or design.'[10] But that is untrue; Psalm 19:1 tells us that the skies proclaim the work of God's hands. To deny God's design is harmful to personal confidence in the truth of the Biblical record and thereby to Christian evangelism.

Evolution and *theistic evolution* can mean several different things. As I write, I wish to acknowledge the logical insights of former geophysicist and philosophy professor, Dr Stephen C. Meyer, written in the first chapter of his book, *Theistic Evolution*, published in 2017 by Crossway. The chapter title is, 'Scientific and Philosophical Introduction: Defining Theistic Evolution'.[11] A big issue arises when we ask, What is the cause of biological change? Is the evolutionary mechanism directed or undirected?[12]

The first meaning of evolution is a process reflecting *change over time*. The fossil record suggests differences between plants and animals from the recent past when compared with plants and animals which existed long ago. Changes in peppered moths or Galapagos finches can take place more quickly. Such changes are due to natural selection and are sometimes referred to as micro evolution. This very unhelpful term leads to confusion because natural selection does not lead to new *kinds* of animals; it is not evolution.

A Christian affirms that God has caused change over time. When God created the world *ex nihilo* (out of nothing), that was a dramatic change. In creating all the different forms of life and in his providential control of human history, God superintended change. There is substantial scientific evidence that change can occur within species. So, for example, the God-designed, inbuilt genetic make-up of the first male and female dogs allowed variation in size or appearance, which dog breeders have utilized. It is important to emphasize that this variation is within limits, i.e., within what Genesis calls *kinds*, dictated by inbuilt genes.

The second implication of the word, 'evolution', is that all organisms are related by common ancestry. The evolutionary claim is that all known, living organisms are descended from a single common ancestor, alive in the distant past. Darwin referred to this as 'one primordial form'. Biology textbooks often have a diagram of

Darwin's tree of life. By implication, there are no limits to the morphological changes which can occur in living organisms, given the billions of years available.

A single common ancestor is clearly contrary to the Genesis account, in chapter 1, of God creating distinct 'kinds' of plants and animals which all reproduce 'after their own kind'. Darwin bred pigeons and knew that he never bred a monkey from a pigeon. Evolutionists, Stephen Jay Gould and Niles Eldridge, were aware that the fossil record did not demonstrate the gradual change of one *kind* of creature into another *kind* of creature, so came up with their theory of 'Punctuated Equilibrium' (see chapter 11) to overcome the problem of missing links.

According to Genesis, Adam was made from the dust of the ground and Eve was made from a rib, taken from Adam. We have noted that, following the Fall, God told Adam, 'Dust you are and to dust you will return' (Genesis 3:19), and again, in Genesis 3:23, God banished Adam from the Garden of Eden 'to work the ground from which he had been taken'. The origin of mankind is clearly described. The creation of Eve is particularly problematical for theistic evolutionists. Unlike all other animal life, where a female gives birth to male and female offspring, Eve came out of the body of Adam. It is for that very reason that Adam called her *woman* (Genesis 2:23). Adam and Eve, as described in Genesis, cannot be squashed into the evolutionary process.

The third mechanism essential to modern Neo-Darwinism is that of random genetic mutations. These were not known to Darwin but are vital to his theory. Evolutionists believe that these mutations are, in fact, the creative power producing new organisms or so-called macro evolution. It is also claimed that natural selection and mechanisms of random mutation give rise to the appearance of design in living organisms. Genetic mutations are actually invariably harmful.

Darwin declared that 'nature', through environmental changes or other factors, could have the same effect on organisms as the intentional decisions of an intelligent designer. When changes in the organism conferred survival or functional advantage, these would be passed on to descendants. Darwin claimed you could have design without a designer.[13] In believing this, he excluded God from his search to understand the Origin of Species. Darwin, in later life, described himself as agnostic but wrote autobiographically, 'I can indeed hardly see how anyone ought to wish Christianity to be true.'[14]

Darwin wrote a letter to Frederick McDermott, in November 1880, in response to a question which McDermott had asked. The letter was short: 'Dear Sir, I am sorry to have to inform you that I do not believe in the Bible as a divine revelation, and therefore not in Jesus Christ as the son of God. Yours faithfully, Ch. Darwin.'[15]

Darwin never professed to be an atheist, but he did write to Thomas Huxley describing him as, 'My good and kind agent for the propagation of the gospel—i.e., the devil's gospel.'[16] It is ironic that he is buried in Westminster Abbey, along with Stephen Hawking who wrote in his posthumous book, *Brief Answers to the Big Questions*, 'There is no God. No one directs the universe.'[17]

Darwin believed that 'nature' had designed all of creation and one hears many modern commentators repeating this view. Theistic evolutionists attempt to reintroduce God, albeit with a very light hand on the steering wheel, even though evolution has made God redundant. Richard Dawkins' 1986 book, *The Blind Watchmaker*, lays claim to the same idea that evolution has made a designer unnecessary and that theistic evolution is a superfluous attempt to 'smuggle God in by the back door'.[18]

As we continue to consider random genetic mutations, a major problem arises for belief in theistic evolution. If design is just an appearance, then logically, the mechanism which produces that appearance must be unguided and undirected. There will, of course, be theistic evolutionists who claim that God could have guided and started the evolutionary process but then left it to its own unguided devices. Design abilities are then attributed to a process working randomly through genetic mutations.

The matter of whether theistic evolution is directed or undirected, divides proponents into two camps. Kenneth Miller, the American cell biologist and author of *Finding Darwin's God*, states that, 'evolution works without either plan or purpose ... Evolution is random and undirected.'[19] Alternatively, leading geneticist, Francis Collins, who led the Human Genome Project and is the Director of the National Institutes of Health in the United States, believes in universal common ancestry but says that evolutionary mechanisms 'could be' directed.[20]

The issue of the appearance of design leads to at least three problems for the theistic evolutionist. The *first* is the intrinsic contradiction in the phrase, *theistic evolution*. God, who is an intelligent being, would not direct an undirected process. As soon as God steps in, even with a light hand on the steering wheel, the process becomes directed. If the theistic evolutionist proposes that God is directing the process, by directing genetic mutations, then this is not neo-Darwinism but a form of intelligent design. If God is the director, then the appearance of design is real not the illusion that Dawkins, Huxley and Crick want us to believe in. Many theistic evolutionists reject intelligent design.

The *second* problem arises when it is denied that God directs natural selection and genetic mutation. This idea, with two variations, is that God designed the laws of nature at the beginning of the universe so that the development of life was inevitable. (While Stephen Hawking believed that there are laws of nature, he did not believe they were designed by God.) The first variation being that God let the laws of nature run their course. The second holds that God, in addition, upholds the laws throughout time. Both ideas make God passive as he watches to see how things turn out.

We end up with God being dependent on the random process of evolution and not even knowing, with any confidence, whether man, created in his image, would ever be born. Nature is given autonomy from God and who knows where that will lead? This idea makes God's foreknowledge, sovereignty, providence, promises and plans all false. If creation is no longer under the direct control of God, then he cannot have foreknowledge; is not sovereign; cannot behave providentially; cannot make promises; and cannot make plans. The God of the Bible sits and watches impotently.

The *third* difficulty for the theistic evolutionist is bound up with the 'appearance of design'. Because theistic evolutionists affirm the creative power of evolution, they usually do not want to allow God any part in directing the process, which, of course, would become intelligent design! Geneticist Francis Collins rejects intelligent design. He hedges his bets, however, by saying evolution 'could be'

378 The Something Delusion

directed. He engages in mental gymnastics explaining, 'Evolution could appear to us to be driven by chance, but from God's perspective the outcome would be entirely specified. Thus, God could be completely and intimately involved in the creation of all species, while, from our perspective ... this would appear a random and undirected process.'[20]

Francis Collins is not explicit but, in confirming that the appearance of design is just that, an appearance only, he seems committed to an undirected process of evolution, though allowing himself a get out clause: 'could be directed'. One wonders how he would explain that to a class of university students. They might mutter, 'He seems to want it both ways—how can the appearance of design be an illusion?'

By denying that there is a designer who was and is responsible for the design of all 'the things that are made' in the natural world, theistic evolutionists are in a head-on collision with the Bible. We are expected to see God's creative power in all that he has made and to attribute glory to Him. Psalm 19:1 tells us that the 'heavens declare the glory of God,' and Romans 1:20 states that anyone who refuses to see the design hand of God in all around us is without excuse.

Jesus, himself, drew attention to birds being fed according to God's plan; to rain and sunshine being sent by God and essential to life on Earth; and to the beautiful design of the lilies of the field. Where would we be if God had not designed photosynthesis? The Bible teaches that there was a designer who was a personality, not a process. As Colossians 1:16 says, 'For by him all things were created.'

This verse draws attention to a personality who made planets and plants, which are visible, as well as gravity, which is invisible.

For me, a significant problem for theistic evolution is that of timescale. What do I mean? It is undisputed that evolution requires a timescale of billions of years. Jesus Christ came to Earth as a man some 2,000 years ago, which means that the division of history into BC and AD is currently a very unequal division for a theistic evolutionist. If time began 13.8 billion years ago, how much longer will the Universe and our solar system remain before the second coming of Jesus Christ?

The Bible teaches us to be alert and ready for the second coming of Jesus at any time. The Bible describes events which will herald the second coming. Some events, such as the restoration of the land of Israel to the Jewish people in 1948, may have already passed. Some current events, such as wars, drought, plagues of locusts and the pestilence of pandemics may also be relevant. Our Lord Jesus told us clearly that no man knows the exact date of his return.

Are theistic evolutionists consciously or subconsciously tied into a very long future by the past evolutionary timescale and does that distort their theology? David Wilkinson, who addressed the 1997 *Nothing but the Truth* meeting, submitted a PhD thesis, 'Christian Eschatology and the Physical Universe'[21], to the University of Durham in 2004. *Eschatology* means that part of theology which is concerned with the end of the world and final events of history. It considers the final destiny of mankind and deals with the second coming of Jesus Christ and the final judgement. David Wilkinson's thesis can be read online.

Wilkinson's thesis begins as follows:

> The scientific picture of the end of the Universe has undergone dramatic changes since 1998, with its future characterized by accelerated expansion and futility. Yet, Christian systematic theology has been largely silent on this, despite the interest in eschatology in popular culture and in theology itself. This thesis argues that Christian theology can learn and contribute to a dialogue with the scientific picture of the future of the Universe.[22]

His reference to 1998 is because, in that year, two teams of cosmologists published evidence that the rate of expansion of the universe is increasing.[23] Distant galaxies are seen accelerating as they recede from the observer. This has led to modifications in scientific models of the beginning and end of the universe.

Wilkinson, in his abstract, explained his approach of exploring Biblical narratives in conversation with scientific discoveries. He said that Christian eschatology must take the relationship between creation and the new creation *(the new heavens and earth described in the Bible—my words)* seriously. In his opinion, this relationship is modelled on the Resurrection and is seen as transformation rather than destruction of this creation.

His abstract describes the universe as having a 'future characterized by accelerated expansion and futility'.'[22] I have explained what current science believes about accelerated expansion but why futility? Collins' *English Dictionary* defines futility as, 'a total lack of purpose or usefulness'.[24] The concept that Creation experiences futility is, of course, biblical.

Following the sin of Adam and Eve, we read, in Genesis 3, of the curse which God declared, leading to the physical and spiritual death of man, to disease and to the decay and bondage of creation.

But it is important to acknowledge that creation was not like that at the beginning. God repeatedly declared during creation week that what he had made was good and, on the sixth day, that it was very good.

The Bible (ESV translation) states in Romans 8:19–22:

> For the creation waits with eager longing for the revealing of the sons of God. For the creation was subjected to futility, not willingly, but because of him who subjected it, in hope that the creation itself will be set free from its bondage to corruption and obtain the freedom of the glory of the children of God. For we know that the whole creation has been groaning together in the pains of childbirth until now.

The Bible describes the consequences of sin: for example, pain in childbirth for the woman and the thorns and thistles that would accompany work for man (Genesis 3:16–19). When Jesus died on the cross, he not only did so to conquer the power of death and disease but, also, to reverse the curse on creation caused by the Fall. It is significant that Jesus wore a crown of thorns when he was crucified. Adam never encountered a thorn before the Fall. The book of Ecclesiastes repeatedly uses the phrase, 'all is vanity', which is translated in the Septuagint version of the Bible, with the Greek word for 'futility'. Futility is a consequence of the Fall; it did not precede it.

When David Wilkinson describes the future of the Universe being characterized by futility, he is influenced by modern scientific theory with a number of possible models to explain 'the end of the world', all of which focus on billions of years in the future.

The theories about the future and end of the universe have

dramatic names. The Big Freeze (Heat Death), The Big Rip, The Big Crunch, The Big Bounce, The Big Slurp and Cosmic Uncertainty.[25] A broad summary of the theories about the future of the solar system sees it either collapsing back to be absorbed by the sun in about 7.5 billion years or continuing in an eternal expansion, causing the temperature to end near absolute zero with all structures being destroyed.

Wilkinson discusses Creationism and Intelligent Design which, he says, 'both attack evolution and the perceived naturalism behind it'. He criticizes these movements because 'they represent a revived form of the design argument'.[26] Theistic evolution holds that design is only apparent. His thesis claims that Creationism and Intelligent Design 'do not take the futility as well as the goodness of the physical Universe into account and therefore have little place for incarnation or resurrection. Such an apologetic strategy is doomed to failure.'[26]

Wilkinson says, 'The creationist case is severely undermined by the futility of the physical Universe. To argue that God created a static, perfect creation some 6,000 years ago does not do justice to *the timescale or future development of the Universe* (my italics). This creation is not perfect but longs for new creation. Creationism, in neglecting the importance of eschatology for the physical creation, is thus undermined by the scientific data.'[26]

Wilkinson denies Biblical chronology, with the beginning of the Universe occurring approximately 6,000 years ago. In addition, when he says, 'This creation is not perfect,' he appears to miss the point that it once was perfect. To follow Wilkinson's line of reasoning we might understand 'the new heavens and new earth' as God's second attempt at perfection—He failed first time!

Wilkinson complains that creationists will either 'argue against the scientific data' or 'argue that the futility is the result simply of a cosmic Fall. While we have acknowledged that the doctrine of the Fall should not be ignored, it is not strong enough to support such creationist claims.'[27] On what basis does he make such a claim? The Bible's historical record is strong enough—how else can we know the truth?

Wilkinson, in drawing attention to Romans 8, distorts its meaning. He wrote, 'consideration of Romans 8 has enabled us to see the futility of the end of the Universe in the context of a renewed and limited natural theology. At the same time, a consideration of space-time models has enabled us to go beyond certain Greek concepts to take more seriously the temporal nature of new creation.'[28]

Natural theology means *knowledge of God based on observed facts and experience apart from divine revelation.* Wilkinson suggests that we have greater scientific knowledge than the apostle Paul and that the Greeks had erroneous concepts about time. He, therefore, suggests that we should move on to a more modern and informed view of the futility of the future of the Universe, measured in billions of years. Wilkinson objects to a perfect static Creation some 6,000 years ago, which is what Genesis describes. He, being wedded to a past and future of millions of years, claims the creationist view does not do justice to *the timescales or future development of the Universe.*[29] This blinkered view of the future leads to a distorted understanding of the chronology of Genesis.

NOTES

1 'Nothing but the Truth', *IDEA*, January–March 1997, pp. 23–24.

2 Denis R. Alexander, 'Idea–the Evangelical Alliance magazine', 1 May 2004.

3 Denis Alexander, *Creation or Evolution–Do We Have to Choose?* (Oxford: Monarch Books, 2008), p. 43.

4 M. A. Jeeves and R. J. Berry Science, *Life and Christian Belief*, (London: APOLLOS (IVP), 1998), p. 116.

5 Charles Hodge, *Commentary on the Epistle to the Romans*, (Grand Rapids, Michigan: Wm B. Eerdmans Publishing Company, 1864), p. 190.

6 Charles Hodge, *What is Darwinism?* (New York: Scribner, Armstrong & Company, 1874). https://www.gutenberg.org/files/19192/19192-h/19192-h.htm

7 Ibid., p. 141.

8 Ibid., p. 177.

9 Sol Tax and Charles Callender, *Evolution after Darwin*, (University of Chicago Press, 1960), p. 45.

10 *Encyclopaedia Britannica*, 'Macropaedia', Volume 7, 1979, p. 23.

11 Stephen C. Meyer, 'Scientific and Philosophical Introduction: Defining Theistic Evolution', in: *Theistic Evolution*, (Wheaton, Illinois: Crossway, 2017), p. 33.

12 Ibid., pp. 46–49.

13 Francisco J. Ayala, 'Darwin's Greatest Discovery: Design without Designer', *Proceedings of the National Academy of Sciences* USA 104, 2007, pp. 8567–8573.

14 Nora Barlow (editor), *The autobiography of Charles Darwin, 1809–1882, with original omissions restored*, (New York: W. W. Norton, 1969), p. 87.

15 *Darwin Correspondence Project*, 'Letter no. 12851', accessed on 8th February 2022. https://www.darwinproject.ac.uk/letter/?docId=letters/DCP-LETT-12851.xml

16 *Darwin Correspondence Project*, 'Letter no. 2893', accessed on 8th February 2022. https://www.darwinproject.ac.uk/letter/?docId=letters/DCP-LETT-2893.xml

17 Stephen Hawking, *Brief Answers to the Big Questions*, (London: John Murray, 2018). https://www.thestatesman.com/supplements/science_supplements/stephen-hawking-no-god-no-one-directs-universe-1503037129.html

18 Richard Dawkins, *The Blind Watchmaker*, (London: Longman, 1986), p. 316.

19 Kenneth R. Miller, 'Finding Darwin's God': An excerpt in *Brown alumni* magazine, November 1999.

20 Francis Collins, *The Language of God: A scientist presents evidence for belief,* (New York: Free Press, 2006), p. 205.

21 David Wilkinson, 'Christian Eschatology and the Physical Universe', PhD thesis University of Durham, 2004. http://etheses.dur.ac.uk/2815/

22 Ibid., Abstract

23 'Accelerating expansion of the universe'—Wikipedia. https://en.wikipedia.org/wiki/Accelerating_expansion_of_the_universe

24 Collins English Dictionary, 'Futility'—definition and meaning, (11th edition, 2011).

25 'Ultimate fate of the universe'—Wikipedia. https://en.wikipedia.org/wiki/Ultimate_fate_of_the_universe

26 David Wilkinson, 'Christian Eschatology and the Physical Universe', p. 186. http://etheses.dur.ac.uk/2815/

27 Ibid., p. 187.

28 Ibid., p. 188.

29 Ibid., p. 187.

30 Theistic evolution, Part 2

Some Christians describe themselves as theistic evolutionists and write in its defence. For example, in the November 2020 edition of *Evangelicals Now*, Professor Paul Ewart asked the question, 'What would life on Venus mean for Christian faith?'[1] Paul Ewart is Professor of Physics at Oxford University and chairman of Christians in Science. He was not asking what it would be like to live on Venus, but what would the finding of life on Venus mean for Christian faith.

Astronomers, led by Jane Greaves of Cardiff University, had observed a change in the intensity of radiation from the atmosphere of Venus at a particular wavelength, that could only be because of the presence of phosphine gas.[2] They believed that phosphine was present in relatively large concentrations. Paul Ewart commented that, on earth, phosphine is produced by biological processes so a mechanism for that to happen on Venus would require 'some kind of microbes—a form of life'.

Paul Ewart wrote that this 'is also another piece of evidence in the search for understanding the origin of life on earth and elsewhere. As Christians we can celebrate this further advance in our understanding of God's Creation. The origin of life is one of the great unsolved mysteries and this discovery is a step, albeit a small one, on the way to discovering how God did it.'[1]

I was disturbed by the suggestion that the origin of life is one of the great unsolved mysteries for a Christian and, by his suggestion, that the finding of phosphine in the atmosphere of Venus was a step on the way to discovering 'how God did it'! I wrote to *Evangelicals Now* to point out that the creation of the world, out of nothing, was *by the spoken word of Almighty God*, as taught in the Bible.

Psalm 148 encourages us to 'Praise the Lord' for his creation. The first six verses indicate that God made the cosmos, including Venus, and verse five indicates that these heavenly bodies are to the praise 'of the Lord for he commanded and they were created'. In Hebrews 11:3, we read a similar statement: 'The Universe was formed at God's command.' Several times, in Genesis chapter 1, the phrase, 'and God said', is followed by, 'and it was so'. God kindly told us how he did it, so that it would not be a great unsolved mystery.

My letter was not published but an excellent one by Geoff Chapman of Creation Resources Trust was! He pointed out that many scientists were sceptical, and one biochemist suggested on BBC News (14 September 2020), that for airborne microbes to survive the sulphuric acid in the Venusian atmosphere, they would have to wear armour which would prevent them eating or exchanging gases! The *New Scientist*, 21 October 2020, reported that a new analysis had suggested there were no signs of gas after all.[3]

The website, *Online Research @ Cardiff*, reported that the authors had informed the editors of *Nature Astronomy* about an error in the original processing of the ALMA Observatory data underlying the work in this article, and that recalibration of the data had had an impact on the conclusions that can be drawn (2nd November 2020).[4]

Geoff Chapman, in his letter, suggested that there is no hint in Scripture that God created life anywhere other than on the Earth. The gospel, as we know it, is earth centred. I share his view but will not discuss this further, apart from commenting that it would save a lot of money being spent on the search for extra-terrestrial intelligence, if this view was more widely adopted!

I recognize that some prominent Christian advocates of theistic evolution believe that 'creationists' do harm and should be silent. At a national Christian conference, in 2018, I attended three seminars about science, given by Professor Tom McLeish PhD, FRS, who was renowned for increasing our understanding of the properties of soft matter (liquids, foams and biological materials). Formerly Professor of Physics in Durham University, he held the inaugural Chair of Natural Philosophy in the Department of Physics at York University. Sadly, Professor McLeish died in February 2023, aged 60 years.

Natural Philosophy was the term used for the study of nature, from the time of the philosopher, Aristotle, until the 19th century. Natural philosophy involved explanations about how nature worked, later becoming quantitative, whereas natural history was descriptive and qualitative. From the 19th century onwards, the term, *science*, with its divisions into physics, biology, chemistry and other disciplines, has been used.

Towards the end of his third seminar, Tom McLeish said that a young earth position on creation must be opposed. It is clear from his book, *Faith and Wisdom in Science* reprinted in 2017, that he did not tolerate believers who differed with him on the issue of Creation.[5] An online Guardian review of his book, stated, 'McLeish has no patience with Young Earth Creationists and other people in "the dark cells of ignorance" who think the Bible offers a story that is literally true.'[6] Writing about the young Earth viewpoint, McLeish referred to 'the so-called "fundamentalist" doctrine of a young (6,000 years or so) Earth and a "literal" interpretation of the first chapter of Genesis. Developed further, it insists that all species were created fully formed by a special *fiat* of God, and are not connected by any evolutionary tree, demonising Darwinian evolution and therefore most of biological science in the process.' He wrote, 'The shallowness and distorted reading of a "6-day" exegesis becomes evident.'[7]

McLeish advocated a confrontational approach to deal with such 'heresy' (*his words*)—'There is no progress to be made by any form of peaceful co-existence with a wilful denial of our path to reconciliation with the natural world.'[8] On the same page he claimed, 'It paralyses the Christian message of reconciliation and hope, plays into the hands of authoritarian power structures, and imprisons the minds of the thousands of honest believers, especially when children, into dark cells of ignorance, when a God-given ocean of truth awaits enjoyment just outside.'[8] To refer to those having a belief in the history of Genesis 1–3 as, 'authoritarian power structures', is extraordinary rhetoric suggesting a lack of respect for other Christians, many of whom are distinguished PhD scientists and professors!

He is not alone in a harsh attitude. N. T. Wright says that young-Earth Christians make it hard for others to be Christians! He was the Bishop of Durham from 2003 to 2010 and is a recognized New Testament scholar with a particular interest in the apostle Paul. He has written over seventy books and, in one of these, *Surprised by Scripture*, he comments, 'I wonder whether we are right even to treat the young-Earth position as a kind of allowable if regrettable alternative, something we know our cousins down the road get up to, but which shouldn't stop us getting together at Christmas.'[9]

He continues: 'And if, as I suspect, many of us don't think of young-earthism as an allowable alternative, is this simply for the pragmatic reason that it makes it hard for us to be Christians because the wider world looks at those folks and thinks we must be like that too?'[9]

Earlier in *Surprised by Scripture* he states, 'The root problem we face as Christians is that in articulating a Christian vision of the cosmos the way we want to do, we find ourselves hamstrung because it is assumed that to be Christian is to be anti-intellectual, anti-science, obscurantist, and so forth.'[10]

N. T. Wright is clear in his view that believing Genesis 1–11 is real history is error. 'That's the danger of false teaching: it isn't just that you're making a mess; you are using that mess to cover up something that ought to be brought urgently to light.'[9]

You can listen to an extract from N. T. Wright's talk, 'Christ and Creation: Exploring the Paradox', given at the 2017 BioLogos conference on the internet.[11] Recognizing that Jesus is described as the Creator of the world, which Scripture of course teaches—for example, in Colossians 1:15–17—he suggests that to understand our origins we should not start with the great act of Creation but look through the lens of Jesus and His vision of the Kingdom. He said, 'We must somehow start with what we know of Jesus' own vision of truth and the kingdom and power and ask what that might mean for creation itself. The results, I think, are striking.'

I would interject, before looking at what N. T. Wright said: how confident do you feel in 'somehow start(ing) with what we know of Jesus' own vision of truth and the kingdom' and resisting the personal ideas of a highly imaginative, world-renowned Bible scholar who proceeds to develop a new theology of creation based on the parable of the Sower? His talk was laced with imaginative phrases, which I highlight in italics in this verbatim record:

> To begin with, if creation comes through the kingdom bringing Jesus, we ought to expect it be *like a seed growing secretly*. That it would involve *seed being sown in a prodigal fashion* in which a lot went to waste, apparently, but other seed producing a great crop. We ought to expect that it be like a *strange, slow process which might suddenly reach some kind of harvest*. We ought to expect that it would involve some kind of *overcoming of chaos*. Above all, we ought to expect that it would be a *work of utter, self-giving love*. That the power which made the world, like the power which ultimately rescued the world, would be the power not of brute force, but of *radical, outpoured generosity*. We ought to expect, in other words, that the creation would not look like *an oriental despot deciding to build a palace, and just throwing it up at speed, with his architects and builders cowering before him*.[11]

Does N. T. Wright's allusion to an oriental despot throwing it up at speed *(I take that to be a dig at six-day creation)* border on blasphemy? In order to adhere to *theistic evolution*, the imagination of a renowned scholar suggests that believing in an all-powerful God who spoke the universe into being is not the sort of God that we should believe in. His suggestion that, in Creation, God adopted a methodology similar to that employed in the parable of the Sower (who generously preached the gospel to some who believe but to many who reject, ignore or are apathetic towards the gospel) is totally unwarranted from reading the Bible. It also belittles the preaching of the gospel, by comparing it to a wasteful, cruel, chaotic and undirected process called evolution.

A further quote from his address shows how he uses Jesus' parables of the Kingdom to justify his view.

> No one in the late 18th or early 19th centuries was doing the kind of fresh work on Jesus and the gospels that would lead to this picture. But various scientists (not least the Darwin family, a century before Charles Darwin), motivated by quite a different worldview—namely, Epicureanism—nonetheless come up with a picture of Origins that looks remarkably like Jesus' parables of the Kingdom: some seeds go to waste, others bear remarkable fruit; some projects start tiny and take forever, but ultimately produce a great crop; some false starts are wonderfully rescued; others are forgotten. Chaos is astonishingly overcome.[11]

Personally, I wonder who wants or needs 'fresh work on Jesus' in the 20th or 21st centuries if this is the outcome.

A third example of strong opposition to a belief that Genesis 1–11 is real history comes from Denis Alexander, a molecular biologist who is the Emeritus Director of the Faraday Institute for Science and Religion at St Edmund's College, Cambridge. He writes in his book, *Creation or Evolution—Do We Have to Choose?*, 'The public promotion of creationism and intelligent design continues to create intellectual barriers for scientists, significantly diminishing the likelihood of their taking the gospel seriously.'[12] He then continues: 'Instead of putting millions of pounds and dollars into publishing glossy magazines attacking evolution, why not put that money into helping the poor, or tackling HIV, or funding orphanages? Ironically, those

Christians who are most enthusiastic at talking about Creation are not always the same people who are most involved in creation care.'[13] He does not provide evidence for either of these remarks.

In chapter 6 of this book, with the title 'Objections to Evolution', Denis Alexander writes, 'Of course that does not mean that Christians cannot have serious questions and objections about evolution, and it is perfectly valid to exchange views on these in a friendly spirit, which is the purpose of this chapter.'[14] In spite of this conciliatory remark, his frustration at that process of debate appears evident from his later comments: 'Christian campaigns against evolution represent a giant "red herring", distracting believers from far more important pursuits.'[15]

In explaining that Christians have broadly two different views about our origins, as Rob Frost and David Wilkinson highlighted at the *Nothing but the Truth* meeting (see previous chapter), I do not wish to engage in a harsh or disrespectful discussion about these matters. However, I believe that many Christians, all over the world, have been brought out of a confused understanding about the reliability of Genesis by examining evidence such as that presented in this book. *Creation* magazine[16] is published quarterly and, in each issue, the correspondence pages record testimonies of individuals who have been blessed by reading the evidence for a young Earth and understanding how God created the Earth.

I have quoted Professor Paul Ewart's article that suggested scientists will be able one day to find out 'how God did it', speaking of Creation. In fact, the Bible tells us that God spoke Creation into being. That is how he did it. Of course, this was a miraculous action by God and I do not believe it can be explained in scientific terms, any more than the raising of Lazarus from the dead, when Jesus said, 'Lazarus come out' (John 11:43).

I cannot, therefore, agree with the late Melvin Tinker who wrote in his book, *Reclaiming Genesis*, 'In principle, my strong biblical belief in a God who is intimately involved in His world actually causes me to expect a thoroughly sufficient scientific explanation of the origin and development of life, as I would expect, in principle, a complete scientific explanation to be given of *every* (his italics) part of God's creation.'[17]

In chapter 25, I referred to the three miracles of Creation, the Incarnation and the Resurrection of Jesus Christ. The Bible's testimony, in Genesis chapter 1, is that God created the Universe by His spoken Word. Jesus' Resurrection is explained in Ephesians 1:19–20, which states that God used 'His mighty strength, which he exerted in Christ when he raised him from the dead'. In explaining the Incarnation of Christ to Mary, recorded in Luke 1:35, the angel Gabriel told her, 'The Holy Spirit will come upon you, and the power of the Most High will overshadow you.' We can have no idea of how God worked these three miracles.

God has told us enough in order to trust him, as Hebrews 11:3 says, 'By faith we understand that the universe was formed at God's command, so that what is seen was not made out of what was visible.' We can believe in what actually happened in real history. It is true that the laws of nature have been given by God for stability in the functioning of our planet and so that scientists can research and learn the workings of the Universe and employ their findings for the good of mankind. However, miracles are miracles and God has retained and reserved to himself this particular mighty power. As previously stated, miracles do not suspend the laws of nature; they are due to God's power which is over and above nature. Jesus Christ regularly demonstrated this power during his earthly ministry. In John 14:11, He claimed to be God because of His union with the Father which was proved by the evidence of miracles.

As I come to the end of this chapter, I would like to recommend three resources which help to show that God did not use evolution to create the world. These uphold the Scriptures of the Old and New Testament as of first importance in this debate.

Dr Stephen Lloyd holds a PhD in Materials Science from Cambridge University and is a pastor of a church in Gravesend, UK. His 30-page booklet, *Adam or death: Which Came First?* is published by Biblical Creation Trust. Theistic evolution claims that death existed before Adam, but 1 Corinthians 15:21 states, 'For since death came through a man, the resurrection of the dead comes also through a man.' Quoting Stephen Lloyd, 'Jesus' resurrection from the dead (the solution) is linked to the problem of death through Adam's sin. Given that the resurrection includes new physical life, Adam's sin must have led to physical death.'[18]

The second resource is a DVD: *Which Gospel? How Long Age Stories Undermine the Gospel*, by Dr Martin Williams, a lecturer at the Reformed Theological College in Melbourne, Australia. The bonus talk: 'Is Creation a Secondary Issue?' is most helpful in showing that a deep-time view of our origins is incompatible with the New Testament's understanding of Jesus' life, death and resurrection.[19]

Finally, I would commend Philip Bell's book, *Evolution and the Christian Faith—Theistic evolution in the light of Scripture*,[20] published in 2018. His book focuses on a defence of biblical Creation from the

Scriptures and highlights that an attempt to see evolution described in the Bible is an error. He shows the impact of evolutionary teaching on the moral and spiritual state of our society.

In chapter 12 of his book, he quotes a book by Bible college lecturer, Rev. C. Leopold Clarke, called *Evolution and the Breakup of Christendom*. Clarke wrote, 'Evolution is the greatest and most active agent of moral and spiritual disintegration. It is a battering-ram of unbelief—a sapping and mining operation that intends to blow religion sky-high.'[21]

Helpfully, Clarke also wrote, 'The one thing which the human mind demands in its conception of God, is that, being Almighty, He works sovereignly and miraculously—and this is the one thing with which evolution dispenses.'[22]

NOTES

1   Paul Ewart, 'What would life on Venus mean for Christian faith?', *Evangelicals Now*, November 2020, p. 26.

2   Jane Greaves et al., 'Phosphine gas in the cloud decks of Venus', *Nature Astronomy*, 2021, 5, pp. 655–664.

3   Geoff Chapman, 'Venus: pie in the sky?' *Evangelicals Now*, December 2020, p. 8.

4   Jane Greaves et al., 'Phosphine gas in the cloud decks of Venus', 20th November 2020, Editor's Note. http://orca.cardiff.ac.uk/id/eprint/134883

5   Tom McLeish, *Faith and Wisdom in Science*, (Oxford University Press, 2017 reprint), pp. 240–241.

6   *Faith and Wisdom in Science* by Tom McLeish, review—rich and discursive', *The Guardian*, 19 September 2014.

7   Tom McLeish, *Faith and Wisdom in Science*, p. 240.

8   Ibid., p. 241.

9   N. T. Wright, *Surprised by Scripture: Engaging with Contemporary Issues*, (London: SPCK, 2014), p. 31.

10 Ibid., p. 26.

11 N. T. Wright, 'Christ and Creation: Exploring the Paradox', *BioLogos conference*, 2017. https://biologos.org/resources/if-creation-is-through-christ-evolution-is-what-you-would-expect

12 Denis Alexander, *Creation or Evolution: Do We Have to Choose?* (Oxford: Monarch Books, 2008), p. 352.

13 Ibid., p. 353.

14 Ibid., p. 131.

15 Ibid., pp. 352–353.

16 *Creation* magazine, published quarterly in Australia. Creation Ministries International Ltd PO Box 4545, Eight Mile Planes, Queensland 4113, Australia.

17 Melvin Tinker, *Reclaiming Genesis*, (Oxford: Monarch Books, 2010), p. 26.

18 Stephen Lloyd, *Adam or death: which came first?* (Rugby, Warwickshire: Biblical Creation Trust, 2017), p. 12.

19 Martin Williams, *Which Gospel? How long age stories undermine the Gospel*, Creation Ministries International DVD.

20 Philip Bell, *Evolution and the Christian Faith—Theistic evolution in the light of Scripture*, (Leominster: Day One Publications, 2018).

21 C. Leopold Clarke, *Evolution and the Breakup of Christendom*, (London: Marshall, Morgan & Scott, 1930), p. 36.

22 Ibid., p. 57.

31 Arthur Rendle Short's struggle: Creation apologetics in its infancy

A rthur Rendle Short (ARS[1] is how his son John referred to him in his book, *Green Eye of the Storm*) was born in Bristol in 1880.[2] In 1855, his grandfather had taken up a position as a teacher at Ashley Down Orphan Homes, recently opened by George Müller. His father, Edward, was a director of 'Fry's', the chocolate manufacturers. ARS was brought up in a Christian home and personally had a strong Protestant evangelical faith. He was strongly influenced by the preaching of his own father and by the life and works of George Müller, who founded schools and orphanages while working as a missionary in Bristol.

In his biography, entitled *Arthur Rendle Short—Surgeon and Christian*, by W. Melville Capper and Douglas Johnson, published in 1954, the final chapter is the testimony of ARS under the title, 'My Road to Faith'.[3] He wrote this testimony two years before his own sudden death in 1953. ARS was a prolific writer with two textbooks on physiology, books on archaeology, science and Biblical apologetics—for example, *Why Believe?*[4] and *The Rock Beneath*.[5] Among his many surgical writings was, *The Causation of Appendicitis,*[6] a book which Mr Dennis Burkitt, the 'Bran Man', found very helpful.

ARS belonged to the denomination known as the *Association of Brethren* which did not have ordained ministers. The men in each congregation took responsibility for teaching and preaching and ARS lived an incredibly busy life, sharing this responsibility in a number of Brethren chapels in Bristol. His obituary, recorded by the Royal College of Surgeons of England, refers to him

> as a man of strong religious principles, but with a keen sense of fun. He was an excellent teacher and surgeon, absolutely self-confident without any vanity or self-seeking. He particularly liked the company of young people and of working men and women. He was a devoted citizen of Bristol, preferring the poor quarters of the old historic town, which were largely destroyed in the Second World War.[7]

His biographers, Capper and Johnson, describe that he had

> an intense love of children. They were quick to detect it and to respond. A retiring nature which shrank from violating the private scruples of anyone else, sometimes appeared almost assertive through its anxiety to recover the values which our generation holds all too lightly *(written in 1954)*. An intense dislike of controversy and an unwillingness to believe evil of anyone were yoked to a fearless telling of the truth and a personal integrity which declined to deviate from principle. In brief, Rendle Short was a unique combination of those great and good characters whom he admired so much in *Pilgrims Progress*.[8]

His father lost money in a bank failure in 1882, but ARS won scholarships in 1894, 1896, 1899 and 1903, which supported his education. It was not unusual for students studying medicine to embark on a BSc in a subject related to medicine during their undergraduate years. ARS chose to study Geology which, as we will see, was a very significant choice.

His academic achievements are noteworthy: his BSc in Geology won the University Gold Medal; he also won a University Gold Medal in Physiology, in Medicine, in Materia Medica and in his 1904 MD. At one time planning to be a medical missionary, he obtained the Diploma of Tropical Diseases with distinction and in the same year, 1908, the FRCS.[9] (Materia Medica is a Latin term for the study of pharmacy and the therapeutic properties of substances used for healing. The more modern terms of Therapeutics or Pharmacology have replaced this term.)

ARS was eager to share his knowledge of physiology and surgery with all around him. However, his greatest teaching desire was to share the Good News concerning Jesus Christ and the offer of salvation from sins. He did that with both adults and children in Bristol and when travelling on speaking engagements throughout the UK. When visiting European cities for medical conferences, he also took the opportunity to speak to students about Christianity.

ARS had to learn Greek and Latin at school and, in addition, taught himself Hebrew. His fiancée, Helen Case, soon after their engagement, was walking in Clifton when one of the senior medical staff from the Royal Infirmary met her. He said, 'I understand that you are the lady who is going to marry the Encyclopaedia Britannica.'[10]

In 1908 he married Helen and he was also appointed to the staff of Bristol Royal Infirmary as a surgical registrar and of University College, Bristol, as a lecturer in Physiology. After the usual long training, he became a consultant surgeon to the Infirmary from

1922 to 1933. In 1933 he was appointed Professor of Surgery at the University of Bristol, serving in this position until his retirement in 1946. During the First World War he served in the Royal Army Medical Corps in France and while there did research into shock.

ARS and Helen had three children; Coralie who, in 1953, became Professor of Obstetrics and Gynaecology at the University of East Africa; Morwenna who trained as a nurse at St Thomas' Hospital, later serving as a nursing sister in the RAF in Cairo and Jerusalem. After working in a number of countries she settled in Cambridge, hosting overseas students and reached her 100th birthday. His son, John, was a paediatrician and became the Foundation Professor of Child Health at the University of Queensland, Brisbane, Australia in 1961.

ARS was a keen student of nature and often spent holidays in Cornwall. His Christian life was active and charitable, and he was a founder of the Inter-Varsity Fellowship—a worldwide evangelical Christian organization for university students. For many years, ARS was a trustee of Müller's Orphan Homes at Ashley Down. A quite large volume, recording Mr Müller's narrative of God's dealings with him, had been edited by Mr G. F. Bergin. Believing the content was important but inaccessible to many people, ARS prepared a condensed form of the narrative, *The Diary of George Müller*[11], published after ARS's death in 1954.

ARS had a brilliant scientific mind. For most of his life he approved of Darwin's *The Origin of Species*[12], apparently because he thought biology and geology could be reconciled in Darwin's theory. Christians like ARS had no doubt that the spiritual part of man was special, created in the image of God. However, the ruling geological paradigm was Lyell's uniformitarianism with millions or billions of years explaining the origin of the Universe and denying the universal flood of Noah. ARS chose to study Geology to get to grips with the evidence. At that time, his interpretation of the first three chapters of Genesis was influenced by the idea that the human body was not the result of direct creation but of millions of years of imperceptible change.

I would like to pause from the story of ARS to explain that, in the early years of the 20th century, there was little public awareness of scientific evidence for Biblical Creation. ARS was an example of a 'man of his time', making the best of the problem of reconciling the Biblical account with current scientific thought. In the 1970s, an increasing amount of apologetic scientific literature and films became available. These showed that it is reasonable and rational to believe in a young earth of approximately 6,000 years. Many had struggled, as did ARS, with the apparent paucity of scientific evidence to defend a young earth position.

Christians are influenced by those with scientific understanding, but theologians and ministers, of course, have great influence as well. One minister, whose influence in the 20th century has been and continues to be significant, was John Stott, Minister of All Souls Langham Place. Some believing in theistic evolution today, regard him as an authority.

In his book, *Understanding the Bible,* he wrote:

> But my acceptance of Adam and Eve as historical is not incompatible with my belief that several forms of pre-Adamic 'hominid' may have existed for thousands of years previously. These hominids began to advance culturally. They made their

cave drawings and buried their dead. It is conceivable that God created Adam out of one of them. You may call them, *Homo erectus*. I think you may even call some of them *Homo sapiens*, for these are arbitrary scientific names. But Adam was the first *Homo divinus*, if I may coin a phrase, the first man to whom may be given the biblical designation 'made in the image of God'.[13]

This view is difficult to reconcile with the statement in Genesis 3:19: 'By the sweat of your brow you will eat your food, until you return to the ground, since from it you were taken; for dust you are, and to dust you will return.' It is suggested, by some, that 'the dust of the earth' may be a metaphor for the evolutionary process—is that really plausible?

Another minister, Dr Martyn Lloyd-Jones, of Westminster Chapel in London, stated the following at an International Fellowship of Evangelical Students conference in 1971:

> We accept the biblical teaching with regard to creation and do not base our position upon theories of evolution. We must assert that we believe in the being of one first man called Adam, and in one first woman called Eve. We reject any notion of a pre-Adamic man because it is contrary to the teaching of the Scripture. Now someone may ask: why do you care about this? Is this essential to your doctrine of salvation? Yes. I would contend that the early chapters of Genesis are given to us as history. We know that there are pictures and symbols in the Bible, but when it presents something to us in the form of history it requires us to accept it as history. The Bible does not merely make statements about salvation. It is a complete whole: it tells you about the origin of the world and of man, how he fell and the need of salvation.
>
> Therefore, these early chapters of Genesis with their history

play a vital part in the whole doctrine of salvation. Take for instance the argument of the apostle Paul (Romans 5:12–21). Paul's whole case is based upon that one man, Adam, and his one sin, and the contrast with the other one man, the Lord Jesus Christ, and his one great act. Similarly in 1 Corinthians 15 the apostle's whole argument rests upon historicity. Indeed, it seems to me that one of the things we have to assert, particularly today, is that *our gospel is not a teaching, nor a philosophy, but primarily a history* (my italics). The works of salvation are God's acts! Salvation is not an idea; it is something that results from actions which have taken place on the concrete plane of history. Historicity is a very vital matter. In addition to that, of course, the whole question of the person of our Lord arises. He clearly accepted this history, he referred to Adam, and in speaking about marriage he clearly accepted the historicity of that portion of Scripture (Matthew 19:4–5). But, quite apart from this, if you do not accept this history and prefer to believe that man's body developed as the result of an evolutionary process and that God then took one of these humanoid persons and did something to him and turned him into a man, you are still left with the question of how to explain Eve, for the Bible is very particular as to the origin of Eve. All who accept the theory of evolution in any form completely fail to account for the being, origin, and existence of Eve.[14]

It is interesting to read, in *Green Eye of the Storm*, that ARS struggled with the origin of Eve[15], as he thought there may have been a pre-Adamic race along the lines that John Stott suggested. ARS also struggled with the Fall of man[14], which brought sin and death into the world and yet the fossils seemed to show a creation groaning for millions of years before man. ARS believed that Noah's flood was local and not worldwide.[16] How blessed he would have been to listen today to the many Creation Geologists who see in the fossil record widespread evidence of a global flood.

In the 1949 edition of his book, *Modern Discovery and The Bible*, ARS wrote about these difficulties and said, 'The reverent Bible student must wait further for the light, and meanwhile hold steadfastly to the doctrines of man's divine creation, his distinction from the beasts that perish, his fall into sin, and the divine institution of marriage.'[17] John Rendle-Short called ARS's struggle, an intellectual impasse, which was evident in much of his writings. How could man be both a rising ape and a fallen image?

In his book, *The Rock Beneath*, ARS's struggle with evolution is made clear in a chapter with the title, 'Problems of Inspiration'. I quote: 'How can the opening chapters of Genesis be reconciled with the established facts of scientific discovery and with the current principles of scientific deduction, such as the theory of evolution? How long has man lived on the earth?'[18]

In the following chapter, entitled 'Scientific Difficulties of the Bible', ARS comments that 'the very princes of science have found it possible to be earnest Christians and believers in the Word of God'. He listed among these 'princes of science': Lord Kelvin, the physicist; Sir James Simpson of chloroform anaesthesia fame; Lord Joseph Lister, the founder of antiseptic surgery; Lord Rayleigh, Sir George Stokes, and James Clerk Maxwell, all physicists; Professor J. H. Gladstone, Sir William Ramsay and Sir William Perkin, all chemists; Professors Boyd Dawkins, Edward Hill, C. J. Prestwich and C. J. W. Dawson, four English geologists; and a large number of famous medical men. Many of these men devoted their spare time, and some their whole lives, to the preaching of the Gospel.[19]

His son, John Rendle-Short, published his book, *Green Eye Of The Storm*, in 1998. John wrote that his father's 'sermon notes seem to indicate that he came ever closer to a straightforward understanding of Genesis'.[20]

ARS died suddenly in Hereford on 14 September 1953, aged 73. Three months later, in December 1953, the Piltdown man was shown to be a hoax. One wonders what impact that would have had on the direction of ARS's thinking. His widow, Helen, chose the verse, Malachi 2:6 from the Authorised Version, for the funeral notice: 'The law of truth was in his mouth, and iniquity was not found in his lips: he walked with me in peace and equity, and did turn many away from iniquity.'[21]

This chapter has been particularly written about the surgeon Arthur Rendle Short and his personal journey struggling to a settled Christian worldview. It would be wrong to end the story there because, in a remarkable way, his son, John Rendle-Short, was not only his biological heir but his spiritual heir. John would become not only a famous paediatrician and innovator but a well-informed champion of Biblical Creationism. He established and was the Foundation Chairman of the Creation Science Foundation (UK) and was World Chairman of the US-based Creation Ministries International.[22]

John Rendle-Short wrote that he, personally, was converted and became a Christian at the age of eight[23] and, for many years, like his father, believed in theistic evolution. In *Green Eye of the Storm*, he describes his own journey to a strong and settled worldview, based on the historicity of Genesis.

In 1974, he attended the International Convention of Christian Physicians in Toronto. As a paediatrician, he was interested to attend a lecture by a well-qualified Professor of Pharmacology, Dr A. E. Wilder-Smith, on 'Drugs of Addiction'. I have written about Dr Wilder-Smith and the debate at the Oxford Union in chapter 15.

On the Sunday of the conference, the delegates were taken to the People's Church in Toronto. He found himself sitting next to Wilder-Smith in the coach and the topic of Creation and evolution came up. John was overwhelmed to hear Wilder-Smith offer his opinion that the world was created in six literal days, as stated in Genesis. John had never heard anyone of scientific integrity say such a thing and, whether from astonishment or because the coach started at that moment, he found himself precipitated onto the floor. The importance of six-day creation was firmly impressed upon him. He did not speak to Wilder-Smith again for another ten years but was able to buy his book, *Man's Origin, Man's Destiny*, published in 1974. This was the first book he had ever seen stating that the days in Genesis chapter 1 were literal days.[24]

It is not my purpose to relate all of his journey of understanding, but it is proper to recognize his personal character and qualities, which endeared him to many in Australia. The UK Royal College of Physicians has a website entitled, 'Inspiring Physicians'.[25] John Rendle-Short is included in this group with the following mention: 'Early in his career he had investigated what was thought to be a rather strange phenomenon—some mothers reported their babies tasting "salty" when they kissed them. The scientific basis for this,

Rendle-Short found, was that a metabolic abnormality in cystic fibrosis produces excess salt in the sweat, thus opening the way for a diagnostic test. He published the findings as "Fibrocystic disease of the pancreas presenting with salt depletion",[26] a paper which became a classic of its time.' The Cystic Fibrosis Foundation website indicates that the sweat test is considered the gold standard for diagnosing cystic fibrosis.

John Rendle-Short was a pioneer in two other paediatric developments—'rooming-in' for mothers in hospitals and research into autism. His book, *A Synopsis of Children's Diseases*, was published in six editions, translated into three languages and used as a standard paediatric textbook on four Continents. In 1981, he was made a Member of the Order of Australia for services to medicine and infantile autism. He wrote eighteen books and hundreds of papers.[27]

John was an esteemed and highly respected paediatrician. About 2,600 doctors graduated from the University of Queensland, having been taught child development and health under his leadership. Since 1984, the Rendle-Short Gold Medal has been awarded to medical students gaining best marks in paediatrics and child health. John's life was guided by his Christian worldview, with his beliefs and values permeating his professional life and guiding key decisions. John died in 2010 at the age of 90.

Both Arthur Rendle Short (ARS) and his son, John Rendle-Short, were Christian men of great character and integrity.

NOTES

1   John Rendle-Short, *Green Eye of the Storm*, (Edinburgh: The Banner of Truth Trust, 1998), p. xi.

2 The name, Rendle, came from family connections in Polperro, Cornwall. Arthur Rendle Short did not have a hyphen between Rendle and Short, but his son, John, used Rendle-Short as his surname. John's first name was actually Tyndale.

3 W. Melville Capper and Douglas Johnson, *Arthur Rendle Short—Surgeon and Christian*, (London: Inter-Varsity Fellowship, 1954), p. 184.

4 A. Rendle Short, *Why Believe?* (London: Inter-Varsity Fellowship 6th edition, 1954).

5 A. Rendle Short, *The Rock Beneath*, (London: Inter-Varsity Fellowship 1st edition, 1955).

6 A. Rendle Short, *The Causation of Appendicitis*, (Bristol: John Wright and Sons, 1946).

7 Short, Arthur Rendle (1880–1953), 'Plarr's Lives of the Fellows', *Royal College of Surgeons of England*, Resource Identifier: 'rcs:E005545'.

8 W. Melville Capper and Douglas Johnson, *Arthur Rendle Short—Surgeon and Christian*, p. 11.

9 Ibid., p. 203.

10 Ibid., p. 171.

11 A. Rendle Short, *The Diary of George Muller*, (Glasgow: Pickering & Inglis, 1954).

12 Charles Darwin, *The Origin of Species*, 1st Edition, (Albemarle Street, London: John Murray, 1859).

13 John Stott, *Understanding the Bible*, Expanded ed., (Grand Rapids, MI: Zondervan, 1999), pp. 55–56.

14 Ranald Macaulay, 'It is essential—what did Lloyd-Jones and Schaeffer say about the scientific interpretation of Genesis 1-3', *Evangelicals Now*, July 10th, 2014.

15 John Rendle-Short, *Green Eye of the Storm*, p. 167.

16 Ibid., p. 282.

17 A. Rendle Short, *Modern Discovery and The Bible*, (London: Inter-Varsity Fellowship, 1942), p. 83.

18 A. Rendle Short, *The Rock Beneath*, p. 78.

19 Ibid., p. 92.

20 John Rendle-Short, *Green Eye of the Storm*, p. 263.

21 Ibid., p. 177.

22 J. Pearn, 'Professor Tyndale John Rendle-Short (1919–2010), British and Australian paediatrician: A life in two domains', *Journal of Medical Biography*, 22(2): 2014, pp. 63–70.

23 John Rendle-Short, *Green Eye of the Storm*, p. 183.

24 Ibid., p. 218.

25 Tyndale John Rendle-Short, 'Inspiring Physicians', Royal College of Physicians. https://history.rcplondon.ac.uk/inspiring-physicians/tyndale-john-rendle-short

26 J. Rendle-Short, 'Fibrocystic disease of the pancreas presenting with acute salt depletion', *Arch Dis Child* 1956, 31: pp. 28–30.

27 Professor John Rendle-Short A.M., M.A., M.B., B.Chir., M.D. (Cantab.), F.R.C.P., F.R.A.C.P. (19 June 1919–21 January 2010). https://creation.com/professor-john-rendle-short

32 Philosophers: searching for the truth

The use of the term, *philosopher*—a 'lover of wisdom'—has been attributed to the Greek thinker, Pythagoras of Samos.[1] Philosophy is the study and development of theories about such basic things as knowledge, reason, thought, the nature of existence and about how we should live.

The ancient phrase, 'Natural philosophy' (the philosophy of nature), embraced the study of the natural and physical universe and was the precursor of modern science. It involved the natural sciences such as astronomy, medicine, and physics and would now also include chemistry, biology and cosmology. At older universities, long-established Chairs of Natural Philosophy are nowadays occupied mainly by professors of Physics.[2]

'Moral philosophy', or *ethics*, is the study of what is right and wrong—what is goodness, justice and virtue. It is the forerunner of the social sciences. 'Metaphysical philosophy', or *logic*, includes the study of being, reason, logic, causation, forms, and the existence of God. This would now include mathematics and the philosophy of science.

Perhaps the earliest well-known Greek philosopher was Socrates (470–399BC) who influenced Plato (approximately 428 –347BC) and his student Aristotle (384–322BC). Socrates left no written record of his ideas, though his beliefs have been passed on by others.[3] Later Roman philosophers, such as Seneca and Cicero, continued to discuss Greek philosophy.

When the early church—which was small, persecuted and surrounded by an established alien culture—began to preach concerning the resurrection of Jesus Christ, of sins forgiven and a future home in heaven, it had to debate and interact with the well-developed Greek philosophies of the day. Actually, there was much in the thinking of Plato and Aristotle that was helpful. They both believed that the Universe was ordered and rational, which was an inspiration for the development of modern science. They affirmed the ideals of truth, goodness and beauty and believed that knowledge was objective.[4]

Socrates had written, 'With such signs of forethought in the design of living creatures, can you doubt they are the work of choice or design?'[5] While Plato agreed with 'the argument from design', his view was distorted, believing that matter pre-existed and could not be fully controlled by a divine designer. The argument from design notes that all the things in the world appear fitted to one another including all the parts of an organism. In addition, when we see design in things, we believe that someone designed and made them. The world must have a designer or creator with greater intellect and power than any human. This is known as the 'teleological argument'—things have been made for a purpose. I discussed this in chapter 6 when Professor Hunt taught us, as medical students, that we must exclude teleology in describing physiological functions. William Paley[6], later, used the teleological argument when he claimed that someone finding a watch for the first time would realize that it was the creation of an intelligent being.

In contrast to Christians, Plato and Aristotle were pagans, believing in many gods.[4] As classical philosophers, they described a strong distinction between matter and spirit. Matter and the material realm were less valuable and sometimes evil when compared to the spiritual realm. They thought that the highest ideal was to liberate the spirit from the material world by denial of physical or psychological desires, in order to attain the spiritual ideal or goal and ascend to God. Later, followers of these views were called *Gnostics*.

I will discuss Plato's views in more detail. Plato regarded *matter* as pre-existing from eternity. Upon this raw material, Plato believed that *form* was imposed from the spiritual realm. Form meant rational ideas which were good—bringing order, harmony and beauty upon matter. Indeed, pure form was more real than the material world. Plato believed that only philosophers had the ability to discern the *forms*.[4]

Plato thought that the Universe was made from the four elements of fire, water, earth and air. The Universe, he proposed, was the handiwork of a kind, divine craftsman and demonstrated purpose and rational thought. Despite the good intentions of the divine craftsman, the material world was the realm of error and illusion. Because matter pre-existed, the creator tried to impose form upon it but was never fully successful. This meant that disorder and irrational behaviour existed in the world. In summary, Plato described two eternal elements prior to the origin of the world: *matter* with inbuilt evil and chaos and *form* representing reason and rationality.[4]

Plato's established views were contrary to what the early church taught. The Bible declares that the only pre-existing eternal 'thing' in the Universe is God. As Hebrews 11:3 reminds us, 'By faith we understand that the universe was formed at God's command, so that what is seen was not made out of what was visible.' God created matter from nothing, not from something which pre-existed—hence the title of my book: *The Something Delusion*. God is a spirit with absolute control over matter. Genesis 1 records Him creating a world which was originally good and without flaw. The good world reflected God's character. Genesis 3 records that sin, death, disease and decay were consequences of the sin of Adam and Eve.

The early church rightly opposed Plato's view that the body (matter) is of lesser value than the spirit, which led to the heresy called *Gnosticism*. In contrast to Plato's view, early Christians believed that the body was to be honoured and taught that bodily exercise was good; that gluttony or drunkenness was to be avoided; and that the weak were to be protected. The incarnation of Christ, who then lived a sinless life in a human body which was resurrected after death, affirms the importance and sacredness of each human body.

I have said that God is a spirit with absolute control over matter. The creation of Adam is recorded in Genesis 2:7: 'The LORD God formed the man from the dust of the ground and breathed into his nostrils the breath of life, and the man became a living being.' Many people, whether Christian or not, accept that we possess an immaterial part which lives on after our bodies die. This second part is called our soul or spirit—words which are often used interchangeably in the Bible. Other people believe the soul and spirit are separate entities.

In the latter view the soul includes man's intellect, emotions and will, which are functions of our mind and consciousness separate

.om the spirit. Wayne Grudem helpfully explains the 'two part' and 'three part' views and their scriptural basis in chapter 23 of his book *Systematic Theology*.[7]

The immortal nature of our spirits is affirmed throughout the Bible. For example, Jesus' words to the dying thief: 'Today you will be with me in Paradise' (Luke 23:43), or Stephen the Martyr's dying words: 'Lord Jesus, receive my spirit' (Acts 7:59). The Bible indicates that we will have a conscious awareness in God's presence before the Second Coming of Christ. Revelation 6:9–11 describes martyrs in heaven calling out to the Sovereign Lord for judgement.

Moving on from the above consideration of man's essential nature, we note that Paul engaged with Greek philosophers in Athens to warn them about a coming day of judgement, guaranteed by the resurrection of Christ from the dead (Acts 17:31). The clear message that we will experience bodily resurrection prior to our meeting Jesus as our judge, was understood and caused a division of opinions. 'When they heard about the resurrection of the dead, some mocked. But others said, "We will hear you again about this." So, Paul went out from their midst. But some men joined him and believed' (Acts 17:32–34).

In introducing his first letter, the apostle John was at great pains to testify that he saw, touched and listened to God the Son, who was alive with a human body and with whom he shared meals. John was a reliable witness, as were others who were still alive. The fact that Jesus chose to become a human being opposes the idea that the body is evil.[8]

People following Gnostic teaching saw no purpose in practising moral restraint, as required by the law of God, and often behaved in an immoral way. In contrast, some of those who wanted to please God and receive His blessing, mistakenly, treated their bodies harshly, practising *Asceticism*. Salvation, for Gnostics, meant the escape from the body, achieved not by faith in Christ but by special knowledge (Greek = *gnosis*). John wrote his letter to counteract this heresy.

The church of Christ always exists in a contemporary world and takes account of this when sharing the truth of Christianity. The apostle Paul engaged with the local culture wherever he travelled. He dialogued with the Athenians and wrote about these matters to the Corinthians. He discussed philosophy and theology with Jewish leaders in their synagogues. The Gnostic error of valuing the spirit as of greater importance than the body still has parallels in modern life. There are those who believe that the mind and emotions can overrule the biological reality of the body.

Turning to 20th century philosophers, let us consider the lives and thinking of Bertrand Russell (1872 – 1970) and then of Jean-Paul Sartre (1905 – 1980). I want to emphasize that how people live is determined by what they think; hence the importance of developing a personal worldview which I discussed in my introduction to this book. Humans are unique in having a mind which can reason and their 'thought world' determines how they act. The New King James Version of the Bible in Proverbs 23:7 states of man, 'For as he thinks in his heart, so *is* he.'

Bertrand Russell was born into an aristocratic family and was talented in many fields. He was known as a mathematician, philosopher, historian and political activist and won the Nobel Prize for literature in 1950. His adolescence was described as

and he contemplated suicide.[9] At the age of 15, when
̤sidering the claims of Christianity, he dismissed free will and
̤ife after death. At the age of 18, he declared himself an atheist.[10]
He would later also describe himself as a socialist, liberal and a
pacifist.

Russell studied Mathematics at Trinity College, Cambridge. At
the age of 22, he supported eugenic policies, suggesting that
prospective parents should be checked to see if they were healthy,
and if so, they would be issued by the state with certificates of
health. He advocated that those considered unfit should have public
benefits withheld. In 1929, he proposed that the 'mentally defective
should be sterilized because of their propensity to produce
enormous numbers of illegitimate children who, as a rule, were
useless to society.'[11]

His comments about voluntary population control, through
educational propaganda, were accompanied by remarks that war
had a disappointing effect on population, though bacteriological
warfare perhaps would be more effective. He suggested that if the
'Black Death' (bubonic plague pandemic) could be spread around
the world once in every generation, then the survivors could
multiply without causing overcrowding.[12]

In 1944, Bertrand Russell wrote, *The Value of Free Thought. How to
Become a Truth-Seeker and Break the Chains of Mental Slavery.* In the
opening paragraph, he writes:

> What makes a freethinker is not his beliefs but the way in which
> he holds them. If he holds them because his elders told him
> they were true when he was young, or if he holds them because
> if he did not he would be unhappy, his thought is not free; but if

he holds them because, after careful thought he finds a balance of evidence in their favour, then his thought is free, however odd his conclusions may seem.

The person who is free in any respect is free from something; what is the free thinker free from? To be worthy of the name, he must be free of two things: the force of tradition, and the tyranny of his own passions. No one is completely free from either, but in the measure of a man's emancipation he deserves to be called a free thinker.[13]

Russell was married four times (and divorced three times) with his last marriage, in 1952, being the only one described as happy. Russell had affairs with a number of women and caused unhappiness to several wives. He confessed, 'I always bring misery to anyone who has anything to do with me.' One mistress described him as a man 'passing from person-to-person, never giving any real happiness, or finding any'. Russell's selfishness led, in his own words, to his experiencing 'so many lonely years'.[14]

As a medical student at Guy's Hospital, I would walk past a small shop at 103, Borough High Street, which was an outlet for the National Secular Society. During my search for a settled worldview, I spotted a small booklet on display: 'Why I am not a Christian',[15] by Bertrand Russell. I bought this for one shilling. I will pick out two quotes from the foreword by David Tribe, which are full of admiration for the author and his message: 'Suburban waverers were relieved to find unbelief respectable when, after 1931, Earl Russell could be cited as a repudiator of Christianity.' The second, commenting on the booklet itself: 'Its abiding qualities are honesty and simplicity. In layman's language, but with all the virtuosity of the professional logician, it powders the philosophical, historical, ethical and emotional edifice Christianity has systematically built up over two thousand years.'[16] Bertrand Russell's atheism did not help him or his family to a happy life or encourage me that his would be a worldview worth embracing.

Jean-Paul Sartre was a French philosopher and one of the leading figures in 20th-century philosophy. He saw a conflict between oppressive, spiritually destructive conformity to rules (*mauvaise foi*—literally, 'bad faith') and an 'authentic' way of 'being'.[17] Atheism was at the core of his philosophy, leading to his belief in absolute personal freedom: 'If there is no God, then there are no rules or commandments, no restrictions placed on human liberty.' We see the out-workings of this philosophy in world affairs as you read this book.

Sartre had an 'open relationship' with the feminist philosopher, Simone De Beauvoir, and they are buried in the same grave in the Montparnasse Cemetery, Paris. Hazel Rowley wrote a sympathetic book, *Tête-à-Tête*, about their relationship, which she thought was inspiring. She believed that young intellectuals wanted partners with whom to share ideas. 'Didn't everyone want to write in Paris cafes amid the clatter of coffee cups and the hubbub of voices, and spend their summer in Rome in complicated but apparently harmonious foursomes? Who wanted monogamy when one could have freedom and stability, love affairs and commitment?'[18] The New York Times Book Review of *Tête-à-Tête* commented: 'Well, you could have it, all right, as long as you did not mind leaving a lot of human wreckage behind. The evidence can be found in Beauvoir's calculatedly frank memoirs and in the many letters between the two, published after their deaths.[19]

Sartre, the apostle of transparency, lied shamelessly to his various mistresses, including to Beauvoir herself—'particularly to the Beaver', he once told an interviewer, using Beauvoir's nickname.[19] He bragged to a friend of having nine women 'on the string' at one time. It is reported that when one of his new books was published, he had copies printed with the dedication made to four different mistresses to facilitate his deceit.

He was awarded the 1964 Nobel Prize in Literature, though it is said that he tried to refuse it. The despair of Sartre's philosophy might be summed up in his comments: 'Everything is indeed permitted if God does not exist,' and, 'That God does not exist, I cannot deny, that my whole being cries out for God I cannot forget.'[20]

Simone De Beauvoir wrote a nihilistic epitaph for the tomb they would ultimately share, ensuring their sad philosophy would go down in history. 'His death does separate us. My death will not bring us together again.'[21] Sartre frankly stated, 'Atheism is a cruel, long-term business: I believe I have gone through it to the end.' He also said, 'Every existing thing is born without reason, prolongs itself out of weakness, and dies by chance' and, 'Life has no meaning the moment you lose the illusion of being eternal.'[22]

Now I will turn to a modern-day Christian thinker, the late American, Dr Francis Schaeffer[23] (FS), who Liz and I met in March 1968 when we attended the *L'Abri* conference at Ashburnham Place. FS did not consider himself to be a philosopher but rather an evangelist and pastor, dedicated to helping people, particularly the young, in developing their worldviews. He engaged with contemporary culture and thinking in both his writing and his films.

His hope was that the truths he expounded would lead men and women to trust Christ as their Saviour.

Francis Schaeffer was converted, in 1930, at the age of 17 while he was a junior in high school. His wife, Edith, wrote about this in her autobiographical book, *The Tapestry*. FS went to a bookshop in search of a beginner's English reading book but returned with a book on Greek philosophy.[24] He found that the philosophers asked lots of questions but that they did not seem to have satisfactory answers to the basic problems of humanity. The liberal church that he attended also seemed devoid of answers. He wondered about discarding the Bible but realized that he had never read it; so, beginning at Genesis he read, night by night, to the end of Revelation.

He did not have anybody to guide him in how to read the Bible but, as a 17-year-old, he had a deep thirst for the answers to life's questions and began to discover the existence of adequate and complete answers right in the Bible! In following what he was later to call 'the flow of biblical history', the answers to the most fundamental questions and problems of human existence were to be found. In the Biblical account of Creation, the Fall, and Redemption, God answered his questions. FS began to develop a Biblical worldview.[24]

FS began his studies at Westminster Theological Seminary in Philadelphia, in 1935. He was greatly influenced by a statement of Geerhardus Vos who wrote that biblical theology is 'the study of the actual self-disclosures of God in time and space'.[25] FS would often say, about his own view of Scripture, 'God is there; he is not silent, but rather he has made himself known to us in space and in time and in history.'[26]

At the 1968 *L'Abri* conference, FS emphasized why it is so important that God has revealed Himself to mankind. If God had not revealed Himself, man would have no knowledge of the true God.

In the first place, there is 'General Revelation' in the creation all around us. So, the facts and the forces and laws of nature speak of God. The working of the human mind, particularly conscience, and the facts of human experience and of history are all part of *general revelation*.

Bible verses explaining general revelation include:

(i) 'The heavens declare the glory of God' and 'Day after day they pour forth speech' (Psalm 19:1–2).

(ii) 'For since the creation of the world God's invisible qualities— his eternal power and divine nature—have been clearly seen, being understood from what has been made, so that men are without excuse' (Romans 1:20).

(iii) 'When Gentiles, who do not have the law, do by nature things required by the law, ... they show that the requirements of the law are written on their hearts, their consciences also bearing witness' (Romans 2:14–15).

In addition, there is 'Special Revelation', found in the written record of Old and New Testaments. This revelation is necessary because sin came into the world, causing man to be spiritually blind, leading to unbelief and a wrong interpretation of Creation. The testimony of Creation, itself, was obscured by the curse, leading to natural disasters. Examples of God's *special revelation* include Him showing Himself to man in fire and clouds of smoke (Exodus 13:21– 22)). God spoke directly to Moses and the children of Israel at Mount Sinai (Deuteronomy 5:4). In the miracles of the Bible, God's power and presence were manifest: for example, in Joshua 10:12–13, when the sun stood still about a full day. Supremely, when the Son of God came to earth in human flesh, God revealed Himself to mankind (Hebrews 1:2). The Holy Spirit speaks into the mind and heart of man to help him understand.

The conference was memorable for many reasons, including the sermon on the Tower of Babel which FS preached, and for the fellowship of many young people. We were privileged to listen to Edith Schaeffer telling the 'L'Abri Story'[27]—how she, her husband and family had settled in Switzerland, opening their home to many visitors who were seeking to learn about God. Dr Hans Rookmaaker, the Professor of the History of Art at the Free University of Amsterdam, also took us on guided tours of the National Gallery, and the Tate Gallery in London.[28] As we looked at a large painting, he explained how the American artist, Jackson Pollock, put his canvases on the floor and dripped different coloured paints on them. You might wonder what paintings and artists have to do with a chapter on philosophers. The answer is in the verse, Proverbs 23:7 (NKJV), quoted earlier: 'For as he thinks in his heart, so *is* he.'

Jackson Pollock's art is a statement about what he thought. A reviewer of his work, Elisa Angelini, wrote in June 2019 on the website, '*Auralcrave*' that, 'Revolutionary, anarchic, irascible and brave, Jackson Pollock is with no doubt the most influential native American artist in the history of pictorial art. ... He lived a short life but free from constraints and conventions.'[29] She writes about a large 1953 painting titled, *Blue Poles*—'a chaotic labyrinth on a metallic grey-black background, in which red and yellow shades intertwine. Even though it's mentioned in the title, blue colour (symbol of peace and serenity) is completely absent. The twisted black poles can be interpreted as an allegory of human efforts to emerge from the chaos of life.'[29]

Did Jackson Pollock's worldview of life free from constraints and conventions, have anything to commend it? As one looks at the chaos in his paintings, it is questionable whether he found personal peace. His relationship with his wife, artist Lee Krasner, deteriorated owing to his infidelity and his alcoholism. Jackson Pollock committed suicide at the age of 44 by drunkenly driving into a tree at 80 mph, killing one passenger, though the other survived.[30]

Francis Schaeffer wrote many helpful books including, *The God Who Is There*.[31] The book I found most helpful is, *He Is There and He Is Not Silent*, answering the question, 'How we know, and how we know we know.'[32] FS wrote that the infinite-personal God is not silent. God spoke to Adam & Eve and continues to speak today through the Bible and by His Spirit. The Logos—the Word, Jesus Christ, has compellingly spoken in these last days. John 1:10–11 declares that, even though Jesus created the world, people in the world did not recognize him. He came to the family that he had created in his own image, 'but his own did not receive him'. Verses 12–13 explain that this blindness can be reversed when individuals are born-again by the Spirit of God.

In 1976, FS wrote, *How Should We Then Live?* which was a description of the rise and decline of Western thought and culture, from Ancient Rome to our present society.[33] The title is based on Proverbs 23:7. His son, Franky, was the inspiration behind making this a cultural and historical documentary film series as well.

Filming took place in many different locations. Liz and I were so impressed with the book that I took a copy of it to 10 Downing Street for Mrs Thatcher, who was then Prime Minister. A member of her staff wrote in February 1980, thanking us for a copy of *How Should We Then live?* They said, 'This is much appreciated.'

Francis Schaeffer and Dr C. Everett Koop (Surgeon General of the United States) wrote the book, *Whatever Happened to the Human Race?* and produced the film series, in 1979.[34] This tackled the issues of abortion, infanticide and euthanasia; all choices which undermined the basic human right to life. It exposed how laws based on God's standards (the Christian worldview) were being replaced by laws based on man's standards. Schaeffer and Koop showed that such humanism was bankrupt.

Everett Koop, according to the British Medical Journal obituary[35] was chief surgeon for decades at the Philadelphia Children's Hospital, where he pioneered neonatal surgical intensive-care and conducted many ground-breaking surgical procedures. He was appointed US Surgeon General, aged 66, serving in the Reagan and Bush administrations from 1982 to 1989. During the first decade of the AIDS epidemic, the obituary describes him 'standing as a beacon of reason amid the maelstrom of ignorance and fear surrounding AIDS'. He issued a report on AIDS, written by himself (involving 17 drafts), and later mailed an eight-page summary of this to every one of the 107 million households in the US. His coordinated education campaign was successful. He called nicotine as addictive as heroin and, through his forceful advocacy, smoking rates in the US fell from 38 per cent to 27 per cent.

Everett Koop was a born-again Christian whose worldview is

explained in the book he wrote with Francis Schaeffer. Dr Anthony S. Fauci is an American physician-scientist and immunologist who serves as the director of the U.S. National Institute of Allergy and Infectious Diseases and recently achieved fame as adviser to President Donald Trump in the COVID-19 pandemic and continues as the Chief Medical Advisor to President Joe Biden. He said of Everett Koop, 'He always seemed to do what was the most correct, honourable, and appropriate thing for the health of the nation and the world.'[35]

Mary Beth Albright worked with Everett Koop for fifteen years. She advised on food systems and managed a White House initiative. She said, 'Koop would carry a $50 bill in his right pants pocket, folded into the shape of a triangle so that he could quickly palm it and slip it to someone in need, with a goodbye handshake. He didn't want to embarrass the person by taking out a wallet.'[35] Everett Koop demonstrated the truth of Proverbs 23:7.

Francis Schaeffer believed the Bible is the revealed 'true truth' about history and the cosmos as well as about spiritual matters, so Genesis chapters 1–11 are real history. He described the confusion which follows if we do not believe that:

> Consider what is lost if the Fall is not a space-time event. First, God is then the author of the sorrows of the present world. Second, if there is no literal Fall, there is a loss of true moral guilt because Adam and Eve would not have passed from obeying God to disobeying him. In such a case, Christ's death as a substitutionary atonement is gone. It becomes an enigma. Third, if all is normal now to what God made it to be, (*i.e., this world is how God first made it—my words*) there can be no way to

say, 'Such and such is really wrong, absolutely wrong.'Along with the secular humanists, we are caught in the relative.[36]

Faith is not believing in what may turn out to be untrue but is believing in what God has told us is certain in the Bible. The possibility that anything other than God existed before the creation, described in Genesis 1, is dismissed by the statement in Hebrews 11:1–3: 'What is seen was not made out of what was visible.' The Bible says that Plato was wrong in regarding matter as pre-existing from eternity and Richard Dawkins was wrong in telling me there must have been *something* there to start with! In fact, there was not something but *Someone*. Theistic evolution is a mistaken worldview in suggesting that there were chapters of history before the creation of Adam.

Paul wrote about philosophers in 1 Corinthians 1:18–25: 'For the message of the cross is foolishness to those who are perishing, but to us who are being saved it is the power of God. For it is written: 'I will destroy the wisdom of the wise; the intelligence of the intelligent I will frustrate.' Where is the wise man? Where is the scholar? Where is the philosopher of this age? Has not God made foolish the wisdom of the world? For since in the wisdom of God the world through its wisdom did not know him, God was pleased through the foolishness of what was preached to save those who believe. Jews demand miraculous signs and Greeks look for wisdom, but we preach Christ crucified: a stumbling-block to Jews and foolishness to Gentiles, but to those whom God has called, both Jews and Greeks, Christ the power of God and the wisdom of God. For the foolishness of God is wiser than man's wisdom, and the weakness of God is stronger than man's strength.'

NOTES

1 Christoph Riedweg, *Pythagoras: His Life, Teaching, and Influence*, Translated from the German by Steven Rendall, first ed. (New York: Ithaca, 2005), p. 92.

2 'Natural philosophy'. https://en.wikipedia.org/wiki/Natural_philosophy

3 'Socrates, Plato, and Aristotle: The Big Three of Greek Philosophy', 2021. https://www.dummies.com/article/body-mind-spirit/philosophy/philosophers/socrates-plato-and-aristotle-the-big-three-in-greek-philosophy-199341

4 Nancy R. Pearcy, *Total Truth, Liberating Christianity from Its Cultural Activity*, (Wheaton, Illinois: Crossway Books, 2005), pp. 74–75.

5 Abby-Jane Hunt, 'Examine the design argument for the existence of God'. https://www.markedbyteachers.com/gcse/religious-studies-philosophy-and-ethics/examine-the-design-argument-for-the-existence-of-god-4.html

6 William Paley, *Natural Theology, Or, Evidences of the Existence and Attributes of the Deity, Collected from the Appearances of Nature*, (Philadelphia: John Morgan, 1802).

7 Wayne Grudem, *Systematic Theology*, (Leicester: Inter-Varsity Press, 1994), pp. 472–483.

8 *Christianity*, 'The church and its history: Early heretical movements'. www.britannica.com.

9 *Bertrand Russell Autobiography*, (London: Psychology Press, 1998), p. 38.

10 *Bertrand Russell Autobiography*, '2: Adolescence', (London: Psychology Press, 1998).

11 Nicholas Griffin, *The Selected Letters of Bertrand Russell: The Private Years, 1884–1914*, (Milton Park, Abingdon: Routledge, 2002), p. 588.

12 Bertrand Russell, *The Impact of Science on Society*, (Milton Park, Abingdon: Routledge, 1951), p. 89.

13 Bertrand Russell, *The Value of Free Thought: How to Become a Truth-seeker and Break the Chains of Mental Slavery*, (Haldeman-Julius Publications, 1944), p. 1.

14 Ray Monk, *Bertrand Russell, The Spirit of Solitude*, (London: Jonathan Cape, 1996), p. 607.

15 Bertrand Russell, 'Why I am not a Christian', *National Secular Society*, (London: The Hatfield Press Ltd, 1967).

16 Ibid., Foreword.

17 Jean-Paul Sartre, *Time note*. https://timenote.info/en/Jean-Paul-Sartre

18 Hazel Rowley, *Tête-à-Tête: The Tumultuous Lives & Loves of Simone de Beauvoir and Jean-Paul Sartre*, (New York: Harper, 2005). http://hazelrowley.com/books/book-2/

19 'Tête-à-Tête: Simone de Beauvoir and Jean-Paul Sartre, reviewed by William Grimes', *The New York Times*, October 7th, 2005.

20 God Does Not Exist Quotes—MoreFamousQuotes.com https://www.morefamousquotes.com/topics/god-does-not-exist-quotes/

21 Michael Dobbs, 'Appreciation', *Washington Post*, 15 April 1986.

22 Donald DeMarco, 'Sartre: "Atheism is a cruel, long-term business ..."', *The Interim Newspaper*, Hamilton Ontario, 22 February 2002.

23 '10 Things You Should Know about Francis Schaeffer.' https://www.crossway.org/articles/10-things-you-should-know-about-francis-schaeffer/

24 'Francis Schaeffer: The Man and His Message—Covenant Seminary.' https://www.covenantseminary.edu/francis-schaeffer-the-man-and-his-message/

25 Charles R. Biggs, 'Outline to the Introduction of Gerrhardus Vos: *Biblical Theology, Old and New Testaments*, "Theology is the science concerning God"', *RPM Magazine*, Third Millennium Ministries. 2016 Vol 18, Number 17, 17–23 April.

26 Todd Kappelman, 'The Need to Read Francis Schaeffer', *Probe Ministries. Francis A. Schaeffer Institute of Church Leadership Development* http://www.truespirituality.org/

27 Edith Schaeffer, *L'Abri*, (San Francisco, CA: Norfolk Press, 1972).

28 Hans Rookmaaker—*Transpositions*. 2011 http://www.transpositions.co.uk/hans-rookmaaker/

29 Elisa Angelini, 'Jackson Pollock: the best paintings and the meaning of his art'. Auralcrave.com June 30th, 2019.

30 'Jackson Pollock Biography, Paintings, and Quotes', www.Jackson-Pollock.org

31 Francis A. Schaeffer, *The God Who is There*, (London: Hodder and Stoughton Ltd, 1968).

32 Francis A. Schaeffer, *The Francis A. Schaeffer Trilogy*, (Westmont, Illinois: Inter-Varsity Press, 1990), pp. 275–350.

33 Francis A. Schaeffer, *How Should We Then Live?* (London: Lakeland, Marshall Morgan & Scott, 1976).

34 Francis A. Schaeffer and C. Everett Koop, *Whatever Happened to the Human Race?* (London: Marshall Morgan & Scott, 1982).

35 C. Everett Koop, 'US surgeon general extraordinaire', *British Medical Journal*, vol 346, 30 March 2013, p. 25.

36 Ranald Macaulay, '"It is essential"—what did Lloyd-Jones and Schaeffer say about the scientific interpretation of Genesis 1-3', *Evangelicals Now*, 10 July 2014.

33 History—God's story

I have always loved history. When faced with the choice of studying History, Geography or Biology as an O-level subject at Epsom College, I chose History. This was in spite of my plan to study A-level Biology to meet the entrance requirements for Medical School. In this chapter I wish to examine the interaction between world history and science.

In 1933, Sir John Hammerton published his 856-page book, *The Outline History of The World*.[1] He lived from 1871 to 1949 and is described in the *Dictionary of National Biography* as, 'the most successful creator of large-scale works of reference that Britain has known'.[2] This prolific writer claimed, in the preface to his book, that he knew of no other single volume of history that contained a thousand pictorial illustrations and described each one as an authentic historical document and not merely the invention of an illustrator.[3] When he claimed authenticity for these illustrations, he may have had in mind the illustrations of 'primitive man' presented in magazines and textbooks—for example, the illustration of Nebraska man and his wife, published in *The Illustrated London News* in 1922, which was based on the finding of a single tooth from a pig.[4]

His belief that historical events should be reliably documented was commendable but, as I will explain, he personally seemed to struggle with the speculations of prehistory. Sir John presented his outline of world history, divided into ten eras, in 850 pages. These were preceded by an introductory sketch of the prehistoric world in 6 pages with the title, 'Before History Began'.[5] I wonder whether his choice of title conveyed personal doubts.

Sir John conceded in his sketch on prehistory that other experts, rather than historians, were needed to delve into the mysterious unrecorded past of our planet. He gave ground to these experts but seemed keen to get on with the real business of known history. He wrote:

> But even to attempt in outline a sequential story of historical events demands at least a preliminary peep into the mysterious unrecorded past of our planet: a realm of fascinating investigation which is shared today by the astronomer, the mathematician, the geologist and the archaeologist, of whose continuous and surprising discoveries the historian must content himself with being recorder. Such a glimpse of the prehistoric world this chapter is designed to supply as briefly as may be, so that our proper business of recording and illustrating the known events of history may proceed.[5]

Sir John explained that the findings of scientists must be accepted as true, but then turned to getting on with the *proper business* of recording and illustrating *the known events of history*. His final paragraph on prehistory, is given the title of 'Beginning of Recorded History'.[6] He wrote, 'It was in Egypt and Mesopotamia less than 6,000 years ago that Man first began to leave conscious records, and "prehistory" *(his inverted commas)* came to an end.' That is the testimony of a reputable historian: history started less than 6,000 years ago—remarkably like the duration of Biblical history!

Sir John continued,

> But there are areas today where in all essentials the native

The Something Delusion **433**

inhabitants are still pre-record men. Moreover, in the remotest of these areas they are still food-gatherers, even if possessing stray elements of a higher culture; and indeed, so primitive that they may be used to illustrate the prehistory of more advanced races. However, as we are concerned in this Outline History mainly with the marshalling and recording of the known facts in the development of the nations of the world, their flourishing and decay, rather than with the data and *speculations of anthropology* (my italics), we shall follow the stream of history proper, from the headwater at which we have arrived, and content ourselves with this very cursory glance at the prehistoric world.[6]

Despite Sir John's comments about the inventions of illustrators and his claim that his book only contained authentic historical documents, his sketch on prehistory contained a speculative diagram prepared by Sir Arthur Keith. He described Sir Arthur as our greatest anthropologist, in a paragraph discussing the earliest discoveries of human remains at least 300,000 years ago. The diagram labelled as 'The Common Genealogical Tree of Mankind, Anthropoids and Monkeys' covered just over 2 million years and included the fraudulent Piltdown man![7]

Included in Sir John's 6 pages of prehistory is his speculation on 'How religion first came to be.' This paragraph seemed to reflect a man writing outside his area of expertise. He ended by saying, 'Finally, religion was born when the tribal god was made guardian and sponsor of the tribal ethics, which are still completely separable from religion in certain backward races, and no less strict on that account.'[8] This remark does not appear to increase our understanding of the origin of religion.

He also describes the timing of the invention of agriculture: 'It was once the fashion to throw it back into a remote past; but while modern research has greatly extended the antiquity of Man, it tends to bring agriculture down to comparatively recent times, say 7,000 to 10,000 years ago.'[6] As Sir John moved into *the known events of history*, his tables of dates[9] suggested the invention of a Solar Calendar in Egypt in 4,241 BC—though the dawn of Egyptian history[10] was recorded as 3,400 BC. These estimated dates for the beginning of history are similar to those of James Ussher (4,004 BC), The Venerable Bede (3,952 BC) and Johannes Kepler (3,992 BC), derived from Biblical chronology and genealogy.

My purpose in drawing attention to Sir John Hammerton's history book is to show the huge pressure put upon historians by scientists, whose interpretation of world history requires the billions of years needed for the evolution of life. Sir John appeared uncomfortable with the speculations of anthropologists but bowed to their self-appropriated authority. As a consequence, he appeared to believe that some races were 'primitive'.[6] He exhibited unease about the 'mysterious unrecorded past of our planet'.[5] But, like so many today, he assumed the reliability of astronomers, mathematicians, geologists and archaeologists. He noted their 'fascinating investigations'[5] and 'surprising discoveries'[5] and contented himself with recording them as 'prehistory'. Sir John died in 1949, just before the Piltdown fraud was exposed.

However, is there a glimmer of truth shining through Sir John's opening remarks and his tables of dates beginning at 4,241 BC? Are historical facts more reliable than scientific speculations?

I introduced you to Dr Voddie Baucham in chapter 10 of this book

and his presentation of 'Why I Choose to Believe the Bible'. He
demonstrated how and why we can rely on Biblical history.

Any study of the history of the world should begin with the
records provided by reliable witnesses. There is excellent evidence
that the Bible is a historical record, effectively dictated by God, the
Creator of the Universe, who was present at the beginning of the
Universe and, hence, a dependable witness of what really happened.
It seems reasonable that God, having created the Earth, as recorded
in Genesis 1, would give mankind a historical account of the event.
In fact, he has graciously given us the Bible of sixty-six books,
describing his interaction with mankind and showing his loving
care for his creatures.

Sir John Hammerton's title for the first chapter of his book is
'Twilight: 4000 to 1580 BC'.[9] He described large, highly organized
societies and civil institutions based on the two great rivers, the
Nile and the Euphrates. He believed that historical records
suggested the dawn of Egyptian history as 3400 BC and the first
contemporary records from the Euphratic, or Mesopotamian area,
were dated at 3000 BC.

Chapter 2, 'Dawn: 1580 to 900 BC'[11], described how Egypt in the
south and the more northern kingdoms of Assyria, Mitanni and the
Hittite Confederacy began to flex their military muscles. Between
these powerful kingdoms lay the land of Syria and, particularly, the
Plain of Megiddo, which was a link or a bridge between the north
and the south. On the Plain of Megiddo (or *Esdraelon*—the Greek
modification of Jezreel), at least thirty-four significant battles[12]
have taken place during the past 4,000 years, with the last, great,
fateful battle of Armageddon possibly still to come. Megiddo and

the Jezreel Valley has been the most important site, in history, of battles which determined the course of civilizations. In the last book of the Bible, we read in Revelation 16:16, 'Then they gathered the kings together to the place that in Hebrew is called Armageddon.' Two verses earlier, we read, 'They go out to the kings of the whole world, to gather them for the battle on the great day of God Almighty.' This is the only mention of Armageddon in the Bible, though the place, Megiddo, is mentioned twelve times in the Old Testament.

The Bible indicates the progress of world history towards the 'great day of God Almighty', in which God will oppose and judge unrepentant sinners and Satan in a final confrontation, known as Armageddon. The Bible records an earlier intervention of God at Megiddo, in Judges 4 and 5, when God miraculously destroyed the enemy armies attacking Israel with a storm and the flooding Kishon River, during the time when Deborah was judge. In the song which she and Barak sang (Judges 5:19–20), we can read, 'Kings came, they fought; the kings of Canaan fought at Taanach by the waters of Megiddo but they carried off no silver, no plunder. From the heavens the stars fought, from their courses they fought against Sisera.' (Sisera was the Canaanite commander.)

The word, *Armageddon*, is a corruption of the Hebrew, *Har Megiddo*, and literally means the Mount of Megiddo. Strictly there is no mount, but there is *a tell* which is a mound or hill created by many generations of people living and rebuilding on the same spot. The site has been extensively excavated with twenty-six main levels of settlement identified on a mound now 21 m high and covering an area of more than 10 acres at the top. The earliest settlement goes back before 3000 BC. Archaeologists have uncovered a Canaanite 'high place'; the city's water supply system; a fortified gateway of a similar pattern to those at Gezer and Hazor; a hoard of carved ivory objects; and stables, probably from King Ahab's time.[13]

A 28-year-old British Army lieutenant (later Field Marshal), Lord Horatio Herbert Kitchener, looked down upon the Plain of Megiddo and wrote these words in 1878: 'It is impossible not to remember that this is the greatest battlefield of the world, from the days of Joshua and the defeat of the mighty host of Sisera, till, almost in our own days, Napoleon the Great fought the battle of Mount Tabor; and here also is the ancient Megiddo, where the last great battle of Armageddon is to be fought.'[14] Field Marshal Kitchener believed the Bible to be true history.

The plain of Megiddo has been described as a rough triangle,[15] with each side 15 miles long. The area is of great strategic importance as the principal north-south route of the ancient world, which the Romans called Via Maris (the way of the sea). This was the ancient trade route linking Egypt to Syria and Mesopotamia. Napoleon Bonaparte declared, 'All the armies of the world could manoeuvre their forces on this vast plain.... There is no place in the whole world more suited for war than this ... the most natural battleground of the whole earth.'[16] It is of interest that, in April 1799, the flooded Kishon River assisted Napoleon's victory over the Turkish army—an event similar to Deborah's and Barak's experience.

Returning to Sir John's book, he describes perhaps the first great empire-builder stepping onto the stage of history. Pharaoh Thutmose III, of Egypt, was considered a military genius but an even

History—God's story

greater statesman. At the time of the death of his father, Thutmose II in 1490 BC, he was only 10 years old, so his stepmother, Hatshepsut, ruled in his place for approximately twenty years. Under her rule, Egypt flourished and she built and restored splendid temples. There were no threats to Egypt at the time and it did not suit her to allow her young stepson to win military honours and take over the throne. When she died and he became the sole ruler, he did his best to remove her memory by deliberately defacing monuments, which has resulted in a degree of obscurity attached to her.[17]

Following her death, in 1479 BC, he immediately set off north with a moderate sized army. Within ten days he was at the eastern foothills of Mount Carmel. On the other side of the mountain lay the town of Megiddo at the northern end of a narrow pass. Thutmose III was expected to approach Megiddo by the main route, skirting the south of Mount Carmel or by an approach from the north. In the event, he approached Megiddo through a very narrow pass in the hills, call the Musmus Pass, where his soldiers and chariots often had to move in single file. His enemies, who were Hittite and Syrian troops, were surprised and the next day were routed. This was the first major battle known in recorded history anywhere in the world. Sir John records that 'the first battle on the field of Armageddon (*Har Megiddo*) had been fought and won, but by no means the last'.[16] Later, Gideon would conduct the first-known night campaign and the Mongols would lose their first major battle ever at Megiddo.[14]

Towards the end of his book, Sir John described General Edmund Allenby, in southern Palestine, dealing a decisive blow upon the Turkish enemy towards the end of the First World War. By a brilliant, well-planned and executed attack, he surprised and practically

The Something Delusion **439**

annihilated the entire Turkish force in Palestine in three days of fighting (September 19th–21st, 1918) at the Battle of Megiddo and then, proceeded to the conquest of Syria. Allenby also led his men through the narrow Musmus Pass, suggesting that he was following Thutmose III's tactics. This is likely, given that he was an avid student of military history and that his plans closely mirrored those of the Pharaoh.[18]

One biographer of Allenby, General Wavell, observed that Allenby consulted books about the Crusades and Herodotus's histories. Wavell stated, 'Certainly no commander ever gave more careful study to the history and topography of the theatre in which he was operating than did General Allenby. Two books he consulted almost daily were the Bible and George Adam Smith's *Historical Geography of the Holy Land*.[19] Field Marshal Allenby later took the title of Viscount Allenby of Megiddo and of Felixstowe.

God actively participates in world history—which has been called His story. Indeed, the Bible declares God directs history. We learn in the Bible that God is gracious and loving towards mankind, particularly in sending Jesus Christ as our Redeemer from sin. If God had not been in control of his plan of redemption, then all mankind would remain under judgement. History is not meaningless or an endless circle of random events. On the contrary, the Bible shows us that it is linear from when God began it until the time when He brings it to an end as Jesus Christ returns in glory. All things will come to pass according to the plan and foreknowledge of God.

Some Bible verses illustrate this, for example in Acts 17:26: 'From one man he made every nation of men, that they should inhabit the whole earth; and he determined the times set for them and the exact places where they should live,' or in Daniel 2:21: 'He changes times and seasons; he sets up kings and deposes them.'

God, at times, used great military powers to chastise his rebellious people, Israel. For example, the Southern Kingdom of Israel (Judah) had been deported by King Nebuchadnezzar II to Babylon in 597 BC. Remarkably, the prophet Isaiah recorded, in Isaiah 44:26–28 and 45:1, 13, that these captives would be allowed to return to Jerusalem in the future and to rebuild the temple, by King Cyrus of Persia. Isaiah made this prophecy 150 years before the events took place or Cyrus had been born. Throughout his book, Isaiah is at pains to show that the God of the Bible can make predictive prophecies about his plans for history. Isaiah records God's words of Cyrus: 'He is my Shepherd and will accomplish all that I please; he will say of Jerusalem, "Let it be rebuilt," and of the temple, "Let its foundations be laid."' Isaiah referred to Cyrus as the Lord's 'anointed' (Isaiah 45:1).

It is of interest that Sir John Hammerton refers to the character of Cyrus as being a man of 'conspicuous humanity attested by his statesmanship, in noble contrast to the old Assyrian ruthlessness, which the last Babylonian Empire had by no means discarded'.[20]

The theme of God's control of history is also illustrated in a sermon preached by the apostle Paul in Antioch of Pisidia and recorded in Acts 13:16–30. I acknowledge the insight of John Piper, in a sermon dated 15 December 1991[21], that in the space of fifteen Bible verses, Paul declares sixteen acts of God in history. All of them are vital to the plan of redemption that God planned for all of mankind.

The Bible passage reads:

The Something Delusion **441**

16 Standing up, Paul motioned with his hand and said: 'Men of Israel and you Gentiles who worship God, listen to me! 17 The God of the people of Israel chose our fathers; he made the people prosper during their stay in Egypt; with mighty power he led them out of that country; 18 he endured their conduct for about forty years in the desert; 19 he overthrew seven nations in Canaan, and gave their land to his people as their inheritance. 20 All this took about 450 years.

After this, God gave them judges until the time of Samuel the prophet. 21 Then the people asked for a king, and he gave them Saul son of Kish, of the tribe of Benjamin, who ruled for forty years. 22 After removing Saul, he made David their king. He testified concerning him: "I have found David son of Jesse, a man after my own heart; he will do everything I want him to do."

23 From this man's descendants God has brought to Israel the Saviour Jesus, as he promised. 24 Before the coming of Jesus, John preached repentance and baptism to all the people of Israel. 25 As John was completing his work, he said: "Who do you think I am? I am not that one. No, but he is coming after me, whose sandals I am not worthy to untie."

26 Brothers, children of Abraham and you God-fearing Gentiles, it is to us that this message of salvation has been sent. 27 The people of Jerusalem and their rulers did not recognise Jesus, yet in condemning him they fulfilled the words of the prophets that are read every Sabbath. 28 Though they found no proper ground for a death sentence, they asked Pilate to have him executed. 29 When they had carried out all that was written about him, they took him down from the tree and laid him in a tomb. 30 But God raised him from the dead.'

So, what are the sixteen acts of God?

- In verse 17: God chose Israel for His own special purposes / made these people very numerous / led them out of slavery in Egypt by mighty actions.

- In verse 18: God was patient with Israel for forty years.
- In verse 19: God defeated seven nations / and then gave the land (which belonged to Him) to Israel.
- In verse 20: God gave them judges as leaders.
- In verse 21: God gave them their first King—Saul.
- In verse 22: God removed Saul / and raised up David, a reliable man, as King.
- In verse 23: God sent Jesus as Saviour just as He had planned and foretold throughout the Old Testament.
- In verses 24–25: we learn God sent John the Baptist to show that Jesus, the Anointed One, is the centre of the story of history.
- In verse 26: we read that God sent the message of salvation to Jews and Gentiles.
- In verse 27: we observe that God uses unbelievers to accomplish his purposes.
- In verse 29: we learn that when many prophecies about Jesus had been fulfilled, His dead body was laid in a tomb.
- Finally in verse 30: God raised Jesus from the dead.

God had been at work from the beginning of Creation; He was at work in the death and resurrection of Jesus; and He continues working today in history. As Jesus said in John 5:17: 'My Father is always at his work to this very day, and I too am working.'

Relevant to a chapter on history is the question, 'How reliable are the historical documents we are reading or using?' Can we be confident of understanding what actually happened in the distant past? The same issue of reliability can be applied to geological findings or the interpretation of archaeological sites and discoveries. It is not my intention to embark on a lengthy presentation of the historical documents supporting the truth and reliability of the Bible. However, this matter is very important and excellent scholarly books are available; I would commend two for your study and believe that they will prove the reliability of the Bible and that you will find them very helpful.

The first book, *Nothing but the Truth*[22] by Brian Edwards, was published by Evangelical Press in 1978. This brilliant book deals among other things with the inspiration of the Bible; the accuracy and authority of the Bible; how and why the thirty-nine Old Testament books and twenty-seven New Testament books were included in the Bible; how the Bible came to us—examining language and text, including the Dead Sea Scrolls and examples of supposed errors in the Bible. Brian Edwards convincingly shows that trust in the authority and sufficiency of the Bible is well placed. Without the Bible, how can we be sure that the God whom we worship is not made up from our own imagination?

The second book, *Can We Trust the Gospels?*[23] is by Dr Peter Williams, the Principal of Tyndale House, a Bible research institute in Cambridge. Crossway published this in 2018. The author set out to write a short book of 140 pages, plus the index, to demonstrate the vast amount of evidence for the trustworthiness of the four Gospels. He was aiming for a general audience and provides information from non-Christian literature and sources, as well as explaining the origins of the four Gospels. The author asks, 'Did the Gospel authors know their stuff?' He examines whether the authors demonstrated familiarity with the time and places they wrote about. If not, the text cannot be trusted historically. He shows that it is wrong to claim that the Gospel authors were too distant from the events they described.

Peter Williams also examines the geographical knowledge and references of the authors. He looks at the names of towns, regions, bodies of water and particular places, such as Gethsemane or Solomon's Colonnade. Descriptions of roads and travel and of gardens are included. He looks at personal names of people who appear in the Gospels and how some of the common names, such as Simon, are qualified by giving a father's name or profession or place of origin. The name, *Jesus*, is also carefully examined. There are lots of other signs of authenticity about the Gospels including botanical terms, financial transactions, local languages and unusual customs, all pointing to the reliability of the Gospel records. Peter Williams answers the questions, 'Has the text changed?' and 'Who would make all this up?'

As I close this chapter on history, I would suggest that the idea of prehistory is fictional! We have to ask, 'Where did the certainty for the period of time known as *prehistory* come from?' Sir John Hammerton listed some scientific disciplines responsible for 'evidence' for long ages and evolutionary theory. We should add palaeontology (the study of prehistoric species using data from fossils) to the list but, perhaps, the most important field contributing to a belief in the long ages of prehistory is geology. I will discuss geology in the next two chapters.[24]

NOTES

1 Sir J. A. Hammerton, *The Outline History of the World*, (London: The Amalgamated Press Ltd, 1933).

2 Bridget Hadaway, 'Hammerton, Sir John Alexander, 1871–1949', *Oxford Dictionary of National Biography*, (Oxford University Press, 2004). https://doi.org/10.1093/ref:odnb/37505

3 Sir J. A. Hammerton, *The Outline History of the World*, (London: The Amalgamated Press Ltd, 1933), p. vi.

4 *The Illustrated London News*, 24 June 1922, pp. 942–3.

5 Sir J. A. Hammerton, *The Outline History of the World*, p. 1.

6 Ibid., p. 6.

7 Ibid., p. 4.

8 Ibid., p. 5.

9 Ibid., p. 8.

10 Ibid., p. 13.

11 Ibid., p. 29.

12 Eric H. Cline, *The Battles of Armageddon. Megiddo and the Jezreel Valley from the Bronze Age to the Nuclear Age*, (Ann Arbor: The University of Michigan Press, 2000), p. 3.

13 Megiddo—Tourist Israel. https://www.touristisrael.com/megiddo/9448/

14 Eric H. Cline, *The Battles of Armageddon. Megiddo and the Jezreel Valley from the Bronze Age to the Nuclear Age*, p. 1.

15 Ibid., p. 7.

16 Ibid., p. 142.

17 Sir J. A. Hammerton, *The Outline History of the World*, pp. 31–33.

18 Ibid., p. 812.

19 Eric H. Cline, *The Battles of Armageddon. Megiddo and the Jezreel Valley from the Bronze Age to the Nuclear Age*, p. 15.

20 Sir J. A. Hammerton, *The Outline History of the World*, p. 80.

21 John Piper, 'History is God's story'. www.desiringgod.org. 15 December 1991.

22 Brian H. Edwards, *Nothing but the Truth*, (Welwyn Garden City: Evangelical Press, 1978).

23 Peter J. Williams, *Can We Trust the Gospels?* (Wheaton, Illinois: Crossway, 2018).

24 In the introduction of this book, I referred to Travels with a Donkey in the Cévennes by Robert Louis Stevenson.24 Sir John Hammerton was a great admirer of Stevenson and published a 255-page book, In the Track of R. L. Stevenson and Elsewhere in Old France, with 92 illustrations in 1907. He declared, 'that the

interest in Stevenson's French travels is still so considerable that any straightforward account of later journeys over the same ground cannot fail to have some attraction for the admirers of that great master of English prose' (J. A. Hammerton, *In the Track of R. L. Stevenson and Elsewhere in Old France*, (Bristol: J. W. Arrowsmith, 1907), p. xii. www.gutenberg.org (eBook #43209).). Sir John's book can be read online at www.gutenberg.org (eBook #43209).

34 Geology, Part 1 — the geological timescale

eologists study the physical nature and history of the Earth's materials and processes. Geology can be divided into *physical geology* (the solid earth, rocks and processes that change the landscape of the planet) and *historical geology* (analysing Earth's past by examining rocks and their formations).[1] It is in this second field of historical geology that claims for long ages, prehistory or deep time, amounting to 4.5 billion years, are made. The reason for devoting this chapter to the Geological Timescale[2] and the next chapter to radiometric dating is because evolution is sustained by the millions and billions of years that the *Geological Timescale* and *radiometric dating* allow, for the slow, undirected process of evolution. Evolutionists will claim that, in light of this science, belief in a young earth is irrational. But are their claims reliable?

I must explain that the Geological Timescale (also known as the Chronostratigraphic Column) refers particularly to the ages attributed to rock layers and fossils by radiometric dating. It can be used as a measure of the relative or absolute duration or age of any part of geological time.

The Geological Column,[3] on the other hand, is the observable succession of rocks and fossils of geological history which does not necessarily have an absolute timescale imposed on it. The column is often described and displayed diagrammatically as a chart. Some geological formations are actually quite small and limited in extent, geographically. In very few areas are more than a few successive geological time periods seen, so the total column is compiled by adding together different rock formations, at different sites, to make one global geological column. Rocks are correlated from different regions to infer a complete sequence.

Geology is a fascinating subject and Liz and I have been blessed to see many amazing geological sights, such as the many volcanoes (Puys) of central France[4]; geysers in Yellowstone Park; recently formed canyons at Mount St Helens; the dramatic layers of the Grand Canyon; and in the north-east of England where we see sedimentary layers and lava flows from the Cheviot volcano. We have walked on the hot rocks of Mount Etna and I, as a medical student, climbed Mount Kilimanjaro in Tanzania and experienced the cold of -7°C at the summit. Geological formations can be sights of great beauty: for example, columnar basalt, often of hexagonal shape, as seen at the Giant's Causeway, Fingal's Cave or on the Allier River in France.

Geologists are helpfully involved in understanding how the Earth will behave in the future: for example, in predicting earthquakes, storms, floods and volcanic eruptions. They look for adequate supplies of resources, such as water, petrol and metals. Agriculture and soil conservation are benefitted so that the environment can be safeguarded. Geology is a very important subject. I have described how the surgeon, Arthur Rendle Short, gained a first-class degree in Geology in 1899, to help him in understanding the Bible and the age of the Earth.

One message of my book is that Charles Darwin's, *The Origin of Species*[5], published in 1859, profoundly changed the way that people regarded world history and the origin of man. But, foundational to everything that Darwin proposed was an established view of geology, which he imbibed by reading Charles Lyell's, *Principles of Geology*[6], published in 1830–1833. Lyell developed the theory of *uniformitarianism* to explain how the Earth's surface changed over time. His view opposed the geological theory of *catastrophism* and particularly the biblical account of Noah's flood. He declared that his geological mission was to 'free the science from Moses'.[7] He claimed that processes occurring in the present at a particular rate are the same as those that occurred in the past, leading to the phrase, 'the present is the key to the past'.

The Christian worldview might put that the other way round: 'The past is the key to the present.' God, in the Bible, wants us to learn how he created the Earth and to learn from the past behavioural mistakes of our ancestors. He contrasts the consequences of sinful lives with the happy and purposeful lives enjoyed when one choses to live according to His design and commandments.

Charles Darwin, aged 22, was given the first volume of Lyell's book just before setting out on his second voyage on HMS Beagle. When Darwin went ashore on the Cape Verde Islands, after reading this book, he saw rock formations which, seen 'through Lyell's eyes', gave him insight into the geological history of the island.[8] At the time, however, there was criticism of Lyell's book, as it focused on a theoretical idea rather than producing empirical geological evidence to substantiate the theory. It should be noted that uniformitarianism was not always associated with belief in evolution. For example, Lyell believed in species fixity until Darwin persuaded him otherwise.

Two famous geologists, contemporary to Darwin and Lyell, argued against the theory of uniformitarianism because of the geological evidence of catastrophic events.[9] They were Adam Sedgwick, Professor of Geology at Cambridge from 1818 to his death in 1873, and the French Baron, George Cuvier, 1769–1832, who established the fields of comparative anatomy and palaeontology.

Cuvier, for example, noted intermittent patterns of sudden fossil disappearance in the geologic record, which is now known as mass extinction.[10] Lyell's dismissive response to Cuvier was to say, 'The geological record was grossly imperfect,'[11] —a phrase regularly used by Charles Darwin to explain the paucity of intermediate varieties in the fossil record. In *The Origin of Species*, he wrote, 'Why then is not every geological formation and every stratum full of such intermediate links? Geology assuredly does not reveal any such finely graduated organic chain.'[12]

Secular world histories had been written well before Lyell and Darwin, with geology enjoying a secular emphasis from its earliest days. In 1749, George-Louis Leclerc, Comte de Buffon, published his *Histoire Naturelle*,[13] which led the way in rejecting biblical history and bringing us to today's natural history, that assumes atheism. Buffon published an estimate of the age of the Earth as 75,000 years but, privately, thought that it might be millions of years old.

Writing in 1779, Horace de Saussure, in his book, *Alpine Travels*,[14] claimed that it was universally accepted that the Earth's past history occupied 'a long succession of ages'. He was born in Geneva into an aristocratic family and is remembered as an original scientist; one of the founders of geology, of physical geography, of meteorology and the initiator of scientific mountaineering.

Abraham Werner, 1749 – 1817, a German geologist, developed an early theory about the stratification of the Earth's crust. Werner believed that an all-encompassing ocean gradually receded to its present location leaving the rocks and minerals of the Earth's crust to either precipitate or be deposited. At the time this was called 'Neptunism'. He is remembered for demonstrating a chronological succession in the rocks and has been dubbed, 'The Father of German Geology'. He wrote that the 'pile of rock masses' represented perhaps millions of years.[15]

Antoine-Laurent Lavoisier, the discoverer of the role that oxygen has in combustion, was a geologist of distinction as well as being called, 'The Father of Modern Chemistry'. His geological achievements included seven years preparing data for a geological atlas of France, published in 1784, and a famous memoir on sedimentary strata in 1788. He believed the Earth's age was in millions of years.[16]

Geologists at the end of the 19th century were describing the Earth as being hundreds of millions of years old and some believed that the Earth had been around forever. A famous Christian physicist, William Thomson, later Lord Kelvin,[17] restrained them with smaller estimates. Kelvin was a devout Christian, attending chapel throughout his life and believing that his Christian faith informed his scientific work. He is most famous for describing the Second Law of Thermodynamics and that the lowest temperature possible is absolute zero at -273.15°C.

Kelvin believed that the Earth, when formed, was a completely molten object at a temperature of 7,000° Fahrenheit and calculated how long it would take for the Earth to cool to its present surface temperature. It was believed that for every 50 feet of descent into the Earth the temperature increased by 1° Fahrenheit. In 1862, Kelvin published his estimate of 20–400 million years for the age of the Earth, which bolstered opposition to uniformitarian geology for a time. This timescale would be insufficient for evolution to have happened. However, Kelvin's calculations did not take account of heat produced by radioactive decay (unknown at that time) or plate tectonics[18] and that nuclear fusion creates the heat of the Sun.[19] So, Kelvin's opinions were later dismissed as incorrect.

Uniformitarian geology argued that sedimentation of rocks occurred very slowly, so the Genesis Flood could not have deposited the volume of sedimentary rocks, found in the Earth's crust, in a short time. However, the catastrophic events of Noah's flood,[20] described in Genesis 7:11, do allow for rapid geological changes. We read, 'On that day all the springs of the great deep burst forth, and the floodgates of the heavens were opened.' In the Bible the 'deep' usually refers to the ocean, so that 'the great deep' being 'broken up' probably refers to great subterranean reservoirs, perhaps both in the oceans and on land, ejecting their contents at the same time. This continued for 150 days. The phrase, 'broken up', implies a great tectonic event, resulting in earthquakes, devastating tsunamis and volcanism which totally restructured the surface of the Earth. During this time and later, as the floodwaters ran off the Earth (recessive stage), sedimentation would have been dramatic and on a worldwide scale.[21]

Modern historical geology, based on uniformitarian theory, overlooks the biblical description of catastrophic geology. It employs a core method of *actualism* to interpret the rock record. Actualism[22] is a fundamental axiom of method, restricting interpretations of the rock record only to mechanisms that are actual i.e., that *can* happen in the present. Hence the idea that the present is the key to understanding the past.

An actualistic comparison of observed modern sedimentation rates to the total volume of Earth's sedimentary rock, supposedly deposited over 4.5 billion years, demonstrates that the real volume of rock is surprisingly small, relative to modern rates of deposition.[23] Rather than accept that this discrepancy means that the method of actualism is wrong, modern geologists respond by inserting 'missing time' between the deposition of two layers.

To challenge the reigning paradigm of uniformitarian geology, we need to ask what geological evidence of catastrophic events can be seen all around us, which may be supportive evidence of Noah's flood. Paul Garner, in his book, *The New Creationism*, has described some of these.[24] On a large scale worldwide, *sedimentary rocks* appear to have formed rapidly. *Turbidites* are layers deposited by fast-flowing, dense underwater currents, capable of covering hundreds of thousands of square miles in hours. Other evidence of a rapid process is *cross-bedding*, which is inclined layering, formed as 'sand dunes' that move across the ocean floor, driven by high-velocity water, often flowing more powerfully than that observed today. *Conglomerates* are rocks formed by pebbles and boulders that have been cemented together. Some of these boulders are very large and the boulder deposits were possibly formed during hurricanes or storms. Sedimentary layers are often widespread, covering hundreds of miles across continents and of a magnitude not seen in present sedimentary environments studied by geologists.

On a smaller scale we can consider fossils as evidence of catastrophic events. Fossil graveyards and some particularly dramatic fossils, such as fossilized fish eating other fossilized fish—displayed in many museums—are evidence of catastrophic events such as Noah's flood. I believe that Noah's flood was a worldwide catastrophic event, explaining many of the plant and animal fossils we find buried in sediment throughout the world. One would expect large numbers of marine creatures to be buried and indeed 95 per cent of the fossil record is of marine creatures. If one includes microfossils (smaller than 1 mm and requiring light or electron microscopy for visualization) then the figure is probably greater.

Examples of catastrophic finds include nine pairs of fossilized turtles mating,[25] discovered in the shale deposits at the Messel Pit in Germany in 2012. This particular site was probably caused by a post-flood catastrophic event. Fossils and marine sediments are found at the top of the highest mountain ranges in every continent of the world, including Mount Everest. The fossil of an ichthyosaur mother, discovered in 2011 in China, shows that she was carrying at least three offspring. One is seen outside the mother's body; a second is waiting to be born; and a third was half-way out of the birth canal as catastrophe struck.[26]

Land creatures would be more likely to float, rot and disintegrate in a flood. In spite of this, many large fossil graveyards are found throughout the world. One such graveyard was found in 1997 in Alberta, Canada, over an area of 2.3 square kms. Several thousand fossil skeletons of *Centrosaurus*—a cow-sized, plant-eating, horned dinosaur—were found. Charles Choi wrote, 'The likely culprit in this scenario was a catastrophic storm.'[27] In the same article, David Eberth, a palaeontologist at the Royal Tyrrell Museum in Alberta, is quoted: 'The landscape basically just drowns.'[27]

In Great Falls, Montana, 10,000 duckbilled dinosaurs were buried in a thin layer of rock over 2.5 square kms; dinosaur footprints and tracks with millions of dinosaur eggs were also found.[28] In 2017, a shepherd discovered an enormous fossil graveyard on the floodplains of the Eastern Cape Province of South Africa.[29] These graveyards are compatible with the rapid burial of many creatures in the turmoil of Noah's flood.

Anyone privileged to have visited the Grand Canyon will have been awestruck by the size: 277 miles long, and the depth of over a mile. Liz and I, when visiting the North Rim in 2011, heard the usual explanation that the canyon was cut by the Colorado River 5–6 million years ago as the Colorado Plateau was uplifted. Equally breath-taking was the suggestion that 2 billion years of Earth's geological history had been exposed. Is that the truth, or was the canyon cut in a short period of time by a massive river? Events at Mount St Helens in 1980, and in the years following, suggest that the usual explanation should be reconsidered.

Liz and I visited Mount St Helens in Washington State in May 2009. Lloyd and Doris Anderson hosted us at the Seven Wonders Museum. We enjoyed two hikes, on the Hummock Trail and to the Sediment Dam, with Lloyd who taught us about the eruption. Seeing the evidence of the destructive power of the volcano, and the resulting geology, was memorable. Thousands of shattered trees formed a floating log raft covering 40 per cent of Spirit Lake's surface, which was still present and may give us insight into coal formation. The newly formed geology is impressive and offers supportive evidence for a young Earth and for a reinterpretation of how the Grand Canyon formed.

The volcano had been dormant for 123 years when it erupted on May 18th, 1980. On the first day of eruption, stratified layers up to 120 feet thick in places, were formed by pyroclastic flows of volcanic ash. Landslides covered 14 miles of the valley of the North Fork Toutle River to an average depth of 150 feet. Layers formed in a few seconds from 1 mm thick to more than a metre high. Later, on June 12th, 1980, one hundred thin layers accumulated in one day. The mechanism for this, known as pyroclastic flow, sees fast-moving currents of hot gas and rock (collectively known as tephra), reaching speeds of up to 450 mph. The gas can reach temperatures of about 1,000 °C.[30]

Geologists have long claimed that stratified layers, such as those found in the geological column, have accumulated over vast periods of time. However, the Mount St Helens' deposits demonstrated that catastrophic processes are able to create similar stratification in a very short period of time.

On March 19th, 1982, a small eruption at Mount St Helens melted the snow that had accumulated in the crater over the winter. The resulting mudflow carved a system of canyons up to 140 feet deep and 17 miles long in a single day. This mudflow cut through the unconsolidated deposits from the 1980 eruptions. The deepest of the canyons is 1/40th the size of the Grand Canyon. The small creek that now flows at the bottom would appear to have carved this canyon over a long period of time. But this witnessed event has demonstrated that rapid catastrophic processes were, instead, responsible.[31]

At Mount St Helens' Johnston Ridge Observatory, a video has been displayed comparing the canyon formed at Mount St Helens with that of the Grand Canyon. The video contrasted a canyon 'formed very quickly' with that formed 'over a long period'. The possibility that the Grand Canyon had also been formed quickly is overlooked, in spite of the dramatic insight which the eruption of Mount St Helens has given into geological formations.

When examining a particular rock formation, such as those at the Grand Canyon, the formation will be assigned to a particular time period by dating methods such as the presumed evolutionary age of its fossil contents or by radiometric dating. A large textbook, *Geologic Time Scale 2020* in 2 volumes[32], is 1390 pages long and contains separate chapters on each geological period and models of how the ages, assigned to each period, are derived. The 80+ authors are at the 'forefront of research' and the purpose of the book is authoritatively described as, 'the creation of an international geologic timescale'. The synopsis of the book remarks, 'As the framework for deciphering the history of our planet Earth, this book is essential for practicing Earth Scientists and academics.'[32]

The reality is that the succession of rocks (known as the Geological Column) has had a timescale imposed on it. Because of the conviction that a prehistory of 4.5 billion years is a reality, so geological history must be of that duration. The geologists who first assembled the timescale in the early 1800s were already convinced of prehistory and deep time. Details in the timescale have been refined but the framework of a long period of prehistory was there from the beginning of modern geology. This framework was not primarily derived from the rocks but from a secular view of history.

We should also note that by using the word, *deciphering*, it is implied that world history is written in a code only geologists can comprehend. This, of course, applies to much of science. Where once the origin of mankind and the timescale of human history could be known by reading the Bible, we now need geologists to decipher the truth for us. Deep time—the basis of historical geology and evolutionary theory—is a closed subject and certainly proved a frustration for Sir John Hammerton (see chapter 31) who, as a historian, had to 'content himself with being recorder' of the expert's discoveries. Whether sedimentary layers represent millions of years of Earth's history or a much shorter length of time, according to Biblical chronology and Noah's flood, is an important question to answer.

Let us discuss some of the evidence geologists have presented to answer this question. Joseph Barrell, 1869–1919, was a US geologist who wrote the classic paper, 'Rhythms and the measurement of geologic time',[33] in 1917. He showed, from studies of sea-level change, that there were only limited time periods when sea-level was rising and sediments could accumulate. He concluded that 'only one-sixth of time is recorded' by sediments. Joseph Barrell proposed that sedimentary rocks were produced by the action of rivers, winds, and ice as well as by marine sedimentation. Prior to this it was generally believed that almost all sedimentary strata were produced by oceans. Joseph Barrell was convinced that at least one-fifth of the land was covered by other types of sediments. He also challenged the idea that the depth of sedimentary layers is directly related to the time necessary to produce them—a fact assumed in modern geology when millions of years are inserted between many of the sedimentary strata.

Joseph Barrell's observations, that sedimentary rock only reflected a sixth of historical time, were largely overlooked until 1973, when Derek Ager DSc, PhD, FGS, a famous Professor of Geology at Swansea University, revealed in his book, *The Nature of the Stratigraphical Record*,[34] that the sedimentary processes should have left us a lot more rocks. He commented that there was 'more gap than record'. He also wrote, 'the sediment pile at any one place on the Earth's surface is nothing more than a tiny and fragmentary record of vast periods of Earth history—the *Phenomenon of the Gap Being More Important than the Record.*' [35] (These were his italics.)

Paul Garner, in his booklet, *99% missing, or where on earth did the time go?* states, 'The inescapable conclusion is that something like 90–99% of the elapsed time inferred from radiometric dating is not represented by rocks, but rather by time gaps.'[36]

Professor Ager's views were considered unlikely at the time, but a review of the third edition of his book, in the *Geological Magazine*, in 1993, stated of 'this remarkable book' that, after twenty years, 'it has dated in only one respect; that Ager's heresies have become orthodoxy'. [37]

A recent paper, from 2010, by Robin Bailey and David Smith[38], implies large numbers of hiatuses, pauses, or breaks in continuity, in the rock record at all scales, most undetectable, and raises the possibility that the rock record is a series of undecipherable 'frozen accidents' at all scales with no causal connection between each other. I personally conclude that there are not enough rocks to justify the timescale usually applied to the geological column. This is rather like the paucity of missing links in the fossil record, which led to the theory of 'Punctuated Equilibrium', sometimes nicknamed, 'Evolution by Jerks'.

Professor Andrew Miall PhD, DSc, former Professor of Geology at the University of Toronto until his retirement in 2020, remains a forthright defender of the Geological Timescale. While recognizing the need to insert theoretical, so-called 'hiatuses' of millions of years in the geological record, Miall noted, 'Notwithstanding observations such as this, stratigraphers have tended to operate as if continuous sedimentation was the rule. For example, many of the independent marker horizons in the GTS (Geological Time Scale) were, at one time, dated by extrapolation or interpolation between well-dated beds (e.g., radiometric dates on bentonites) by assuming a constant sedimentation rate.'[39] *Bentonite* is a naturally occurring material that is composed predominantly of the clay mineral, smectite. Most bentonites are formed by the alteration of volcanic ash in marine environments and occur as layers sandwiched between other types of rocks.

Can one trust the geological timescale of billions of years imposed on the geological column, when five-sixths of it is missing? Is this real science? Andrew Miall, elsewhere, quotes Ager: 'It may seem paradoxical, but to me the gaps probably cover most of earth history, not the dirt that happened to accumulate in the moments between. It was during the breaks that most events probably occurred.'[40]

In a newly established journal, *Stratigraphy*, Andrew Miall published a paper, 'Empiricism and model building in stratigraphy:

The historical roots of present-day practices.'[41] In his introduction, he wrote,

> Geology is historically an empirical science, firmly based on field data. Hallam has claimed that 'Geologists tend to be staunchly empirical in their approach, to respect careful observation and distrust broad generalization; they are too well aware of nature's complexity.'[42] However, interpretive models, including the modern trend towards numerical modelling, have become increasingly important in recent years.[41]

My conclusion from his introduction is that, because empirical evidence for the uniformitarian model of geology is deficient, then experts retreat into interpretive models, reflecting the prevailing worldview of prehistory. Dr Gadi Kravitz, a researcher of the philosophy of natural science and of geology at Haifa University, has written, 'Geologists' knowledge of the past is based on ... assumptions ... (and) they are products of the geologists' imagination.'[43] Is historical geology empirical science or is the Geological Timescale built on tenuous predictions?

Jesus described wise and foolish house builders in Matthew 7:24–27. He said, 'Therefore everyone who hears these words of mine and puts them into practice is like a wise man who built his house on the rock.' In contrast he warned, 'But everyone who hears these words of mine and does not put them into practice is like a foolish man who built his house on sand.' When the rain came and the streams rose and the winds blew, only the rock foundation was secure. It is not surprising that Jesus knew a thing or two about geology and foundations, given that He is the Creator of the world and the first cause of all Geology. However, Jesus was speaking about more than geology. He was stating that, if we build our lives on the wrong foundation, then we will come to ruin. His message is foundational to this book.

Before leaving the Geological Timescale, I must draw your attention to the horizontal lines between the individual sedimentary rock layers, seen from the rim of the Grand Canyon. These junctions are known as contacts. If there is *thought to be a gap in time* between the deposition of the two layers, it is called a 'nonconformity'. On the other hand, if the two layers are thought to have been laid down one after the other without a time gap, then it is referred to as 'conformable'.

The lowermost of the horizontal layers at the Grand Canyon is known as the *Tapeats Sandstone* and is given an age of about 508 million years. Over the next 250 million years, it is suggested that multiple cycles of advancing and retreating seas formed further horizontal sedimentary layers, visible today. Some layers higher up, such as the *Coconino Sandstone*, were interpreted as having been deposited as windblown sand, though research has shown this is also marine in origin.[44]

We see little evidence of erosion at the junctions between the layers where water and other erosional agents should have removed material. There is some evidence—for example, channels carved into the top of the Muav Limestone—but the amount of erosion is much less than expected for the timescale of millions of years supposedly involved.[45] A different interpretation than the layers being deposited over millions of years is the Biblical explanation that there was a catastrophic global event with water and sediment running off the land.

Most of the nonconformable contacts in the Grand Canyon are said to represent from 5 to 145 million years of missing time, according to conventional geology. A dramatic example of a perfectly smooth junction is seen between the Hermit Formation and the Coconino Sandstone, with the latter supposedly deposited 5–10 million years later. There should be significant evidence of erosion between these two layers of the Grand Canyon, but what is seen is totally inadequate if this formation took 10 million years to be deposited.

While considering the matter of erosion, there is a lot of material missing from the Canyon. The Colorado River is 1,450 miles long and there are 900 cubic miles of missing material. Why isn't there an enormous delta at the mouth of the Colorado River? In addition, geologists—whatever their worldview—agree that sometime in the past there was a mile of sedimentary rock layers on top of the Kaibab Limestone, which is at present the top layer at the rim of the Canyon. This conclusion is drawn from the sedimentary rocks seen in the Grand Staircase to the north of the Canyon.

In 2011, Liz and I travelled on our coach tour through this immense sequence of sedimentary rock layers that stretches south from Bryce Canyon National Park and Grand Staircase-Escalante National Monument, through Zion National Park, and into the Grand Canyon National Park. If one adds the removed layers to the present visible layers of the Grand Canyon, there would be a total depth of at least 2 miles. Conventional theory suggests that these rocks were removed by a slow process over millions of years. In contrast, the Biblical account of the recessive stage of Noah's flood suggests that they were removed by catastrophic events such as have been seen more recently at the Little Canyon at Mount St Helens.

The sedimentary layers of the Grand Canyon can be traced for hundreds and, in some cases, thousands of miles across the North American continent. For example, the Tapeats Sandstone stretches from Mexico to eastern Canada and north through the Arctic Circle. In different places, these layers have been labelled with different names that were given when the layers were first discovered. These continent-sized rock units imply continent-wide geological processes: testimony to the catastrophic processes expected in a global flood.

In the next chapter we will consider the subject of *Radiometric Dating*.

NOTES

1 'What are the Basic Differences Between Physical and Historical Geology', *Geology Degree*, 27 May 2019. https://geologydegree.org/physical-vs-historical-geology/

2 John K. Reed, *Rocks aren't Clocks—A Critique of the Geologic Timescale*, (Powder Springs, Georgia: Creation Book Publishers, 2013), pp. 28–36.

3 Ibid., pp. 36–38.

4 Noel Graveline and Francis Debaisieux, *Known & Little-known Volcanoes of the Massif central*, (Beaumont, France: Editions Debaisieux, 2016), p. 14.

5 Charles Darwin, *The Origin of Species*, 1st Ed., (Albemarle Street: John Murray, 1859).

6 Charles Lyell, *Principles of Geology: Being an Attempt to Explain the Former Changes of the Earth's Surface, by Reference to Causes Now in Operation*, (London: John Murray, in three volumes 1830–1833).

7 *Life, Letters and Journals of Sir Charles Lyell, Bart., vol. 1*, (London: John Murray, 1881), p. 268.

8   Charles Lyell, https://en.wikipedia.org/wiki/Charles_Lyell

9   'Principles of Geology—Criticism'. https://en.wikipedia.org/wiki/Principles_of_Geology

10 Norman D. Newell, 'Crises in the History of Life', *Scientific American* Vol. 208, No. 2, 1963. pp. 76–95. https://www.jstor.org/stable/e24936467

11 Michael Rampino, 'Re-examining Lyell's Laws', *American Scientist*, 105 (4) 2017, pp. 224–231.

12 Charles Darwin, *The Origin of Species*, p. 280.

13 George-Louis Leclerc, Comte de Buffon, *Histoire Naturelle, générale et particulière*, 36 volumes, (Paris: *Imprimerie royale*, 1749–1788).

14 Horace de Saussure, *Voyages dans les Alpes*, 4 volumes (Neuchâtel: Samuel Fauche, 1779–1796).

15 M. J. S. Rudwick, *Bursting the Limits of Time: The Reconstruction of Geohistory in the Age of Revolution*, (Chicago: University of Chicago Press, 2005), p. 84.

16 A. V. Carozzi, 'Lavoisier's fundamental contribution to stratigraphy', *Ohio Journal of Science*, 1965, Vol 65, pp. 71–85.

17 William Thomson, 1st Baron Kelvin https://en.wikipedia.org/wiki/William_Thomson,_1st_Baron_Kelvin

18 The National Geographic Society describes 'plate tectonics' it as 'a scientific theory that explains how major landforms are created as a result of Earth's subterranean movements.' https://education.nationalgeographic.org/resource/plate-tectonics/

19 Evelyn Lamb, 'Lord Kelvin and the Age of the Earth', *Scientific American*, 26 June 2013. https://blogs.scientificamerican.com/roots-of-unity/lord-kelvin-age-of-the-eart/

20 Steven A. Austin (Ed.), *Grand Canyon: Monument to Catastrophe*, (Santee, California: Institute for Creation Research, 1994), pp. 33–35.

21 Michael J. Oard, 'Flood processes into the late Cenozoic: part 2—sedimentary rock evidence', *Journal of Creation* 30(2) 2016, pp. 1–9.

22 John K. Reed, *Rocks aren't Clocks*, pp. 78–79.

23 John K. Reed and Michael J. Oard, 'Not enough rocks: the sedimentary record and deep time', *Journal of Creation* 31(2) 2017, pp. 84–93.

24 Paul Garner, *The New Creationism*, (Darlington: Evangelical Press, 2009), pp. 82–87.

25 Michael Le Page & Jeff Hecht, 'Stunning fossils: Turtles caught in the act', *New Scientist*, 18 February 2015.

26 Michael Le Page & Jeff Hecht, 'Stunning fossils: Mother giving birth', *New Scientist*, 18 February 2015.

27 Charles Q. Choi, 'Dinosaur graveyard unearthed in Canada; could be world's largest', *The Christian Science Monitor*, 23 June 2010.

28 Michael Oard, *Dinosaur Challenges and Mysteries*, (Atlanta: Creation Book Publishers, 2011), p. 15.

29 Pumza Fihlani, 'How a South African shepherd found a dinosaur graveyard', *BBC News*, Qhemega, 16 December 2018. https://www.bbc.com/news/world-africa-46511196

30 John Morris & Steven A. Austin, *Footprints in the Ash*, (Green Forest, AR: Master Books, 2003), pp. 50–53.

31 Ibid., pp. 74–77.

32 F. M. Gradstein et al., *Geologic Time Scale 2020: Vol 1 & 2*, (Amsterdam: Elsevier Science Publishing Co, 2021).

33 Joseph Barrell, 'Rhythms and the measurement of geologic time', *Geological Society of America Bulletin*, 1917, 28, p .797.

34 D. V. Ager, *The Nature of the Stratigraphical Record, 3rd ed.*, (Chichester, West Sussex: John Wiley & Sons, 1993), p. 53.

35 P. L. Gibbard and P. D. Hughes, 'Terrestrial stratigraphical division in the Quaternary and its correlation', *Journal of the Geological Society*, 178, 2020, p. 134.

36 Paul Garner, *99% missing, or where on earth did the time go?* (Ely: Biblical Creation Trust, 2019), p. 8.

37 'Reviews: Ager, D.V. 1993: The Nature of the Stratigraphical Record, 3rd ed, John Wiley & Sons, Chichester', *Geological Magazine* 1993, 130 (6), pp. 857–858.

38 R. J. Bailey & D. G., 'Smith Scaling in stratigraphic data series: implications for practical stratigraphy', *First Break*, 2010, vol 28, pp. 57–66.

39 A. D. Miall, 'Updating Uniformitarianism: Stratigraphy as just a set of 'Frozen Accidents', In: Smith, D. G., Bailey, R. J., Burgess, P. M., and Fraser, A. J. (Eds.), *Strata and Time: Probing the gaps in our understanding*, Special Publication 404, (London: Geological Society, 2015).

40 Andrew D. Miall, *Stratigraphy: A Modern Synthesis*, (Springer, 2016), p. 373.

41 Andrew D. Miall, 'Empiricism and model building in stratigraphy: The historical roots of present-day practices', *Stratigraphy* 2004, vol. 1, no. 1, pp. 3–25.

42 A. Hallam, *Great geological controversies 2nd edition*, (Oxford University Press, 1989), p. 244.

43 Gadi Kravitz, 'The thermodynamics time arrow and the logical function of the uniformity principle in geohistorical explanation'. In: Baker, V. R. (Ed.), *Rethinking the Fabric of Geology*, (Boulder, CO: Geological Society of America, 2013, Special Paper 502), p. 21.

44 John Whitmore & Paul Garner, 'The Coconino Sandstone 2018. (Permian, Arizona, USA): Implications for the origin of ancient cross-bedded Sandstones'. In: J. H. Whitmore (ed.), *Proceedings of the Eighth International Conference on Creationism*, (Pittsburgh, Pennsylvania: Creation Science Fellowship, 2018), pp. 581–627.

45 Paul Garner, *99% missing, or where on earth did the time go?* p. 9.

35 Geology, Part 2 – radiometric dating

It is widely assumed by the public that radiometric dating produces cast-iron evidence for millions and billions of years of prehistory. However, as with the Geological Timescale, inappropriate assumptions are made. Sometimes conflicting dating results are produced when the same material is subjected to different radioisotope tests.[1] In chapter 28, I have discussed radiocarbon (^{14}C) dating, which can be used for items theoretically no more than 50,000 years old.

There are several other radiometric dating methods used today that give ages of millions or billions of years for rocks. These techniques, unlike carbon dating, mostly use the relative concentrations of parent and daughter products in radioactive decay chains. For example, potassium-40 decays to argon-40; uranium-238 decays to lead-206 via other elements such as radium; uranium-235 decays to lead-207; rubidium-87 decays to strontium-87. These techniques are applied mostly to igneous rocks, formed through the cooling and solidification of magma or lava. Dating is normally believed to give the time since solidification. 'Absolute ages' can be obtained and applied to adjacent geological strata, allowing the reconstruction of a theoretical time sequence of events.

In order to improve the accuracy of dating results, several

minerals in the same sample can be dated, producing so-called *isochron* dates.[2] Another alternative is to use more than one isotopic dating system to check dates.

Modern geology has grappled with the evidence of catastrophic geological events and, in the 1970s and 1980s, began to recognize their role in the geological record. This view is known as *neocatastrophism* and recognizes, among other things, asteroid impacts in the past leaving large craters. Conventional geology usually attributes millions or billions of years to the age of these craters. Due to erosion over the years, the exact size of the asteroids is often uncertain. Possibly the largest crater is in South Africa; the Vredefort Crater has an estimated radius of 118 miles. Another, the Chicxulub Crater on the Yucatán Peninsula in Mexico, is believed by evolutionists to have caused or contributed to the extinction of the dinosaurs.

One pivotal issue relevant to all evolutionary thinking is the age of the Earth and the Universe. When asteroids enter the atmosphere of the earth, they often burn and break up into smaller parts, which land as meteorites. Scientists have investigated these and believe that some are particularly useful for estimating the age of the solar system. The current estimate of 4.55 billion years for the age of the Earth is based on investigations made by Clair Cameron Patterson, published in 1953, on several meteorites, including the Canyon Diablo meteorite which landed in the Barringer Crater in Arizona.[3] The particular technique he used was uranium–lead isochron dating, though he modified this to a technique called lead–lead dating. The basis of this is that uranium breaks down into only two isotopes of lead 206 and 207. Another lead isotope, 204, is fixed in quantity since no element breaks down into it. So, to determine a sample's age, Patterson could compare the ratio of lead isotopes created by decay to those that occur naturally.[4]

The reason why rocks from the Earth are unsuitable for determining the age of the Earth is because crustal rocks from the Earth are constantly recycled as a result of weathering, erosion and tectonics.[5] This means that the oldest rocks on Earth do not go back to the very beginning. The oldest rocks are dated about 4 billion years, but meteorites are thought to represent unaltered, primordial material from the time of the origin of the solar system –the material from which the Earth, itself, accreted.

In writing about Lord Kelvin's sincere calculations in the last chapter, we were reminded that he clearly did not have all the information needed to come to the correct conclusion. As we look at radiometric dating, we must recognize that several doubtful assumptions are made in the technique and wide variations in results are obtained.

Before looking at faulty assumptions about the technique, I will mention some erroneous results produced by radiometric dating. The first involves dating rocks from the lava dome of Mount St Helens. In June 1992, Dr Steve Austin, a geologist then at the Institute for Creation Research in Dallas, climbed up to the lava dome of Mount St Helens, with others, and collected 7kg of dacite from high on the lava dome. The lava dome was known to be only ten years old. Part of the sample was crushed into a fine powder. Another piece was crushed and the various mineral crystals within it were separated out. The rock powder and four separate mineral concentrates were sent for potassium-argon dating to Geochron

Laboratories of Cambridge, Massachusetts, a reliable radioisotope-dating laboratory. The laboratory was told that the samples were of dacite and that 'low argon' levels should be expected. The five results obtained by the laboratory ranged from 340,000 years to 2.8 million years![6] Very different from the real age of ten years and with wide variation.

Other faulty radioisotope dates were obtained for lava flows from Mt. Ngauruhoe in New Zealand, which erupted on three occasions between 1949 and 1975. By the potassium-argon dating method, results of 0.8, 1.0, 1.3 and 3.5 million years were obtained.[7,8]

Dating of lava from volcanoes on the north rim of the Grand Canyon using the rubidium-strontium isochron method produced a result of 1.34 billion years.[9] Geologists look upon these volcanoes as some of the youngest rocks in the canyon and only a million or so years old. Not only was the result 'too old' but it was older than an igneous rock formation, the Cardenas Basalt, which is at the bottom of the canyon, dated as having an age of 1.07 billion years by the same radioisotope method.

We must remember that a scientist cannot do repeatable experiments on events that happened in the distant past. Scientists do not measure the age of rocks, they measure radioisotope concentrations, and make assumptions leading to estimates of age, which can be faulty. While radioisotope concentrations can be measured extremely accurately. the rock 'age' is calculated using three un-provable assumptions about the past and the specimens examined.

Firstly, the starting conditions are known; either there was no daughter isotope present, or we know how much there was at the start. The *second* assumption is that decay rates have always been constant over time and *finally,* that the systems are closed or isolated so that no parent or daughter isotopes were lost or added. If any of these assumptions is wrong, then the results cannot be considered accurate.[10]

If the dating methods are an objective and reliable means of determining ages, different dating techniques should consistently agree. However, with radiometric dating, the different radioisotope techniques often give quite different results, as shown in the above examples.[7,8]

In 1993, another example came to light. During construction of the Crinum Colliery in Queensland, Australia, when employees were sinking the upcast ventilation shaft, some charred wood was found in Tertiary basalt, clearly buried in the lava flow that formed the basalt.[11] The wood was 'dated' by radiocarbon (14C) analysis at about 37,500 years old, but the basalt was 'dated' by the potassium-argon method at 47.5 million years old! One dating method produced a result more than a thousand times greater than the other, though the charred wood and basalt were 'frozen together' at the same time.[12]

Attempts have been made to improve the accuracy of the standard radiometric dating techniques. 'Isochron dating' endeavours to overcome inaccuracies which may be introduced by not knowing the initial composition of a rock. This really could only be known by having actually sampled the rock at the time of its formation. The details of isochron dating are complicated but essentially it makes use of the fact that, in some cases, in addition to the daughter isotope (the radiogenic isotope), there is another naturally occurring, stable isotope (the non-radiogenic isotope or sister isotope) of the same element as the daughter. The isochron technique assumes an unknown amount of radiogenic daughter isotope and of non-radiogenic sister isotope to be present in the rock sample, but in a ratio independent of the concentration of parent isotope.[13]

Isochron dating is used to analyse several different samples that are considered to have formed at the same time but might have different initial compositions. These might be whole rock samples or different minerals separated from a single rock sample. However, for the technique to work properly, the initial ratio of daughter isotope to sister isotope must be the same for all samples. Over time, the ratio of the daughter to non-radiogenic isotope will become larger, while the ratio of parent to daughter will become smaller. These ratios are measured (not the initial ratios—the ratios today) using solid-source mass spectrometers and the isotope ratios can be determined with great accuracy. So what results are obtained when using this technique?

When the isochron technique was applied to the lava from the three eruptions of Mt Ngauruhoe, mentioned above,[7,8] the results were actually worse than those from the potassium-argon method. Three different isotope techniques gave dates of 133 ± 87, 197 ± 60 and $3,908 \pm 390$ million years. Given that the lava was formed between 1949 and 1975, the assumptions behind isochron dating did not hold, in this case at least.

As mentioned above, the current estimate of 4.55 billion years for the age of the Earth was made by Clair Cameron Patterson.[3,4] It is based on the lead isochron method of radiometric dating. In their

2011 book, *Arguing for Evolution: An Encyclopedia for Understanding Science*, authors Sehoya Cotner and Randy Moore state that 'Five different meteorites and a deep-sea marine sediment had the same age. ... Studies of moon rock, tens of meteorites and thousands of rocks and sediments have yielded remarkably similar results.'[14]

Palaeontologist, Niles Eldredge, noted in his book, *The Monkey Business*, 'We now have literally thousands of separate analyses using a wide variety of radiometric techniques. It is an interlocking, complex system of predictions and verified results—not a few crackpot samples with wildly varying results, as some creationists would prefer to believe.'[15]

Cotner and Moore summarize that the 'Earth is approximately 4.55 billion years old. This age easily accommodates evolution by natural selection as a major force for the generation of life's diversity'.[16] The authors do particularly address creationists' critical views of radiometric dating. They dismiss creationist claims as *contradicting decades of research by competent mainstream physicists.*[17]

So, what should we believe? I would comment that just because dating of five meteorites and a deep-sea marine sediment plus moon rocks and other rocks have produced 'remarkably similar results' is no reason to believe the deduced ages of these items, particularly if the techniques used to date them are inaccurate. One might suggest that they are consistently wrong.

The results from the lava dome of Mount St Helens; from Mount Ngauruhoe; from the Crinum Colliery in Queensland, Australia; and the younger age of the top of the Grand Canyon compared to the bottom by 270 million years, are all significant inaccuracies and are hardly a few 'crackpot samples'.

When evolutionary scientists consider the results of published research, they are influenced by their own preconceptions about the long ages of Earth's history and the first appearance of man. An example of this kind of thinking is found in a report in *Science* magazine, published in 2005 with the title, 'Ancient Human Footprints Found in Mexico—Controversial find suggests humans were in Americas 40,000 years ago.'[18]

A team of British scientists, headed by geochronologist Silvia Gonzalez of Liverpool John Moores University, had found over 250 footprints in an abandoned quarry near the shore of an ancient lake in the Valsequillo basin in central Mexico. The findings were presented in London on July 4th, 2005, at a press conference at the Royal Society's Summer Science Exhibition. The team believed that the prints may have been caused by humans walking across a layer of fresh ash, deposited by a nearby volcano. Some prints showed toes and some tracks showed left and right steps along a line. Also reported were footprints of a dog, a cat and cloven-hoofed animals. Radiocarbon and electron spin resonance dating of nearby sediments gave an age of about 40,000 years. Given that scientists believe that man did not arrive in the Americas until 13,000 to 20,000 years ago, this led to initial controversy about their conclusions.[19]

Soon there was a further challenge to this research. In the December 1st, 2005, issue of the prestigious journal, *Nature*, Paul Renne, adjunct professor of earth and planetary science and director of the Berkeley Geochronology Center, and his colleagues reported their own conclusions about the rock in the abandoned quarry in the Valsequillo basin.[20] Their argon/argon dating technique gave an age for the rock of about 1.3 million years. Renne concluded that, 'You're really only left with two possibilities; one is that they are really old hominids—shockingly old—or they're not footprints.'

As this chapter has highlighted, there is a third possibility; their result of 1.3 million years is wrong. Radiometric dating is based on assumptions about the past, which cannot be checked, and is therefore open to erroneous results. It is not uncommon for dates to be challenged or dismissed if they do not fit with preconceptions.

Professor Chris Stringer, head of human origins at the Natural History Museum in London, wrote:

According to Gonzalez, the dates reported by Renne's group need to be replicated and independently confirmed. 'It is not clear from where exactly they took their samples and which fraction was dated. We took our samples directly from the footprint horizons,' said Gonzalez. 'Even if we are wrong and the ash is indeed 1.3 million years old, that is not automatically a reason to disregard interpretation of the features reported as footprints, simply because they are not in agreement with the established models for the settlement of the Americas,' she says. 'The new dating is far beyond any credible evidence of humans in the Americas.' Some experts had questioned whether the prints were indeed human, and this issue will now have to be re-examined very carefully.[21]

The British team included scientists from Liverpool John Moores University, Bournemouth University, the University of Oxford and the Australian National University. They were thorough in using multiple methods of assessment of different samples from the research site, employing laboratories in Britain and Australia. Their results should not be dismissed lightly.

The estimate of 40,000 years was a rational conclusion. While it does not fit with an evolutionary timeline, nor does it fit with the Biblical chronology suggesting 6,000 years as the approximate age of the Earth. While there is scientific evidence that vast amounts of radioactive decay have occurred in the past, we might ask if the assumption that there has been a *constant slow decay rate* is possibly wrong? Of course, this is one of the three assumptions mentioned above on which radiometric dating is based. So, is there any scientific evidence that radioactive decay was faster at any time in the history of the Earth? Yes, there is.

In 1997, a $1.25 million research project was begun by the Institute for Creation Research (ICR) and the Creation Research Society (CRS) in the USA. The project is known as the 'Radioisotopes and the Age of The Earth' (RATE) project. In 2000, an introduction and outline of the research plan was published as Volume I of RATE. The technical results were published in November 2005 in Volume II and presented to an audience of 2,000 people in El Cajon, California.

Evidence was presented that showed it is erroneous to assume that radioactive decay at today's rates has been constant throughout history. The RATE group found evidence that one or more periods of accelerated radioactive decay had occurred in the past. The group considered the possibilities that there had been more rapid decay during Creation Week and/or more rapid decay at the time of Noah's flood.

One RATE paper[22] examined helium retention in zircons. When uranium decays to lead, helium is formed as a by-product. This very light, inert gas escapes easily from the rocks. In very deep granitic rocks there are crystals, called zircons, in which uranium has partly decayed into lead. By measuring the amount of uranium and radiogenic lead in these crystals, an age of about 1.5 billion years is obtained, assuming a constant decay rate.

Surprisingly, there are significant amounts of helium still found inside the zircons. Are the zircons actually young? Given that helium easily escapes from the crystal structure and leaks into the atmosphere, there should be very little left in the rocks. To draw a conclusion from this, one must confirm the actual rate at which helium leaks out of zircons.

Samples were sent by the RATE group to a world-class expert to measure the rate of helium leakage. The consistent result was that the helium seeps out quickly over wide-ranging temperatures. Because of the amount of helium still in the zircons, it was concluded that the granitic rocks could not be older than between 4,000 and 14,000 years. So, in only a few thousand years, 1.5 billion years' worth of radioactive decay looks to have occurred. A later updated result gave a date of 5,680 ± 2,000 years.[22] The expert who made the measurements of helium leakage was not a young-Earth creationist.

There are scientific and theological problems which the RATE group continue to address. The first of these is theological: if a lot of radioactive decay occurred during Creation Week, how could God call that 'very good'? However, if one changes the word, 'decay', to 'transformed', then a negative implication in the word, 'decay', is overcome. If there was significant radioactive activity in creating the Earth and Universe, that does not have to be considered a bad thing.

A second problem would arise if there was significant radioactive activity during the time that Noah and his family were in the Ark. The radiation could have killed them, as well as the animals. The water of the flood would provide some protection but perhaps not enough. We do not know whether, during the geological and meteorological upheaval of the flood, there was increased radioactive activity, though we might presume that there was if decay rates have accelerated as the RATE project suggests.

Thirdly, increased radioactivity during the flood might have produced enormous amounts of heat, which could have melted the whole of the Earth's crust and boiled away the oceans!

Efforts are being made to rigorously quantify the amount of radiogenic heat which may have been produced during Noah's flood. Creation researcher, Dr Russell Humphreys, has proposed a means by which this excess heat may have been dispersed. In 2018, he suggested a new mechanism for accelerated removal of excess radiogenic heat.[23]

As I conclude this chapter, it should be acknowledged that there are real problems with the reliability of radiometric dating. As I described in Chapter 28, ^{14}C radiocarbon has been found in dinosaur bones in spite of the general belief that they became extinct 65 million years ago. The finding of blood cells, haemoglobin, osteocytes, proteins and soft tissue, such as collagen and nerves plus short segments of DNA in dinosaur bones, all indicate a younger age than radiometric dating suggests.[24, 25]

Evidence has been presented to show that radioactive decay rates may not be the slow steady rates assumed by scientists. Radiometric dating, which is thought to support the long ages of prehistory, may be based on false assumptions so that its reliability cannot be assumed.

NOTES

1 Paul Garner, *The New Creationism*, (Darlington: Evangelical Press, 2009), pp. 98–99.

2 Ibid., pp. 93–96.

3 William Dicke, 'Clair C. Patterson, Who Established Earth's Age, Is Dead at 73', *New York Times*, 8 December 1995, p. 18.

4 Clair Patterson, 'Rocks from Space, and Metal in the Air', *Magpie's Miscellany*, 15 August 2014. https://magpiesmiscellany.wordpress.com/2014/08/15/1728/

5 'Age of Earth'—Wikipedia https://en.wikipedia.org/wiki/Age_of_Earth

6 Steve Austin, 'Excess argon within mineral concentrates from the new dacite lava dome at Mount St Helens volcano', *J. Creation*, 1996, 10(3) pp. 335–343.

7 A. Snelling, 'Andesite flows at Mt Ngauruhoe, New Zealand, and the implications for potassium-argon "dating"', Presented at the Fourth International Conference on Creationism, Pittsburgh, PA, 3–8 August 1998.

8 A. Snelling, 'Radioactive "Dating" Failure', *Creation*, 2000, 22(1), pp. 18–21.

9 S. A. Austin (ed)., *Grand Canyon: Monument to Catastrophe*, (Santee, California: Institute for Creation Research, 1994), pp. 111–131.

10 Paul Garner, The New Creationism, pp. 92–93.

11 Anonymous, 'Rare find unearthed at Crinum', *BHP Australia Coal Newsline*, December 1993–January 1994, p. 1.

12 A. Snelling, 'Conflicting "Ages" of Tertiary Basalt and Contained Fossilised Wood, Crinum, Central Queensland, Australia', *CEN Technical Journal*, 2000 (14) 2, pp. 99–122.

13 Paul Garner, *The New* Creationism, pp. 93–96.

14 S. H. Cotner & Randy Moore, *Arguing for Evolution: An Encyclopedia for Understanding Science*, (Westport, CT: Greenwood, 2011), pp. 34–35.

15 Niles Eldredge, *The Monkey Business: A Scientist Looks at Creationism*, (New York: Washington Square Press, 1982), p. 108.

16 S. H. Cotner & Randy Moore, *Arguing for Evolution: An Encyclopedia for Understanding Science*, p. 35.

17 Ibid., p. 34.

18 Mason Inman, Ancient Human Footprints Found in Mexico Controversial find suggests humans were in Americas 40,000 years ago, 5 July 2005. https://www.science.org/content/article/ancient-human-footprints-found-mexico.

19 'The Fertile Shore', *Smithsonian Magazine*, Science, January 2020. https://www.smithsonianmag.com/science-nature/how-humans-came-to-americas-180973739/

20 P. Renne et al., 'Age of Mexican ash with alleged "footprints"', *Nature*, 2005, 438, E7–E8 https://doi.org/10.1038/nature04425

21 Rossella Lorenzi, 'First Americans left their mark, but when?' *ABC (Australian Broadcasting Corporation) News in Science*, Thursday, 1 December 2005.

22 D. Humphreys et al., 'Helium diffusion rates support accelerated nuclear decay', www.icr.org/pdf/research/Helium_ICC_7-22-03.

23 Humphreys, D.R., 2018. New mechanism for accelerated removal of excess radiogenic heat. In: J.H. Whitmore (ed.), *Proceedings of the Eighth International Conference on Creationism*, (Pittsburgh, Pennsylvania: Creation Science Fellowship, 2018), pp. 731–739.

24 Mary Schweitzer et al., 'Soft-tissue vessels and cellular preservation in Tyrannosaurus rex', *Science* 307, 2005, pp. 1952–1955.

25 Mary Schweitzer et al., 'Molecular analyses of dinosaur osteocytes support the presence of endogenous molecules', *Bone*, 52 (1) 2012, pp. 414–423.

36 Finally...

As I begin this last chapter of *The Something Delusion,* I hope that you will have been stimulated to consider your own worldview and journey to that worldview. Has some of the evidence for your beliefs been challenged by what you have read? Worldviews can be held, despite a lack of evidence, because of a desire to live life in a particular way. An extreme example would be Aldous Huxley's statement: 'I had motives for not wanting the world to have a meaning; consequently, assumed that it had not.'[1]

The Christian worldview claims that, in addition to what we can learn from history and science, mankind has received information about the world from Almighty God the Creator. This information is authoritative and so to be trusted, being the testimony of the only witness to the origin of the Universe and of all the historical events on this planet. The information, recorded in the Bible, enlightens our minds and understanding.

The opening verses of John's Gospel describe the role of Jesus Christ, the second person of the Trinity, who was with God the Father in the beginning. Verses 3–5 state, 'Through him all things were made; without him nothing was made that has been made. In him was life, and that life was the light of men. The light shines in the darkness, but the darkness has not understood it.' Verse 9 continues: 'The true light that gives light to every man was coming into the world.' Jesus, personally, later stated, 'I am the light of the world. Whoever follows me will never walk in darkness, but will have the light of life' (John 8:12).

Francis Schaeffer, in Appendix A of his book, *He Is There and He Is Not Silent*, entitled, 'Is Propositional Revelation Nonsense?'[2] explains how the Bible shines light into man's spiritual darkness. I quote from his appendix, which is only five pages long and can be read in its entirety at this reference.[3]

'The Christian presupposition is that there was a personal beginning to all things—someone has been there and made all the rest. This someone would have to be big enough, and this means being infinite.'[2]

We all have a choice to either believe in an infinite Someone with the intelligence and power to create everything out of nothing (the God of the Bible) or to share the view of Stephen Hawking and Leonard Mlodinow who wrote, 'Because there is a law such as gravity, the universe can and will create itself from nothing.'[4]

It is surely intellectually unsatisfactory to claim that a law like gravity exists without an explanation of why it exists. In addition, at least two masses would need to exist for the force of gravity to be operative. No explanation is given of where gravity or the masses came from.

I described, in chapter 19, how Richard Dawkins told me, 'Don't be so silly, there had to be something there to start with.' Richard Dawkins and Stephen Hawking believe(d) the same 'Something Delusion'.

In contrast, the Christian worldview believes that God—that is Someone—has given mankind information about the origin and history of the world. We can describe this under four headings (i) through nature (or creation)—Romans 1:19–20; (ii) through God's written Word, the Bible—Luke 24:27 and 2 Timothy 3:15–16; (iii) through Jesus Christ, God made flesh—Hebrews 1:1–2, and all that he did, recorded in the Gospels; (iv) through our consciences—Romans 2:15.

God, by His Holy Spirit, awakens saving faith in an individual, as the gospel is made known and understood. The Holy Spirit uses the Law of God to reveal our sin to us and leads us to repentance. By the death of Christ and his resurrection, forgiveness of sins can be received. The Christian believer's faith is built not on human wisdom but on the power of God. We call this change in an individual, *regeneration* or being *born-again*. I have described my own experience of this in chapter 9.

Before leaving the matter of spiritual enlightenment, I would mention what a blessing physical light is. In the daytime, we can see where we are going and the sun provides energy as heat for photosynthesis and, more recently, for solar panels to generate electricity. Genesis 1 indicates that during the first twenty-four-hour period God said, 'Let there be light' and there was light. God saw that the light was good, and he separated light from darkness calling the light, 'day', and the darkness, 'night'.

In passing, we should note that physical darkness can also be a blessing, allowing us to rest and sleep and maintain our healthy diurnal rhythm. Spiritual darkness, however, should be feared. We read in John 3:19–20, 'Light has come into the world, but men (*people*) loved darkness instead of light because their deeds were evil. Everyone who does evil hates the light, and will not come into the light for fear that his deeds will be exposed.'

It was not until the fourth day of creation week that God made the sun, moon and stars. This of course raises a scientific issue. Most people would assume that light has to come from the sun. However, the day-night cycle only requires a rotating Earth and a source of light coming from one direction. Just as we are told, in Genesis 1, that God made light before he made the sun, so we read that in the new heavens and earth there will be no need for sun or moon—'for the Lord God will give them light' (Revelation 22:5).

I wrote earlier in this book that 'a naturalistic worldview believes that all knowledge of the properties of the universe falls *only* within the reach of scientific investigation. By implication, no truth about the origin of the universe can come from anywhere else.' Richard Dawkins and Stephen Hawking consciously refuse(d) to consider the testimony of the one reliable witness, who does have the answers to our biggest questions. They argue(d) that there is no chance that the 'Someone' who witnessed the beginning of the Universe could have left an account or testimony of that event.

When I was a senior registrar, I had the sad task of breaking bad news to a female patient on whom we had operated. She had inoperable advanced cancer. I spoke to her in the privacy of the ward sister's office, in the company of one of the staff nurses. I explained that our findings during the operation had now been confirmed by microscopy and there was no drug or radiotherapy treatment which could alter the course of the cancer.

She accepted the news bravely, explaining she had had a suspicion that her condition was serious. As is often the case in such circumstances, she asked how long she might live. I suggested that doctors can get such predictions wrong, but it was likely the prognosis was several weeks or a few months. We talked for a little while about her family and she commented that she did believe that our souls live on after the death of our bodies.

She said she believed in heaven, having attended Sunday school and church for a number of years, but that her attendance had lapsed in recent years. I encouraged her that when the prodigal son returned to his father there was no discussion about his behaviour 'in recent years'. The father in the parable, of course representing her heavenly Father, would receive her with open arms.

Some weeks after she went home, I received a letter from her daughter, which I have kept. She wrote, 'I thought perhaps that you would like to know that mother died peacefully at home after taking communion for the first time in many years. She had said that she wanted to go with Jesus. All the family are grateful for the time you spent on us and just want to say thank you.'

It is not necessary to be at death's door to turn to Jesus Christ in repentance and faith, although impending death may lead to a sense of urgency to get right with God. However, it is wiser to consider these matters while we have a clear mind. Paul wrote in 2 Corinthians 6:2, 'I tell you, now is the time of God's favour, now is the day of salvation.'

As I draw to the end of a surgeon's journey, I invite you to consider a painting which, in the early 20th century, was possibly better known than the great paintings of the Renaissance. I refer to Holman Hunt's painting, *The Light of the World*, which is based on Revelation 3:20. Holman Hunt painted the picture three times; the first, begun at the age of 21, took him eight years to complete. Hunt went to great lengths to capture the moonlight seen in his painting.

He actually travelled to the Holy Land and there made dangerous and difficult journeys to find the inspiration for his work.

This first painting was purchased and donated to Keble College, Oxford, where a fee was charged to view the painting. His painting was very popular and so he spent five years painting another version, which can be seen in the Manchester City Art Gallery. Hunt's meticulous preparation for his painting is illustrated by his having a physical lamp made to his design which he then copied in his paintings.

About fifty years later, Hunt, with the help of Edward Hughes, painted a larger version, which went on a world tour from 1905 to 1907. In Australia, it was said that 80 per cent of the population saw the painting. It was seen by millions in Canada, South Africa and in other lands. The painting was purchased by Charles Booth and donated to St Paul's Cathedral, where it hangs in the crypt. St Paul's describes it as the most travelled artwork in history.

The verse which Holman Hunt based his painting on, Revelation 3:20 (ESV), reads: 'Behold, I stand at the door and knock. If anyone hears my voice and opens the door, I will come in to him and eat with him, and he with me.'

In chapter 6, I quoted the evolutionary biologist, Richard Lewontin, who died on 4th July 2021. I drew your attention to his statement: 'We cannot allow a Divine Foot in the door.' Could it be that he had this painting or verse in mind when he made his frank admission about the *Divine Foot*?

He wrote,

> Our willingness to accept scientific claims that are against common sense is the key to an understanding of the real struggle

between science and the supernatural. We take the side of science in spite of the patent absurdity of some of its constructs, in spite of its failure to fulfil many of its extravagant promises of health and life, in spite of the tolerance of the scientific community for unsubstantiated just-so stories, because we have a prior commitment, a commitment to materialism. It is not that the methods and institutions of science somehow compel us to accept a material explanation of the phenomenal world, but, on the contrary, that we are forced by our *a priori* adherence to material causes to create an apparatus of investigation and a set of concepts that produce material explanations, no matter how counter-intuitive, no matter how mystifying to the uninitiated. Moreover, that materialism is absolute, for we cannot allow a Divine Foot in the door.[5]

At the end of this last chapter of 'The Something Delusion', I repeat God's words in Jeremiah 29:13: 'You will seek me and find me when you seek me with all your heart.' I found that promise to be true in the journey that I travelled, and I commend both the promise and the Lord Jesus Christ to you as you continue your journey to your own worldview.

NOTES

1   Aldous Huxley, *End and Means*, (New York: Garland Publishers, 1938), p. 270.
2   Francis A. Schaeffer, *Francis A. Schaeffer Trilogy—He Is There and He Is Not Silent*, Appendix A: 'Is Propositional Revelation Nonsense?' (Leicester: Inter-Varsity Press, 1990), pp. 343–347.
3   Francis A. Schaeffer, Appendix A: 'Is Propositional Revelation Nonsense?' https://www.crossway.org/articles/is-propositional-revelation-nonsense
4   Stephen Hawking & Leonard Mlodinow, *The Grand Design*, (New York: Bantam Books, 2010), p. 180. https://www.theguardian.com/science/2010/sep/02/stephen-hawking-big-bang-creator

5 Richard Lewontin, *Billions and Billions of Demons*, 9 January 1997. www.nybooks.com.

Bibliography

Books

Ager, D. V., *The Nature of the Stratigraphical Record, 3rd ed.*, (Chichester, West Sussex: John Wiley & Sons, 1993).

Aitken, J. T. J. Joseph; Causey, G.; and Young, J. Z., *A Manual of Human Anatomy, Vols 1–5, Second edition*, (Edinburgh: E. & S. Livingstone Ltd, 1964).

Aitken, Robin, *The Noble Liar*, (London: Biteback Publishing Ltd, 2018).

Alberts. Bruce et al., *Molecular Biology of the cell 3rd Ed.*, (New York and London: Garland Publishing, 1994).

Alexander, Denis, *Creation or Evolution—Do We Have to Choose?* (Oxford: Monarch Books, 2008).

Austen, Jane, *Pride and Prejudice*, (Whitehall: T. Egerton, Military Library, 1813).

Austin, Steven A. (Ed.), *Grand Canyon: Monument to Catastrophe*, (Santee, California: Institute for Creation Research, 1994).

Barlow, Nora (editor), *The autobiography of Charles Darwin, 1809–1882, with original omissions restored*, (New York: W. W. Norton, 1969).

Barnham, Denis, *Malta Spitfire Pilot: A Personal Account of Ten Weeks of War, April–June 1942*, (S. Yorkshire: Frontline Books, 2011).

Barr, James, *Escaping from Fundamentalism*, (London: SCM Press, 2012).

Bayliss, Dr L. E., *Living Control Systems*, (London: The English Universities Press Ltd, 1968).

Beauchamp, Tom L. and Childress, James F., *Principles of Biomedical Ethics, 8th ed.*, (Oxford University Press USA, 2019).

Behe, Michael, *Darwin's Black Box: The Biochemical Challenge to Evolution*, (New York: Free Press, 2006).

Bentley, Wilson and Humphreys, W. J., *Snow Crystals*, (New York: Dover Publications Inc., First published 1931, Republished 1962).

Bidwell, Kevin (Ed.), *Westminster Shorter Catechism*, (Welwyn Garden City, UK: Evangelical Press, 2019).

Binding, Karl and Hoche, Alfred, *Die Freigabe der Vernichtung Lebensunwerten Lebens*, (The Project Gutenberg eBook, 1920).

Book of Common Prayer, (Oxford University Press, 1928 edition).

Bowden, Malcolm, *Ape-Men—Fact or Fallacy?* (Kent: Sovereign Publications, 1977).

Bowden, Malcolm, *True Science Agrees With The Bible*, (Bromley: Sovereign Publications, 1991).

Brassett, Cecilia; Evans, Emily; & Fay, Isla, *The Secret Language of Anatomy*, (Chichester: Anatomy Boutique Books, 2017).

Bryson, Bill, *A Short History of Nearly Everything*, (London: Black Swan, 2004).

Burkitt, Denis, *'Where Are You Going?'* (London: Christian Medical Fellowship, 1982).

Cameron, Nigel M. de S. (Ed.), *Embryos and Ethics: Warnock Report in Debate*, (Edinburgh: Rutherford House Books, 1987).

Cameron, Nigel M. de S., *Creation and the Christian response to Warnock, a symposium*, (Rugby: Biblical Creation Society, 1985).

Cameron, Nigel M. de S., *The New Medicine—the Revolution in Technology and Ethics*, (London: Hodder and Stoughton, 1991).

Capper, W. Melville and Johnson, Douglas, *Arthur Rendle Short— Surgeon and Christian*, (London: Inter-Varsity Fellowship, 1954).

Carroll, Patrick, *Assessing the Damage*, (London: Pension and Population Research Institute, 25 October 2007).

Chambers *20th Century Dictionary*, (Edinburgh and London: W & R Chambers, 1901, reprinted 1950).

Chapman, Colin, *The Case for Christianity*, (Chicago Illinois: Lion Publishing Ltd, 1981).

Chesterton, G. K., *The Defendant*, (London: J.M. Dent & Sons, 1901).

Chesterton, G. K., *The Everlasting Man, Part 1*, (Connecticut: Martino Fine Books, 2010).

Chippendale, Thomas, *The Gentleman and Cabinet-Maker's Director*, (New York: Dover Publications, 1754).

Churchill, Winston S., *Second World War Volume II, Their Finest Hour*, (London: Cassell & Co Ltd, 1949).

Churchill, Winston S., *The Second World War, Volume 1*, (Boston, Massachusetts: Houghton Mifflin, 1948–53).

Cline, Eric H., *The Battles of Armageddon. Megiddo and the Jezreel Valley from the Bronze Age to the Nuclear Age*, (Ann Arbor: The University of Michigan Press, 2000).

Collins, *English Dictionary*, 'Futility'—definition and meaning, (11th edition, 2011).

Collins, Francis, *The Language of God: A scientist presents evidence for belief*, (New York: Free Press, 2006).

Cotner, S. H. and Moore, Randy, *Arguing for Evolution: An Encyclopedia for Understanding Science*, (Westport, CT: Greenwood, 2011).

Creation magazine, published quarterly in Australia. Creation Ministries International Ltd PO Box 4545, Eight Mile Planes, Queensland 4113, Australia.

Crick, Francis, *What Mad Pursuit: A Personal View of Scientific Discovery*, (New York: Basic Books, 1988).

Darwin, Charles, *The Descent of Man*, (Albemarle Street, London: John Murray 1871).

Darwin, Charles, *The Origin of Species, First Edition*, (Albemarle Street, London: John Murray Publishing House, 1859).

Darwin, Francis (ed.), *The life and letters of Charles Darwin, including an autobiographical chapter. vol. 2 & 3.* (New York: D. Appleton and Co., 1899).

Dawkins, Richard and Wong, Yan, *The Ancestor's Tale: A Pilgrimage to the Dawn of Life*, (London: Weidenfeld & Nicolson, April 2016).

Dawkins, Richard, *A Devil's Chaplain, Selected Essays*, (London: Orion, 2003).

Dawkins, Richard, *An Appetite for Wonder: The Makings of a Scientist*, (Transworld Digital, September 2013).

Dawkins, Richard, *Climbing Mount Improbable*, (New York: WW Norton & Co, 2006).

Dawkins, Richard, *River Out of Eden*, (New York: Basic Books, 1995).

Dawkins, Richard, *The Blind Watchmaker*, (New York: W. W. Norton & Company, 1986).

Dawkins, Richard, *The God Delusion*, (New York: Bantam Books, October 2006).

Dawkins, Richard, *The Selfish Gene: 30th Anniversary Edition*, (Oxford University Press, 2006).

Denton, Michael, *Evolution: A Theory in Crisis*, (Burnett Books, 1985).

Dirckx, Sharon, *Am I just my brain?* (Epsom: The Good Book Company, 2019).

Donne, John, *MEDITATION XVII Devotions upon Emergent Occasions*, 1624.

Doolittle, Russell F., *The Evolution of Vertebrate Blood Clotting*, (University Science Books, 2012).

Edwards, Brian H., *Nothing but the Truth*, (Welwyn Garden City: Evangelical Press, 1978).

Einstein, Albert, *The World As I See It*, (New York: Philosophical Library, 1949).

Eldredge, Niles, *The Monkey Business: A Scientist Looks at Creationism*, (New York: Washington Square Press, 1982).

Enoch, Hannington, *Evolution or Creation*, (Welwyn Garden City: Evangelical Press, 1966).

Enoch, Hannington, *Where Did Man Come From?* (Republished Union of Evangelical Students of India, 2004).

Frame, John, *Medical Ethics—Principles, Persons and Problems*, (New Jersey: P&R Publishing Co, 1988).

Frame, John, *The Doctrine of the Christian Life*, (New Jersey: P&R Publishing Co, 2008).

Gardner, Rex, *Abortion—the personal dilemma*, (Milton Keynes: The Paternoster Press, 1972).

Garner, Paul, *99% missing, or where on earth did the time go?* (Ely: Biblical Creation Trust, 2019).

Garner, Paul, *The New Creationism*, (Darlington: Evangelical Press, 2009).

Gould, Stephen Jay, *Ontogeny and Phylogeny*, (Cambridge, Massachusetts: Harvard University Press, 1977)

Gower, D.B., *In Six Days—Why 50 Scientists Choose to Believe in Creation*, Dr John Ashton (Ed.) Chapter 28 (Green Forest, Arkansas: Master Books, 2007).

Gradstein, F. M. et al., *Geologic Time Scale 2020: Vol 1 & 2*, (Amsterdam: Elsevier Science Publishing Co, 2021).

Grant, W. B., *We Have a Guardian: Some Instances of Divine Intervention in British History*, (County Durham: Covenant Publishing Co. Ltd, 2011).

Graveline, Noel and Debaisieux, Francis, *Known & Little-known Volcanoes of the Massif central*, (Beaumont, France: Editions Debaisieux, 2016).

Griffin, Nicholas, *The Selected Letters of Bertrand Russell: The Private Years, 1884–1914*, (Milton Park, Abingdon: Routledge, 2002).

Griffith, Leonard, *This is Living*, (Nashville, Tennessee: Abingdon Press, 1966).

Grove A. J. & Newell G. E., *Animal Biology*, (London: University Tutorial Press Ltd, 1964, 6th edition reprint).

Hadaway, Bridget, 'Hammerton, Sir John Alexander, 1871–1949', *Oxford Dictionary of National Biography*, (Oxford University Press, 2004).

Haldane, J. B. S., *Possible Worlds and Other Essays*, (London: Chatto and Windus, 1927).

Hallam, A., *Great geological controversies 2nd edition*, (Oxford University Press, 1989).

Ham, Ken, *The Lie*, (Green Forest, AR: Master Books, 1996).

Hamilton, W J (ed.), *Textbook of Human Anatomy 2nd edition*, (London: The Macmillan Press Ltd, reprinted in 1982).

Hammerton, J. A., *In the Track of R. L. Stevenson and Elsewhere in Old France*, (Bristol: J. W. Arrowsmith, 1907) www.gutenberg.org (eBook #43209).

Hammerton, Sir J. A., *The Outline History of the World*, (London: The Amalgamated Press Ltd, 1933).

Hawking, Stephen and Mlodinow, Leonard, *The Grand Design*, (New York: Bantam Books, 2010).

Hawking, Stephen, *Brief Answers to the Big Questions*, (London: John Murray, 2018).

Henley, William Ernest, *Invictus*, 1875. https://www.scottish poetrylibrary.org.uk/poem/invictus/

Hinde, Julia, *'Does God Exist?' Big Questions in Science*, Ed., Harriet Swain, (London: Jonathan Cape, 2002).

Hodge, Charles, *Commentary on the Epistle to the Romans*, (Grand Rapids, Michigan: Wm B. Eerdmans Publishing Company, 1864).

Hodge, Charles, *What is Darwinism?* (New York: Scribner, Armstrong & Company, 1874).

Honeysett, Marcus, *Meltdown: Making Sense of a Culture in Crisis*, (Leicester: Inter-Varsity Press, 2006).

Hopwood, Nick, *Haeckel's Embryos—Images, Evolution, and Fraud*, (University of Chicago Press, 2015).

Hoyle, Fred and Wickramasinghe, Chandra, *Evolution from Space*, (London: J.M. Dent, 1981).

Hoyle, Fred, *The Black Cloud*, (London: Penguin Books reprint 1964).

Hoyle, Fred, *The Intelligent Universe*, (London: Michael Joseph, 1983).

Hoyle, Fred, *The Nature of the Universe*, (London: Pelican Books, 1963).

Hull, David, *Philosophy of Biological Science, Foundations of Philosophy Series*, (Englewood Cliffs, New Jersey: Prentice Hall, 1973).

Humphreys, D.R., 2018. 'New mechanism for accelerated removal of excess radiogenic heat'. In: J.H. Whitmore (ed.), *Proceedings of the Eighth International Conference on Creationism*, (Pittsburgh, Pennsylvania: Creation Science Fellowship, 2018).

Huxley, Aldous, *End and Means*, (New York: Garland Publishers, 1938).

Huxley, Julian, *Evolution in Action*, (London: Chatto and Windus, 1953).

Jeans, James, *The Mysterious Universe*, (Cambridge University Press, 1930).

Jeeves, M. and Berry, R., Science, *Life and Christian Belief*, (Westmont, Illinois: Apollos, imprint of IVP, 1998).

Johnson, Boris, *The Churchill Factor: How One Man Made History*, (London: Hodder & Stoughton, October 2014).

Johnson, Donald E., *Programming of Life*, (Alabama: Big Mac Publishers, 2010).

Johnson, Phillip E. and Lamoureux, Denis O., *Darwinism Defeated?* (Vancouver: Regent College Publishing, 1999).

Johnston, T. B., *Synopsis of Regional Anatomy*, (London: Churchill Publishing House, 1968).

Katz, Michael J., *Templets and the explanation of complex patterns*, (Cambridge University Press, 1986).

Kenyon, Dean H. and Steinman, Gary, *Biochemical Predestination*, (New York: McGraw-Hill, 1969).

Keown, John, *Euthanasia in the Netherlands: sliding down the slippery slope?* (London: Centre for Bioethics and Public Policy, 1995).

Kipling, Rudyard, 'Chapter 5, The Elephant's Child', *Just So Stories for Little Children*, (London: Macmillan, 1952 reprint).

Klotz, John W., *Genes, Genesis and Evolution*, (St Louis, Missouri: Concordia Publishing House, 1955).

Koenig, Harold G.; McCullough, Michael E.; Larsonet, David B., *Handbook of Religion and Health*, (Oxford University Press, 2001).

Krauss, Lawrence, *A Universe from Nothing: Why There is Something Rather than Nothing*, (New York: Atria Books, 2012).

Kravitz, Gadi, 'The thermodynamics time arrow and the logical function of the uniformity principle in geohistorical explanation'. In: Baker, V. R. (Ed.), *Rethinking the Fabric of Geology*, (Boulder, CO: Geological Society of America, 2013, Special Paper 502).

Lane, Sir Allen, *The Literary Shed*, (2013). https://www.theliteraryshed.co.uk/read/the-literary-lounge/penguin-original-ten-the-first-titles-published-by-allen-lane

Lavoisier, Antoine Laurent, *Traité Élémentaire de Chimie—tome premier*, (Paris: Chez Cuchet, 1789).

Lawton, Graham, with introduction by Stephen Hawking, *New Scientist: The Origin of (almost) Everything: from the Big Bang to Belly-button Fluff*, (London: John Murray, 2016).

Leclerc, George-Louis Comte de Buffon, *Histoire Naturelle, générale et particulière, 36 volumes*, (Paris: Imprimerie royale, 1749–1788).

Lee, R.S., *Freud and Christianity*, (London: Pelican Books, 1967).

Leiser, Erwin, *A pictorial history of Nazi Germany*, (London: Pelican Books, 1962).

Lewis, C. S., *Essay Collection: and other short pieces,* (New York: Fount / Harper Collins; First Edition 2000).

Lewis, C.S., *Miracles*, (Glasgow and London: Fontana, 1974).

Lewis, C. S., *The Case for Christianity*, (Nashville, Tennessee: B&H Publishing Group, March 1999).

Lewontin, Richard, *Billions and Billions of Demons*, www.nybooks. com, 9 January 1997.

Lisle, Jason, *Logic & Faith—discerning truth in logical arguments*, (Petersburg, Kentucky: Answers in Genesis, 2016).

Lloyd, Stephen, *Adam or death: which came first?* (Rugby, Warwickshire: Biblical Creation Trust, 2017).

Lloyd-Jones, David Martyn, *Authority*, (Westmont, Illinois: Inter-Varsity Press, 1958).

Long, Maureen, *Birthright? A Christian woman looks at abortion*, (London: Triangle SPCK, 1985).

Lyell, Charles, *Life, Letters and Journals of Sir Charles Lyell, Bart., vol. 1*, (London: John Murray, 1881).

Lyell, Charles, *Principles of Geology*, (London: Penguin Classics, 1997).

Lyell, Charles, *Principles of Geology: Being an Attempt to Explain the Former Changes of the Earth's Surface, by Reference to Causes Now in Operation*, (London: John Murray, in three volumes 1830–1833).

Mahkorn, Sandra, *Life Matters: Pregnancy From Rape*, (Washington DC: Secretariat of pro-life activities United States conference of Catholic Bishops, 1979).

Mandela, Nelson, *Long Walk to Freedom*, (Abacus, Little, Brown Book Group, 2007).

McDowell, Josh, *Evidence That Demands a Verdict, Volume 1: Historical Evidences for the Christian Faith*, (Orlando: Campus Crusade for Christ, 1972).

McLeish, Tom, *Faith and Wisdom in Science*, (Oxford University Press, 2017 reprint).

Meyer, Stephen C., 'Scientific and Philosophical Introduction: Defining Theistic Evolution', in: *Theistic Evolution*, (Wheaton, Illinois: Crossway, 2017).

Miall, A. D., 'Updating Uniformitarianism: Stratigraphy as just a set of 'Frozen Accidents', In: Smith, D. G., Bailey, R. J., Burgess, P. M., and Fraser, A. J. (Eds.), *Strata and Time: Probing the gaps in our understanding*, Special Publication 404, (London: Geological Society, 2015.

Miall, Andrew D., *Stratigraphy: A Modern Synthesis*, (Springer, 2016).

Miller, K.R., *Only a Theory: Evolution and the Battle for America's Soul*, (New York: Viking Penguin, 2008).

Milne, A. A., *Winnie the Pooh*, illustrated E. H. Shepard, (London: Methuen, 1926).

Monk, Ray, *Bertrand Russell, The Spirit of Solitude*, (London: Jonathan Cape, 1996).

Moore, Patrick, *Space in the Sixties*, (London: Pelican books, 1963).

Morison, Frank, *Who Moved the Stone?* (Milton Keynes: Authentic Lifestyle, 1983).

Morris, Desmond, *The Naked Ape: A Zoologist's Study of the Human Animal*, (London: Jonathan Cape, 1967).

Morris, Henry M., *The Genesis Record*, (Ada, Michigan: Baker Books, 1976).

Morris, John and Austin, Steven A., *Footprints in the Ash*, (Green Forest, AR: Master Books, 2003).

Muggeridge, Malcolm, 'The humane holocaust', Cited in: Ronald Reagan, *Abortion and the conscience of the nation*, (Nashville, Tennessee: Thomas Nelson Publishers, 1984).

Murray, Iain H, *David Martyn Lloyd–Jones; The Fight of Faith 1939–1981*, (Edinburgh: The Banner of Truth Trust, 1990).

Murray, Iain H., *The Undercover Revolution—How Fiction Changed Britain*, (Edinburgh: The Banner of Truth Trust, 2009).

Nagel, Thomas, *Mind and Cosmos—Why the Materialist Neo-Darwinian Conception of Nature Is Almost Certainly False*, (Oxford University Press, 2012).

Nagel, Thomas, *The Last Word*, (Oxford University Press, 1997).

Numbers, Ronald L., *The Creationists: From Scientific Creationism to Intelligent Design*, (Harvard University Press, 2006).

Oard, Michael, *Dinosaur Challenges and Mysteries*, (Atlanta: Creation Book Publishers, 2011).

Paley, William, *Natural Theology, Or, Evidences of the Existence and Attributes of the Deity, Collected from the Appearances of Nature*, (Philadelphia: John Morgan, 1802).

Patterson, Colin, *Evolution*, (London: British Museum, Natural History, 1978).

Pearcy, Nancy R., *Total Truth, Liberating Christianity from Its Cultural Activity*, (Wheaton, Illinois: Crossway Books, 2005).

Playfair, John, *Illustrations of the Huttonian Theory of the Earth*, (Cambridge University Press, 2011).

Popper, Karl R., *The Logic of Scientific Discovery*, (Abingdon-on-Thames: Routledge Classics, 2nd Ed, 2002).

Prothero, Donald, *Bringing Fossils to Life: An Introduction to Paleobiology*, (Columbia University Press, 2013).

Quinones, Sam, *Dreamland: The True Tale of America's Opiate Epidemic*, (London: Bloomsbury Press, 2015).

Qureshi, Nabeel, *Seeking Allah, Finding Jesus: A Devout Muslim Encounters Christianity*, (Grand Rapids, Michigan: Zondervan, February 2014).

Ramachandran, Vilayanur, *The Tell-Tale Brain: A Neuroscientist's Quest for What Makes Us Human*, (London: William Heinemann, 2011).

Reardon, David, et al (Ed.), *Victims and Victors: Speaking Out About Their Pregnancies, Abortions, and Children Resulting from Sexual Assault*, (San Diego: Acorn Publishing, January 2000).

Reed, John K., *Rocks aren't Clocks—A Critique of the Geologic Timescale*, (Powder Springs, Georgia: Creation Book Publishers, 2013).

Remmelink report: Dutch government,—Remmelink 1991. https://archive.org/details/RemmelinkReport

Rendle Short, A., *Modern Discovery and The Bible*, (London: Inter-Varsity Fellowship, 1942).

Rendle Short, A., *The Causation of Appendicitis*, (Bristol: John Wright and Sons, 1946).

Rendle Short, A., *The Diary of George Muller*, (Glasgow: Pickering & Inglis, 1954).

Rendle Short, A., *The Rock Beneath*, (London: Inter-Varsity Fellowship 1st edition, 1955).

Rendle Short, A., *Why Believe?* (London: Inter-Varsity Fellowship 6th edition, 1954).

Rendle-Short, John, *Green Eye of the Storm*, (Edinburgh: The Banner of Truth Trust, 1998).

Respect for life—A Symposium, (London: Christian Medical Fellowship Publications, 1984).

Riedweg, Christoph, *Pythagoras: His Life, Teaching, and Influence*, Translated from the German by Steven Rendall, first ed. (New York: Ithaca, 2005).

Robinson, John A.T., *Honest to God*, (London: SCM Press, 1963).

Rowley, Hazel, *Tête-à-Tête: The Tumultuous Lives & Loves of Simone de Beauvoir and Jean-Paul Sartre*, (New York: Harper, 2005).

Rudwick, M. J. S., *Bursting the Limits of Time: The Reconstruction of Geohistory in the Age of Revolution*, (Chicago: University of Chicago Press, 2005).

Russell, Bertrand, 'Why I am not a Christian', *National Secular Society*, (London: The Hatfield Press Ltd, 1967).

Russell, Bertrand, *A History of Western Philosophy*, (London: Allen & Unwin, 1946).

Russell, Bertrand, *Autobiography*, (London: Psychology Press, 1998).

Russell, Bertrand, *The Impact of Science on Society*, (Milton Park, Abingdon: Routledge, 1951).

Ryle, Bishop J. C., *Christian Leaders of the 18th Century*, (Edinburgh: The Banner of Truth Trust, 2017).

Saussure, Horace de, *Voyages dans les Alpes*, 4 volumes (Neuchâtel: Samuel Fauche, 1779).

Sayers, Dorothy L., *The Man Born to be King*, (San Francisco: Ignatius Press, 1999).

Schaeffer, Edith, *L'Abri*, (San Francisco, CA: Norfolk Press, 1972).

Schaeffer, Francis A., *Francis A. Schaeffer Trilogy—He Is There and He Is Not Silent*, (Leicester: Inter-Varsity Press, 1990).

Schmidt, Alvin, *How Christianity Changed the World*, (Grand Rapids, Michigan: Zondervan Publishing House, 2001).

Seymour-Jones, Carole, *A Dangerous Liaison*, (London: Arrow Books, 2008).

Shakespeare, William, *Macbeth*, Act 5 Scene 5, lines 26–28. https://myshakespeare.com/macbeth/act-5-scene-5

Shapiro, Robert, *Origins: A Skeptic's Guide to the Creation of Life on the Earth*, (Portsmouth, New Hampshire: William Heinemann Ltd, 1986).

Silverthorn, D., *Human Physiology: An Integrated Approach*, (London: Pearson, 6th Ed., 2012).

Simpson, George Gaylord, *The Meaning of Evolution. A study of the history of life and of its significance for man*, (Yale University Press, 1950).

Sims, Andrew, *Is Faith Delusion? Why religion is good for your health*, (London: Bloomsbury Publishing, 2009).

Sims, Andrew, *Symptoms in the Mind: An Introduction to Descriptive Psychopathology*, 3rd Edition, (Edinburgh: Saunders, 2003).

Singer, Peter (Ed.), *'Persons and non-persons', in Defence of Animals*, (Oxford: Basil Blackwell, 1985).

Singer, Peter, *Practical Ethics*, (New York: Cambridge University Press, Third Edition, 2011).

Smith, Joseph, *Book of Mormon*, (Palmyra, USA: E. B. Grandin, 1830).

Spencer, Frank, *Piltdown. A Scientific Forgery*, (New York: Natural History Museum Publications and Oxford University Press, 1990).

Stark, Rodney, *The Triumph of Christianity*, (New York: HarperCollins, 2011).

Stevenson, Robert Louis, *Prayers Written at Vailima and a Lowden Sabbath Morn*, (London: Chatto & Windus, 1916).

Stevenson, Robert Louis, *The Pentland Rising: a page of history, 1666*, (London/Delhi: Pranava Books, 2020).

Stevenson, Robert Louis, *Travels with a Donkey in the Cevennes*, (Imprint Illyria Books, February 2009).

Stott, John, *Understanding the Bible*, Expanded ed., (Grand Rapids, MI: Zondervan, 1999).

Sunderland, Luther, *Darwin's Enigma: fossils and other problems*, (El Cajon, CA: Master Books, 1988).

Tattersall, Ian, 'Human Evolution: Personhood and Emergence', cited in: M. Jeeves & D. Tutu (Ed.), *The Emergence of Personhood: A Quantum Leap?* (Grand Rapids, Michigan: Eerdmans, 2015).

Tax, Sol and Callender, Charles, *Evolution after Darwin*, (University of Chicago Press, 1960).

Ten Boom, Corrie, *The Hiding Place*, second impression, (London: Hodder and Stoughton, 1976).

Thomas, Brian, 'Collagen remnants in ancient bone', PhD thesis, University of Liverpool, 2018.

Tinker, Melvin, *Reclaiming Genesis*, (Oxford: Monarch Books, 2010).

Trench, Richard C., *Notes on the Miracles of Our Lord—Popular Edition*, (Grand Rapids, Michigan: Baker Book House, 1949).

Tripp, Paul David, *Come Let Us Adore Him*, (Wheaton, Illinois: Crossway, 2017).

Ussher, James, *The Annals of the World*, (printed by E. Tyler for J Crook at the Sign of the Ship in St Paul's Churchyard, 1658).

Vermes, Dr Geza, *The Complete Dead Sea Scrolls in English*, 7th Ed, (London: Penguin Classics, 2011).

Vesalius, Andreas, *De Humani Corporis Fabrica Libri Septem*, (Padua: School of Medicine, 1543).

Warnock, Mary, *Dishonest to God: On Keeping Religion Out of Politics*, (Bloomsbury Continuum, 2010).

Watson, David C. C., *Myths and Miracles—A new approach to Genesis 1–11*, (Worthing: H. E. Walter Ltd, 1976).

Watson, David C. C., *The Great Brain Robbery*, (Worthing: H. E. Walter Ltd, 1975).

Wells, H. G., *First & Last Things: A Confession of Faith and Rule of Life*, (London: Cassell & Co Ltd, 1917).

Wells, H. G.; Huxley, Julian; and Wells, G. P., *The Science of Life*, 3 vols, (Glasgow: The Waverley Publishing Company Ltd, 1931).

Wells, H. G., *Mind at the End of Its Tether*, (Portsmouth, New Hampshire: William Heinemann Ltd, 1945).

Wells, H. G., *The Fate of Homo Sapiens*, (London: Secker & Warburg, 1939).

Whitmore, John and Garner, Paul, 'The Coconino Sandstone 2018. (Permian, Arizona, USA): Implications for the origin of ancient cross-bedded Sandstones'. In: J. H. Whitmore (ed.), *Proceedings of the Eighth International Conference on Creationism*, (Pittsburgh, Pennsylvania: Creation Science Fellowship, 2018).

Wiedersheim, Robert, *The Structure of Man: An Index to His Past History*, 2nd Ed Translated by H. and M. Bernard, (London: Macmillan and Co, 1895).

Wilkinson, David, 'Christian Eschatology and the Physical Universe', PhD thesis University of Durham, 2004.

Williams, Peter J., *Can We Trust the Gospels?* (Wheaton, Illinois: Crossway, 2018).

Woodward, Thomas, *Doubts about Darwin: A History of Intelligent Design*, (Ada, Michigan: Revell, a division of Baker Publishing Group, 2003).

Wright, N. T., *Surprised by Scripture: Engaging with Contemporary Issues*, (London: SPCK, 2014).

Wright, Verna, *Relevance of Christianity in a Scientific Age*, (Christian Medical Fellowship, 1981).

DVDs

Stein, Ben and Frankowski, Nathan, *Expelled: No Intelligence Allowed*, (DVD), (Timeless International Christi, January 2010).

Williams, Martin, *Which Gospel? How long age stories undermine the Gospel*, Creation Ministries International DVD.

Wright, Verna, *Monkey to Man?* DVD, (Chesterfield: Two by Two Worship Ltd, 1980).